PEASANTS AND I.......

Manchester University Press

Manchester Medieval Studies

SERIES EDITOR   Professor S. H. Rigby

The study of medieval Europe is being transformed as old orthodoxies are challenged, new methods embraced and fresh fields of enquiry opened up. The adoption of interdisciplinary perspectives and the challenge of economic, social and cultural theory are forcing medievalists to ask new questions and to see familiar topics in a fresh light.

The aim of this series is to combine the scholarship traditionally associated with medieval studies with an awareness of more recent issues and approaches in a form accessible to the non-specialist reader.

ALREADY PUBLISHED IN THE SERIES

Peacemaking in the middle ages: principles and practice
Jenny Benham

Money in the medieval English economy: 973–1489
James Bolton

Reform and the papacy in the eleventh century
Kathleen G. Cushing

Picturing women in late medieval and Renaissance art
Christa Grössinger

The Vikings in England
D. M. Hadley

A sacred city: consecrating churches and reforming society in eleventh-century Italy
Louis I. Hamilton

The politics of carnival
Christopher Humphrey

Holy motherhood
Elizabeth L'Estrange

Music, scholasticism and reform: Salian Germany 1024–1125
T.J.H. McCarthy

Medieval law in context
Anthony Musson

Constructing kingship: the Capetian monarchs of France and the early Crusades
James Naus

The expansion of Europe, 1250–1500
Michael North

Medieval maidens
Kim M. Phillips

Approaching the Bible in medieval England
Eyal Poleg

Gentry culture in late medieval England
Raluca Radulescu and Alison Truelove (eds)

Chaucer in context
S. H. Rigby

Lordship in four realms: The Lacy family, 1166–1241
Colin Veach

The life cycle in Western Europe, c.1300–c.1500
Deborah Youngs

MANCHESTER MEDIEVAL STUDIES

PEASANTS AND HISTORIANS
DEBATING THE MEDIEVAL ENGLISH PEASANTRY

Phillipp R. Schofield

Manchester University Press

Copyright © Phillipp R. Schofield 2016

The right of Phillipp R. Schofield to be identified as the author of this work has been asserted by him in accordance with the Copyright, Designs and Patents Act 1988.

Published by Manchester University Press
Altrincham Street, Manchester M1 7JA

www.manchesteruniversitypress.co.uk

British Library Cataloguing-in-Publication Data
A catalogue record for this book is available from the British Library

Library of Congress Cataloging-in-Publication Data applied for

ISBN 978 0 7190 5377 1 hardback

ISBN 978 0 7190 5378 8 paperback

First published 2016

The publisher has no responsibility for the persistence or accuracy of URLs for any external or third-party internet websites referred to in this book, and does not guarantee that any content on such websites is, or will remain, accurate or appropriate.

Typeset by
Servis Filmsetting Limited, Stockport, Cheshire
Printed in Great Britain
by Bell & Bain Ltd, Glasgow

For Jane

CONTENTS

Acknowledgements *page* viii

Introduction 1

1 Early contributions 33

Part I Themes

2 Population, resources and the medieval English peasantry 59
3 Lords and peasants 84
4 Peasants and markets 117

Part II Debates

5 Demography and the medieval peasantry 151
6 Family, household and gender 172
7 The village community and the nature of peasant society in medieval England 196
8 Peasant culture 223

Conclusion 254

Guide to further reading 264
Index 272

ACKNOWLEDGEMENTS

The idea of writing this book was first mooted by Professor Stephen Rigby in 1996. For too long, thereafter, it existed in the half-life of a book conceived of but not yet written. That it has been published is due very much to the input of two people. One is Steve Rigby who, as series editor, has been always reassuring and, in the final stages, commenting on a number of drafts, has been the most assiduous, informed and critical (in the best sense of the word) editor. This book would be much less a contribution without his invaluable input. The other person was my wife, Jane, who died in March 2013. Jane did not let me forget that I was expected to complete this book and was gently encouraging and persistent in helping to ensure that I did. As in so much else, I owe this book to Jane and, with love, I dedicate it to her. Our children, Bethany and Thomas, are a source of constant inspiration and support, as are their grandparents (Jane's Dad and my Mum), and they have helped me more than they will ever know. At Manchester University Press, Emma Brennan has been the most patient and considerate of editors. I would also like to thank Dee Devine, production editor at Manchester University Press, and John Banks, the volume's copy-editor, for their careful work seeing this through to publication. Versions of chapters were given at the following meetings: sections of Chapter 4, Social Science History Association, Portland, Oregon, November 2005; introductory sections, Cardiff University/Historical Association, March 2009, and the University of Girona, February 2010. I am very grateful for the comments of those attending these meetings.

PRS
26 October 2015

Introduction

This book is an examination of the themes and approaches employed by historians in their discussions of the medieval English peasant, and most particularly in the period from the end of the eleventh to the beginning of the sixteenth century. In it we will set out and discuss the principal issues or questions which have been applied to that study and, in so doing, offer an overview and assessment of the development of work on medieval peasants since the close of the nineteenth century. Above all a presentation and a synthesis of arguments and debates relating to the medieval peasantry, the book can also be read as a case-study of historiographical development and an example of the ways in which historical theses are applied and revised both in response to current historical scholarship but also in the context of wider and more far-reaching developments.

In this introductory chapter, the broad thrust of the book is identified through both an assessment of the themes and approaches employed in the study of the medieval English peasantry and a sketch of the key historiographical phases in this area of research and writing. This sketch is also supported by a discussion of a range of possible causes of changes and developments in writing on the medieval English peasantry. Finally, with this context to the fore, we will consider historical reflection upon the term 'peasant' and its appropriateness. While most historians working on medieval English peasants do not appear to have expressed a great deal of anxiety over definitions of the term 'peasant' or its applicability in this period, there are some notable exceptions to this and it will be useful to consider the issue of definition and its historiographical framing at the outset.

The historiography of the medieval English peasantry: main features

In the most general terms, the historiography of the medieval English peasantry from the end of the nineteenth century, when we can first detect an attempt to examine matters pertaining to the medieval peasantry in ways that generally look to conform to the expectations of a modern historiographical tradition,[1] until the present replicates some of the broader patterns of Western historical writing for the same period. While not all elements of the pattern are to be observed in the peasant historiography, with very little for instance that is avowedly postmodern, the basic structure is a familiar one, with shifts from an institutional, legal, constitutional and administrative history through an early economic history to a greater splintering of approach, a recourse to other disciplines and some, but in this respect limited, flirtation with econometrics and cultural and gender history. So, in the pioneering studies of the medieval English peasantry, there is a pronounced focus on the institutional setting of the peasantry; in fact, much late nineteenth-century historical literature is actually directed at the institutions and the peasants appear in relation to that. For example, publications by Vinogradoff on the manor, Maitland on customary law and, at about the same time, Seebohm and Gomme on village communities were the product of interests in the development of forms and structures much more than they were examinations of the material lives of the peasantry *per se*.[2]

Much of the early twentieth-century discussion of the medieval economy, and of the peasant's role within it, was located within and was explained by institutional structures. Some of the more important studies of medieval agrarian history produced in the later nineteenth and early twentieth centuries were directed at lordship but thereby admitted a detailed investigation of peasants as tenants. Thus, for example, A.E. Levett's examination of the Black Death on the Winchester estates has much to say about the changing obligations of the tenantry but rather less to say about peasant experience of those obligations or associated matters of 'peasant life' *per se*.[3] This persistence in the broad theme of lordship continued for far more than a generation, until the last quarter of the twentieth century, with important studies of individual lordships, and especially the greater ecclesiastical and monastic lordships and their estates, providing significant comment upon, *inter alia*, tenants and their forms of tenure and of land transfer.[4] In similar vein major county and regional volumes, including the *Victoria County Histories*, added to the discussion of the economy of the countryside and by extension the peas-

INTRODUCTION

antry, but again chiefly in terms that were framed by discussion of institutional forms, including those of manor and lordship.[5] This tendency was also, inevitably, reflected in the more general studies of the medieval economy produced in the later nineteenth and early twentieth centuries; thus, for instance, the index to Lipson's exploration of the economic history of England, first published in 1915 and reissued in new editions in the next two decades, included only two page references to 'peasantry' but referred the reader to 'see also freeholders, tenants (free), and tenants (unfree)', under which headings a number of page references and further cross-references could be found.[6] W.J. Ashley's often subtle and informed discussion of the medieval village and its development, part of a general economic history of England, draws extensively on published primary sources, in order to describe tenurial change, he also has plenty to say on the internal organisation of the medieval village and its operating structures but he has less to say on the peasantry *per se*.[7]

With the development of economic history in the last decades of the nineteenth century and the first years of the twentieth century we witness the first stirrings of a new departure in the study of the medieval English peasantry.[8] While historians of the medieval village and of the medieval agrarian economy maintained a familiar focus upon lordship, rent, tenure and the associated 'institutional' features of medieval rural history, we also detect the introduction of different research agendas. It is most obviously in the work of R.H. Tawney, and particularly his consideration of the agrarian problem of the sixteenth century, that we encounter a closer, more tenant-focused, interest in the peasant and small-holder. Tawney's emphasis upon the economic dealings of the peasantry, which he explores for the middle ages as well as the early modern period, remains one of the most significant discussions of the premodern agrarian economy and reflects a partial change of emphasis in terms of historical attention and of explanations of historical agency.[9]

In other respects also, a developing economic literature, which had at its heart a strong interest in rent, labour and commutation as well as developments in agriculture and land use, presented further opportunity for discussion of the peasantry, at least by extension, but again within the ambit of discussion of institutional form. Thus, for instance, Gray's study of the commutation of villein services, published in 1914, was a response to an ongoing debate about the chronology of commutation of labour services into money rents encouraged, but certainly not initiated, by T.W. Page's examination of what he termed the 'end of villeinage', a work published at the turn of the century.[10] Later commentators on this theme, and

3

especially on the historical investigation of rent, including M.M. Postan and E.A. Kosminsky, also brought their own agendas to their study and developed explanations that moved the study in new directions, reassessing, in the case of Postan, the issue of linearity in economic development and, in Kosminsky's work, the feudal nature of rent and its distribution.[11]

Earlier discussion of rent and its changing nature can also be found in the work of one of the first significant contributors to medieval economic history in England, James E. Thorold Rogers.[12] A keen advocate of the economic interpretation of history, and one who, in the last decades of the nineteenth century, directly and deliberately challenged the primacy of political and constitutional history, Rogers had a great deal to say on the condition of the medieval peasantry and considered a firm grasp of the effective income and outgoings of a peasantry to be fundamental to the understanding of 'the social state of any country'.[13] What is striking about Rogers's analysis is his insistence, even if he detects little substantial change, upon the need at least to consider change over time and to quantify that change, or at least to evaluate its trends through the use of, for instance, price and wage data.[14] In this respect also, the high and late medieval English peasantry offered him opportunity to reflect with conviction upon the advantage and relative disadvantages of the labourer and farmer at the close of the nineteenth century.[15]

In the early decades of the twentieth century, other historians, notably G.G. Coulton and H.S. Bennett, also offered commentaries upon medieval rural life. These works, and especially that of Coulton, published in the mid-1920s, and based on a series of lectures delivered at Aberystwyth, were enthusiastic discussions of the peasantry but retained some of that generality and lack of analytical focus which had also characterised earlier work, such as that of Jessop and Gasquet.[16] In fact, as Coulton explains in the introductory chapter to his volume on the *Medieval village*, his purpose was to draw out distinctions in the experience of the medieval peasantry and to illustrate the differences from the present.[17] Part of the reason for this rather hazy agenda may be taken to lie in the fact that there was less evidently an analytical or historiographical framework with which authors such as Coulton could grapple; that, however, would not, as we have seen, be entirely correct. Instead, it is clear that Coulton and Bennett sought to describe rural society rather than to engage in a close analysis of its changing features. Ada Levett's review of Coulton's survey of the medieval village, published in the first volume of the *Economic History Review*, is subtly critical of this failure to engage with detailed earlier work and prior analysis of the sort of which she was herself an author.[18] Levett condemns Coulton for possessing the 'loving observation of the artist rather than the mentality of the lawyer' when, according to her, 'the perfect historian is produced by a combination of the two'.[19] Bennett, writing a decade later, adopts, in his *Life on the English manor*, a rather less general approach than that favoured by Coulton and his predecessors; his is also a study based on a fairly close reading of the published primary material. However, the emphasis on a literary approach and one which offers a commentary upon rather than a close dissection of rural life identifies this still-popular work as of its time but also, and more importantly, of a particular tradition. As was the case with Coulton so also with Bennett: reviewers of a different and essentially more economic bent sharpened their quills. T.A.M. Bishop in particular applauded the sympathetic description of peasant life but bemoaned the timelessness of the discussion of rural life and the failure to engage with a growing literature on economic change. In his most caustic comment, clearly one excited by reading that Bennett would give up any number of cartularies, accounts, assize and court rolls for one brief peasant diary of the fourteenth century, Bishop retorted:

> If medieval history continues to attract scholars and students, it will be owing to and not in spite of the impersonal and circumstantial nature of much of the evidence, which calls for patient scientific examination, and does not encourage short cuts to truth.[20]

The timelessness of rural life in the middle ages remained though a theme for some of the more significant works appearing in mid-century. Undoubtedly one of the most important of these was G.C. Homans's study of English villagers of the thirteenth century, a work generally recognised to be important and one that, with a different emphasis, shared noticeable traits with the work of Coulton and Bennett.[21] Many of the main themes and topics of interest are the same, and there is some going over of the same ground. Where Homan's study differs from those earlier works however is in the particularity of Homan's interest and his choice of emphasis, especially his focus upon family form and inheritance. Homans was a Harvard sociologist who brought to his study a keen awareness of family structure and inter-familial relations. His introduction of the language and approach of a different discipline into the study of the medieval peasantry generated both acclaim and criticism, but it certainly brought a particular emphasis for later researchers, as we shall also discuss below.[22] In the second half of the twentieth century narrative accounts were increasingly set aside in favour of a *longue-durée* view of the medieval economy, and the study of the medieval English peasantry came initially to be dominated by two main approaches: Marxist and social scientific or demographic.

A Marxist or quasi-Marxist discussion of lord–tenant relations encouraged further research into the kinds of themes already evident in an earlier phase of the discussion, especially that pertaining to rent and to commutation of labour services. This, in its various forms, has maintained some clear relevance until the present time but undoubtedly its strongest moments came in the middle years of the century, and especially from the 1940s through to the 1970s. Led and epitomised by the work of Rodney Hilton but ably supported by other historians, especially those working at the University of Birmingham, a Marxist investigation of the medieval peasantry generated much that was familiar from non-Marxist research, including regional and estate studies which examined the experience of the peasantry as one significant feature of a changing economy and society. The extent to which the peasantry were themselves agents in that change was of major importance for this research, as a glance at the bibliographies of Hilton, Dyer and others illustrates, but what was also important, especially for Hilton, was the changing nature of feudal rent, a theme of crucial relevance to earlier generations of historians as already noted and one given renewed emphasis by the work of Dobb and others in the so-called 'transition debate', the last significant manifestation of which was the Brenner debate of the 1970s.[23] In this respect also, it is worth noting here that the persistence of themes pertaining to the transition debate, which was never wholly a Marxist project, continued in other respects into the last decades of the twentieth century, with in particular work on the relationship of peasants with the market and with a developing economy a central strand of recent research.[24]

The second of the two main strands in the second half of the twentieth century was one born out of the social sciences and 'new social history'. We have already noted the introduction by G.C. Homans of a sociological approach to the study of the medieval English peasantry, and it is evident that Homans's efforts sowed a seed in the work of the generation that followed him, especially in North America. In Toronto, J. Ambrose Raftis and his students employed sociological techniques, in particular, in describing and examining social structure as revealed by the available historical material, in this instance the manorial court rolls from the Ramsey Abbey estates.[25] Here, in the most immediate and obvious ways, investigation was directed at the peasantry and some of the hitherto defining features of the sub-discipline, especially the relationship of lord and tenant, were chiefly set aside.

INTRODUCTION

Social scientific history also prompted other kinds of investigation of the peasantry, including demographic and social structural studies of the peasantry, studies of kin and kin structures, of replacement rates and of family size and population change within local communities. As we shall see in later chapters, a social scientific approach, associated especially with cohorts of academics working in particular departments and universities, gained significant force in the 1960s and 1970s. Outside of North America, where Raftis and his colleagues in Toronto had pioneered investigation of social distinction and interaction in the medieval village, academics in Cambridge adopted social science methodologies and research questions hitherto unapplied to the medieval village in a bid to examine questions of propinquity, legitimacy, inheritance and so on within this context, as well as to bring an additional analytical dimension to issues, such as the peasant family, already subjected to some level of analysis.[26] Most importantly, in establishing a theoretical context in which such work might operate, M.M. Postan, examination of whose work will sit at the heart of a later chapter, had, by the 1950s, posited an explanation for change in the medieval economy founded upon the movement of population and thereby encouraged investigation of the medieval peasantry in terms of its demography and especially of changing mortality rates.[27]

Themes

Is there then a series of broad and persistent questions or foundations of analysis which dominate discussion of the medieval English peasantry? We can certainly detect within the historiography of the medieval peasantry certain phases and emphases which merit attention and which, loosely, we might think of as themes. These, in the broadest terms, we might list as follows, by sub-period and theme:

- A later nineteenth-century tradition founded on institutional and legal history persists in a variety of subtle transformations throughout the last century and to the present
- Developing almost alongside this, if generally a little later, is an economic tradition which has, at its core, an interest in rent and the changing nature of rent and obligation across the high and late middle ages. This theme persisted in a variety of forms throughout the twentieth century, including a Marxist approach founded on the discussion of the transition from feudalism to capitalism, but generated a strong and dedicated programme of research in the early twentieth century.

7

It remains alive until the present, as evidenced, for instance, in recent work on changes in tenure on the estates of Durham priory and of the bishops of Durham.[28] We can also associate discussion of commercialisation and the growth of the market in this period, which of necessity involves consideration of the role of peasants as producers and consumers, with this phase of historiographical development.

- We can identify a social history or sociological aspect to the discussion incorporating both general narrative social histories of the medieval village as well as more particular investigations aimed at adding to our understanding of, for instance, inheritance, the nature of the family and household, marriage, kinship, demography and gender history – in all respects topics for investigation that have taken their inspiration from the social sciences.

But it is also important to note that there was seldom, in the study of the medieval English peasantry, an overarching intellectual paradigm or shared and unchallenged view regarding the subject of study unless that is we are to identify the 'normal science' of historical approach and enquiry as the paradigm itself. Instead, as some of the comments and reviews already mentioned here illustrate, the study of the medieval peasantry across the last century and more reflected a diversity of approaches, not all of which combined easily; in fact, particular strands of research could persist without real intersection or absorption. Thus, for instance, the social structural approach of Raftis and others, with its emphasis upon limited family reconstitution and categorisation, persisted and persists amongst historians working within the same Toronto tradition but has been subjected to quite aggressive criticism and rejection by some historians operating within other 'schools'.[29] In other cases, as for instance in the relatively early discussion of commutation and its significance in the medieval rural economy, issues of debate enjoyed brief and energetic moments only to subside fairly quickly, sometimes to be resurrected and at other times not.[30] Given this, changes in the historiography of the medieval English peasantry are most likely best explored as development of *themes* rather than shifts in *paradigms*. As is well known, Thomas Kuhn established an explanatory model for the development of scientific theory; in his examination of what he termed 'scientific revolutions', Kuhn identified a nexus of collectively identified problems and recognised approaches capable of being employed in their solution, in other words, a paradigm. Paradigms persist, according to Kuhn, for as long as they are perceived as useful and necessary to the furtherance of effective study; in a scientific context, and Kuhn was a physicist, this tends to mean for as long as they continue to generate results that are capable of being reconciled with the paradigm rather than being wholly anomalous. Once a sufficient weight of anomalous and irreconcilable results is generated, then the shared paradigm fails or collapses, and fragmentation follows; normality, a return to 'normal science', occurs again only when a new dominant paradigm can be established, typically through the introduction of a new shared problem by an individual or a community of individuals.[31] In what follows we will see that, further to Kuhn's view that paradigms were 'incommensurable', no paradigm capable of co-existing with another, we cannot make such a claim for the various approaches and nodes of discussion adopted in the study of the medieval English peasantry.[32] Not only did various intellectual strands co-exist, they sometimes came each to support the other, either directly or, as often, indirectly, in helping to establish a fuller understanding of the main issue at hand, the historical experience of the medieval English peasantry.

In general terms, it is not especially difficult to identify some shared if fairly broad approaches to the study of the medieval English peasantry, of a kind that we might wish to label as 'paradigmatic'; these paradigms though relate far less, indeed not at all, to the unique study of the medieval English peasantry but instead to the wider conception of the study of history *per se*. In the first instance, historians have, for the greater part but certainly not with any consistency, accepted that change over time in the medieval village is important and that the condition of the medieval peasantry is likely to have altered over time, though they have differed over the extent of that change and, most especially, the causes of that change. Secondly, they have mostly agreed upon the evidential base that permits study of the medieval peasantry and have tended to place the greatest emphasis on documentary sources and, most especially, seigneurial records from the mid-thirteenth century onwards. The impact of archaeology on the study of the medieval English peasant has, by extension, been relatively limited – at least in the research and writing of historians, a point to which we will return in the concluding chapter to this volume. This has also meant that, thirdly, much of the emphasis of relevant research has either been directed at understanding in some form the relationship of lord and tenant or has been set within the context of seigneurial structures, most obviously the manor and the manorial economy.

If we reflect upon the current historiographical position, we would certainly identify the persistence of these typical approaches but also some significant testing of the parameters of study and a degree of challenge to their perceived centrality. Thus, unsurprisingly, identification and discussion of change over time remains an accepted and vital component of study in this area; historians also remain committed to the value of the main seigneurial sources (court rolls, rentals, account rolls etc.) in pursuing research in this area but there have been recent attempts to pursue 'new' intellectual approaches using the same kind of material (notably, a return to a legal-historical investigation of manorial court rolls) as well as to seek out new materials, as for instance in the later medieval and early modern investigations of individual account books and of documents issuing from the parish rather than the manor.[33] Finally, there has also been no abandonment of the importance of the relations of lord and tenant as foundations to our investigation of the medieval peasant but there has been some greater movement away from the perception that the peasantry were largely defined by those kinds of relationship; instead, historians have tended, often in more recent work, to place some greater emphasis upon exploration of other kinds of influence, be that the state, towns and merchants, or the church, points again to which we will return and examine at greater depth in later chapters. Obviously, as we have discussed earlier, it would be unwise and most probably incorrect to identify these as paradigm shifts; instead, such developments reflect changes in theme and intellectual approach and it is these 'shifts' that will sit at the core of the discussion in this book.

How then do such historiographical developments occur? There seems little doubt that, as might reasonably be expected and indeed hoped, individual historians are capable of diverting the research agenda. These considerations are important because they speak to the intellectual motive and the driving force of the research. Of course, all historians are, to a greater or lesser extent, influenced by their circumstances, their characters, environment, gender, sexuality, their political convictions, to identify, research and write on particular topics. The approach they bring to their work, the opportunities they do or do not enjoy, the message they convey from the material, cannot help but be conditioned in such ways. The great political events of the twentieth century, including the two world wars, influenced the writing of history in a myriad ways (including the changed life experiences of historians, a retreat from national histories and the extension of university education and the franchise to larger bodies of men and to women); we cannot chart all of these developments here but neither should we overlook them. Some of these, including 'household, sex and marriage', are so personal and immediate as to be often beyond our detection, though they are hinted at and sometimes described in the writings and memoirs of historians.³⁴ Others reflect the determined efforts of historians to direct and to adjust the historical agenda.

For instance, Homans's examination of the medieval villager in the thirteenth century, with its strong emphasis upon a sociological approach and the employment of sociological categories for investigation, helped develop a new direction in the study of the medieval peasantry.³⁵ M.M. Postan acknowledges as much in his sometimes sniffy review of Homans's work, noting that, while a considerable amount of what Homans had to offer replicated, in some degree or other, that which had gone before, his emphasis upon the peasant family, and its placing in centre stage reflected a real difference of approach and one that 'may not be as colourful as Dr Coulton's nor as intimate as H.S. Bennett's, but ... is probably more accurate than the former, more analytical than the latter, and more deliberate than either'.³⁶ Similarly, and in some sense an extension of the inroads made by Homans, work by J. Ambrose Raftis and historians based in and around the Pontifical Institute at Toronto, the so-called 'Toronto School', developed a social science approach to the study of the medieval peasantry which, with its particular focus on social stratification, persisted as a vibrant theme until at least the early 1980s, and enjoyed a heyday in the 1960s and 1970s.³⁷ Most obviously, and as we shall discuss in the some detail in later chapters, the work of Rodney Hilton and of M.M. Postan provided major impetus to investigations of the medieval English peasantry, in terms of, respectively, class struggle and the political as well as socio-economic relations of lords and tenants and the chronology of population change and its relationship with resources, not least peasant resources.³⁸

An earlier generation of historians had also seen in the medieval peasantry an opportunity ripe for comparisons with the social conditions pertaining in their own society. With this agenda in mind, some few early forays into medieval English social, more than economic, history identified the lives of rural-dwellers as objects worthy of intellectual study, and of contemporary moral purpose. The peasantry of the high and late middle ages was served up as a battle-ground for those who sought to define their own political and social agendas thereby, and in so doing these commentators began to test out themes and approaches that would resurface in more recent and often more sophisticated historical research and writing. Thus, for instance, the Reverend Augustus Jessop's strictly paternalistic account of Norfolk village life c.1280 addresses the condition of the peasantry.³⁹ So, for instance, he identifies the various tenurial conditions applying on the manor and distinguishes between the likely experiences of different kinds of tenant, the physical nature of the village, the travails of contemporary life, including poor weather and flooding, and particular aspects of the material condition of life in the thirteenth and fourteenth centuries. All of these features he exhibited to his rural audience – attenders at an evening lecture at Tittleshall, Norfolk, in about 1880 – as evidence of the advantages they enjoyed relative to their 'rude forefathers' who 'were more wretched in their poverty, ... incomparably less prosperous in their prosperity, ... worse clad, worse fed, worse housed, worse taught, worse tended, worse governed'.[40] His near contemporary, J.E.T. Rogers comes to the opposite conclusion, one closely informed by his political conviction that his own society was failing in its duty to the poor, that little had changed in the condition of the villager and labourer since the thirteenth century and that, in certain respects – and here his focus is upon the material condition of the peasant and the extent to which she or he enjoyed opportunities for betterment or social aspiration – the thirteenth-century villager was better placed than his or her equivalent in the nineteenth century.[41] Taking a far rosier view, Cardinal Gasquet, also basing his observations on the recently published rolls of the Durham Priory Halmote, wrote at the turn of the twentieth century of 'medieval village life among the tenants of the Durham monastery' as 'some Utopia of dreamland', and one that exhibited 'many of the things that in these days advanced politicians would desire to see introduced into the village communities of modern England, to relieve the deadly dullness of country life'.[42] Some endeavours, informed by contemporary political concerns, helped set the agenda for the study of the medieval peasantry and, especially in the work of Rogers, who allied his commentaries with prodigious amounts of data gathering and compilation,[43] helped provide foundation to later investigation in this area.

Further, the historical agenda has certainly been influenced by historical emphases operating in different national and linguistic contexts. In some instances, the potential impact of non-English writing on the medieval peasantry has been limited; while relevant work undoubtedly had considerable resonance within the author's own country and/or language group, the likely subtleties of their research have tended to be hidden in favour of English-language syntheses. This has sometimes evidently been the case for work published in Russian and in Japanese, where a fair amount of relevant research has been undertaken, far greater in fact than that translated into English.[44] Where linguistic barriers have, for reasons of relative linguistic familiarity or through translation, been less difficult to overcome, there has been a considerable exchange of ideas and it is evident that work by historians working in different national traditions as well as often in different languages has informed the development of an Anglophone historiography. Peter Gattrell has described the ways in which later nineteenth- and early twentieth-century Russian historians, with a keen and far more immediate interest in serfdom, offered significant comment on the nature and development of serfdom and villeinage, important elements of which work were available to non-Russian readers, through either the author writing in English (Vinogradoff) or the work appearing in subsequent translation (Kosminsky).[45] French and German work on the Peasants' Revolt, for instance, has also been absorbed into English writing in this area while, more generally, persistent disciplinary relations with historians in continental Europe has added nuanced and comparative reference to much of the relevant historiography.[46] In recent years, through conferences and joint publications, work on important topics in medieval economic and social history, including that pertaining to the peasantry, consumption and the peasant land market, has been closely informed by such comparative reference.[47] Earlier generations of European historians had developed schema aimed at comprehending the operation of the medieval rural economy that were clearly informed by shared ideas and a general consensus; so, for instance, M.M. Postan's model of an English rural economy driven by population change is also reflected in the work of contemporary continental historians such as Wilhelm Abel (Germany), B.H. Slicher-Van Bath (Low Countries) and Georges Duby (France), the latter's work translated into English by Postan's wife, Cynthia Postan.[48]

But it is also clear that the individual or collective initiative of scholars was not and could not be wholly responsible for the changes which have been sketched so far. Thus, for instance, the influence of other disciplines has encouraged new research agendas. In the last half century, historians, in particular, have been keen to draw upon the questions and methodologies of disciplines other than history, and especially the social sciences, in order to frame their own research agendas and to set out new approaches to relevant sources and their study. As we have already seen, certain historians, such as Homans and Raftis, were particularly adept at such inter-disciplinary approaches to the investigation of the medieval English peasantry. In a keynote article, intended to set out the ways in which peasant society might be studied through the use of manorial court rolls, Raftis identifies the importance of the larger and wealthier village families as dominant in the village society and economy. In a largely positive view of the capacity of court rolls to shed light on rural society and its structures,

Raftis encourages future students 'to resort to many more tools made available by the modern social scientist, perhaps particularly to those of social anthropology'.[49] However, developments of this kind were not led only by the initiatives of individual historians. In the first instance, of course, such inter-disciplinarity was dependent upon the appropriate development of those other disciplines. We think especially of the emergence of 'new social (scientific) history' in the 1960s as the product of such cross- and inter-disciplinary exchanges. As we shall discuss more fully in later chapters, students of the medieval English peasantry have willingly absorbed such developments, not least in the investigation of social structure and demography. Thus, for instance, detailed investigation of medieval rural populations, emergent in the literature from the late 1950s and coming to involve argument based upon model-life tables or the calculation of male replacement rates, was dependent upon intellectual agendas and theoretical approaches introduced through the social sciences.[50] Similarly, for example, Smith's study of kinship patterns in a medieval Suffolk village illustrates the ways in which techniques developed elsewhere, again in the social sciences and in geography, helped introduce new approaches to the study of medieval rural society.[51]

Such developments have not always persisted or necessarily flourished, of course, and some have more often than not remained the approach of only a handful of practitioners; that said, the conclusions arising from such work have often enjoyed a more general influence on the commonality of historical views in this area. If, for instance, relatively few historians have adopted a close engagement with the techniques of demographers and social scientists in their research on medieval peasant society it would, despite this, now not be possible to offer an informed view of that society which did not take account of issues arising from such an approach.

We might also reasonably observe that inter- and cross-disciplinarity has worked in other, and not always wholly positive, ways for the study of the medieval English peasantry. To take possible instances here: in the first place, it is possible to suggest that the study of the medieval peasantry has been confined within an agenda determined, for the greater part of its historiography, by the precepts of legal history and, more evidently, economic and social history. As we will see more fully below, and has been briefly outlined above, the persistence of an investigation founded upon economies of exchange, labour, rent, landholding and lord–tenant relations, essential to our understanding of the medieval peasantry and its context, has conceivably left less space for the development of other approaches to the study of medieval peasants.

INTRODUCTION

On occasion, historians sought to challenge the hegemony of such disciplinary conventions. This has been especially noticeable in some of the more vigorous claims by North American historians that areas of potential investigation, as well as of pre-existing historiography, have been overlooked, hidden by editors and authors whose intellectual outlook has been conditioned by other more dominant views of the past and its operation. Thus, for instance, Judith Bennett has been strongly critical of the neglect of areas of research, including that of women and peasant women in particular, and has identified in that neglect a degree of wilfulness.[52] Sherri Olson, whose research on medieval rural society has offered a quite distinctive approach to the study of the medieval society by seeking to show that surviving records and especially court rolls present opportunities to investigate peasant mentality and peasant culture, has been sharply critical of more quantitative, institutional and 'conventional' readings of the surviving material.[53] Kathleen Biddick also laments what she characterises as a forced categorisation of medieval English peasants, issuing from a nineteenth-century reconstruction of an imagined medieval society. Founded upon particular types of historical source, distilled by modern conceptions of peasant societies and without any or great regard for what she terms 'the chinks and cracks they [peasants] created as they traversed the disciplinary places of emplacement', Biddick suggests that we need to look for other hints and more subtle suggestions regarding peasant identity and agency.[54]

In other respects, close engagement with and adoption of new and discrete disciplinary techniques has redirected historical discussion in other ways, occasionally channelling it into rather closed methodological discussion from which it can emerge the stronger but where it may also languish and die.[55] One striking feature of new approaches – and one that would accord with Kuhn's model of scientific revolution – is the occasional and sometimes open hostility to new methodological and conceptual approaches. The introduction of new terminology and of new ways of framing the discussion is often challenged on the basis of its usefulness, meaning or applicability, as is evident in reviews of some of the more distinctively novel approaches to the study of the medieval peasantry undertaken to date, including most obviously techniques and modes of investigation introduced from other disciplines. Challenges of this kind – and there have in fact been relatively few such in this area of research – have also presented those historians researching in the area and representing more strictly orthodox approaches with the opportunity to restate the importance of shared and persistent paradigms, notably in this instance in affirming the need for a solid understanding of those institutional and legal structures which underpin the main sources, essentially manorial documentation.[56]

It is also worth noting here that, just as research questions and parameters of the possible might change, so a change in research focus was also determined by the application of certain source types. Investigation of lordship, of the demesne, of the agrarian economy and of productivity both prompted and was encouraged by detailed work on the central and local fiscal records of the great estates, including cartularies, extents and, above all, accounts, both obedientary and manorial. Kosminsky also effected a partial shift of focus by examining the Hundred Rolls of the later thirteenth as a source for the later medieval economy.[57] While information on peasants and aspects of the peasant economy can certainly be gleaned from such a body of material, it has been above all the close investigation of manorial court rolls that has provided the more particular focus upon the peasantry *per se*. While historians such as Seebohm and Maitland had early drawn attention to the worth of manorial court rolls, especially as sources of legal and institutional/constitutional history, extensive detailed study of manorial court series, with notable exceptions,[58] was a product of work on courts of the Ramsey Abbey estates, begun by Raftis in the late 1950s and early 1960s, with its important antecedent in the study of G.C. Homans as discussed above.[59] In many respects Raftis epitomises that transition, his earliest work a study of the estate of Ramsey itself before he shifted his view to the tenantry.[60] It was his own students, as we shall discuss later in this volume, who extended that court-roll-based discussion and offered even fuller examination of the peasantry *per se*, often in the process writing lords almost entirely out of the narrative.

However, the sorts of advantages which encourage new research – new and unexplored source materials, different and nuanced approaches to the topic and so on – might also help serve to contain growth. Any postgraduate attempting a manor-based or estate-based study of the medieval English peasantry, of the kind undertaken with some degree of regularity over the last half century and more, is certainly faced with challenges in the present day. Allied to the considerable, and increasingly involved expectations placed upon any such researcher in terms of historical, economic and/or demographic skills, including a capacity to read the medieval sources, to gather and store data capable of being analysed and to apply careful analysis to the same, including perhaps some level of statistical analysis, there are also now strictly enforced constraints upon the time needed to conduct such work. In Britain, for instance, increasing 'institutional' pressures on PhD students to complete their doctoral research within three to four years, driven by closely policed submission data gathered by the research funding councils, cannot but influence the planning by students and their supervisors of the proposed research and the scale of topic conceived as achievable. In such a context, most students and supervisors might be forgiven for being wary of more complex or involved areas of research, a reflection of the difficulties of the enterprise proportionate to the potential research rewards.[61]

It is also likely to be the case that most research postgraduates will have had relatively little formal encounter with the study of medieval peasants prior to that stage of their studies. Most historians, certainly in Britain, encounter medieval peasantry and the study of rural society relatively late in their education, and that has almost certainly been the case for most of the last century or more. While a 'traditional' view of the medieval village may now be discussed at an early stage of historical work in the classroom, and often long before the all but ubiquitous regimen of twentieth-century dictatorships is administered to students in their mid-teens, there is little formal opportunity for return to the topic until postgraduate study.[62] Nor do most university departments in the West employ medieval social and economic historians, which means that opportunities to choose research-led modules, or write undergraduate dissertations, on medieval rural society are relatively limited. Most medievalists who come to the study of the medieval English peasantry tend then to come through one of two routes – through largely independent study at or before university leading to approaches to relevant supervisors in order to pursue postgraduate work or in the following of relevant courses in those relatively few universities where directed study of medieval rural society appears on the curriculum, again followed by postgraduate study. In most instances though, very few young historians, in their twenties say, approaching the study of the medieval peasant are likely to have encountered the topic in any great detail or to any great extent in their previous formal education. While that may mean that new researchers approach the topic with enthusiasm and an openness to any number of possible approaches, it also suggests that the pool of potential researchers encouraged by their previous encounters will be small and certainly dwarfed by the oceans of new scholars studying topics at the heart of the historical curricula at secondary school and as undergraduates at university.

In a different way, but one that is also related to the institutional context and framing of research, we can also suggest that the persistence of particular research themes and the relative immutability of some topics

– a point we will find illustrated in what follows – is sustained by the structures put in place to support postgraduate research at university. This is, of course, hardly a novel observation and it is one that has been made frequently by those interested in the development of a discipline or an idea, including Kuhn.[63] Certainly, when we consider the longevity of themes such as, for example, the importance of rent in the high and late middle ages, we are witness both to a recognition by historians that this is an important and accessible topic, but also to the influence of supervisors, directing their students to topics or general approaches with which they have also grappled or perhaps helped to establish and to literature with which they are particularly familiar and to which they will have contributed. Thus, for instance, we can trace the persistence of such routes, often through the same archives but with changing emphases reflecting the input of developments in the historiography, through two, three or more intellectual generations, often to the extent that we can identify particular 'schools' or at least traditions or approaches (theoretical and empirical) to the study of the medieval peasant. Shared intellectual agendas of this kind evidently help to generate research focus and a committed programme of study, as was clearly the case for the detailed research on the Ramsey Abbey estates which emerged from the Pontifical Institute from the 1950s to the 1980s. That said, the association of the so-called 'Toronto School' with a social scientific bent or of historical research at Birmingham University with a uniquely Marxist approach to the study of the medieval peasantry, risks a too-easy characterisation of the work of practitioners within any such institution; at the same time, and in contrast to the last point, association with a particular 'school' may encourage a collective defensiveness to assaults on the 'school's' position and a resistance to change from an inherited or long-cherished position.[64]

It is also worth reflecting here upon the kinds of institutional distinctions that might also serve to break the mould and to lead students in new directions; it is striking that certain particular approaches to the study of the medieval peasantry – which were certainly departures from a more conventional institutional or legal view – tended not to occur in the older, established universities' history faculties. It was in the newer, provincial universities, most obviously Birmingham from the mid-twentieth century, that class-based investigation of medieval peasants was initiated, while in universities outside of Britain (of which, as already noted, the chief instance is Toronto (Pontifical Institute)) social science approaches were most enthusiastically applied to this area of study. Other key developments in the study of medieval peasants took place in departments other than history departments. So, for instance, demographic study of the medieval English peasantry was greatly promoted in research undertaken in the department of geography at Cambridge in the 1970s as well as at the Cambridge Group for the History of Population and Social Structure, in the 1970s and 1980s.

Institutional developments of a different kind have also encouraged the distribution of relevant work and the transmission and sharing of ideas in this, as of course in other, areas of study. It is as true for economic and social history more generally as it is for the study of the medieval English peasantry that the development of the sub-discipline was dependent on the introduction of new avenues for the publication of relevant research. R.H. Tawney, for instance, found it difficult to publish some of his earliest work in Britain as there was not a natural home for its publication and had turned instead to German journals.[65] It is certainly striking to what extent the earliest investigations of medieval social and economic history in Britain were dependent upon mainstream journals. A simple search of key terms in the journal literature of the first decades of the twentieth century illustrates how, in the first instance, historians working on, for instance, 'villeinage' had to compete in order to place their work in the main historical journals (and often managed to do so); with time, however, historians working in these areas found, and in some instances created, new outlets in dedicated journals, at which points submissions on such themes appear to have declined as in, for instance and most obviously, *English Historical Review*.[66]

Furthermore, work inspired by agendas that operated beyond immediate subject boundaries and particular intellectual concerns could also rebound to the benefit of study in this area. Most obviously, changes in wider political and social context are clearly relevant in these respects. Hilton, in the introduction to his 1973 Ford lectures on the medieval English peasantry, attempts a brief assessment of the changing historiographical interest in peasantry and, of course, the medieval peasantry in particular. Striking in his contemporary observation on the state of peasant studies is his placing of the then enthusiasm for such research in terms of a context defined by decolonisation and a process of economic change in developing countries.[67] Hilton notes that, since the Second World War, historians, as well as those more immediately engaged in development and related policy, had come to recognise the potential advantages in applying a comparative approach to peasant society. At least some of the research undertaken in the second half of the twentieth century, and especially in its third quarter, was encouraged and pursued with just such a remit in mind. Hilton suggests, for example, that the Second International Conference of Economic History (Aix-en-Provence, 1962) was guided by such considerations.[68] M.M. Postan's plenary lecture at the Second International Conference of Economic History was also not only or indeed very much about medieval history's absorption of ideas but rather a survey of the applicability of historical enquiry to the postwar development of economies in a contemporary context. For Postan, such work was crucial not least because, if historians did not attempt to make considered associations between the present and the past, others, i.e. non-historian policy makers, would continue to do so; what is more, they would do so poorly and with consequent and potentially disastrous implications for policy and development programmes.[69] Almost a century earlier than such developments, Rogers, a Liberal Party member and an MP in the 1880s, an advocate for a system of public education and someone who had witnessed a great deal of rural poverty in the Oxfordshire countryside of the 1850s, examined the medieval rural condition as a touchstone for modern politics and economic policy making.[70]

Further, and in a manner that is familiar from other studies in the development of historiography and its possible causes, we can find plentiful evidence for the influence of external, 'political' factors upon the study of the medieval peasantry. Anecdotally, for instance, Rodney's Hilton renewed interest in resistance and revolt was encouraged by the student sit-ins of 1968 at his own university at Birmingham.[71] In this respect, the growth of a feminist historiography in general also, as we shall discuss, had its impact in this area of the historiography as others, a development explicable in terms of feminism *per se* but also in the particular influence of highly motivated historians, often able and very willing to encourage each other.[72] Maxine Berg has also shown how, in Britain, female economic historians encouraged each other and, through a combination of particular institutional settings, notably Girton College, Cambridge, and then the London School of Economics, and shared agendas and contacts, both found and nurtured a distinct identity and contribution in the early development of economic history.[73] Whilst not necessarily promoting the study of women or a feminist historical agenda, women, often encouraged by fellow women historians, found a niche in the newly developing economic history, including the history of the medieval English peasantry and some of the most significant contributions to this area have from its first stirrings been offered by female historians to a degree not always evident in other parts of the discipline. It is striking in this respect that the first publication in the *American Historical Review* by a woman was Nellie Neilson's essay on boon services on the estates of Ramsey Abbey, based on her doctoral work and published in 1897.[74]

It is also important to ask if the work of medievalists has been taken up beyond its particular research base: has historical investigation of the medieval English peasantry informed study in other areas of history but also in other subject areas or indeed has it had an influence beyond the academy, for instance in policy terms? In some cases, the answer to the question is probably 'no'; much of the historical work in this area, valid as it is, has tended to stay within the initial intellectual parameters of the research area. There is, for instance, little evidence that close investigation of, say, commutation or the peasant land market has preceded much beyond its own precincts. However, in other instances, it is entirely clear that the detailed research undertaken on medieval peasantry has reached a long way beyond its original research base at certain moments and come to inform particular agendas, as for instance in wider discussion of peasant revolt; this extended beyond the immediate interest of medievalists. This was not confined solely to an intellectualised discussion of the medieval peasantry; Hilton notes, for instance, that the International Institute of Labour Studies organised seminars in the 1960s, including those on medieval peasant movements, with a view to establishing a more coherent view of the long-term relationship between peasant movements and social change.[75]

Medieval 'peasants'?

Lastly, and before we turn to historiographical discussion of the medieval English peasantry, we should address some highly significant and potentially vexed issues which also relate to the comparative nature of peasant studies: who were 'peasants' in the middle ages and, indeed, were there 'peasants' in medieval England at all? While it remains far from clear that historians have always employed a shared definition of the medieval peasant in their work, it is at least evident that the term has been applied and used freely by historians from the nineteenth century until the present in order to describe a cohort of rural dwellers which included both the wealthier villein and free tenants of lords as well as those who were their economic and social inferiors, including cottagers, smallholders and even labourers with small plots of land. On other occasions, as we shall see in the following chapters, historians have used terms other than 'peasant' not evidently because they have rejected the term but because the object of their investigation was sometimes narrower, especially where the focus was upon the tenantry. Where historians have used other and often more general and less easily defined terms, such as 'villager', the explanation for that choice is typically not explained and may be as much stylistic as conceptual.[76]

In short, most historians who work or who have worked on the medieval English peasantry have not evidently given such matters a great deal of thought. As we have seen in this chapter and will have cause to consider further in the next chapter, historians writing on topics germane to the study of the medieval English peasant in the late nineteenth century tended not to direct their work to the subject of peasants *per se* but to sub-groups of peasants defined less by their 'peasantness' and more by their mode of tenure and their obligations to their lords. When, in the first decades of the twentieth century in particular, historians began to use the term 'peasant' as the generally applicable term interchangeable with such terms as 'tenant' or 'serf' it was typically used without definition. As Hilton notes, in reflecting upon the work of Rogers and Seebohm as well as subsequent contributors, the use of such term as 'peasantry, or whatever word they have chosen to use' has been far from consistent.[77] Those relatively few historians who have sought to put some flesh on the bones of the bare term have tended to be consistent, if often understandably vague, in applying a working definition. So, for instance, R.H. Tawney, writing in the second decade of the twentieth century, was content to use the term 'peasantry' as a broad identifier and one capable of accommodating considerable variety.[78] It was not until the late 1970s that any historian working on the medieval English peasantry turned to a close examination of the term 'peasant' and its applicability in this context. It fell at that time to a non-medievalist not only to dissect the term, making use of theorisations recently constructed in the burgeoning field of peasant studies, but also to set it in the context of wider studies of peasantry including modern and contemporary peasantries and to declare that peasants, so defined, did not exist in medieval England. Alan MacFarlane's well-known assault on the applicability of the term 'peasantry' when applied to rural dwellers in medieval England was founded upon the observation that medieval English peasants, when compared with modern peasants as defined by modern commentators such as Daniel Thorner and Teodor Shanin, did not conform to type.[79] MacFarlane's critique of the term was founded upon his own view that research on medieval England had shown medieval rural dwellers to be individualistic rather than family-centred and drawn into market relations to an extent that stretched the term 'peasant' well beyond its correct usage. It was in other words a development in the historiography, notably a heightened interest in an apparently competitive land market in eastern England from at least the later thirteenth century, that encouraged MacFarlane to this redefinition. Few if any historians were sufficiently convinced by this characterisation to abandon use of the term; instead, and this does not take us very far at all from the breadth of definition acknowledged by Tawney over a century ago, medievalists have tended to assume that modern working definitions of peasant, as proposed by Thorner *et al.*, are sufficiently accommodating as to make room for a medieval English peasantry, broadly defined, and to conceive of a peasant society operating in medieval England.[80] It is within this broad conception of a medieval peasantry that the bulk of the historiography discussed in this volume is set.

Notes

1 It would not be correct to suggest that there was no 'historical' research and writing germane to the topic of English medieval peasants prior to the later nineteenth century; estate studies, from at least the seventeenth century, included discussion of matters pertaining to rent and tenure that would certainly accord with some of the themes which have been central to a more recent historiography. See, for instance, John Smyth, *Lives of the Berkeleys* (1883), vol. 2 of *The Berkeley manuscripts*, ed. J. Maclean (1883–85) which includes a considerable deal of detail on the tenantry, changes in tenure and forms of rent etc.; Smyth, the greater part of whose research and writing took place at Berkeley in the early seventeenth century, has been described as 'one of the earliest social historians', Andrew Warmington, 'Smyth, John (1567–1641)', *Oxford Dictionary of National Biography*, Oxford University Press, 2004; online edn, Jan 2008 (www.oxforddnb.com/view/article/25836, accessed 20 May 2014). On the broader theme of early modern historical writing, with particular reference to county and local studies, see K. Tiller, *English local history. An introduction* (Stroud: Alan Sutton, 1992), pp. 7–18; also the essays in L. Fox, ed., *English historical scholarship in the sixteenth and seventeenth centuries* (Dugdale Society, 1956), and especially there, chapter 7, a multi-authored discussion of 'The value of sixteenth- and seventeenth-century scholarship to modern historical research', pp. 115–27.
2 See below Chapter 1, pp. 44–7. Material culture and standard of living, particularly in relation to housing, feature in these discussions in so far as they have relevance to the discussion of communal organisation in past and, in some comparative instances, present societies.
3 A.E. Levett, *The Black Death on the estates of the see of Winchester* (Oxford: Oxford University Press, 1916).
4 See, for instance, F.M. Page, *The estates of Crowland Abbey* (Cambridge: Cambridge University Press, 1934); R.H. Hilton, *The economic development of some Leicestershire estates in the fourteenth and fifteenth centuries* (Oxford:

Oxford University Press, 1947); E. Miller, *The abbey and bishopric of Ely. The social history of an ecclesiastical estate from the tenth to the early fourteenth century* (Cambridge: Cambridge University Press, 1951); J.A. Raftis, *The estates of Ramsey Abbey. A study in economic growth and organization* (Toronto: Pontifical Institute of Mediaeval Studies, 1957); F.R.H. DuBoulay, *The lordship of Canterbury. An essay on medieval society* (London, 1966); E. King, *Peterborough Abbey, 1086–1310. A study in the land market* (Cambridge: Cambridge University Press, 1973); B.F. Harvey, *Westminster Abbey and its estates in the middle ages* (Oxford: Oxford University Press, 1977); C. Dyer, *Lords and peasants in a changing society: the estates of the bishopric of Worcester, 680–1540* (Cambridge: Cambridge University Press, 1980); E. Searle, *Lordship and community: Battle Abbey and its banlieu, 1066–1538* (Toronto: Pontifical Institute of Mediaeval Studies, 1974); I. Kershaw, *Bolton Priory. The economy of a northern monastery, 1286–1325* (Oxford: Oxford University Press, 1973). On secular estates, their lordship and tenantry, see G.A. Holmes, *The estates of the higher nobility in fourteenth-century England* (Cambridge: Cambridge University Press, 1957); J.M.W. Bean, *The estates of the Percy family, 1416–1537* (Oxford: Oxford University Press, 1958); J. Hatcher, *Rural economy and society in the Duchy of Cornwall, 1300–1500* (Cambridge: Cambridge University Press, 1970); P.D.A Harvey, *A medieval Oxfordshire village. Cuxham, 1240 to 1400* (Oxford: Oxford University Press, 1965).

5 See, for example, W. Page, ed., *A history of the county of Bedford: volume 2* (London: Victoria County History, 1908); W. Page, ed., *A history of the county of Buckingham: volume 2* (London: Victoria County History, 1908) and discussion below, pp. 34, 50; for regional studies, rather than those based closely on lordships, see D.C. Douglas, *Social structure of medieval East Anglia* (Oxford: Oxford University Press, 1927); H.C. Darby, *The medieval fenland* (Cambridge: Cambridge University Press, 1940); R.H. Hilton, *A medieval society. The west midlands at the end of the thirteenth century* (Cambridge: Cambridge University Press, 1966). There has been something of a return to regional and/or county-based study in more recent decades, as for instance, G. Platts, *Land and people in medieval Lincolnshire* (Lincoln: Society for Lincolnshire History and Archaeology, 1985); A.J. Winchester, *Landscape and society in medieval Cumbria* (Edinburgh: John Donald, 1987); M. Bailey, *A marginal economy? East Anglian Breckland in the later middle ages* (Cambridge: Cambridge University Press, 1989); L.R. Poos, *A rural society after the Black Death: Essex 1350–1525* (Cambridge: Cambridge University Press, 1991); M. Bailey, *Medieval Suffolk. An economic and social history, 1200–1500* (Woodbridge: Boydell, 2007).

6 E. Lipson, *The economic history of England. Volume 1. The middle ages* (7th edn, London: Adam and Charles Black, 1937), p. 662.

7 W.J. Ashley, *An introduction to English economic history and theory. Part I. The Middle Ages* (London: Rivingtons; 1st edn, 1888), pp. 3–49.

8 On the development of English economic history in the early twentieth century, see P.R. Schofield, 'British economic history, c.1880–c.1930', in P. Lambert and P.R. Schofield, eds, *Making history: an introduction to the history and practices of a discipline* (London: Routledge, 2004), pp. 65–77.

9   R.H. Tawney, *The agrarian problem in the sixteenth century* (Oxford: Longmans, 1912).
10 H.L. Gray, 'The commutation of villein services in England before the Black Death', *English Historical Review* 116 (1914); T.W. Page, *The end of villeinage in England* (New York: Macmillan, 1900); first published in German in 1897 as *Die Umwandlung der Frohndienste in Geldrenten in England* (Baltimore, 1897).
11 E.A. Kosminsky, 'Services and money rents in the thirteenth century', *Economic History Review* 5 (1935), 22–45; M.M. Postan, 'The chronology of labour services', *Transactions of the Royal Historical Society* 20 (1937), reprinted in M.M. Postan, *Essays on medieval agriculture and general problems of the medieval economy* (Cambridge: Cambridge University Press, 1973), pp. 89–106 (from which subsequent references are taken). For further discussion, see below Chapter 3, pp. 85–91.
12 J.E. Thorold Rogers, *Six centuries of work and wages* (1884); J.E. Thorold Rogers, *The economic interpretation of history* (1888). W.J. Ashley, 'James E. Thorold Rogers', *Political Science Quarterly*, 4 (1889), 381–407, questions, somewhat testily, Rogers's claims to the role of pioneer: 'Mr. Rogers has sometimes been looked upon as standing absolutely alone in his acquaintance with early English economic history – a mis-conception which his own language did nothing to weaken.' He notes also the earlier 'social antiquarians' as well as the publications of government departments and societies as early and important contributors (p. 381); as also discussed above, p. 23, n. 1.
13 J.E. Thorold Rogers, 'Rural England – social life', in J.E. Thorold Rogers, *Six centuries of work and wages*, p. 62.
14 Rogers, 'Rural England – social life', pp. 63, 68–9.
15 Rogers, 'Rural England – social life', pp. 68–9.
16 G.G. Coulton, *The medieval village* (Cambridge: Cambridge University Press, 1925); H.S. Bennett, *Life on the English manor. A study of peasant conditions 1150–1400* (Cambridge: Cambridge University Press, 1937). Coulton is himself deeply critical of Gasquet, Coulton, *The medieval village*, pp. 444–6. On Gasquet and Jessop, see below, pp. 11–12.
17 Coulton, *Medieval village*, pp. 1–7.
18 A.E. Levett, review of Coulton, *The medieval village*, in *Economic History Review* 1 (1927), 352–5.
19 Levett, review of Coulton, *The medieval village*, pp. 353–4.
20 T.A.M. Bishop, review of H.S. Bennett, *Life on the English manor. A study of peasant conditions 1150–1400* (Cambridge: Cambridge University Press, 1937), in *Economic History Review* 8 (1938), 193–4, quote at p. 193. For Bennett on the same, see Bennett, *Life on the English manor*, p. vi; compare a similar observation by H.E. Hallam, 'The life of the people', in H.E. Hallam, ed., *The agrarian history of England and Wales, vol. ii, 1042–1350* (Cambridge: Cambridge University Press, 1988), p. 845, and below, p. 221, n. 72. For a more sympathetic review of Bennett, see N. Neilson, *American Historical Review* 43 (1938), 838–40.
21 G.C. Homans, *English villagers of the thirteenth century* (Cambridge, Mass.: Harvard University Press, 1941).

22 See for instance, N. Neilson, review of Homans, *English villagers of the thirteenth century*, in *American Historical Review* 47 (1942), 576–7, who muttered that 'common sense would get us as far as technical phrases and abstractions' (p. 576).
23 R.H. Hilton, ed., *The transition from feudalism to capitalism* (London: Verso, 1976); T.H. Aston and C.H.E. Philpin, eds, *The Brenner debate. Agrarian class structure and economic development in pre-industrial Europe* (Cambridge: Cambridge University Press, 1985). For one of the latest examinations of relevant themes, see also the essays in C. Dyer, P. Coss and C. Wickham, eds, *Rodney Hilton's Middle Ages. An exploration of historical themes* (Past and Present Supplement, 2007); see also S.H. Rigby, *Marxism and history. A critical introduction* (Manchester: Manchester University Press, 2nd edn, 1998), pp. 160–5
24 See, for instance, R.H. Britnell, *The commercialisation of English society, 1000–1500* (Cambridge: Cambridge University Press, 1993; repr. Manchester: Manchester University Press, 1996); C. Dyer, *An age of transition? Economy and society in England in the later middle ages* (Oxford: Oxford University Press, 2005).
25 For instance, E. Britton, *The community of the vill: a study in the history of the family and village life in fourteenth century England* (Toronto: Pontifical Institute of Mediaeval Studies, 1977); E.B. DeWindt, *Land and people in Holywell-cum-Needingworth* (Toronto: Pontifical Institute of Mediaeval Studies, 1972).
26 As, for instance, in R.M. Smith, 'Kin and neighbors in a thirteenth-century Suffolk community', *Journal of Family History* 4 (1979), 219–56.
27 For Postan, his work and responses to it, see below, pp. 59–77.
28 A. Brown, 'Estate management and institutional constraints in pre-industrial England: the ecclesiastical estates of Durham, c.1400–1640', *Economic History Review* 67 (2014), 699–719.
29 Z. Razi, 'The Toronto School's reconstitution of medieval peasant society: a critical view', *Past and Present* 29 (1979), 141–57.
30 On commutation, see for instance, T.W. Page, *The end of villeinage in England* (New York: Macmillan, 1900); H.L. Gray, 'The commutation of villein services in England before the Black Death', *English Historical Review* 29 (1914), 625–56, and below, pp. 38–9, 85–7.
31 T.S. Kuhn, *The structure of scientific revolutions* (Chicago: University of Chicago Press, 1962); revised ed. 1970. For brief discussion of the same, P. Lambert and P. Schofield, 'Introduction', in P. Lambert and P. Schofield, eds, *Making history*, pp. 2–3.
32 On the issue of incommensurability and for a general discussion of Kuhnian paradigms and weaknesses in Kuhn's theoretical perspective, see A.F. Chalmers, *What is this thing called science?* (Buckingham: Open University Press, 3rd edn, 1999), pp. 104–29.
33 On recent approaches to law in manorial courts, see, for instance, C.D. Briggs, 'Manor court procedures, debt litigation levels, and rural credit provision in England, c.1290–c.1380', *Law and History Review* 24 (2006), 519–58; J. S. Beckerman, 'Procedural innovation and institutional change in medieval English manorial courts', *Law and History Review* 10 (1992), 198–252; L. Bonfield, 'The

nature of customary law in the manor courts of medieval England', *Comparative Studies in Society and History* 31 (1989), 515–34; P.R. Hyams, 'What did Edwardian villagers mean by "law"?', in Z. Razi and R.M. Smith, eds, *Medieval society and the manor court* (Oxford: Oxford University Press, 1996), pp. 69–102; P.R. Schofield, 'Peasants and the manor court: gossip and litigation in a Suffolk village at the close of the thirteenth century', *Past and Present* 159 (1998), 3–42. On the potential of individual account books to shed much light on later medieval rural dwellers, see especially C. Dyer, *A Country Merchant, 1495–1520: trading and farming at the end of the middle ages* (Oxford: Oxford University Press, 2012). See also below, pp. 211–12, 230–1, 255, for further discussion of these issues.

34 See, for instance, Bonnie G. Smith, *The gender of history. Men, women and historical practice* (Cambridge, Mass.: Harvard University Press, 1998), p. 71.
35 That said, Homans's research found its most receptive audience in the 1960s and 1970s, by which stage a new social history offered a platform for his work and a stimulus to further research along the same lines.
36 M.M. Postan, review of G.C. Homans, *English villagers in the thirteenth century*, in *Economic History Review* 15 (1945), 88–92, quote at p. 89.
37 As discussed above, pp. 6–7 and below, pp. 207–9. The sense of mission is clear in DeWindt's conclusion to DeWindt, *Land and people*, pp. 281–3; also Raftis, *Tenure and mobility*, pp. 11–12; for reflections on the initial enthusiasm with which this approach was greeted, see I. Blanchard, review article of C. Dyer, *Lords and peasants in a changing society*, and Z. Razi, *Life, marriage and death in a medieval parish*, in *Social History* 7 (1982), 340: 'A wind of change was blowing through the medieval village sweeping away legal stereotypes and revealing the peasant against the backcloth of the Breughelish patterns of village life. A sense of excitement of what could be achieved, through using the new methodology, spread in British and American academic circles, and works from the Pontifical institute were eagerly awaited during the late 1960s and early 1970s.'
38 For discussion of the work of Hilton and Postan, see especially Chapters 2 and 3 below.
39 A. Jessop, 'Village life six hundred years ago', in A. Jessop, *The coming of the friars* (London: Fisher Unwin, 1889). Originally published in *The Nineteenth Century*.
40 Jessop, 'Village life', pp. 53, 111.
41 Rogers, 'Rural England – agriculture', pp. 84–6.
42 Gasquet, *English monastic life* (London; Methuen and Co., 1904), p. 199, quoted and cited in G.G. Coulton, *The medieval village*, p. 444.
43 J.E.T. Rogers, *A history of agriculture and prices in England* (Oxford: Oxford University Press, 7 volumes, 1866–1902).
44 On Japan, see, for instance, the unpublished paper by Yoko Miyoshi summarising Japanese research on the rural history of later medieval Europe undertaken between 1967 and 1987: Y. Miyoshi, 'Recent Japanese studies in rural history of later medieval Europe' (unpublished paper; available on-line at http://medsociety.or.kr/layouts/MLT_Simple_sub/file/1988-04-9.pdf; last accessed 1 September 2014). Yoko Miyoshi's own research on the Suffolk manor of Rickinghall is a

case in point: Y. Miyoshi, *A peasant society in economic change: a Suffolk manor, 1279-1437* [Japanese with English summary] (Tokyo: University of Tokyo Press, 1981); much of Miyoshi's work is available in Japanese though she has published shorter pieces and summaries of her work in English.

45 P. Gattrell, 'Historians and peasants: studies of medieval English society in a Russian context', *Past and Present* 96 (1982), reprinted in T.H. Aston, ed., *Landlords, peasants and politics in medieval England* (Cambridge: Cambridge University Press, 1987), pp. 394-422 (subsequent references taken from this reprint).

46 On the Peasants' Revolt, see, for example, A. Réville, *Le soulèvement des travailleurs d'Angleterres en 1381: Études et documents publiés avec un introduction historique* (Paris: Picard, 1898), one of the earliest 'modern' discussions of the Peasants' Revolt which includes much material and comment subsequently cited by Anglophone historians of the revolt. Marc Bloch's discussion of the relationship between agrarian revolt and seigneurial regimes clearly informed Rodney Hilton's thinking; he returns to Bloch's key quote on this topic (in *French rural history* (1966; English edition, London: Routledge and Kegan Paul), p. 170) in more than one publication throughout his career: R.H. Hilton, 'Peasant movements in England before 1381', *Economic History Review*, 2nd series, 2 (1949), 117, 118; R.H. Hilton, *Bond men made free. Medieval peasant movements and the English rising of 1381* (London, 1973; republished with a new introduction by C. Dyer, London: Routledge, 2003), pp. xviii-xix; xxi.

47 See, for example, the various essays on the peasant land market and the general introduction in L. Feller and C. Wickham, eds, *Le marché de la terre au Moyen Âge* (Rome: École Française de Rome, 2005); for recent reflection upon this exchange, see M. Bourin, F. Menant and Ll. To Figueras, 'Les campagnes agraires avant la peste. Préliminaire historiographiques pour de nouvelles approaches Méditerranéennes', in M. Bourin, F. Menant and Ll. To Figueras, eds, *Dynamiques du monde rural dans la conjuncture de 1300* (Rome: École Française de Rome, 2014), pp. 9-101.

48 For relevant work, see W. Abel, *Agricultural fluctuations in Europe from the thirteenth to the twentieth centuries* (trans. O. Ordish, London: Methuen, 1980); B.H. Slicher-Van Bath, *The agrarian history of Western Europe, AD 500-1850* (trans. O. Ordish, London: E. Arnold, 1963); G. Duby, *Rural economy and country life in the medieval West* (trans. C. Postan, London: E. Arnold, 1968). See also the brief comments in R.H. Britnell, 'Commercialization, stagnation and crisis, 1250-1350', in J. Drendel, ed., *Crisis in the middle ages. Postan-Duby: the destiny of an historical paradigm* (Turnhout: Brepols, 2015), p. 15; J. Munro, '"Money matters": a critique of the Postan thesis on medieval population, prices and wages', in Drendel, ed., *Crisis in the middle ages*, p. 127.

49 J.A. Raftis, 'Social structures in five East Midland villages: a study of possibilities in the use of court roll data', *Economic History Review* 18 (1965), 83-100 (quote at p. 100).

50 See, for instance, S. Thrupp, 'The problem of replacement rates in late medieval English population', *Economic History Review*, 2nd series., 18 (1965); L.R. Poos,

'The rural population of Essex in the later middle ages', *Economic History Review* 38 (1985), 515-30.
51 Smith, 'Kin and neighbours'.
52 See, for instance, J.M. Bennett, 'Review of Z. Razi and R.M. Smith, *Medieval society and the manor court* (Oxford: Oxford University Press, 1996)', *Journal of Interdisciplinary History* 29 (1998), 99-101; also Bennett, 'England: women and gender', in S.H. Rigby, ed., *Blackwell companion to later medieval Britain* (Oxford: Blackwell, 2002), pp. 98-9, where she also suggests, following Miri Rubin, that British historians have been constrained by archival research and 'bound by the nationalistic imperatives that still haunt the historical profession'.
53 For an instance of her intellectual approach, see S. Olson, *A mute gospel. The people and culture of the medieval English common fields* (Toronto: Pontifical Institute of Mediaeval Studies, 2009), pp. 1-51. On her criticism of other forms of approach, see, for instance, Olson's review of M.K. McIntosh, *Controlling misbehavior in England, 1370-1600* (Cambridge: Cambridge University Press, 1998) in *Speculum* 75 (2000), 216-19; see also her review of Z. Razi and R.M. Smith, eds, *Medieval society and the manor court* (Oxford: Oxford University Press, 1996), in *Speculum* 74 (1999), 818-20, in which she perceives the editors' endorsement of a return to the legal-historical approach of Maitland to be 'backward-looking', 'not progressive' and 'divisive' (p. 820).
54 K. Biddick, 'Decolonizing the English past: readings in medieval archaeology and history', *Journal of British Studies* 32 (1993), 1-23, quote at p. 19.
55 See, for instance, the fairly stern critique of M.M. Postan and J.Z. Titow, 'Heriots and prices on Winchester manors', *Economic History Review*, 2nd series, 11 (1959); reprinted in Postan, *Essays in medieval agriculture*, pp. 150-85, by G. Ohlin, 'No safety in numbers: some pitfalls of historical statistics', in R. Floud, ed., *Essays in quantitative economic history* (Oxford: Oxford University Press, 1974), pp. 73-7 (also below, Chapters 2, p. 64, and 5, pp. 155, 162). Note also the comment of Bennett, 'Review of Razi and Smith, *Medieval society and the manor court*', p. 100, who, in discussing the republication of a debate about the use of court rolls in constructing population estimates, concludes, 'This heated, technical, and largely negative debate seems to have had a deadening effect on research'.
56 See, for example, Postan's review of Homans, *English villagers of the thirteenth century* (*Economic History Review* 15 (1945), 88-92); it is a tolerant though hardly enthusiastic reading of Homans's sociological approach: 'on the whole his anthropological bias does no violence to his facts and does not strain the historical sense of his readers. On the contrary many a medievalist will read his sociological summaries with the comfortable feeling of the *bourgeois* gentilhomme at his first confrontation with prose' (p. 89).
57 E.A. Kosminsky, *Studies in the agrarian history of England in the thirteenth century* (Oxford: Oxford University Press, 1956).
58 For early work using manorial court rolls, see, for instance, F.G. Davenport, *The economic development of a Norfolk manor, 1086-1565* (Cambridge: Cambridge University Press, 1906; reprinted, London: Frank Cass 1967); Tawney, *Agrarian problem*, pp. 54-173; A.E. Levett, 'The Black Death on the estates of the see of

Winchester', in P. Vinogradoff, ed., *Oxford studies in social and legal history. Volume V* (Oxford: Oxford University Press, 1916); W. Hudson, 'The prior of Norwich's manor of Hindolveston: its early organisation and the right of the customary tenants to alienate their strips of land', *Norfolk Archaeology* 20 (1919–20), and the works identified in Z. Razi and R. Smith, 'Introduction. The historiography of manorial court rolls', in Razi and Smith, eds, *Medieval society and the manor court*, pp. 3–15.

59 See above, pp. 6, 11, 13–14.

60 J.A. Raftis, *The estates of Ramsey Abbey. A study in economic growth and organization* (Toronto: Pontifical Institute of Mediaeval Studies, 1957); J. A. Raftis, *Tenure and mobility: studies in the social history of the medieval English village* (Toronto: Pontifical Institute of Mediaeval Studies, 1964); J. A. Raftis, *Warboys: two hundred years in the life of an English medieval village* (Toronto: Pontifical Institute of Mediaeval Studies, 1974).

61 Theses on medieval topics, completed between 1970 and the present and identified as 'economic history' by the Institute of Historical Research record of theses completed suggest a degree of decline, with 32 theses recorded in the 1970s, 29 in the 1980s and 25 in the 1990s. No medieval theses were identified as listed under 'economic history' for the decade or more after 2000, though this is also more obviously a feature of data recording rather than of an absolute trend in theses completed. Source: www.history.ac.uk/history-online/categories (last accessed 16 September 2014). It would certainly not be correct to suggest that students and researchers have been entirely discouraged in the last decade or so, as for instance, J.L. Phillips, 'Collaboration and litigation in two Suffolk manor courts, 1289–1364' (unpublished PhD thesis, University of Cambridge, 2005); M. Stevens, 'Race, gender and wealth in a medieval Welsh borough: access to capital, market participation and status in Ruthin, 1312–22' (unpublished PhD thesis, University of Wales, 2005); A. Sapzonik, 'Peasant agriculture at Oakington, Cambridgeshire, c.1290–1400' (unpublished PhD thesis, University of Cambridge, 2010); A. Brown, 'Recession and recovery in the north-east, 1450–1540' (unpublished PhD thesis, Durham University, 2011).

62 The teaching of the medieval agrarian economy to primary school children, between the ages of 4 and 11, is anticipated, in highly general terms, in the current primary school curriculum for the UK: www.education.gov.uk/schools/teachingandlearning/curriculum/primary/b00199012/history/ks2 (accessed 3 May 2013). There is also some limited scope for discussion of aspects of medieval society and economy, potentially including the medieval village, in the secondary level history curriculum, for 11-year-olds and older: www.education.gov.uk/schools/teachingandlearning/curriculum/secondary/b00199545/history/programme/range (accessed 3 May 2013). It is also evident that some teaching of the medieval economy, including the medieval village and rural society, has been anticipated by authors and publishers, with general surveys and more specific texts aimed at children in schooling at all age groups. See, for instance, D. Hartley and M.M. Elliot, *Life and work of the people of England. The fourteenth century* (London: Batsford, 1928); M.E. Reeves, *The medieval village* (London: Longman, 1954), the work of

the latter author also discussed in D. Cannadine, J. Keating and N. Sheldon, *The right kind of history. Teaching the past in twentieth century England* (Basingstoke: Palgrave-Macmillan, 2011), p. 121. At different moments in the twentieth century curriculum designers encouraged or were indifferent to the childhood study of such issues, as discussed in general terms in Cannadine *et al.*, *The right kind of history*.

63 Kuhn, *Structure of scientific revolutions*.
64 See, for instance, the comments on Raftis's later work, below, pp. 123-4.
65 Schofield, 'Emergence of British economic history', p. 6, and references there.
66 For instance, rather more articles or reviews were published on villeinage, or with the word 'villeinage' appearing in the text of the *English Historical Review*, up until 1950 (63 in total) than in the last 60 years or so of the same journal's history (34 appearances). The combined 97 individual references to the word 'villeinage' in the *English Historical Review* are in any case a meagre total in comparison to, say, the 6,760 unique references to 'parliament' or the 2,754 to 'baron' (http://ehr.oxfordjournals.org/; last accessed 15 October 2014).
67 R.H. Hilton, *The English peasantry in the later middle ages. The Ford lectures for 1973 and related studies* (Oxford: Oxford University Press, 1975), p. 4. See also R.H. Hilton, 'Medieval peasants: any lessons?', in R.H. Hilton, ed., *Class conflict and the crisis of feudalism. Essays in medieval social history* (London: Hambledon, 1985), pp. 114-21.
68 Hilton, *English peasantry*, p. 5.
69 M.M. Postan, 'Agricultural problems of the under-developed countries in the light of European agrarian history', in *Second international conference of economic history. Aix-en-Provence, 1962. Volume ii: Middle ages and modern times* (Paris: Mouton, 1965), pp. 9-24, and especially p. 10.
70 See, for instance, W.A.S. Hewins (revised A. Kadish), 'Rogers, James Edwin Thorold', *Oxford Dictionary of National Biography* (Oxford: Oxford University Press, 2004; online edn, May 2006), http://www.oxforddnb.com/view/article/23979 (accessed 4 March 2009).
71 C. Dyer, 'Obituary: Rodney Hilton', *The Guardian*, 10 June 2002, available online at www.theguardian.com/news/2002/jun/10/guardianobituaries.humanities (accessed 8 September 2015).
72 See, for instance, the autobiographical reflections of Judith Bennett in J.M. Bennett, *History matters. Patriarchy and the challenge of feminism* (Philadelphia: University of Pennsylvania Press, 2006), pp. 1-2.
73 M. Berg, 'The first women economic historians', *Economic History Review* 45 (1992), 308-29.
74 J. Des Jardins, *Women and the historical enterprise in America: gender, race, and the politics of memory, 1880-1945* (Chapel Hill: The University of North Carolina Press, 2006), p. 41, N. Neilson, 'Boon-services on the estates of Ramsey Abbey', *American Historical Review* 2 (1897), 213-24.
75 R.H. Hilton, *The English peasantry in the later middle ages* (Oxford: Oxford University Press, 1975), p. 5; *Bond men made free*, pp. xvi-xvii.
76 As, for instance, Homans, *English villagers of the thirteenth century*.

77 Hilton, *English peasantry*, p. 3.
78 Tawney, *Agrarian problem*, pp. 55-9.
79 A. Macfarlane, *The origins of English individualism* (Oxford: Blackwell, 1978).
80 P.R. Schofield, *Peasant and community in medieval England 1200-1500* (Basingstoke: Palgrave, 2003), p. 6; J. Whittle, *The development of agrarian capitalism. Land and labour in Norfolk, 1440-1580* (Oxford: Oxford University Press, 2000), pp. 11-16; S.H. Rigby, *English society in the later middle ages. Class, status and gender* (Basingstoke: Macmillan, 1995), pp. 22-5.

1

Early contributions

In this first chapter we will examine the earliest attempts, in terms of a modern historiography dating from the second half of the nineteenth century, to discuss the medieval English peasantry. This will involve consideration of the various issues that encouraged historians in the late nineteenth and early twentieth century to turn to matters relating to the medieval English peasantry. As we will see, this sometimes meant that peasants, in these first iterations, were dealt with *en passant*, as adjuncts to another main topic of study. In other instances, the peasantry were closer to centre stage in historical investigations. It will also be evident that this early discussion of medieval peasants prefigures important themes that came to dominate the later historiography of the medieval peasantry. This in some instances reflects a continuity of broad themes, illustrative both of persistent intellectual currents in the relevant historiography and the inevitable directions in which researchers have been led by the predominant bodies of source materials. In what follows we will consider the emergent themes in the late nineteenth and early twentieth centuries and consider the contributions of their historians. We can begin with one of the most resilient of the themes in the historiography of the medieval English peasantry: lordship. Thereafter we will explore the following main themes from this early period, in particular, economy, population and demography, and, finally, the village community.

Lordship

In many of the earliest examples of work making reference to medieval peasants, the chief intellectual programme of their authors was to explore the institutions to which the peasants owed service.[1] For instance,

F.W. Maitland's analysis of the records of the manor of Wilburton offers one of the first close discussions of the movement of rent and of the management of the demesne from the thirteenth century through to the early sixteenth century. There is a great deal here on the changing condition of the tenantry, measured through the manorial accounts, but the underlying emphasis is upon the adjustments to the management of the demesne in response to the changing economic environment of the later middle ages. Maitland outlines the diminution in seigneurial management of the manor in the later fourteenth and fifteenth centuries, and the reduction in its dependence upon labour services, as well as the growth of valuable and secure copyholds by the sixteenth century.[2] The earliest of the *Victoria County Histories* also contain a good deal of comment on tenurial structures, manorial descents, the obligations which lords might expect to receive from their manors. There is though far less on the tenantry or, more generally, the peasantry.[3] The same is broadly true of some of the earliest estate studies, though, as we will see, a good number of such do contain plentiful discussion on the condition and, more particularly, the obligations of the tenantry.

So also Maitland's pioneering investigation of customary law, published in 1889 as the first volume of the publications of the Selden Society, emphasises the legal and administrative developments associated with the manor court and above all lordly rights associated with the holding of manorial courts far more than it does the use of the court and the local-level law of peasant litigants.[4] It is hardly surprising to discover such an emphasis: the records, seigneurial records with their content a response to the administrative and managerial requirements of a landed estate and its assets, inevitably and appropriately encourage just such an approach. Writing in the first decade of the twentieth century, Frances Davenport laments the lack of evidence directly available for the study of the economic condition of the tenantry but notes that the manorial accounts 'though primarily treating of the demesne, incidentally furnish material from which some inferences regarding the economic position of the tenants of the manor may be drawn'.[5] Similarly, while there is quite a considerable if largely incidental study of villeinage and its tenurial implications in Maitland's principal work on English law in the middle ages, serfdom features as an instance of the range and nature of law and its development.[6] In his magisterial study of Domesday Book, written a few years after *The history of English law*, and drawing on material originally intended for but not in the end included in that work, tenurial distinctions and the significance of serfdom and villeinage feature far more prominently.[7] In this study, which is both pioneering and evidence for intellectual agendas shared with one or two other significant contemporaries (notably J.H. Round and P. Vinogradoff), Maitland offers a thorough investigation of the earliest English statements on agrarian tenure as well as their mutation in the following centuries. His emphasis is on the legal significance and foundation to the condition of medieval men and women; there is far less here, explicitly, upon the actual condition of men and women or the relations of lords and their tenants.[8] There is however much in Maitland's study that encourages such questions but they do not sit at the heart of his own investigation; instead his remit was to establish some sense of the forms and development of tenure and its relationship within law.

Most obvious in this respect was the contribution of Paul Vinogradoff, whose two major works, on the manor and on villeinage, inevitably include significant comment on lord–tenant relations.[9] To a considerable degree, Vinogradoff's discussion focuses upon the terminology of tenurial status and the distinctions between free tenure and serfdom.[10] Thus he considers in some detail the sorts of tenurial distinction evident in Domesday Book and then seeks to trace the successive use and development of the same in high and later medieval sources. While in many respects he was content to describe the condition of villeinage, although also closely engaged in discussion of change over time and especially in terms of the ways in which tenure is defined in the record, Vinogradoff also from time to time grappled with the implications of unfree tenure for the tenantry and the nature of the relationship between lords and their servile tenants.[11] By the end of the thirteenth century, as Vinogradoff describes, these sorts of terminological distinction, while still evident in the contemporary record, were far from easy to apply in reality. Instead, as he notes, it is the more general condition of servitude which tended to hold a more general sway, and this he describes in some detail.[12]

In considering the significance of villeinage for the society and economy of the medieval countryside, something that does occupy his interest to a certain extent, Vinogradoff is not prepared to attach the greatest social or economic significance to the object of his study. Instead he dismisses as 'preposterous' the notion that the 'formula of disability ... [while] by no means a dead letter or a meaningless fiction ... [was] the one regulating factor of rural life'.[13] In fact, relative to other external factors that played upon the peasant's world, Vinogradoff is keen to stress the relative insignificance of servile status. 'There is', he writes, 'no question of the arbitrary rule of stewards or of the caprice of slaveowners'.[14] In both dismissing the capacity of lords and their officers to order the affairs of their serfs and stressing the ways in which servile peasants were capable of managing their own resources, engaging with royal courts, buying and selling according to their own volition and so on, Vinogradoff adopts a perspective upon servility and its incidence which, as we shall see in a later chapter on lordship, chimes with some of the most recent discussions of this topic.[15] It was however not an approach he was particularly keen to adopt as an agenda for further research. Above all, Vinogradoff's perspective was an intellectualising one: he was interested in the definition of villeinage as much as or more than its everyday implication for those who held their land under it. In this respect also Vinogradoff was interested not only in unfree tenure and servility. As part of his investigation of his villein tenure, he was led to consider the free tenants and the cottagers who stood as points of comparison with the neifs and customary tenants who were his primary object of interest.[16] Again, in addressing these subjects, it is chiefly in the nature of their tenure and its antecedents that his main concerns lie; and, again, where there is an interest in change over time it largely resides in an emphasis on the persistence of terminology and distinctions in the meaning of tenurial terms.

Other historians, also writing at the end of the nineteenth and the beginning of the twentieth centuries, took broadly similar perspectives. In ways that are most likely a conscious extension of Vinogradoff's own work and one certainly informed by its emphases and broader intellectual approach, Nellie Neilson's discussion of customary rent, edited by Vinogradoff for Oxford Studies in Social and Legal History and published in 1910, presents a detailed and careful study of a variety of forms of rent, charting their etymology, their antecedents and their later medieval form.[17] At no point does Neilson offer a view on the significance of the rents she is describing for those who paid them; instead, she offers a study in the history of the kinds of rent, and a focus on their extraordinary variety. Her doctoral study of the estates of Ramsey Abbey, published over a decade earlier in 1898, was also arranged by discussion of rent and the kinds of obligation owed by the tenantry to their lord. As such the discussion, rich, detailed and thorough, tends to a descriptive account, though with some reflection on the changing incidence of villein obligations over time, Neilson proposing that villein obligations increased between the twelfth and thirteenth centuries as lords extended boon works while maintaining other rents.[18] In her research, Neilson displays though a deep and abiding interest in changes in the form and structure of rents of a kind which was more directly reflected in other studies, from the first decades of the twentieth century, also aimed at the investigation of rent.

Of course, historians in the later nineteenth and early twentieth centuries were writing within an academic context which encouraged just such an approach. Legal, constitutional and, increasingly, administrative history sat at the very core of the historical endeavour, as we have already discussed, and historians such as Neilson saw the gathering of such data, transcribed in detail in her doctoral thesis for instance, as an important, in fact vital, element in a scientific engagement with the past; as she noted in the introduction to her *American Historical Review* article on boon services, 'facts are at present more needed than conclusions'.[19] It would take some significant adjustment in the focus of historical enquiry for historians of the medieval countryside to shift attention from lords to their tenants and, then, to the peasantry more broadly. That, of course, this did occur we are already aware and these adjustments in focus will be the subject of later chapters.[20] For now, we can consider a little more fully the ways in which the study of lords and their estates in the middle ages also encouraged investigation of their tenantry and helped to establish a crucial line of enquiry in the historical discussion of the medieval peasantry. In the first place, it would certainly be incorrect to suggest that some of these earliest studies did not venture beyond a description of manor or estate and the place of the tenantry within it, or to examine law and institutional and tenurial structures in ways that were essentially antiquarian and lacking an intellectual agenda. As we have already seen, historians such as Vinogradoff and Maitland, as well as laying crucial foundations for their area of study, also presented their work according to a rigorous intellectual schema, and one chiefly directed at establishing a chronology of change. While some of this earliest work was clearly constrained by its pioneering role, and the necessary fact that there was little or no other research and writing with which to engage and perhaps to take issue, by at least the first years of the twentieth century historians were also using their research in manorial and estate records to test the changing nature of the relationship between lord and tenant.[21] Thus, Davenport's volume on the manor of Forncett (Norfolk) is both a study of the demesne from the thirteenth to the later sixteenth and seventeenth centuries and an investigation of the tenantry in approximately the same period.[22] As Maitland, so Davenport in her discussion of the tenantry chiefly contents herself with relaying the evidence for changing tenurial conditions across the later middle ages and early modern period. She also though offers some limited prosopographical analysis of peasant families, reconstructing certain details of familial holdings, and provides an assessment of the decline of villeinage and its possible causes, drawing upon her research on Forncett and, with only the most oblique of references, challenging the work of Edward P. Cheyney on the same topic.[23] In her challenge to Cheyney's contention that the servile tenantry of the later middle ages was largely static, she employs data from Forncett to argue the opposite and, in a series of observations that accord with much later work in this area, illustrates a significant turnover in servile families as well as offering some comment on their out-migration from the manor, suggesting that tenants often went to neighbouring manors.[24] Such a brief exchange serves to remind us that, even in the earliest stirrings of research into the medieval rural economy and society, there were important debates regarding matters pertaining to lords' rights over their tenantry. This was especially the case in relation to the investigation of the history of serfdom and its disappearance.

One of the more significant contributions to this debate, which took place mostly in the first years of the twentieth century, was made by T.W. Page. Page argued for a relatively late disappearance of serfdom and proposed that a deliberate policy exercised by landlords in the post-plague era was instrumental in achieving this decline. He contended that labour service declined significantly after the Black Death but that there had been little movement in the direction of such a change in the years before the mid-fourteenth century.[25] H.L. Gray, in response to Page, offered a detailed and forensic examination of the original data as well as new source material. Testing Page's argument, Gray used the records of inquisitions *post mortem* in order to pursue the issue of the commutation of villein services. Gray was far less interested in the significance of this process for an understanding of lord–tenant relations than he was in examining the chronology of change and its implications for the rise of a money economy in medieval England. The process of commutation (the formal release of tenants from servile tenure in return for some form of payment by the tenant to his or her lord) was, for Gray, an important index of the changing significance of money in the countryside; he took issue with Page's suggestion that commutation developed rapidly after the arrival of plague in the mid-fourteenth century and suggested that, in fact, there was good evidence for much earlier commutation.[26] In this argument, as he acknowledged, Gray returned to the earlier conclusions of Rogers, who had also found evidence for a significant pre-plague retreat from labour services and a more general process of commutation.[27] Much like Gray, Rogers was at least as interested in the nature of the economy and its capacity to shift from rent in labour and kind into a system built upon money rent as he was in commutation *per se*. Rogers was also keen to stress the moral and societal benefits of commutation as well as linking the process of commutation to the death of serfdom, which he sees as generating a coming together of different kinds of tenure and obligation with the consequence that the separate identity and potency of serfdom was effectively reduced.[28] With Rogers and his interest in the function of the medieval economy in mind, it is then to early discussion of peasant involvement in the economy that we should turn.

Economy

In examining earlier conceptualisations of the economy of the medieval English peasantry, its operation, its ambit and its significance for the wider economy, we can see that, while some historians sought to emphasise the market-orientation of certain members of peasant society, the tendency was, perhaps unsurprisingly given the tenor of our discussion to date, to reduce the role of the market in the lives of the peasantry relative to such other apparent 'constants' as lordship.

As we have already considered, historians writing in the decades either side of 1900 and who expressed an interest in medieval rural society, were inclined to dwell upon the medieval English peasantry not as a direct subject for investigation but as an adjunct, even if an important adjunct, to the object of their primary research. Most evidently, the peasantry was not discussed in its entirety but instead it was those peasants who were tenants of lords who attracted particular interest. Discussion of the economy of the peasantry was therefore most often directed at the economy of the tenantry and this, inevitably, in relation to the manorial economy. A good deal of the earliest investigation of lord–tenant relations was measured in terms of obligations and their extraction, especially in terms of rent and the changing nature of rent.

If, for instance, we review the work of Maitland and Vinogradoff we find a good deal of emphasis upon obligations, and especially rents and services associated with particular categories of tenant. Thus, for instance, Maitland's discussion of serfs, villeins and sokemen in the centuries after Domesday is founded upon an investigation of their changing status and the developing law *vis-à-vis* their tenurial obligations.[29] Vinogradoff, though he has much to say about the commutation of rent and makes some small comment upon the developing English economy in this period, also concentrates his attention upon the nature of obligation relative to customary arrangements. Where he anticipates the possibility of, for instance, an economically active peasantry it is largely in relation to the free peasantry and those more evidently associated with the payment of fixed money rents.[30] Both Maitland and Vinogradoff were certainly aware of the potential for a peasant economy to operate in ways that were not wholly dominated by tenure and the obligations owed to lordship; in fact they allude to it from time to time. Vinogradoff suggested instead that the demands of lordship played against a backdrop of external and internal dealings, some involving their lord and some not.[31] Such issues were however of importance only in so far as they might illustrate the elements of a different thesis, the changing extent of lordship and the nature of its demands upon the tenantry.

Similarly, there was, amongst late nineteenth-century historians, some discussion of the transfer of land, including the buying and selling of land. Maitland, in his broad survey of the court rolls and accounts for late medieval Wilburton (Cambridgeshire), noted the terminology of surrender and admittance in the case of villein holdings. He did not subject this to close analysis however; in fact, his opportunity to research the records of a 'midlands-type' manor,[32] where fragmentation and alienation of virgated holdings appear to have been restricted throughout the period, undoubtedly conditioned his view of the peasant land market.[33] Vinogradoff also, in his survey of villeinage in medieval England, is disinclined to challenge common law theories of villeinage. Instead, he mostly contents himself with blanket statements on the incapacity of villeins to alienate their land, this as a further indication of their servile condition.[34] While both Maitland and Vinogradoff employed manorial records in their assessments of villeinage and of tenurial development in the high and late middle ages, it was in the researches of the next generation that a peasant land market, especially in villein land, was first fully described and subjected to close analysis, points to which we will return in a later chapter.[35]

It is clear that very few historians from this era recognised clearly that a peasant economy might involve interaction with markets and with commerce. Most obviously Rogers, whose work was truly pioneering in this respect and who quite deliberately set out his research as a contrast to all other historical study in the later nineteenth century, identified peasant market involvement as important and attempted to provide a model of a domestic budget for the medieval peasant family.[36] Concentrating his attention on the small-holder, Rogers examined in some detail the income and expenditure of the peasant household and laid no particular stress upon the demands of lordship. Instead, he chose to emphasise the importance of the market in determining the small-holder's budget, and in his analysis identifies the purchase of grain as the main demand upon this domestic budget.[37] While Roger's inclination to identify the market as a major determinant of the domestic economy of the peasantry sets him apart from many historians writing in this area before at least the 1980s, he was not however entirely alone. R.H. Tawney, a historian of the early modern period with rather more than just a passing interest in the later medieval rural economy, was also keenly aware of the dynamics of the market and market-forces operating within the medieval and early modern village. In the first decade of the twentieth century Tawney wrote at some length about the medieval village and, while he was far more inclined than was Rogers to minimise the role of the market relative to the insularity and self-supporting economy of the medieval village, he also discussed the potential for market forces and in particular the pervasiveness of what he perceived as relatively new entrepreneurial and capitalistic tendencies to effect changes in the local economy. Thus, for instance, Tawney wrote of the influence of the village money-lender as essentially a negative one; referring to the creditor as monopolistic and a 'bugbear', Tawney saw such limited injection of capital as an indication of the weakness and impermanence of markets and the general lack of sufficient usable capital.[38] Writing of the fifteenth and sixteenth centuries, Tawney reflected that 'to the mass of the peasantry in our period the commercial side of agriculture offered no problem, because for the mass of the peasantry it did not exist'.[39]

Yet at the same time Tawney also recognised that trade and commerce could and did influence the economic tenor of rural life and might lead to significant differences in the material experience of the peasantry.[40] He reflected upon the opportunities presented to the peasantry in the decades after the mid-fourteenth-century epidemics, the investment in landholding, the stability of customary rents relative to the increased income of the peasant household in this period; in other words, Tawney detected and described some features of proto-capitalist activity within the village consistent with a peasant economy not solely or even largely defined, in the later middle ages and sixteenth century, by the demands of lordship but in certain measure protected by it and by the custom of obligation.[41] In fact, what Tawney described was a burgeoning market in land which, encouraged by a move in the direction of an increasingly commercialised agricultural economy by the early modern period, aggravated economic divisions within the peasant economy and helped to polarise rural society.[42] Other relatively early commentators could conceive of involved and precocious market-orientated activity, as for instance in Kosminsky's discussion of the market in grain in the high and late middle ages; however his analysis, despite his awareness of the extensive money rents paid by peasant tenants, was restricted to the seigneurial sector and, for Kosminsky, engagement with the market by lords served only to reinforce their demands upon their tenantry, especially in terms of labour services.[43] N.S.B. Gras, in his study of the medieval and early modern grain trade, also identified a pull of the market amongst the wealthier peasantry from the twelfth and thirteenth centuries, a feature of peasant society he also associated with resistance to seigneurial demands as unfree peasants sought greater opportunities for market engagement in the later middle ages.[44] Similar strands of peasant engagement with the market are also strongly evident in Eileen Power's published 1939 Ford lectures on the medieval wool trade in which she quickly and forcefully dismissed the notion of a natural and self-sufficient economy and located the peasantry within a world of international commerce.[45]

Population and demography

As in historical discussion of lordship and the economy in the later nineteenth and early twentieth centuries, so also study of a loosely demographic kind in this period tended to be couched in terms conditioned by the normal expectations of the study of rural society. Thus, writing in this context, Maitland's early exploration of the development of the manorial history of the manor of Wilburton, based upon a broken series of manorial records, does not encourage further reflection on population change, epidemic crises and their impact upon the organisation of the manorial economy. Instead, the potential effects of the Black Death are fairly speedily dismissed by Maitland and a narrative of change is offered more than an attempt at its explanation.[46] The same tendency to narrate is also generally true in other work from around the same period but historians other than Maitland also showed a great deal of interest in the impact that the Black Death could have had upon later medieval society.

A debate in the *Fortnightly Review* between Rogers and Seebohm, in the 1860s, was founded upon the extent of the English population and the likely change in that population with the onset of plague.[47] Other historians at the end of the nineteenth century and in the first decades of the twentieth century also set out to identify plague mortality in the medieval countryside through inventive use of sources. Gasquet, writing in 1893, used manorial documentation in order to illustrate the progress of the disease and to provide evidence of its severity.[48] Authors such as Gasquet, and also Jessop, revealed through their work the potential of manorial documentation, and especially the record of tenants' deaths recorded as heriots in court and account rolls, to cast light on the extent of mortality.[49] In this earliest work, however, the greater tendency appears to have been to describe the increases in deaths in fairly general terms more than it was to subject the data to close analysis, even if, as Jessop's largely qualitative discussion of East Anglian court rolls illustrates, estimates of mortality in the region of 50 per cent were highly plausible. In addition, as in Rees's work on the Black Death in Wales, published in the first quarter of the twentieth century, the data, rigorously presented, were intended to describe the widespread, but also to some degree varied, impact of plague mortality and to set out the structural changes and, in terms of rent and services, the economic consequences of the first and subsequent epidemics; Rees describes what would become a largely familiar pattern of adjustment in the wake of plague, with a greater tendency for lords to lease both their demesnes and at least some of their tenanted holdings. The longer-term effect upon population or consideration of other and potentially related demographic consequences was though beyond the purview of Rees.[50] Subsequent to the assertions of Rogers and Seebohm that plague's consequences were revolutionary, most commentators writing in the early twentieth century preferred to see change as evolutionary, and not the result of a single cataclysmic event. This is perhaps most directly argued in Ada Levett's dissection of the manorial economy of the bishop of Winchester's estates, a study published in the second decade of the twentieth century.[51] Levett began by pondering the extent of plague mortality and the general as well as the local death rate. Concluding that there was little that could be said about total populations and the proportion of those who had died, Levett did consider the question of the extent of mortality occasioned by the Black Death. Having explored some possibilities, including the lack of evidence on total tenant populations and of those who were not tenants as well as what she perceived to be significant local and regional variations in mortality, Levett concluded that, while the proportion of total deaths could be great or small, 'The general impression gained from an attempt to make any such calculations is that they are singularly useless'.[52] What Levett's brief attempt to define her population group and the impact of mortality upon it illustrates is a preparedness to make an attempt at such an estimate as well as the recognition that such information would be useful; that Levett soon lost patience with the exercise and returned to the relative familiarity and accessibility of the tenurial history of individual tenant holdings is evidence both of reasonable judgement on her part and the lack of an analytical and methodological framework in which she could adequately set her research. Published a decade earlier, F.G. Davenport's study of the Norfolk manor of Forncett in the middle ages and early modern period also addresses the issue of population change and has some comment on mortality, but for the greater part this was not an analysis based upon or attempting to offer quantification. Instead, Davenport, in terms that are suitably circumspect, looked to the manorial documents to find evidence of changing tenurial structures consistent with a population reduced by the later fourteenth and fifteenth centuries from its early fourteenth century peak. In this respect Davenport was also offering some late reflection on the debate between Seebohm and Rogers on the extent of the pre-plague population and its reduction by the second half of the fourteenth century.[53] All such discussions were framed in terms of a debate that had, however, little to do with demography but a great deal to do with lordship and the management of the agrarian economy in the high and later middle ages. In such a context, as in the work of Levett and Davenport, the discussion of population and demographic change is of relevance for the authors in so far as it adds to their understanding of change in the economy and society under study.

Village community

One of the more vibrant themes in later nineteenth-century historiography of the medieval peasantry was the nature and development of the village community. Political theorists and historians in the middle decades of the nineteenth century sought to identify long-term continuums and the interconnectedness of village communities over time.[54] Frederic Seebohm in his study of the English village community, which was part of a wider exploration of the origins of the economy of England and of Britain, set out a series of observations upon that which he identified as the archetypal village community of the middle ages. His view was fixed firmly upon the regulated open fields, systems of land use that stood in contrast to the 'tribal' systems of land organisation which he observed for the same period in the more westerly parts of the British Isles.[55] For Seebohm the defining characteristics of the medieval village, at least in central and eastern England, were those typically associated with the nucleated villages of the open fields, with holdings of standard size and a villein population owing labour services, the expectations of which were limited by custom.[56] Seebohm's purpose, in establishing this view of the medieval village, was then to test it against earlier conditions and against those found in other contexts in mainland Europe and in other parts of Britain. His agenda here was also overtly political, his belief in the superiority of the British condition encouraging him to the argument that the British success story, which had arrived at its apogee in the late nineteenth century, could provide a blueprint for other, emerging nations.[57] An additional consequence of his work was to help establish a very particular view of the medieval English village which has persisted as a stereotype until the present, as any Web-based search of the 'medieval English village' will quickly reveal. Certainly Seebohm's discussion informed other nineteenth-century discussion of the medieval village. So, for instance, the later nineteenth-century folklorist G.L. Gomme examined the medieval English village in contrast to, and as a stage in the development of, primitive society.[58] For Gomme, building upon Seebohm's work, the customary nature of village society, whether in medieval England or in the village societies of nineteenth-century India or Fiji, was an example of its primitive and early condition, a consequence of practices handed down rather than practices created or modified in order to encourage advance.[59] This, he characterises as 'primitive economics' and identifies in the middle ages in England and Britain, in a period after the centralising influence of the Roman Empire had been lost and before a new wave of state government and developed trade had taken hold, an intensely localised and inward-looking village community.[60] For Gomme also, independent of such developments, there was, within the community itself, a common, pre-Christian bond of mutuality and inter-dependency which forged the kinds of localism which he describes. Modern economic historians would be inclined to describe such communal organisations as 'risk-averse', their relative but far from absolute security in maintaining their condition never being gambled against the potential benefits of seeking change.[61] For Gomme, the characteristics of the village community persisted for centuries; the characteristics themselves, again according to Gomme, were explicable in terms of kinship and religious and/or cultural affinities, and it was the former in particular which defined the village community as well as its economy. At the heart of kinship was the domestic unit, the hearth or homestead, 'the basis of all rights in the village'.[62] Importantly, both for its relevance to later studies of the medieval village and for its general relevance to discussion of peasant society, Gomme argues that the basic unit of the village community was not the individual but the family; it was from the well-spring of the family that law, custom and the culture of the village flowed.[63]

Both Gomme and, most obviously, Seebohm sought to engage directly with historical evidence from the medieval village and both were able to identify evidence which seemed to support their view of a self-sustaining, inward-looking and essentially timeless village community of the middle ages. Seebohm, for instance, uses fourteenth-century manorial court rolls from Winslow (Buckinghamshire), the Hundred Rolls, surveys from Battle Abbey and St Paul's, cartularies, and custumals in order to test his proposition that villeinage continued to operate at the heart of the village community and that the custom and the organisation of the open field were forces crucial to the integrity and operation of the same.[64] Interestingly, theirs is not a particularly cosy view of the corporate community;[65] instead it is a view premised upon the notion that the premodern community was backward, 'primitive', its customary organisation and the persistence of long-held beliefs, its mutuality and sense of collective responsibility evidence of a general weakness and lack of development of historical process or progress. Their work reflects a different kind of preoccupation from that with which later historians of the medieval village would come to engage; their chief concern, the early development of societies in comparative perspective, is not one which has drawn later commentators to the subject. Writing in the late 1880s Rogers believed that the main work on medieval village communities was still to be done, especially work founded upon the records of manorial courts which, though he does not make this same point, were not exploited in any significant degree by Gomme and Seebohm.[66] This is not, though, to say that the influence of such early work has been limited; in fact, as Smith has discussed, if an early, albeit incomplete and often inaccurate, characterisation of the medieval village had relevance it was in helping to establish a general view and expectation of the nature of medieval communal society, a prior assumption from which later scholarship sometimes struggled to shake free and, on occasion, even adopted quite enthusiastically.[67]

Early discussion of the village community also placed considerable store by the topography of the manor, the organisation of field-systems and the associated regulation of farming practices. Studies of the village community by Maine, Seebohm and Gomme all identified the organisation of the farming landscape as a major factor in the regulation and nature of the village community.[68] The perception of Seebohm, for instance, was that lords in Anglo-Saxon England had imposed an order on to the landholding of their tenantry and strove hard to maintain that order both by insisting on the persistence and integrity of servile holdings and of their organisation throughout the common fields.[69] It was the distribution of land by holding and family throughout the open fields, with land sub-divided rather than held in blocks, that also impressed Seebohm and suggested to him a communal consensus in its organisation.[70] Maitland also, though opposed to some of the overall interpretations of Gomme and Seebohm, not least in their desire to chart long-term developments from the antique period to the modern, also recognised the potential importance of collective agriculture for the functioning and nature of the village community. However, Maitland also refused to accept that open-field agriculture necessarily implied a strong force for communalism and was equally comfortable with the notion that individual membership of communal organisations might as conceivably be the determining force for collective arrangements in agriculture. In other words he proposed that membership of a community is a product of landholding by individuals and their families; by extension landholding also, of necessity, requires some kinds of communal co-operation on the part of the landholder.[71]

We should also note that Maitland's antagonism toward the theories of Maine, Gomme and Seebohm reflects a concern about both historical interpretation and the appropriateness, in a historical context, of terms such as 'communalism' and 'individualism'. For Maitland, it was law that mattered, far more than inference drawn from later sources and the seemingly communal agrarian practices persisting into the early modern and modern period. As we shall see below, this intense reflection on the nature of community and its constituent parts, which displays an impassioned discourse on the nature and direction of contemporary society at the close of the nineteenth century, has persisted for more than a century and permeates much writing on rural society in the middle ages as well, of course, as in later periods.[72] In this, writers in the later nineteenth and early twentieth centuries were themselves also reflecting a long-standing tradition; in particular, the view that open-field agriculture, though uneconomical and a product of a barbarous past, was a necessary evil imposed by lords and essential to the organisation of communities in the middle ages, appears to have been widespread in the later eighteenth and early nineteenth centuries, during the last great period of enclosure.[73]

Finally, whilst the early historiography of the peasantry established themes which have persisted to the present day, it ignored other themes, more obviously the product of subsequent developments in the historiography, which hardly feature at all in this early work. So, for instance, reference to family in this early historiography is particularly evident in discussion of the Domesday tenantry, the extent of its landholding and the distinctions to be drawn between the various kinds of tenant identified there.[74] There is though little in this early work which is aimed at identifying the extent or the form of the household or family in this period, of itemising and quantifying the family and household membership itself. Maitland proposed five as a best guess for the average family or household size in Domesday England.[75]

Gender is also a theme largely absent from this first tranche of writing on the medieval peasantry and related issues. Peasants and rural dwellers were discussed not so much as men or women but as often as not as tenants, villeins, the free and so on. Implicit, and sometimes of course explicit, in this was the assumption that most if not all tenants were male and that the main subject of any discussion of a servile or free tenantry was an adult male. Thus, for instance, Vinogradoff has a great deal to say on tenantry but little to offer on the subject of men and/or women, save in so far as gendered distinctions occur in discussion of obligation, as for instance in the payment of marriage fine (merchet) or licence for the son of a villein to enter holy orders.[76] Of most nineteenth-century commentators, Maitland, in his discussion of family law, comes amongst the closest to a detailed consideration of gendered distinctions in his discussion of marriage and the relative positions of husbands and wives. Little of Maitland's discussion of these themes can be said to have been directed at the peasantry and is instead a more general reflection on common law development and the position of free tenants overall; that said, some of Maitland's observations have been applied to such issues as the rights of widows and married women in the medieval village, points to which we will return below.[77] Even Rogers, a precociously perceptive commentator on the social and economic condition of late medieval England with a keen interest in the condition of labourers and artisans in town and countryside has little to say directly on the subject of male and female employment patterns, for example.[78]

Peasant culture was another topic which received little attention from these early historians. The Reverend Augustus Jessop's assessment of village life in medieval Norfolk may stand as indicative of a mind-set that tended to dismiss the notion of a peasant culture capable and indeed worthy of study. In a thesis intended to reassure his audience of late nineteenth-century villagers as to the real benefits they presently enjoyed, and certainly relative to those enjoyed by their forebears, Jessop passes quickly over any vestiges of high medieval peasant culture:

> I can tell you nothing of the amusements of the people in those days.
> I doubt whether they had any more amusement than the swine or the

cows had. Looking after the fowls or the geese, hunting for the hen's nest in the furze brake, and digging out a fox or a badger, gave them an hour's excitement or interest now and again.[79]

In the same essay he laments the general poverty of the peasant's lot and rejects any notion that their material possessions were more than the most basic.[80] Rogers, in reflecting upon the 'social life' of the rural dwellers in the middle ages, also includes some comment on the condition of life in later medieval villages. While he has little to say on 'culture' *per se*, and suggests that the general condition of life was low, and that the movable goods acquired by peasants were basic, he does allow that peasants might look beyond their immediate condition and aspire to education and social elevation.[81] Although not always expressed so stridently, these were views that persisted in the next century. Both Bennett and Coulton, writing, in the first decades of the twentieth century, general studies of the medieval village, were certainly inclined to look for some indications of activities beyond the confines of labour and subsistence. Their work though stands in deliberate opposition to an earlier and imagined 'merrie England' of nineteenth-century novelists and commentators; while both Bennett and Coulton acknowledge that some time was spent in play and leisure in the medieval village, certain details of which they look to detect and describe, they contend that any such activity was limited and set against a constant backdrop of toil and anxiety.[82] When Bennett imagines the thoughts of a middle-aged peasant gazing across his familiar village landscape, it is again matters of work, land and family that dominate his meditations while Coulton encourages his readers to shun the 'superficially picturesque' and any nostalgic yearning for a long-lost rural idyll of dance and merry-making.[83] Other early twentieth-century commentators, including amateur historians such as Henry Montagu Doughty, expressed similar views, contrasting their present with the imagined sheer awfulness of the medieval village and what they assumed must have been the severe limitation on villagers' quality of existence, including their food and living conditions.[84] Elsewhere, late nineteenth- and early twentieth-century historians had little at all to say on such matters; so, unsurprisingly given their emphases and the intellectual agendas they had set, neither Maitland nor Vinogradoff find room in their discussions of law, the tenantry and the development of tenure for wider reflections on village culture or the cultural history of the peasantry.[85] The same is also generally true of manorial and estate studies, as for example Davenport's discussion of the Norfolk manor of Forncett, the focus of which, as we have already considered earlier in this chapter, is also tenurial.[86] We should not though berate these pioneers for failing to deal in detail with themes that emerged only in the later twentieth century and, in some instances, such as that of peasant culture, have yet fully to emerge as significant themes within this historiography. In fact, as we will see in the following three chapters, the main themes of a peasant historiography for most of the twentieth century remained closely located within a general framework established by these first contributors.

Notes

1 Historical discussion of the medieval peasantry in terms defined by the relationship of lord and peasant does not begin in the later nineteenth century of course. Most obviously, Karl Marx includes comment on the medieval peasantry and especially the development of waged labour and the encroachment of capitalist farming into the countryside with the consequence that the landholding of the peasantry was expropriated during the fifteenth century, K. Marx, *Capital. A critical analysis of capitalist production, volume 1*, trans. S. Moore and E. Aveling and ed. F. Engels; 4th edn., ed. and trans. by D. Torr (London, 1887), pp. 740–1, 767; Marx had little of detail to offer on the medieval peasantry, however, and his focus was more upon the development of the bourgeoisie in this and later periods, for comment on which see, for instance, H.J. Kaye, *The British Marxist historians. An introductory analysis* (Basingstoke: Macmillan, 1995), pp. 81–2.
2 F.W. Maitland, 'The history of a Cambridgeshire manor', in H.M. Cam, ed., *Selected historical essays of F.W. Maitland* (Cambridge: Cambridge University Press, 1957), pp. 16–40.
3 See, for instance, the discussion of individual parishes for the county of Bedford, W. Page, ed., *A history of the county of Bedford: Volume 2* (London: Victoria County History, 1908). It is also the case that later volumes of the *Victoria County History* (VCH) have not shifted significantly from this approach, though a greater regard for the obligations of the tenantry is a feature of some more recent volumes, such as R.B. Pugh, ed., *A history of the county of Cambridge and the Isle of Ely: Volume 4: city of Ely; Ely, N. and S. Witchford and Wisbech hundreds* (London: Victoria County History, 2002). In this last volume, discussion of the early development of a money economy on some of the Cambridgeshire manors suggests the injection of recent historiographical trends, and notably Edward Miller's research on the abbey and bishopric of Ely which includes the same observations, into the VCH's account. Miller was also one of the section authors for this volume; his work on Ely is discussed below, pp. 90, 117–18. 165 volumes of the VCH are available on-line through British History Online at www.british-history.ac.uk/catalogue.aspx?type=1&gid=153 (last accessed 8 July 2014).
4 *Select pleas in manorial and other seigniorial courts*, ed. by Frederic W. Maitland (Selden Society, 2, 1888).

5 F.G. Davenport, *The economic development of a Norfolk manor, 1086–1565* (Cambridge: Cambridge University Press, 1906; reprinted, London: Frank Cass, 1967), p. 62.
6 See, for instance, Sir F. Pollock and F.W. Maitland, *The history of English law before the time of Edward I* (2 vols, Cambridge: Cambridge University Press, 2nd edn, 1968), i, pp. 356–83; 624–8.
7 F.W. Maitland, *Domesday Book and beyond. Three essays in the early history of England* (1897; republished Cambridge: Cambridge University Press, 1987).
8 For instance, Maitland, *Domesday Book and beyond*, pp. 36–66.
9 P. Vinogradoff, *Villainage in England. Essays in English mediaeval history* (Oxford: Oxford University Press, 1892); P. Vinogradoff, *The growth of the manor* (London: Sonnenschein, 1905).
10 Vinogradoff, *Villainage in England*, pp. 140–50.
11 For instance, Vinogradoff, *The growth of the manor*, pp. 332–65.
12 Vinogradoff, *The growth of the manor*, pp. 345–52; *Villainage in England*, p. 150, for the same general point.
13 Vinogradoff, *The growth of the manor*, p. 348.
14 Vinogradoff, *The growth of the manor*, p. 349.
15 See below, pp. 106–8.
16 Vinogradoff, *The growth of the manor*, pp. 354–60.
17 N. Neilson, 'Customary rent', in P. Vinogradoff, ed., *Oxford Studies in social and legal history*, ii (Oxford: Oxford University Press, 1910).
18 N. Neilson, *Economic conditions on the manors of Ramsey Abbey* (Philadelphia: Bryn Mawr, 1898); parts of this work also appear in N. Neilson, 'Boon-services on the estates of Ramsey Abbey', *American Historical Review* 2 (1897), 213–24, in which she elaborates her view on boon rents and the extension of villein obligations.
19 See above, pp. 2–3. For comment on Neilson in this respect, see J. Des Jardins, *Women and the historical enterprise in America: gender, race, and the politics of memory, 1880–1945* (Chapel Hill: University of North Carolina Press, 2006), p. 32; see also Neilson, *Economic conditions*, pp. 86ff, for an example of the systematic gathering of the tools of historical research, and for the above quote, Neilson, 'Boon-services', p. 213.
20 See below, pp. 84–108, 117–41.
21 Some works on lord–tenant relations and serfdom were essentially descriptions of tenurial obligations, offering little in the way of historiographical or temporal context, as for instance, A. Clark, 'Serfdom on an Essex Manor, 1308–1378', *English Historical Review* 20 (1905), 479–83.
22 Davenport, *Economic development of a Norfolk manor*.
23 Davenport, *Economic development of a Norfolk manor*, pp. 96–7. The reference is to E.P. Cheyney, 'The disappearance of English serfdom', *English Historical Review* 15 (1900), 20–37, and the chapter draws extensively on Davenport's earlier article, 'The decay of villeinage in East Anglia', *Transactions of the Royal Historical Society*, new series, 14 (1900), 123–41, and in particular pp. 140–1, where the same critique of Cheyney's work is included.

24 Davenport, *Economic development of a Norfolk manor*, pp. 96-7.
25 T.W. Page, *The end of villeinage in England* (New York: Macmillan, 1900), p. 39.
26 H.L. Gray, 'The commutation of villein services in England before the Black Death', *English Historical Review* 29 (1914), 625-56. For earlier comment, also taking issue with Page and presenting data from a manorial study, see K. G. Feiling, 'An Essex manor in the fourteenth century', *English Historical Review* 26 (1911), 333-8.
27 See, for instance, J.E.T. Rogers, *Six centuries of work and wages. The history of English labour* (London: Sonnenschein, 1908), pp. 218-19; see also Page, *End of villeinage*, pp. 37-9, for discussion of this earlier historiography.
28 'These commutations ... would tend to assimilate the tenure of the serf ... with that of the free tenant', Rogers, *Six centuries*, p. 219.
29 Maitland, *Domesday and beyond*, pp. 26-79.
30 Vinogradoff, *Villainage in England*, pp. 138-220, and see especially pp. 180-4 for discussion of the ways in which the commutation of labour rent helps to generate an economically and socially independent body of peasants.
31 Vinogradoff, *Growth of the manor*, p. 348.
32 For fuller discussion of manorial types, including 'Midlands-type' manors, see below, pp. 198-201.
33 Maitland, 'History of a Cambridgeshire manor', pp. 18, 39.
34 Vinogradoff, *Villainage in England*, p. 159, 'The villain has no property of his own, and consequently he cannot transmit property.'
35 See below, Chapter 4, pp. 128-33.
36 Rogers, *Six centuries*, pp. 175-8.
37 Rogers, *Six centuries*, p. 176.
38 R.H. Tawney, *The agrarian problem in the sixteenth century* (London: Longmans, 1912), pp. 105-10.
39 Tawney, *Agrarian problem*, p. 111.
40 Tawney, *Agrarian problem*, pp. 84-5.
41 Tawney, *Agrarian problem*, pp. 76-97.
42 Tawney, *Agrarian problem*, pp. 136ff.
43 Kosminsky, *Agrarian History*, pp. 323-8, and above, Chapter 3, pp. 85-9.
44 N.S.B. Gras, *The evolution of the English corn market from the twelfth to the eighteenth century* (Cambridge, Mass.: Harvard University Press, 1926), pp. 24-31.
45 E. Power, *The wool trade in English medieval history* (Oxford: Oxford University Press, 1941).
46 Maitland, 'History of a Cambridgeshire manor', pp. 25, 39-40. The essay was first published in the *English Historical Review* (1894).
47 F. Seebohm, 'The Black Death', *Fortnightly Review* (1865 and 1866); J.E.T. Rogers, 'England before and after the Black Death', *Fortnightly Review* (1866). See also the relatively early discussion of these same contributions in W.A. Cunningham, *The growth of English industry and commerce during the early and middle ages* (Cambridge: Cambridge University Press, 1910), pp. 331-4, and

especially p. 331, n. 4. For general discussion of these themes and developments in the relevant historiography see also N. Hybel, *Crisis or change. The concept of crisis in the light of agrarian structural reorganization in late medieval England* (Aarhus: Aarhus University Press, 1989), pp. 1–19.
48 F.A. Gasquet, *The Great Pestilence (AD 1348–9)* (London: Simpkin Marshall, 1893), pp. 166–70.
49 A. Jessop, 'The Black Death in East Anglia', in A. Jessop, *The coming of the friars* (London: Fisher Unwin: 1889), pp. 196–207; see also on the same the comments of Cunningham, a near contemporary historian who was impressed by the use of such material and included an instance as an appendix to his general survey of the medieval economy, Cunningham, *Growth of English industry and commerce*, pp. 330–1, 610–14. Jessop's work with manorial court rolls in order to produce crude mortality statistics also found approval from medical practitioners. see anonymous review in *British Medical Journal* 1 (1889), 1469.
50 W. Rees, *South Wales and the March, 1284–1415* (Oxford: Oxford University Press, 1924), pp. 241–69; W. Rees, 'The Black Death in Wales', *Transactions of the Royal Historical Society* 3 (1920), reprinted in R.W. Southern, ed., *Essays in medieval history* (London: Macmillan, 1968), pp. 179–99.
51 A.E. Levett, 'The Black Death on the estates of the See of Winchester', in P. Vinogradoff, ed., *Oxford studies in social and legal history. Volume V* (Oxford: Oxford University Press, 1916).
52 Levett, 'Black Death on the estates of the see of Winchester', pp. 76–81 (quote at p. 81).
53 Davenport, *Economic development of a Norfolk manor*, pp. 98, 104–5.
54 Both Marx and Engels had earlier suggested that medieval peasants were capable of organised resistance to lords, their communal structures founded on pre-medieval tribal systems; see, for instance for discussion and references, S.H. Rigby, 'Historical materialism, social structure, and social change in the middle ages', *Journal of Medieval and Early Modern Studies* 34 (2004), 487.
55 F. Seebohm, *The English village community examined in its relation to the manorial and tribal systems and to the common or open field system of husbandry. An essay in economic history* (London: Longmans, 1883).
56 Seebohm, *English village community*, pp. 76–81.
57 See, for instance, Seebohm, *English village community*, pp. vii–ix.
58 G.L. Gomme, *The village community with special reference to the origin and form of its survival in Britain* (London: Walter Scott, 1890).
59 Gomme, *The village community*, c. 1.
60 Gomme, *The village community*, pp. 46–8.
61 For economists' discussion of communal organisation and the significance of risk in the same, see below, p. 200.
62 Gomme, *The village community*, pp. 56–68, and especially pp. 64–5.
63 Gomme, *The village community*, p. 65.
64 Seebohm, *English village community*, pp. 17–81.
65 Although there are occasional suggestions of such, for instance, Seebohm, *English village community*, p. 18, citing *Piers Plowman*.

66 J.E. Thorold Rogers, 'The economical interpretation of history', in J.E. Thorold Rogers, *The economic interpretation of history* (Oxford, 1889), pp. 3–4.
67 Smith, 'Corporate medieval village', pp. 154ff.
68 H.S. Maine, *Village communities* (4th ed., London, 1881), pp. 131–47; see, also for example, Gomme, *The village community*, pp. 147–56.
69 Seebohm, *English village community*, pp. 176–8.
70 Seebohm, *English village community*, pp. 117–25, referring to the Welsh laws as an instance of this organisation of the land and its ploughing; see also R. Dodgshon, 'The interpretation of sub-divided fields: a study in private or communal interests?', in T. Rowley, ed., *The origins of open-field agriculture* (London: Croom Helm, 1981), pp. 131–2.
71 F.W. Maitland, 'The survival of archaic communities', in H.A.L. Fisher, ed., *The collected papers of Frederic William Maitland* (Cambridge, 3 vols, 1911), ii, pp. 352–3.
72 On the nineteenth-century context in which 'community' was debated, see especially C. Dewey, 'Images of the village community: a study of in Anglo-Indian ideology', *Modern Asian Studies* 6 (1972), 292–5.
73 See, for instance, Maine, *Village communities*, pp. 90–4, citing William Marshall's treatise of landed property (1804).
74 See, for instance, Vinogradoff, *English society*, pp. 446–8.
75 Maitland, *Domesday Book and beyond*, p. 437. On the same, see also Hilton, *A medieval society*, p. 91.
76 Vinogradoff, *Villainage in England*, pp. 156–7.
77 Pollock and Maitland, *History of English law*, ii, pp. 364–436. For more recent observation upon women's property rights in the medieval village, see R.M. Smith, 'Women's property rights under customary law: some developments in the thirteenth and fourteenth centuries', *Transactions of the Royal Historical Society* 36 (1986), 165–94; R.M. Smith, 'Coping with uncertainty: women's tenure of customary land in England, c.1370–1430', in J. Kermode, ed., *Enterprise and individuals in fifteenth-century England* (Gloucester: Alan Sutton, 1992), pp. 43–67.
78 Rogers, *Six centuries*, pp. 159–87. Rogers makes some few comments suggestive of the view that women enjoyed wage parity with men in some roles in the medieval countryside, *Six centuries*, pp. 77, 329. Though what he had to say enjoyed some resonance and infuriated later commentators, especially in his suggestion that women enjoyed a degree of wage parity in the later middle ages. For discussion of the same, see S. Bardsley, 'Women's work reconsidered: gender and wage differentiation in late medieval England', *Past and Present* 165 (1999), 3–29, and especially 5–6, and below.
79 A. Jessop, 'Village life six hundred years ago', in A. Jessop, *The coming of the friars* (London: Fisher Unwin, 1889), p. 103.
80 Jessop, 'Village life', pp. 88–91, 94.
81 Rogers, *Six centuries of work and wages*, pp. 67–8.
82 H.S. Bennett, *Life on the English manor. A study of peasant conditions 1150–1400* (Cambridge: Cambridge University Press, 1937), pp. 257–74; G.G. Coulton, *The medieval village* (Cambridge: Cambridge University Press, 1925), pp. 93–6.

83 Bennett, *Life on the English manor*, pp. 23-4; Coulton, *Medieval village*, pp. 103-4.
84 H.M. Doughty, *Chronicles of Theberton. A Suffolk village* (London: Macmillan, 1910), pp. 79-80.
85 Vinogradoff, *Villainage in England*; Maitland, *Domesday Book and beyond*.
86 Davenport, *Economic development of a Norfolk manor*.

PART I

Themes

In this first section, we will consider the ways in which the historical study of the medieval English peasantry has, after its first stirrings, tended to be confined within three broad themes. These main themes have become associated with a more all-encompassing discussion of change in the medieval economy. So, historians have tended to see the economy as driven by one of or a combination of the following 'supermodels':[1]

- population movement and its determining factors (demographic and non-demographic)
- the demands and constraints of the seigneurial economy and of resistance to the same
- the development of commerce and the market.

In the second half of the twentieth century, these broad approaches were employed with varying degrees of emphasis to make sense of the peasant experience and to help identify and explain change over time, especially in the period from 1200 to 1500. This also, as we will see, generated a good deal of debate as advocates of one or other model clashed; at different moments, different models have also tended to be more or less to the fore, their prominence a product of, *inter alia*, the contribution of particularly active and compelling historians and the perceived rigour of their argument, as well as political trends (such as the rise and subsequent decline of far left politics in the West) and wider socio-economic contexts (for instance, the expansion of global capitalism and the rise of market economies in the 1980s and 1990s). To apply a broad chronology to these developments, we can suggest that a population-driven model, associated especially with the writing of M.M. Postan, was highly influential in the third quarter of the twentieth century but lost significant ground to a more 'commercial model' during the 1980s. The importance of lordship and the seigneurial economy to the peasantry has never been in doubt but the significance of lordship as a determining factor has been debated since the middle years of the twentieth century. The inclination to dignify lord–tenant relations with a primary role in determining economic change is not now one shared by many historians, and this model, as with that founded on population change, has lost ground to the 'commercial' model.

There is less evidence in writing from the later nineteenth and early twentieth centuries of attempts to conceive of determining factors of economic change, even though historians did conceive of change over time, for instance in discussing adjustment to money rent and labour rent, points to which we can return. However, some of the themes later fashioned into models already had their antecedents in the more particular research of nineteenth- and early twentieth-century historians. Thus, for example and again as we shall see below, the demands of lords as regards their villein tenants were an important topic for investigation of historians wishing to explore the conventions of medieval lordship and, for instance, to contrast medieval villeinage with contemporary modern serfdom in Russia, long before similar work was used to underpin models of long-term economic change.

The following three chapters are organised then according to the initial significance and overall dominance of particular main themes. It is perhaps a moot point as to whether, in terms of a strict chronology as applied to the historiography, discussion of lordship and lord–tenant relations should have come before rather than after the chapter on population and its relation to peasant resources, especially given the focus on rent and lord–tenant relations in that form from some of the first contributors to the economic and social history of the medieval peasantry. The choice of order is proposed here on the basis that Postan's thesis of population relative to resources, which will be discussed in the first chapter of this section, has, judging by the direction and framing of much relevant writing in this area, some significant claim to be the defining model of the relevant historiography, even if it was, as we shall see, as much reacted against as promoted.

Note

1 See, for instance, the discussion in J. Hatcher and M. Bailey, *Modelling the middle ages. The history and theory of England's economic development* (Oxford: Oxford University Press, 2001).

2

Population, resources and the medieval English peasantry

Since the mid-twentieth century, much of the discussion of the medieval English peasantry has, in some form or another, been determined by consideration of the overarching theme of population and the availability of resources relative to the peasant's capacity to cope in his or her world. Some aspects of population history, such as the components of demographic change (mortality, fertility, mobility) or social structure and the family, are topics for discussion in later chapters but the theme of population movement and the relationship of the peasantry to that movement has been of key importance to historians' understanding of the way in which the medieval economy operated.[1] Research aimed at defining the role of the peasantry in the wider economy, the general condition of the peasantry, the changing power of lordship *vis-à-vis* peasant labour and obligation, has all been couched in terms dependent upon a model of population movement. As such, therefore, a conception of the medieval English peasantry as being fundamentally conditioned and constrained by fluctuations in population has been central to the modern historiography. As importantly, the demographic experience of the population, of which the rural population was the largest constituent part, has been taken to be a major and, in some cases, the single greatest factor in explaining the behaviour of the economy in the high and late middle ages. It is not an exaggeration to suggest that much other work, at least since the middle decades of the twentieth century, has been undertaken in response to or in refutation of this main principle.

As discussed in the preceding chapter, historians writing in the late nineteenth and early twentieth century recognised that the population history of the medieval English peasantry was subject to change and that such change could influence the condition and role of peasants.[2] Within their historical view, however, change was principally determined by other causes (notably institutional causes and especially the demands of government, the courts and landlords). It was the work of M.M. Postan, writing between the 1920s and the 1970s, which effected a crucial shift in the study of the medieval peasant by introducing a broad thesis of economic change based upon the relationship between population and resources.

In Postan's discussion of the medieval economy, his earliest work, in the 1920s and 1930s, had most to say on the significant topic of the time: the rise of a money economy. In this, Postan was keen to illustrate the non-linear processes of economic change, and one that challenged an earlier generation of historians, such as W.A. Cunningham who had viewed the rise of a money economy as an inevitable process of change without significant deviation. Cunningham and historians of his generation, such as W.J. Ashley, were reflecting the thesis of Adam Smith who, in *The wealth of nations*, had proposed that the growth of the market would inevitably promote economic change. As the market grew so the mode of exchange adjusted, with kind giving way to money so that certain types of institution, such as manors and estates operating on the basis of labour rent and other rents in kind, had to adjust to money rent and to adapt to the prevailing economic conditions.[3] The tenor of this early work is then more closely associated with the institutional and manorial history of a generation of historians previous to Postan's own, and to whom Postan was responding.[4] Thus, in his chronology of labour service and his identification of a generalised but far from universal pattern of ebb and flow in the twelfth and thirteenth centuries, Postan was content chiefly to describe that chronology and to explore its process and, where he sought to engage with it, it is in relation to the rise and consequence of a money economy.[5] But important in that work, for what follows, is the contention that there is no steady and inevitable retreat of labour rent and an inexorable rise of money rent.[6]

Postan was not alone in recognising that a linear view of such development was neither consistent with the historical record nor explicable solely in terms of changing economic structures, such as the growth of the market or the extent of coin in circulation. For instance, even E.A. Lipson, while certainly addressing change in the medieval English economy and the end of villeinage in particular, and writing within a tradition of Smithian economics and indeed indirectly identified by Postan as one 'drawn into the prejudices of his time',[7] also questions its main precept and especially notes that any change driven by a rise of a market economy would have been 'an infinitely slower process' but for the arrival of plague in the mid-fourteenth century.[8] However, whilst earlier historians may have recognised such non-linearity, in Postan's work, this recognition was to provide the foundation for a new view of economic change, one in which population, rather than trade or money, was the driving force. Postan's elaboration of a population-resources model would not appear in print until the early 1950s and it was really thereafter, and especially in work published in the early 1960s and later, that it played upon his study of the medieval peasantry.[9]

Here we will begin with a discussion of Postan's thesis of population movement before exploring it both in relation to his own views on the medieval English peasantry and, further, the application of that thesis by a generation of historians writing subsequent to Postan. This overview of Postan's work and its response summarises what can, with some justification, be described as the predominant explanatory model for the historiography of the medieval English peasantry. Much of the work of historians in the second half of the twentieth century has been conducted in response to this early formulation and will need to be considered within that context in later chapters.

Population and resources: the Postan thesis

In a series of articles and more general reflections, the latter written in the last two decades of his life, Postan explored the relationship between population and resources in the high and late middle ages. He proposed a general pattern of population movement for the period, a movement evidenced by a number of indices which he examined, described and sought to explain. In his approach, Postan has been characterised as a man of his time and place, especially in not adopting a Keynesian economic approach and in being instead wedded to classical and neo-classical economics, of a kind associated with Alfred Marshall, the neo-classical economist of the later nineteenth century, and the earlier 'classical' thesis of population relative to resources proposed by Thomas Malthus and David Ricardo. Both Malthus and Ricardo elaborated theories of diminishing resources in relation to population; Malthus had proposed that population increased only to levels capable of being sustained by the available resources and that once population growth exceeded available resources it would decline. An important cause of the inelasticity of resources which prevented them from matching population growth was the tendency, identified by Ricardo, towards diminishing returns in agriculture. In short, doubling the labour input on land will not, in normal circumstances, generate a double return in output from that land. So, as population grew, the capacity of land to provide the kinds of food resources necessary to support that population, diminished, a function of, for instance, the expansion of farmed land beyond areas of maximum productivity or the reduced yields arising on overworked land.[10] In its political dimension, Postan's approach, especially given its *de facto* reduction of the role of institutions, a stance contrary to both Keynesian economics and Marxism, as agents of change – and thereby obviating the historical endeavour intended to assess the strengths and weaknesses of institutions – has been described as 'neutralist'.[11]

Postan described a general pattern of population movement for the middle ages: it is one of apparently accelerating growth, dramatic decline and then a return to relative calm or stagnation. Thus, from the Anglo-Saxon period until the end of the twelfth century, to follow Postan, there was considerable though far from accurately quantifiable population growth, followed in the thirteenth century by what may have been a greater leap forward in the size of population. By the end of the thirteenth century a population that, judging by localised studies, had swollen by a factor of two or three since the eleventh century faced an enormous struggle simply to survive. Population retrenched in the early fourteenth century and was then cut back with ferocity in the middle years of that century by the Black Death. Recurrent plague continued to force retreat and stagnation upon the medieval population but, to follow Postan, the trend of declining population had been established half a century before plague's arrival.[12]

The causes of that growth and then decline and retreat were, of course, many but Postan, whilst acknowledging the potential multiple factors, preferred to identify control over resources as of singular importance. It was the ability to generate resources sufficient to support a larger population that explains growth in the earlier part of the period just as the subsequent decline is explicable in terms of a reduction in resources and a failure to enhance productivity. The ability of medieval men and women to restore their numbers in the mid- and late fourteenth centuries was curtailed by recurrence of plague at a time when their regained control of resources is already evident in, for instance, a decline in the price of basic foodstuffs. In invoking plague at this juncture, Postan was effectively including an autonomous factor in his model since the assumption is that plague's incidence was wholly independent of the relative state of resources.[13] It was, chiefly for Postan, the relationship between the population and its resource, above all the ratio of land to men, which determined population levels and behaviour. In turn, it was the behaviour of population that dominated the economic situation.[14]

For Postan, such a model of population behaviour, one explicable in terms of the relationship between population size and available resources, had major implications for his own studies of the medieval English peasantry. In terms of his corpus of work, Postan wrote relatively little that was explicitly directed at the topic of the medieval peasant but all that he did write on this subject, at least from the 1950s onwards, was informed by his basic model of the nature and development of the medieval economy. What is more, Postan's writing in this area, and particularly that with regard to peasants and their landholding, had an unmistakable influence on the later study of other medievalists.[15]

Postan and the Postan thesis

The implication of Postan's thesis, as more than one critic has been keen to point out, is that, ultimately, medieval lives were conditioned by factors largely beyond the control of those who lived them.[16] The vagaries of experience are in part explicable in terms of attempts to respond to external factors, such as soil quality, but any fundamental cause of process and change resides not in people or institutions but in some other base, essentially the available resource. Thus, in his survey of village livestock, Postan employs detailed taxation assessment data from the thirteenth century to illustrate the relative paucity of livestock held by villagers in three discrete regions.[17] Postan contends that, despite the high numbers of stock held by some few villagers, the *per capita* number of livestock was low and that, irrespective of region, the paucity is to be explained in terms of land-hunger in the face of population increase: 'land was scarce and getting scarcer, and men in search of sustenance were forced to till the lands which in other more spacious periods would and should have been used as pasture'. Striking is Postan's desire to 'play down' the large flocks and herds of the more substantial villagers; instead, it is the very few animals of the middling peasant that dominates Postan's view. This 'inability of the humbler villagers to maintain sufficient livestock' is portrayed as 'characteristic of an age in which the frontier between corn and hoof had moved very far, indeed too far, cornwards'. Intriguingly Postan concludes this article by suggesting that the importance of the material he has been exploring lies less in its detailed evidence of husbandry within the regions outlined but rather as testimony to 'the main working hypothesis on which historians of the thirteenth-century agriculture must operate', presumably suggesting, though it is no more than hinted at in Postan's discussion, that a low livestock density with a consequent lack of manure limited arable output and made villagers precariously dependent upon a potentially diminishing grain yield.[18]

The same themes, and especially the plight of the large proportion of small-holders in the medieval village of the thirteenth and early fourteenth centuries, also appear in Postan's earlier study, written with Jan Titow, of tenant mortality on the estates of the bishop of Winchester.[19] The frequency and, to Postan, socially discrete patterns of what he took to be evidence for tenant deaths encouraged a view of a society where a significant proportion of the population was at risk, cast afloat on a tide of volatile prices and poor harvests.[20] The explanations of their vulnerability were not hard to find and were identified as a push to the margins of available land and the sub-division of holdings into tiny units incapable of sustaining those who lived upon them. While the weather, the failure of the soil and the utilisation of poorer land might all help explain the crisis of this period, it was population increase that lay at the foundation of this precarious demographic edifice.[21]

Published at around the same time as these articles, that is to say c.1960, Postan's introduction to an edition of the *Carte Nativorum*, a mid-fourteenth-century cartulary from Peterborough Abbey recording a series of land transactions from the late thirteenth century, also illustrates the impact of his thinking on population upon his research into the medieval peasantry.[22] Postan's essay 'The Charters of the Villeins' is a long and involved study of the nature and origins of the peasant land market. An important, indeed central, theme of that work is the relative timelessness of the market which, while it responded to external stimuli, including the demands of commerce and fluctuation in demand occasioned by population shifts, and could be constrained by custom and by lordship, was chiefly determined 'by certain abiding features of peasant life'.[23] For Postan, these features were, for the greatest part, explicable in terms of the natural respiration of the peasant family, its natural buyers and sellers, acquiring and shedding land according to the demands of the family.[24] Implicit in such a thesis is the issue of resource, here confined within a model of the domestic economy; the expansion and reduction of the family, and thereby the extent of land sufficient to sustain a single family (*terra unius familie*), were conditioned by the family's success relative to others in securing an advantage in terms of resources which would permit such growth or decline. There is clearly much in this thesis that acknowledges the role of people, of institutions and of customs and practice, but, as before, the underlying principle is the hegemony of resource in relation to population numbers.

Finally, Postan's views on the relationship between population and peasant resource find their fullest and most generalised exposition in his essay for the *Cambridge economic history of Europe*, published in 1966.[25] A survey of the agrarian history of England in the high and late middle ages, Postan's full contribution to the collection of essays offered an opportunity to draw together the previous two decades of his thinking and writing on this topic.[26] The main headings and sub-headings of his opening sections illustrate his sense of priorities: land (reclamation; land-hunger; deterioration of the land) and population (colonisation; the lure of aggregates; the rising trend; the decline). In a final section Postan concentrates his attention on the 'villagers' while it is in the earliest sections that he rehearses his views on the motive force of the medieval economy. Having set out his thesis of population change in relation to available resource, Postan then considers the village society and economy in relation to this broad schema. He makes a series of important observations regarding the medieval peasantry: that their society and economy were stratified but that stratification within the village was not dependent on legal tenure alone; that the relativities of freedom and serfdom, while potentially significant, may have mattered less than the size and quality of holding;[27] that family size was also a feature of importance but that family wealth was ultimately a function of landholding.

These features are established in relation to Postan's own model of how the economy functions. Thus, land distribution is seen as a function of population change. A growing population in the earlier centuries led to fragmentation of holdings whilst lowered population in the late fourteenth and fifteenth centuries led to a degree of accumulation. But, for Postan, the product of that accumulation was not economic differentiation; instead, an improved opportunity for land acquisition led above all to the promotion of middling villagers, rather than a small class of exceedingly rich and dominant landholders, so that the proportion of larger holdings increased at the expense of the smaller holdings but did not result in an intensive polarisation of landholding. Social differentiation could, for the historian who looked at these things in the right way, to paraphrase Postan, be as evident in the high middle ages as in the late middle ages.[28] As before, this is a model driven by population: growing populations and declining populations led to relative increases and decreases in the extent of pressure upon resources. Rents, prices and wages responded accordingly and the response of the peasantry was modified accordingly. Importantly, for

Postan other potential causative factors, such as the role of the market and of commerce, or such institutional factors as lordship or government, are to be downplayed. Thus, to give one example, Postan considered the role of the cloth industry in supporting small-holders in the countryside and, thereby, its effect upon wage levels in the period between 1200 and 1500 but dismissed the idea that the industry was of sufficient scale to influence wage levels or to affect greatly the lives and security of the majority of the population; instead, once again, it is population that drives such indices as wage levels.[29] That such activity is reduced in its significance by Postan means that his view of the peasantry is conditioned accordingly with inevitable consequences for his identification of the determining features of medieval peasant life.

The Postan thesis in application

We can therefore identify a series of themes in relation to population movement, its explanation and its relevance for historical change in the rural economy which emerge from Postan's work. These are themes which have dominated and, to a degree, continue to dominate historical writing on the medieval English peasantry. This is not to say that the themes necessarily dominate in ways that are consistent with or in full agreement with the Postan thesis; while Postan's arguments certainly hold sway in some quarters of the historiography, his work has also proved a sounding board against which alternative theses have been tested and contrary approaches developed. It is especially the following categories for investigation which have retained a strongly Postanian perspective: explanations for population movement; peasant resources and standard of living; technology; the nature of the peasant land market.[30]

Peasant demography and explanations for population change
Postan's model of population change is founded upon the assumption that population is essentially driven by factors beyond the control of the subject population. Thus, for Postan and for many historians working after him, the medieval population's movement was mortality-driven, the mortality itself occasioned not by direct human impact but by factors typically beyond their control, especially environment (soil conditions, weather, disease and so on). For Postan himself, as we have seen, the significant feature of this mortality regime was, at least until the later middle ages, the extent of the available resource. The movement of population was cyclical, a response to changing levels of resources which were in turn a con-

sequence of changing population levels.[31] Broadly speaking, historians working subsequent to Postan have headed in two directions, promoting the roles of either mortality or fertility as determinative in explaining the behaviour of population in this period. We will return to a fuller discussion of these issues in a later chapter but, for now, it will be useful to reflect on the ways in which explanations of population change have been refined and new elements introduced.

Historians have long been familiar with the role of mortality in explaining change in medieval society. Postan's own model, explaining the behaviour of population in relation to resources, has not attracted the continued focus of historians interested in mortality. While there has been some discussion of the impact of the famines and dearths of the thirteenth and early fourteenth century upon population, this has been relatively light in comparison with research upon the single most important demographic event of the high and later middle ages, and one that does not sit comfortably with Postan's model of population resources.[32] Whilst the plague epidemics of the mid-fourteenth century have sometimes been linked with poor nutrition and limited food availability, the general consensus is that the virulence of the Black Death was such as to make the nutritional status of its victims relatively insignificant.[33] Discussion of the immediate impact of the Black Death in terms of a population and resources model is therefore largely irrelevant, though, as we will consider in a little more detail, historians have proposed a close relationship between the mid-century fall in population caused by plague and the subsequent behaviour of the post-plague population, though they have not always agreed on the nature of such a relationship.

The impact of the Black Death on the later medieval population, in terms of both its initial effect and its subsequent consequence for population movement and recovery, has attracted considerable interest. Research upon morbidity and mortality-driven regimes, evident especially in particularly good source material from monastic communities, has generated important information about the low life-expectancies of populations in the later middle ages and has illustrated how, even in an era of generally increased opportunity and improved standard of living, the impact of disease helped ensure that population levels remained low.[34] In the fifteenth-century countryside, as Gottfried has attempted to show, there is some reasonable evidence to suggest that the opportunities occasioned by trade and an expansion of the economy also brought with them disease, while urban historians also point to the severe infection risks occasioned by urban living.[35]

In this context, as more than one historian has noted, a reduced population with greater food availability and a heightened quality of living should have recovered in the later fourteenth and fifteenth centuries; that it did not suggests that factors other than the extent of available resource played an important role. As already noted, for some historians it was a continued mortality regime, dominated both by high levels of background mortality (high infant mortality and the prevalence of endemic diseases) and crisis mortality (the recurrence of epidemics of more than one disease), that directed the movement of population. For other historians, the explanation for population's behaviour resided instead in changing levels of fertility, issues we will discuss in a later chapter.[36]

Peasant resources and standard of living

In Postan's model, the relation between population and available *per capita* resource was central to explanation of long-term economic change. The extent of individual and collective peasant resource was, for Postan, determined chiefly by the productive capacity of the individual peasant and peasant family. Potential determinants of peasant standard of living, including the role of the market and the demands of landlords, tended to be downplayed. Postan argues, for instance, that the majority of peasant producers in the late fourteenth and fifteenth centuries were 'more or less insulated from the effects of both the low prices and the high wages'.[37] In Postan's model, peasants did not buy a great deal from the market and nor did they sell extensively there. When they did enter into the market this was, not infrequently, because of extra-economic compulsion, their sale of produce, such as wheat as a cash crop, being induced by the need to meet the fiscal expectations of lord or state.[38] Similarly, peasant labour found its greatest outlets in agriculture, either for lords or for other peasants. Neither was sufficient to employ the bulk of those seeking work or to retain men and women in work throughout the year.[39]

Postan quite clearly struggled to fit the changes evident by the end of the middle ages into his own model. In wholly acknowledging the considerable relative advantages which the medieval population enjoyed by the later middle ages, Postan explained the change in cycle in terms of his population-resources model. The Black Death, he argued, 'aggravated' the change but did not cause it; by applying the same line of reasoning, he suggested that population's stagnation in the later fourteenth and fifteenth centuries reflected the incapacity of the population 'to repair the damage done to the land in previous generations'.[40] Further to this, Postan stressed the continued significance of agrarian activity over and above trade in the later middle ages. He finds little evidence for new growth, in terms either of urbanisation or of developing proto-industry in the countryside. Instead, he detects a persistent reliance on a faltering agrarian structure; if wages and, by extension, standard of living rose in the later middle ages this was because, according to Postan, the proportion of wage earners in the countryside had declined and not because of any general expansion in economic opportunity: higher wages meant a reduced population; a reduced population was ultimately a consequence of diminished resource.[41]

In some contrast to the Postanian perspective on the condition of the later medieval economy, some historians have taken a rather different view of the economy's capacity to help effect a recovery in the population, or at least to encourage a different interpretation of the way in which the population's immobility in the later middle ages should be explained. In an early challenge, Barbara Harvey questioned the evidential base for Postan's conclusion that a declining population had prompted a retreat from marginal land by the early decades of the fourteenth century. Reviewing evidence for rents, wages, land use and the extent of change in land use, Harvey concluded that the historical record did not point towards a collapse in population in the period before the Black Death or towards a general failure in the agrarian economy in the face of severe weather conditions.[42] Others, whilst accepting Postan's identification of a period of crisis in the early fourteenth century, have proposed different explanations for the disruption, including warfare, both relatively local and more international in its character, as well as its associated costs including taxation.[43]

As already noted, a number of authors have also described the increase in urban and rural markets in the middle ages, and especially an explosion in their number from the beginning of the thirteenth century.[44] This is especially evident in the work of Richard Britnell, who, in a number of publications, suggested that a greater focus or emphasis upon market growth helps to modify our understanding of the functioning of the medieval economy. As he perceptively notes, such an adjusted emphasis is less dependent upon new research than it is upon new interpretations: Postan was aware of markets and their potential significance but, as also noted above, he did not view commercial activity as of primary importance.[45] We are also aware of other market-led developments across the period, including the growth in the importance of finished product, especially cloth in the later middle ages, and an increase in the market for relative luxuries, as well as a more generally available protein-enriched diet. Such advances can be taken to illustrate the potential of a society to generate surplus and thereby to cope with at least some vicissitudes.[46] Market growth of this kind is not always identified only as a consequence of population increase but can be seen as a stimulus to the same, and there is some suggestion that the population of the thirteenth and early fourteenth centuries was able to sustain its relatively high levels not because of essentially independent agrarian resources but because of the market's capacity to generate a greater resource. Such generation of resource came, for instance, in the stimulus to production which urban and commercial demand gave to rural dwellers, which can be identified in terms of changing labour patterns, the development of proto-industry in the countryside and adjusted agrarian productivity aimed at meeting the needs of neighbouring towns.[47]

That said, it cannot be easily shown that market growth and commercial development enabled population growth; it is also difficult to argue that the presence of active markets eased the effects of demographic crises of the high and later middle ages. We could, for instance, point to rural out-migration as one significant instance of urban and, by extension, market growth; in the early fourteenth century, for instance, we are aware that poorer rural dwellers sought support, employment and escape from the difficulties of the countryside by moving into towns.[48] It is also supposed that, throughout the later middle ages, the presence of towns and the labour markets they offered, especially in terms of service, may have had other demographic consequences, especially in inhibiting population growth and, especially, recovery in the later fourteenth and fifteenth centuries, points to which we shall return in subsequent chapters.[49]

Technology

Discussion of technology offers one further strand in the argument that, rather than essentially operating within a population that was driven exogenously, medieval rural dwellers were capable of some degree of self-determination and that population movement might also have responded to endogenous stimuli. That said, to date a great deal of the discussion of technological development within the medieval countryside has been directed at the investigation of changes in the management of demesnes more than it has at peasant holdings. There are good and obvious reasons for this, not least the far greater availability of source material which offers insight into the responses of lords to the husbandry of their own directly managed portions of their estates but provides far less information on peasant agriculture. We know, for instance, that lords, in a period of direct management, especially in the thirteenth and early fourteenth centuries, attempted a series of measures aimed at improving the efficiency of their estates, including the rotation of crops, changes in seeding rates, programmes of weeding and manuring, selective breeding of livestock, improvements to drainage and so on.[50] It is not entirely clear if peasants adopted the same methods, or indeed were in a position to do so, though relatively small pieces of evidence suggest at least that there were both common and discrete elements between seigneurial and peasant agriculture in the high and late middle ages. Thus, for instance, we tend, from the limited evidence available including tithe data, to find that peasants generally favoured the same grains as did their lords.[51] Most interestingly, recent research by Ben Dodds and Alexandra Sapoznik has been able to prod the tithe data a little further in ways that permit more detailed insight into peasant cropping strategies. Sapoznik, using an unusually detailed set of tithe data from the Crowland Abbey manor of Oakington (Cambridgeshire), argues that peasant productivity was higher than that of their lords in the second half of the fourteenth century (from the period for which relevant records survive). This she explains not so much in terms of crop choice – as tenants at Oakington tended to sow greater proportions of low-yielding grains – but in the relatively intensive cropping patterns employed by peasants.[52] Dodds's examination of Durham tithe data illustrates the ways in which peasant choices as regards cropping were most likely informed by market conditions, their choice of crop and the extent sown seemingly closely responsive to shifts in market price.[53] In both studies, which reflect some of the most recent work in this area, we can detect trends that stand in contrast to an earlier, Postanian orthodoxy and its emphasis on the lack of innovation and the inelasticity of output, and most especially in the ways in which significant weight is given both to peasant agency in agriculture and to the close relationship between the market and peasant agrarian activity.[54]

These distinctive features of a peasant-led agriculture have been noted in other studies published in recent years. Taxation data, including highly detailed lay subsidy assessments from the later thirteenth and early fourteenth centuries, as well as the few surviving peasant inventories and listings of movable property recorded in manorial court rolls, also suggest features consistent with seigneurial husbandry while at the same time hinting at novelties in terms of peasant investment.[55] In addition, as Dyer has noted, it also seems clear that peasants were at the forefront of the more extensive campaigns aimed at extending the agrarian acreage in the thirteenth and early fourteenth centuries, in terms of both drainage works and the conversion of relatively poor land, the waste, into farming land.⁵⁶ In the high and later middle ages we are also aware of attempts to exploit the rural labour force and landscape in ways that were other than purely agricultural. Thus, for instance, technological injections of other kinds, including the development of technologies associated with the cloth industry, especially fulling mills, as well as a more general introduction from the twelfth century of windmills, helped to enhance the economic productivity of rural areas.⁵⁷ Investment in particular kinds of livestock by peasants also indicates a peasant economy able to adapt to circumstance and to seek to improve agricultural outputs; thus, John Langdon has described a changing pattern of investment in horses, and in particular significant use of horse-power by small-holders in later medieval England. Langdon also notes, however, that such take-up was sometime sluggish and some peasant holdings still maintained oxen throughout the period, a persistence he considers explicable in terms of an array of potentially significant factors, including environment and ecology, the relative influence of commerce and the demesne sector, and shared contemporary views on continuity and change in medieval agriculture.⁵⁸

To what extent have historians, writing subsequent to Postan, suggested that such attempts to improve output had any effect on the behaviour of the medieval rural population? Perhaps most significantly, Bruce Campbell, the historian who has engaged most closely with issues of agrarian output and seigneurial agriculture, especially in the thirteenth and early fourteenth centuries, and with the attempts of lords to improve the productivity of their demesne, has concluded that output was not significantly improved in this period. Instead, he argues that population movement c.1300 was tied closely to what was essentially a poor yield of cereals.⁵⁹ He notes however that, in some parts of the country in parts of eastern England, a combination of factors including propitious environmental and institutional conditions, uniquely helped generate higher yields, as for instance those he describes for the estates of the priors of Norwich.⁶⁰ Elsewhere in the country however, according to Campbell, such a combination did not pertain and there was relative stagnation of yields; like Postan, he finds no evidence in this period for a wider attempt to invest to good effect in agrarian output. Instead the English agrarian economy exhibited features that were generally extensive rather than intensive.⁶¹ This he explains also in terms of the main constraints which operated in the medieval agrarian sector; thus, as regards the 'supply side', agrarian output was inevitably constrained by, *inter alia*, variable soil conditions and tillage, the relatively poor grain types available and the ubiquity of pests, diseases and weeds. In terms of the 'demand side', Campbell rejects the possibility that any but the most significant urban markets could have exerted a significant impact upon agrarian production, especially in terms of generating intensification or specialisation. In such conditions, where local markets for a common generality of products and especially foodstuffs existed, it was not ignorance or backwardness that held back major investment in agriculture but chiefly a lack of market opportunity. England, in the high middle ages, while developing important elements of a commercial infrastructure, lacked the major urban centres which might have helped jolt the rural economy towards justifiable economic risk by investing in other than raw product and in the intensive production of raw product.[62] While it is clear that rural investment, including many of the commercialising features identified as necessary by Campbell if the agrarian economy was to be transformed by the market, increased in the later middle ages, and especially in the period after the Black Death, most commentators would acknowledge that the market was insufficiently robust to drive economic change single-handedly in the later middle ages.[63]

While, though, Campbell has used his own argument for the relative slowness of the agrarian economy in order to suggest that England's population c.1300 could not have been as large as some historians had hitherto suggested, David Stone has proposed that peasant agriculture responded rather differently from demesne agriculture, and that peasant yields, on account of different cropping patterns and more intensive labour inputs, might actually have been higher than demesne yields.[64] We cannot, at this point in research on peasant agriculture, claim with absolute confidence that peasants generally and actively invested differently from lords in the high middle ages and that, in general terms, their pattern of agriculture was significantly different from that of lords. However, Stone at least has argued that differences in the cropping of grains did have measurable consequences for the behaviour of population c.1300, the output on peasant-cropped land producing a yield significantly in excess of that proposed by Campbell and one capable of sustaining a population of 5.5 million, a million more than that suggested by Campbell for the same period.[65] In addition, John Langdon and James Masschaele, using extents from the twelfth and thirteenth century, propose an earlier phase of population growth linked to energetic commercial activity and consequent enhanced fertility, something they propose may serve as 'a replacement – or at the very least a supplement – to the population-resources model'.[66] Their proposal, to which return will be made in a later chapter, is predicated upon the assumption that commercial growth is encouraged by and encourages population growth through the extension of families in periods of relative prosperity, a proposal obviously at odds with some of the key tenets of Postan's population-resources model.[67] By contrast, Gregory Clark has quite recently provided support for Postan's thesis; extrapolation from Clark's calculations of the 'marginal product of labour' (essentially wages divided by an index of prices) suggest to him that wages moved closely with population and that it was population, evidenced through the availability of labour, that dictated employers' responses and, thereby, economic change before the early modern period. Furthermore, and contrary to Campbell, he argues for a larger population, closer to the six million c.1300 originally proposed by Postan, by contending both that the extent of land available for cultivation was greater than that suggested by Campbell and that there was limited evidence for efficiency gains in the middle ages of a kind that would encourage population growth.[68]

Peasants, markets and the land market

It will be evident from the discussion so far that Postan approached the study of the market and the village economy anticipating that it would not be commercial exchange that drove peasant interaction or, indeed, that commerce was not of sufficient importance to have a determining influence upon the direction of the economy or the welfare of the general population. For Postan, exchange directed at and led by the market could help to draw out social and economic distinctions within the medieval peasantry, helping for instance a vulnerable small-holder class to survive perilously close to disaster; the overall influence of the market was, however, relatively muted. His view, given its fullest expression in his discussion of the peasant land market, was that the functioning of the medieval village was relatively timeless and that its motion and direction were above all determined by demographic factors.[69] Postan recognised that aspects of the peasant land market could be influenced by other factors and that the peasant economy was not divorced from other, more complex and commercially orientated features of the wider medieval economy.[70] Postan also identified features of inter-peasant dealing consistent at least with commercial and market-led exchange, where the focus of activity was less upon a reallocation of resources and more to do with one individual profiting from the relative disadvantage of another. Thus, for example, Postan recognises that wealthier peasants might sub-let their land to poorer villagers and could also serve as creditors, employing their surplus capital as well as their excess of landholding to their own economic benefit.[71] This was also true, for instance, in terms of the village labour market and the range of crafts which can be identified in the medieval village, both consistent with employment beyond or, at most, associated with agriculture.[72] Postan also recognised the possibility that the wealthier peasants might consume goods beyond their immediate needs, including luxury items.[73] Despite this, Postan saw such instances of medieval market-dependency as of secondary importance. Thus, for Postan, there is little evidence for excessive consumption on the part of wealthier peasants, just as we cannot easily detect a sophisticated market in credit; nor, to follow Postan, could by employment offer significant and consistent support for the relatively poor village labourers and small-holders.[74] There is also little in Postan's work that speaks to peasant involvement with neighbouring market-towns and markets at a further remove. Instead, Postan tends to see the major markets and trades of the middle ages as operating almost independently of the later medieval peasantry, the domain of merchants more than of petty producers.[75]

Historians contemporary or near-contemporary to Postan and writing about peasant conditions and matters pertaining to the peasantry were also influenced by the same view of a limited and constrained peasant economic agency. Thus, in the first instance, studies of peasant economic interaction beyond the manor or in terms of inter-peasant dealing were, as already noted, relatively few before the last decades of the twentieth century. G.C. Homans, for instance, finds little room for the market and the wider economy in a discussion founded on the family and household as keys to unlocking the nature of village society in the thirteenth century;[76] a number of other commentators, from the 1960s through to the 1980s, not all issuing from the same intellectual backgrounds or subscribing to the same models, also tended to base their working hypotheses and underlying assumptions regarding the nature of and change within the medieval village upon the importance of family size and structure.

In work published in the 1970s, for example, Rodney Hilton suggested, in drawing conclusions that were not wholly inconsistent with the position adopted by Postan, that a market in land, especially in small plots, was occasioned far less by 'unequal market opportunities' than by a 'long term cyclical movement by which the family labour force tended to increase faster than agricultural productivity'.[77] The intellectual association between a Postanian model and explanation of economic change, which obviously placed population movement in the foreground, and historians inclined to accept the social structural and demographic explanations for change in the medieval village, is certainly evident in the work of more than one historian writing in the generation after the publication of Postan's main contributions. We can, for instance, detect this in discussions of the peasant land market completed as doctoral theses in the 1960s and 1970s and republished as a collection of extended essays in the early 1980s. In this, the interpretative framework is closely allied to that proposed earlier by Postan; thus, Janet Williamson's investigation of the land market in Norfolk in the thirteenth century employs a population-driven explanation for the patterns of fragmentation, redistribution and accumulation she describes.[78] Rosamund Faith's study of later medieval Berkshire, while more than identifying the potential for wealthier peasants to take full advantage of changes in opportunity occasioned by demesne leasing on the part of lords, also couches much of the discussion within a demographically determined context.[79] Andrew Jones also, while describing in some detail the speculation of wealthier merchants and townsmen in Bedfordshire within the local land market by the end of the middle ages, concludes that much of the movement in customary land was, especially where it was further away from the reach of market towns, quite sluggish and determined by population movement.[80] This is a description of a later medieval midlands-type land market dominated by large holdings and with relatively little small-scale and frequent exchange of land of a kind also described earlier by Rodney Hilton for fourteenth- and fifteenth-century Leicestershire. While Hilton promotes the agency of the peasantry in relation to the policy of lords as determining factors of such developments,[81] as with Jones and other contributors on the peasant land market, there is no suggestion that a market or constituent features of involved economic exchange were wholly absent, but it is rather more the case that the focus of historical investigation was not directed at them. This is also evident in Tim Lomas's contribution on south-east Durham in the later fourteenth and fifteenth centuries. Lomas describes significant economic dealing in basic foodstuffs redolent of an active economy where exchange within a market was important but also argues against a commercial motive as the defining feature of the local economy; instead it appears, from Lomas's analysis, that the region was defined by a localised and largely demographically determined economy.[82]

A major departure in such an approach came in the 1980s and 1990s, as a series of publications, mostly on eastern England and East Anglia in particular, illustrated the ways in which aggressive policies of accumulation could be undertaken by a discrete group of wealthy villagers, topics to be considered later in this volume when we turn to discussion of commercialisation.[83] A decade earlier than the first appearance of studies of this kind, Paul Hyams had provided a critique of a Postanian approach to the peasant land market in which he offered direct challenge to some of the main contentions set out in Postan's introduction to the *Carte Nativorum*.[84] In particular, Hyams emphasises the discrete regional chronologies in the development of a land market and the need for historians to identify the means by which capital might be generated in order to support the buying and selling of land, most especially by acknowledging the role of leases in support of mortgages.[85] Subsequent work has in fact found it less than straightforward to associate mortgages with a peasant land market and the extension of security, the evidence of court rolls from the later thirteenth and fourteenth centuries tending to suggest that even quite extensive credit agreements were not secured on land, though it is also recognised that leasing might conceivably be used debtors to secure funds sufficient to pay off third-party creditors.[86] In fact, Hyams recognised that there was a large number of routes to generating capital through a land and/or lease market and it is evident that historians have, in their discussion of the peasant land market, taken up his call to investigate more fully the relationship between capital, the land market and the external market-led factors that may, as or more than changes in total population, have contributed to its stimulation and/or contraction.[87]

This chapter, by outlining the main views of M.M. Postan, his population-resources model and its application to the medieval peasantry, has identified what may be seen as the major operating theme in this area of historical research. The relationship between the medieval peasants and their environment and their incapacity to escape its control was most fully formulated by Postan. In addition, his proposed chronology of population change, relative to available resources, framed and continues to frame the discussion of the medieval peasantry but also wider society and economy in this period. It is no great overstatement to suggest that the greater extent of work on the medieval peasantry in the last fifty and more years has been conducted in Postan's shadow. Some of that work has been undertaken in flat contradiction of Postan's own thesis; other of it has been intended to test and develop it. Very little of it has been carried out without any regard to Postan at all. In the following two chapters we will consider the two other significant competing major themes in relation to the medieval English peasantry, the relations between lords and peasants, and peasant engagement with the market.

Notes

1 See below, Chapters 5, pp. 151–67, and 6, pp. 173–82.
2 See for instance Maitland's discussion of changing conditions on a Cambridgeshire manor: F.W. Maitland, 'The history of a Cambridgeshire manor', in H.M. Cam, ed., *Selected historical essays of F.W. Maitland* (Cambridge: Cambridge University Press, 1957), pp. 16–40.
3 For a useful summary, see S.H. Rigby, *English society in the later middle ages. Class, status and gender* (Basingstoke: Macmillan, 1995), pp. 61–2; also J. Munro, '"Money matters": a critique of the Postan thesis on medieval population, prices and wages', in J. Drendel, ed., *Crisis in the middle ages. Beyond the Postan–Duby paradigm* (Turnhout: Brepols, 2015), pp. 131–3. See also Sir W.J. Ashley, *An introduction to English economic history and theory. Part I. The middle ages* (London: Rivingtons, 1888).
4 See below, Chapter 3, pp. 85–6, for fuller discussion of this issue.
5 M.M. Postan, 'The chronology of labour services', *Transactions of the Royaal Historical Society*, 4th series, 20 (1937); also published in M.M. Postan, *Essays on medieval agriculture and general problems of the medieval economy* (Cambridge: Cambridge University Press, 1973), pp. 89–106.
6 See also M.M. Postan, 'The rise of a money economy', *Economic History Review* 14 (1944); also published in Postan, *Essays on medieval agriculture*, pp. 28–40, especially p. 34.
7 Postan, 'Rise of a money economy', p. 29 and n. 2 there.
8 E. Lipson, *An introduction to the economic history of England. I. The middle ages* (London: Adam and Charles Black, 1915), pp. 94–129 (quote at p. 103).
9 M.M. Postan, 'The economic foundations of medieval society', in *Rapports, Libraire Armand Colin* (Paris: Libraire Armand Colin, 1950), repr. in Postan, *Essays on medieval agriculture*, pp. 3–27.
10 For discussion of these issues see, for instance, Rigby, *English society*, pp. 66–9; also Munro, '"Money matters"', pp. 133–4.
11 D.C. Coleman, *History and the economic past. An account of the rise and decline of economic history in Britain* (Oxford: Clarendon Press, 1987), pp. 91–2, 101–7; N. Cantor, *Inventing the middle ages. The lives, works and ideas of the great medievalists of the twentieth century* (Cambridge: Lutterworth, 1991), pp. 390–1.
12 See, for a succinct overview of this thesis, M.M. Postan, *The medieval economy and society. An economic history of Britain in the middle ages* (Harmondsworth: Penguin, 1972), c. 3.
13 See also below, pp. 67–9
14 Postan, *Medieval economy and society*, p. 44.
15 See below, pp. 74–7
16 R. Brenner, 'Agrarian class structure and economic development in pre-industrial Europe', in T.H. Aston and C.H.E. Philpin, eds, *The Brenner debate. Agrarian class structure and economic development in pre-industrial Europe* (Cambridge, Cambridge University Press, 1985), pp. 15–17.
17 M.M. Postan, 'Village livestock in the thirteenth century', *Economic History*

Review, 2nd series, 15 (1962); also published in Postan, *Essays on medieval agriculture*, pp. 214-48.

18 Postan, 'Village livestock', p. 247, for this and previous direct quotations in this paragraph. For critical comment on Postan's analysis, see for instance J. Masschaele, *Peasants, merchants and markets. Inland trade in medieval England, 1150-1350* (Basingstoke: Macmillan, 1997), pp. 42-4.

19 With J.Z. Titow, 'Heriots and prices on Winchester manors', *Economic History Review*, 2nd series, 11 (1959); reprinted in Postan, *Essays in medieval agriculture*, pp. 150-85.

20 For a counterview of this material and its potential for interpretation, see G. Ohlin, 'No safety in numbers: some pitfalls of historical statistics', in R. Floud, ed., *Essays in quantitative economic history* (Oxford: Oxford University Press, 1974), pp. 73-7, and below, Chapter 5, p. 162.

21 Postan and Titow, 'Heriots and prices', p. 174.

22 C.N.L. Brooke and M.M. Postan, *Carte Nativorum, a Peterborough Abbey cartulary of the fourteenth century* (Northants Record Society, 1960).

23 M.M. Postan, 'The charters of the villeins', in Brooke and Postan, eds, *Carte Nativorum*, pp. xxviii-lxv; reprinted in M.M. Postan, *Essays in medieval agriculture and general problems of the medieval economy* (Cambridge: Cambridge University Press, 1973), pp. 107-49, especially p. 114.

24 Postan, 'The charters of the villeins', pp. 114-15.

25 M.M. Postan, 'Medieval agrarian society in its prime. England. F. The village rich', in M.M. Postan, ed., *The Cambridge economic history of Europe. I. The agrarian life of the middle ages* (Cambridge: Cambridge University Press, 2nd ed., 1966), pp. 548-632.

26 See, for instance, the dismissal of the notion that 'sheep-farming regions' existed in thirteenth-century lowland England and the suggestion that 'the typical small man was not a sheep-farmer but a cottager with "three acres and a cow"', 'Medieval agrarian society', p. 556, a view that draws heavily upon the arguments of Postan's earlier article on village livestock, discussed above.

27 Postan, 'Medieval agrarian society', p. 616.

28 Postan, 'Medieval agrarian society', pp. 631-2.

29 Postan, 'Medieval agrarian society', p. 568. For discussion of these indices, see also M.M. Postan, 'Some agrarian evidence of declining population in the later middle ages', *Economic History Review* 2 (1950), reprinted in Postan, *Essays on medieval agriculture*, pp. 188-213.

30 For a succinct and highly effective commentary upon Postan and the Postan thesis as well as an assessment of its durability, see R.H. Britnell, 'Commercialization, stagnation and crisis, 1250-1350', in J. Drendel, ed., *Crisis in the later middle ages. Beyond the Postan-Duby paradigm* (Turnhout: Brepols, 2015), pp. 15-34.

31 For an overview of this, see above, pp. 61-3 and Postan, *Medieval economy and society*, pp. 30-44.

32 For discussion of famine-related mortality and some evidence for population decline in the early fourteenth century, see L.R. Poos, 'The rural population of Essex in the later middle ages', *Economic History Review* 38 (1985), 515-30;

Z. Razi, *Life, marriage and death in a medieval parish. Economy, society and demography in Halesowen, 1270-1400* (Cambridge: Cambridge University Press, 1980), pp. 39-41; I. Kershaw, 'The great famine and agrarian crisis in England 1315-1322', *Past and Present* 59 (1973); reprinted in R.H. Hilton, ed., *Peasants, knights and heretics. Studies in medieval English social history* (Cambridge: Cambridge University Press, 1976), pp. 85-132.

33 For attempts to associate pre-plague nutritional deficiencies with the epidemic, note for instance the recent article by Dewitte and Slavin, the ultimate conclusion of which appears to be that there is as yet insufficient evidence to associate early fourteenth-century nutritional failings with mid-fourteenth century plague mortality, S. DeWitte and P. Slavin, 'Between famine and death: England on the eve of the Black Death – evidence from paleoepidemiology and manorial accounts', *Journal of Interdisciplinary History* 44 (2013), 37-60, especially at pp. 57-8. That plague is identifiably a disease of the poor, and by extension malnourished, has been explained by other authors chiefly in terms of the social and environmental factors pertaining at the time of an epidemic, as for example F. Audouin-Rouzeau, *Les chemins de la peste. Le rat, la puce et l'homme* (Rennes: Presses Universitaires de Rennes, 2003), pp. 339-57.

34 J. Hatcher, 'Mortality in the fifteenth century: some new evidence', *Economic History Review* 39 (1986), 19-38; B.F. Harvey, *Living and dying in England 1100-1540. The monastic experience* (Oxford: Oxford University Press, 1995), pp. 112-45.

35 R. Gottfried, *Epidemic disease in fifteenth-century England. The medical response and the demographic consequences* (Leicester: Leicester University Press, 1978); G. Rosser, *Medieval Westminster 1200-1540* (Oxford: Oxford University Press, 1989); also C. Dyer, *Standards of living in the later Middle Ages: social change in England c.1200-1520* (Cambridge: Cambridge University Press, 1989), pp. 192-3.

36 For discussion of which see below, Chapter 5, pp. 165-7.

37 Postan, 'Some agrarian evidence', p. 194.

38 Postan, 'Medieval agrarian society', pp. 600-1. This is an important theme for Marxists in their own analysis of peasant standard of living and seigneurial exaction, for which see below, pp. 118-23

39 Postan, 'Medieval agrarian society', p. 624.

40 Postan, *Medieval economy and society*, pp. 42-4.

41 Postan, 'Some agrarian evidence', pp. 196-202.

42 B.F. Harvey, 'The population trend in England between 1300 and 1348', *Transactions of the Royal Historical Society* 16 (1966), 23-42.

43 As, for instance, John H. Munro, 'Industrial transformation in the north-west European textile trades, c.1290 – c.1340: economic progress or economic crisis', in B.M.S. Campbell, ed., *Before the Black Death. Studies in the 'crisis' of the early fourteenth century* (Manchester: Manchester University Press, 1991), pp. 120-40, and also references at n. 104, p. 140.

44 R.H. Britnell, 'The proliferation of markets in England, 1200-1349', *Economic History Review* 34 (1981), 209-21; see also John Langdon and James Masschaele,

'Commercial activity and population growth in medieval England', *Past and Present* 190 (2006), 43–9.

45 As, for instance, Britnell, 'Commercialization, stagnation, and crisis', p. 24. For Britnell's major discussion of this issue, see especially R.H. Britnell, *The commercialisation of English society, 1000–1500* (Cambridge, 1993; republished by Manchester University Press, 1996).

46 Postan was not wholly dismissive of the notion that wealthy peasants might stimulate a market in relative luxury goods but he saw little or no evidence for it and suspected that reinvestment of any peasant surplus was likely to be directed at land, Postan, 'Agrarian society in its prime', p. 625.

47 See, for instance, B.M.S. Campbell, J.A. Galloway, D. Keene and M. Murphy, *A medieval capital and its grain supply: agrarian production and distribution in the London region, c.1300* (London: Institute of British Geographers, 1993).

48 E. Rutledge, 'Immigration and population growth in early fourteenth-century Norwich: evidence from the tithing roll', *Urban History Yearbook 1988*; R.M. Smith, 'Demographic developments', in B.M.S. Campbell, ed., *Before the Black Death: essays in the crisis of the early fourteenth century* (Manchester: Manchester University Press, 1991), p. 75.

49 See below, Chapter 5, pp. 165–6.

50 See, in particular, B.M.S. Campbell, *English seigniorial agriculture, 1250–1450* (Cambridge: Cambridge University Press, 2000) and D. Stone, *Decision-making in medieval agriculture* (Oxford: Oxford University Press, 2006).

51 B. Dodds, *Peasants and production in the medieval north-east. The evidence from tithes, 1270–1536* (Woodbridge: Boydell, 2007), pp. 132–61; Stone, *Decision-making*, pp. 262–72.

52 A. Sapoznik, 'The productivity of peasant agriculture: Oakington, Cambridgeshire, 1360–99', *Economic History Review* 66 (2013), 518–44.

53 Dodds, *Peasants and production*, pp. 132–61.

54 On this point, see also M. Bailey, 'Peasant welfare in England, 1290–1348', *Economic History Review* 51 (1998), 228–9.

55 D. Stone, 'The consumption of field crops in late medieval England', in C. Woolgar, D. Serjeantson and T. Waldron, eds, *Food in medieval England: diet and nutrition* (Oxford: Oxford University Press, 2006), p. 19.

56 C. Dyer, *An age of transition? Economy and society in England in the later middle ages* (Oxford: Oxford University Press, 2005), p. 90; P.R. Schofield, *Peasant and community in medieval England* (Basingstoke: Palgrave, 2003), pp. 25–6. The colonisation of new land could also be driven by population pressure and failing resources, as Postan also suggested; see, for instance, M. Stinson, 'Assarting and poverty in early fourteenth-century western Yorkshire', *Landscape History* 5 (1983), 53–67.

57 J. Langdon, *Mills in the medieval economy. England 1300–1540* (Oxford: Oxford University Press, 2004); Edward J. Kealey, *Harvesting the air: windmill pioneers in twelfth-century England* (Woodbridge: Boydell and Brewer, 1987); Richard Holt, *The mills of medieval England* (Oxford: Oxford University Press, 1988); see also the discussion of the thirteenth-century rural cloth industry, in E. Miller,

'The fortunes of the English cloth industry in the thirteenth century', *Economic History Review* 18 (1965), 64-82; Langdon and Masschaele, 'Commercial activity and population growth', pp. 51-2; Dyer, *Age of transition?*, pp. 92-4.

58 J. Langdon, *Horses, oxen and technological innovation. The use of draught animals in English farming from 1066-1500* (Cambridge: Cambridge University Press, 1986), pp. 172-253, 255-65.

59 B.M.S. Campbell, *English seigniorial agriculture 1250-1450* (Cambridge: Cambridge University Press, 2000), p. 386.

60 For instance, Campbell, *English seigniorial agriculture*, p. 420.

61 Campbell, *English seigniorial agriculture*, pp. 411-14.

62 Campbell, *English seigniorial agriculture*, pp. 424-30. For further reflection on restricted urban demands and explanations for it, see also S.H. Rigby, 'Introduction. Social structure and economic change in late medieval England', in R. Horrox and W.M. Ormrod, eds, *A social history of England, 1200-1500* (Cambridge: Cambridge University Press, 2006), pp. 28-9.

63 See, for instance, Dyer, *Age of transition*, pp. 176-8; also Bailey, 'Peasant welfare', 233-8.

64 Stone, *Decision-making*, pp. 262-72.

65 Stone, 'Consumption of field crops', pp. 19-25.

66 Langdon and Masschaele, 'Commercial activity and population growth', pp. 56-77.

67 See below Chapter 4, pp. 140-1.

68 G. Clark, 'The long march of history: farm wages. Population, and economic growth, England 1209-1869', *Economic History Review* 60 (2007), pp. 97-135.

69 Postan, 'The charters of the villeins', p. 114, and above, this chapter, pp. 64-6; see also P.R. Schofield, 'Peasants and contract in the thirteenth century: village elites and the land market in eastern England', in Schofield and Lambrecht, *Credit and the rural economy in north-western Europe, c.1200-c.1800* (Turnhout: Brepols, 2009), pp. 129-30; also, in the same volume, G. Béaur, 'Credit and land in eighteenth-century France', pp. 153-4; also, P.R. Schofield, 'M.M. Postan and the peasant economy', in Drendel, ed., *Crisis in the later middle ages*, pp. 73-93.

70 Postan, 'Charters of the villeins', p. 114: 'Some of the inducements [i.e. that were capable of stimulating a market in land held by peasants – PS] were purely economic; they might even be described as commercial.'

71 Postan, 'Medieval agrarian society', pp. 626-8.

72 Postan, 'Medieval agrarian society', pp. 622-3.

73 Postan, 'Medieval agrarian society', p. 625.

74 Postan, 'Medieval agrarian society', pp. 622-32.

75 M.M. Postan, 'The trade of medieval Europe: the north', in M.M. Postan, *Medieval trade and finance* (Cambridge: Cambridge University Press, 1973), pp. 140-1.

76 G.C. Homans, *English villagers of the thirteenth century* (Cambridge, Mass.: Harvard University Press, 1941), pp. 337-8.

77 R.H. Hilton, 'Reasons for inequality among medieval peasants', in R.H. Hilton, ed., *Class conflict and the crisis of feudalism. Essays in medieval social history* (London: Hambledon, 1985), p. 147.

78 J. Williamson, 'Norfolk: thirteenth century', in P.D.A. Harvey, ed., *The peasant land market in medieval England* (Oxford: Oxford University Press), pp. 59–60.
79 R. Faith, 'Berkshire: fourteenth and fifteenth centuries', in Harvey, ed., *Peasant land market*, pp. 159–60.
80 A. Jones, 'Bedfordshire: fifteenth century', in Harvey, ed., *Peasant land market*, pp. 222–3 and, by contrast, pp. 248–51.
81 R.H. Hilton, *The economic development of some Leicestershire estates in the fourteenth and fifteenth centuries* (Oxford: Oxford University Press, 1947), pp. 94–105, and below, pp. 118–19.
82 T. Lomas, 'South-east Durham: late fourteenth and fifteenth centuries', in Harvey, ed., *Peasant land market*, pp. 308–9, 311–14, 317–27.
83 R.M. Smith, *Land, kinship and lifecycle* (Cambridge: Cambridge University Press, 1984), and below, Chapter 4, pp. 129–33.
84 P.R. Hyams, 'The origins of a peasant land market in England', *Economic History Review* xxiii (1970), pp. 18–31, and above, pp. 64–5.
85 Hyams, 'Origins of a peasant land market', pp. 26–31.
86 See, for instance, Schofield, 'Peasants and contract', pp. 129–52; C. Briggs, *Credit and village society in fourteenth-century England* (Oxford: Oxford University Press, 2009), pp. 158–64.
87 Hyams, 'Origins of a peasant land market', pp. 30–1, and below, Chapter 4, pp. 128–33.

3

Lords and peasants

In the previous chapter we saw how historians have discussed the peasantry in terms of the population and its movement. Here we will explore the ways in which historians have engaged with the peasantry chiefly as tenants, and especially in terms of the relationship between lord and peasant-tenants. This concentration on lord–tenant relations has sometimes narrowed the historical focus to dwell upon sub-sets of the peasantry, namely those, especially the unfree, who held land from lords on particular kinds of tenure and were thereby especially visible in seigneurial records. However, at other junctures, especially in consideration of revolt and 'class struggle' and of peasants and their socio-political superiors (lords, the church, the state), it has also broadened the category. In particular, there are those historians who have identified the peasantry as a 'class', existing chiefly in resistance to the institutions through which its members were obliged to operate. The most significant of these institutions was certainly lordship, and discussion of the medieval English peasantry has seldom been entirely discrete from discussion of the peasant's lord.

While, inevitably, historical focus on the relationship between lord and peasant is directed towards tension, dispute and, on occasion, open revolt, the earliest work on the medieval English peasantry drew attention to lordship from a slightly more prosaic perspective. While, as we have already seen in an earlier chapter, it would be correct to state that some 'early' work on the medieval peasantry, such as that by J.E.T. Rogers and R.H. Tawney, was carried out on topics which were not defined by the parameters of lordship, it is clear that most research and writing was conducted within such a seigneurial context. In this approach to the study of the rural economy, the 'peasantry', that is in the most general terms almost all rural dwellers below the level of minor knights, gentry, clergy and so on, including the sub-sets of wealthy villeins, free tenants, cottagers but also those occupying very small plots of land, as well as their families and those who worked for them in so far as the latter also issued from the same socio-economic base,[1] featured far less directly in general than did the important sub-set of country dwellers, the 'tenantry', in other words those holding directly from their lords as tenants. The range of study has often been confined to units of seigneurial administration – the estate or the manor – as a consequence. Furthermore, the chief focus for investigation was lordship, rather than the tenantry itself; in other words, initial investigation of the medieval peasant was typically conducted as an adjunct to an institutional history of medieval lordship, its administration and estate organisation or in relation to careful histories of the legal development of tenure and the obligations of the tenantry. As we had cause to mention in the preceding chapter in discussing Postan's earliest work and his response to a previous generation of historians, it was also conducted within a context dominated by investigation of the rise of the money economy, a topic that necessarily encouraged interest in the changing nature of rent and the shift from rents in kind and in labour to money rent.

Lords, tenants and rent

This interest in the changing nature of rent as a significant indicator in the quality and capacity of the medieval economy persisted into the second quarter of the twentieth century and beyond, most evidently, in its first reappearance, in the work, published in the 1930s, of M.M. Postan and also of the Russian historian E.A. Kosminsky. Both historians engaged closely with the prior debate, and both were particularly keen to interpret the movement in labour services in novel ways.[2] To begin with Postan, whose study of labour service and its changing incidence in the high middle ages, written in the late 1930s, was amongst his earliest published contributions to the field of medieval economic history, is to continue to engage with the long-standing discussion of the significance of commutation of labour service for an historical understanding of the rise of a money economy.[3] Striking in his analysis, however, is his emphasis upon the long-standing causes underlying the general chronology in the use of labour services. Postan notes a tendency amongst earlier historians to treat some of their investigations as local studies without a great deal of wider application, lacking the overall theoretical argument that might permit broader sense to be made of their discoveries, and to be constrained by their own views of the nature of the high medieval agrarian economy in ways that prevented them from drawing the obvious conclusions.[4] In gathering information for a wider chronology of labour services, Postan offers a chronology of change which sees an increase in labour services before the twelfth century, followed by a process of commutation during the twelfth century, and then a return to labour service in a period of increased population and economic growth in the long thirteenth century. Postan locates his discussion within the bounds of the debate regarding the rise of the money economy and is eager to emphasise the prevalence of labour services even during a period of economic growth, the absence of a cheap and available labour force, for Postan, explaining lords' increased reliance on their own bonded labour.[5] There is then much in his discussion which reflects upon the relationship of lords and tenants, as well as some consideration of the capacity of lordship to adjust to changed local and more general circumstance. Important in any such development, according to Postan, was the will of the tenant's lord even if that will was necessarily constrained and conditioned by a multiplicity of factors, including regional conditions, population, climate and so on. In his later discussion of the demesne labourer, the *famulus*, in the twelfth and thirteenth century, Postan is, for instance, eager to show that the changing context of labour was determined by seigneurial policy and that, as direct management of demesnes grew apace, lords sought to supplement labour on their demesne with the employment of waged labour.[6] Indeed, most of the potential decisions taken in terms of management of rent and labour, as set out by Postan, were evidently those of lords and their estate managers. While Postan has some comment to make upon the potential impact of such changes upon the tenantry itself, this was not, as we have seen, his main concern and neither was the relationship between lord and tenant *per se*. Rodney Hilton, in his review of Postan's study of the *famulus*, notes this lack of discussion of a wider context in reflecting both upon the significantly larger proportion of the high medieval wage-labour sector created by peasant employers and, what is likely to have been of greater importance for Hilton, upon the links between unfree status and the obligation to serve as *famuli* on the lord's demesne.[7] In this last point, he stresses the lack of correspondence with modern wage labour and contends instead that *famuli* were, at least in some contexts, likely to have been constrained to work on their lords' estates, observations that he feels had eluded Postan.

E.A. Kosminsky, whose article on labour services and money rents was published a couple of years before Postan's investigation of the chronology of labour services, also engages directly and fully with the earlier discussion of labour services and commutation characterised by the work of Page, Gray and others.[8] In certain respects, Kosminsky's discussion was grounded in earlier historiographical concerns but he also brought new ideological perspectives to the investigation of lord–tenant relations and the study of rent. In the first instance though, Kosminsky's approach returns us to the earliest discussions of terminology and close definitions of tenure evident in the work of Vinogradoff and Seebohm at the close of the nineteenth century. Thus, he argues that some of the money rents evident by the thirteenth century were not the product of commutation in, say, the twelfth century (so-called *mal, mol* or *mail*) but were instead *gafol*, far more ancient money payments.[9] For Kosminsky, the necessary point of departure for an analysis of this kind is the relationship between money and labour rent pertaining in the middle years of the thirteenth century. By making use of material surviving from this period, and especially the inquisitions *post mortem* (inquests conducted into the estates of the major secular landholders – the tenants-in-chief – upon their deaths)[10] and Edward I's Hundred Rolls of 1279–80, a national survey of the rights pertaining to landlords, Kosminsky offers a comparison of the relative significance of money and labour rent and notes some striking features, notably an association of labour rent with those areas characterised by heavy population and relatively heightened economic activity.[11] In this Kosminsky arrives at the general conclusion which was also supported a year or two later by Postan, namely that economic precocity, good management and seigneurial ambition were not antithetical to the extension of labour service as had been assumed by those who equated economic progress with the rise of a money economy. Instead, Kosminsky stresses the capacity of lordship to effect a change in tenure and rent which created both economic opportunity for the landlord and complaint from the servile tenantry; it was, for Kosminsky, the most powerful and successful landlords who sought to retain and, where possible, extend labour services in the thirteenth century; a move to money rent reflected rather more a 'policy' of obligation on the part of the middling and lesser lords, who operated within the strictures of small-holders and freemen as their tenants and with relatively little in the way of coercive machinery available to adopt any different and more demanding a strategy.[12]

In this respect Kosminsky's analysis, which was developed more fully in his book-length study of the same material and was published in Russian in 1935 before being translated into English twenty years later, is important in the development of a historiography of lord–tenant relations in this period.[13] His discussion, for what were undoubtedly deep-rooted political and ideological reasons, was the first to stress the tension which seigneurial policy might generate in the tenantry. Employing a Marxist analysis in the final sections of his article on labour service and money rent, Kosminsky argues that it was the pressures of labour service imposed by lords, who sought further and better opportunities, that occasioned resistance from the tenantry; he, in fact, goes further and suggests that it was in these areas of strong and demanding lordship that the seeds of resentment sown in the thirteenth century were reaped in the Peasants' Revolt in the later fourteenth century.[14] In what is, in many respects, a subtle and informed discussion, Kosminsky offers the first important attempt at employing evidence for the economic experience of the medieval English countryside as a model of the process of transition from feudalism to capitalism. Interestingly, Rodney Hilton, in his introduction to the 1956 English translation of Kosminsky's book on the agrarian history of England in the thirteenth century, draws a firm and critical line between Kosminsky's contribution to the study of rent and 'many previous writings' which, he at least implied, were less theoretically charged in their approach:

> [Kosminsky's] emphasis on rent is not simply due to a more or less arbitrary selection for special attention of one among a number of important topics. It results from the conception that in the payment of rent are embodied the essential features of the social relations between the two basic classes of feudal society – landlords and peasants.[15]

For Kosminsky, as Hilton points out, it was the human and social interaction, embodied in the competing claims over rent, that was central and essential to our historical understanding of social and economic change in the middle ages.[16] Kosminsky himself also identifies this departure in the historiography, setting out a useful overview of the preceding literature on commutation of labour services and money rent before offering a view on the rise of money rent that admitted the capacity of lords to reintroduce labour rent even when the rising tide of money rent was in full flood.[17] Important, for Kosminsky as also for Postan, was the non-unilinear development of money rent, a disjointed chronology of change reflective of different expectations which were themselves the consequences of a variety of factors, including changing market conditions and the associated demands of lordship.[18] These differences were also evident between regions, the persistence of labour rent in eastern counties an inversion of the standard thesis, namely that economic development in the more densely populated and more prosperous parts of England would serve to drive out labour rent. Kosminsky rejects, in his explanation of this feature, the notion that a quasi-capitalism drove these developments; instead he contends that it was the demands of lordship that prompted such shifts in rent just as it was peasant resistance that eventually overcame them.[19]

This intellectual focus, namely on the seigneurial use of labour rent relative to money rent, itself allied to an understanding of adjustments to the management of demesne and estates in a changing economic climate, remained an important consideration in studies of the agrarian economy throughout the twentieth century. Postan's own interpretation was subjected to close scrutiny in a series of studies and debates which followed the publication of his 1937 article on the chronology of labour services. This was especially marked for a generation or so after Postan set out his initial thoughts on labour service. Early contributors to this theme included Reginald Lennard, whose study of late eleventh- and early twelfth-century rural England, published in his retirement in 1959 but the summation of a lifetime's research in this area, clearly reflects a preoccupation with similar concerns for the earliest part of the period.[20] He has, for instance, much to say on the organisation of the eleventh- and twelfth-century tenantry, the distinctions between types of tenant and the obligations owed to their lords. In his account, Lennard illustrates the variety of tenures already in evidence in the late eleventh century. By the twelfth century, as Lennard points out, estate surveys permit some identification of the distinctions in the peasants' obligations to their lord as well as offering evidence of the variety, across estates, regions and within individual manors, that argues against any simple assessment of rent and its changing significance; even so he concludes that, for the later eleventh and early twelfth centuries, the combined information is insufficient to permit 'a complete account of the obligations of any individual peasant or the means of measuring the relative importance of labour services, money payments, and renders in kind for any class in any part of the country'.[21] A good deal of historical discussion in this area was in fact founded upon the problems of extracting from medieval sources data of a kind capable of supporting explanations of economic change. When, in the early 1950s, Postan attempted to return to his earlier discussion of the chronology of labour services and to use the twelfth-century surveys of Glastonbury Abbey as evidence for a period of retreat from direct demesne farming by lords and a consequent extension of tenanted land, his conclusions were challenged by Lennard. The latter contended that the surveys did not permit the kinds of conclusions drawn from them by Postan, who had also tried to use evidence of an apparent diminution in plough teams to suggest that heavy labour services, including ploughing services, were giving way to money rents. Lennard's argument was not so much that the demesnes might not have contracted but rather that the evidence put forward by Postan did not sustain it, a view evidently supported by Harvey and Stone in their preface to Lennard's 'rejoinder', published posthumously in the early 1970s.[22]

Writing at about the same time as Lennard, Edward Miller, in his subtle and insightful study of the estates of the abbey and bishopric of Ely in the long thirteenth century, adopts a similar general focus on the evolving nature of rent, his use of extents in the mid-thirteenth century suggesting to him, for instance, that villein rents had, by then, become fixed and an insufficiently elastic source of labour supply. Given this, it was adjustments by the lord and his officials – the trading between labour rent and money rent, the introduction of new money rents and the growing reliance of leasing on the Ely estates – which sit at the core of Miller's investigation.[23] In all of this, peasants feature as tenants and as colonisers of new land (assarts), but it is the policy of the lord that is central to the discussion. As with Postan's and Lennard's discussion of twelfth-century rural society, so Miller's own investigation of the peasantry is mostly couched in terms of land and landholding; this is, after all, the essential preoccupation of the sources, chiefly surveys and extents, which shed most light on the topic in this earlier period. The distinctions between types of tenant and their obligations are set out fully and the discussion is presented in terms of patterns of landholding and the ways in which these, according to tenure, the will of the lord and the ambition of the tenantry, might be adjusted in the thirteenth century. In fact, a number of estate studies written between the 1940s and 1970s display similar concerns. These studies, typically informed by a general discussion of changes in the quantity and quality of rent between the eleventh and fifteenth centuries, tend to reflect fairly typical trends but also describe an inconsistent chronology, reflective of regional differences and variable estate policies. As E.M. Halcrow noted in concluding one such discussion of direct management of the demesne by the lord at Durham Cathedral Priory's estates, further studies were required in order to establish a fuller understanding both of the patterns and their explanation.[24] Importantly, in this context, the debate in these estate studies tends to be conditioned by the agenda established in the last years of the nineteenth century and the first decades of the twentieth century: most obviously, tenurial obligations and their distinctions, the causes and chronology of commutation, and the leasing of the demesnes.[25]

There is also piecemeal evidence for the durability of such themes as well as a tendency for a somewhat sporadic re-emergence; the last significant contribution in this particular respect, by Rosamund Faith, was published in the 1990s.[26] Faith, in a study of the relationship between the demesne and labour rent on the estates of St Paul's Cathedral from the eleventh century through to the early thirteenth century, concluded that Postan's chronology of the development of labour services, which included analysis of some of the St Paul's evidence, was flawed. Her contention, that leasing from the demesne in the long twelfth century intensified rather than diminished the use of labour rent, is an important adjustment of the much earlier thesis proposed by Postan. In reinterpreting the ways in which land held in demesne was released to tenants, through permanent alienation as assized rent or by temporary lease *de dominio*, Faith contends that, in the latter case especially, land leased by lords from the demesne was often held by labour rents rather than money rents and that, thereby, lords increased labour input of their tenants even during a period when parts of the demesnes were not in their hands.[27] She also suggests that lords were able to expand the labour input on demesnes by dividing holdings and increasing the number of their tenants; land-hunger and a rising population were the motors that drove this development.[28] In this fairly recent engagement, Faith illustrates the persistence of a line of historical discussion and its potential to offer new insights; while sometimes in abeyance and seldom occupying the attention of more than a handful of historians, discussion of rent and its development in the high and late middle ages has retained its significance as a main strand within the study of the agrarian economy, lordship and the tenantry in this period.

Serfdom, class-consciousness and the transition debate

An original intention of historical discussion of rent was to chart the development of serfdom, with a view to exploring the origins of servility in medieval England. While the material focus of this discussion, conducted by historians in the later nineteenth century and discussed in an earlier chapter, was similar to that employed by historians working in later generations, namely, evidence for rent and other kinds of obligation in manorial, estate and legal records, the central purpose of the work itself was quite different. To a considerable degree the original focus and motive of many of the historians engaged in study of lordship and the obligations of tenantry was not upon the 'political' nature of the relationship of lord and tenant but rather on the formal and institutional relations created by those obligations. This was not at all a generational distinction but, as we have discussed, historians of seigneurial estates have maintained that focus into recent decades. Other historians and especially Marxist historians, while often drawing upon the same work, issues and approach, have looked to rent and its history as a key index of the changing relationship of lord and tenant, with rent the mechanism for our understanding of an unequal distribution of power. If, as we have considered earlier in this chapter, Kosminsky was the first historian, at least writing in English,[29] to explore this relationship in these terms, within a few years other historians working in Britain and elsewhere had entered into the debate over the transition of the medieval economy, a debate that still, obviously, had a great deal to do with the economic and political relations of lord and tenant. In ways that both draw upon a tradition founded in the study of lordship and yet in some respects sit outside of that tradition, the most evident and, arguably, the most important strand in the study of medieval relations between lord and tenant is that founded in a Marxist tradition. In terms of the historiography of the medieval English peasantry, the two most significant figures in this tradition, Rodney Hilton and Robert Brenner, illustrate quite discrete trajectories in the ways in which their own contributions were established; we will reflect here upon the work of both historians as well as the ways in which they either stand for or stand in some contrast to the historiographical trends already outlined in this chapter.

Hilton in particular, and Brenner as a later contributor, were both engaged in what has been referred to as the 'transition debate', a long-standing discussion of the processes that explain change in the European economy and which sought to identify a primacy of causes for that change.[30] Often associated with Marxist historians, the debate was not in fact confined to an internalised discussion based upon Marxist precepts. Instead, the transition debate, though instigated by Marxist historians, such as Maurice Dobb, attracted the attention of historians keen to explore a variety of causal factors in making sense of change over time.[31] As might be expected, therefore, a good deal of the discussion focuses upon potential measures of the changing economy, including, once again, rent, its extent and the capacity of lordship to extract it. Just as earlier generations of Russian historians had found much of comparative and theoretical relevance in the nature and decline of serfdom in medieval England, so historians engaged in the transition debate followed Marx in identifying the same period as a crucial example of the processes by which an economy might emerge from feudalism into capitalism.

Hilton's own contribution, as an important and early figure in this debate, was to argue that a feudal mode of production (tenants paying rent to lords in an essentially coercive relationship founded upon seigneurial power) predominated in the high and later middle ages and that, therefore, a transition from feudalism to capitalism was dependent on the collapse of seigneurial authority over their tenantry; in other words, if the power of lords remained paramount then a new mode of production, based upon the relationship of employer and employee rather than lord and tenant, could not emerge.[32] By identifying this mode of production as key, Hilton's studies were necessarily directed towards certain kinds of enquiry and to particular topics of research, not least of which, of course, were the relations of lord and tenant as well as changes in that relationship over the centuries of the high and late middle ages. Hilton was applying a Marxist analysis to his research and was not alone in this approach or indeed the first to apply it to the medieval English economy, but he was the only medievalist of his generation to base his research in this area – economic and agrarian history – so directly and purposefully upon such intellectual foundations.[33] A generation later Brenner, to whose work we shall return below, also argued that the mode of production was central to our historical understanding of change in the medieval economy and the same process of transition, and, as Hilton, identified an end to serfdom with the elimination of 'the lord's right and ability to control the peasantry, *should they desire to do so* [author's italics]'.[34]

While evidently theoretically charged, and clearly informed by his Marxism, Hilton's work on the medieval peasantry, which commenced just before the Second World War and was taken up again after the war, can be located, especially in its earliest contributions, within that long-standing British tradition of estate and lordship studies which we have already described in this chapter.[35] Thus, in ways that were generally consistent with other contemporary research projects in the same area, Hilton's earliest research was upon the economic history of seigneurial estates in the high and later middle ages. Most obviously, Hilton's study of the economic development of estates in Leicestershire in the fifteenth and sixteenth centuries, published in 1947, can be set within a corpus of broadly similar work on the changing patterns of lordship in a period of significant economic adjustment. As such, this may have allowed it to be accepted by many who were not themselves Marxists. Significantly though, Hilton is eager to stress the ways in which his research is intended to move beyond a regional study and is instead an exploration of the processes and explanations of economic change in this period, and especially of a transition from a feudal economy to capitalism.[36]

In other studies of rural society in this period, Hilton never loses sight of this, for him, core issue. In his discussion of midlands rural society, he offers a detailed and informed assessment of rural life, the nature of the village community and the relation between lords and tenants. In all of this, his assessment is measured according to his theoretical perspective and he continually, though sometimes obliquely, tests the central proposition that lordship constrained the economic development of the peasantry in this period.[37] For instance, in his discussion of entry fines and other kinds of relatively arbitrary exaction, Hilton detects the capacity of lords to redefine exactions according to the expectations of their own domestic economy and current needs. He in particular draws attention to the potential impact of irregular dues (*consuetudines non taxatas*, as he identifies them), such as entry fines or *gersuma*, upon the income and surplus of the peasant household, arguing that these exactions, which allowed lords to sidestep some of the more regular and relatively immutable rents, were potentially disproportionately heavy.[38] Inevitably, then, Hilton was drawn into discussion of rent. Thus, for instance, his thorough survey of medieval rural society in the midlands of the thirteenth century has much to say on the process of commutation of labour rents into money rents in the twelfth century, and is a continuation of earlier debate, particularly that identified with Kosminsky. As is discussed in the following chapter, Hilton identified rent as an obligation that effectively reduced to nothing any peasant surplus;[39] he was especially keen to pinpoint the role of additional arbitrary exactions, such as entry fines, marriage fines (merchet), fines to leave the manor (chevage) and their like, as the precarious and piecemeal burdens that served to exact a high economic and political cost on his tenantry. The extraction of rent, both the fixed elements of labour-rent and money-rent as well as these additional exactions (the *consuetudines non taxatas*) which could supplement the lord's income to a significant degree, Hilton saw as political acts, as statements of power.[40]

From an early stage of his work, Hilton's study, though framed by lordship, is also defined by class, and it is the nature of class structure, its development and its implications for longer-term economic change which is at the heart of his discussion. Historians before Hilton had used the word 'class' in discussing at the least groups within the medieval English peasantry, but it is striking that the use of the term was largely apolitical, 'class' tending to signify a tenurial sub-set and not intended, as far as can be understood by its use, to convey a sense of a political amalgam necessarily in conflict with other identifiable classes. Thus, for instance, Vinogradoff identifies these sub-sets and, while he refers quite generally to the 'peasantry', and sometimes describes the peasantry as a 'social class', he consistently emphasises important tenurial distinctions between them as their defining qualities, identifying these as 'classes'.[41] So also Maitland uses 'class' in terms of 'classification'; thus, for him, Domesday Book refers to five 'classes' of tenant: *villani, servi, cotarii, liberi homines, sochemanni*. In this sense Maitland's use of the term, as Vinogradoff's, is almost scientific; later in the same discussion Maitland interchanges 'class' with 'species' and distinguishes between the two 'genera' of free and unfree.[42] Page, in describing the efforts made by villeins to escape their servile bonds in the later fourteenth century, also refers to villeins as 'a class of the rural population'.[43] Tawney also suggested that tenurial distinctions were, by the sixteenth century, poor guides to 'class' but that in earlier centuries such distinctions as 'villein' might be treated by the historian as economic 'class' divisions.[44] He also distinguishes between economic and political classes within the peasantry, noting that opportunities for advancement were, by the fourteenth century, more available to 'a rural middle class'.[45] Reginald Lennard also, in discussing peasants of the eleventh and twelfth centuries, warns against the imposition of a single 'class' upon the totality of the peasantry, suggesting instead that tenurial distinctions militated against a 'class consciousness' which, along with 'class war', he considered 'a crudity … misleading to the interpretation of the period'.[46] In fact, this approach is also partly reflected in Hilton's doctoral work on the estates in the county of Leicester in the later middle ages in which he employs 'class' often to denote a distinction between types of peasant and in which he charts the evolution of a wealthy peasant class in the later middle ages.[47]

While then Hilton's first use of 'class' as a term, perhaps partially informed by Lennard, his doctoral supervisor at Oxford, was relatively muted, though clearly informed by a broader interest in the transition from a feudal economy to a capitalist one and by a Marxist agenda,[48] he came to employ the term rather more directly and was increasingly prepared to apply it to more than just tenurially distinct groups. In more than one study, Hilton set out his view on the peasanty as a class. He contended that, in relation to other social groups, the gentry and the nobility, richer and poorer villagers were effectively united in their shared ambitions and identities as well as in their separateness from those who identified them as their social inferiors.[49] While then Hilton, like Tawney a generation before him, was closely aware of social and economic stratification within the medieval village, and had discussed it in a number of his publications, he did not see this as a fundamental barrier to the existence of a peasant class.[50] For Hilton, as also for Brenner, members of the peasantry ultimately identified themselves as an economically inter-dependent group or class in relation to other groups of classes. In terms of co-operation or resistance it was natural for peasants, even those of different economic and social status within their class, to combine in support, typically against a common class enemy, particularly a landlord. Hilton's application of this constant theoretical perspective is predicated upon his intellectual commitment to the Marxist concept of the mode of production. If lords controlled the feudal mode of production, and power resided with lords, then those without power, the tenants, were necessarily engaged in a struggle to overcome it; their identity was defined by that struggle and by the expectations of those who held them in thrall.[51] Hilton suggests that evidence for class-consciousness amongst the medieval peasantry can be detected in their resistance and their claims against their lords; in particular he cites the demands that villeinage be abolished, an important refrain in the Peasants' Revolt of 1381, also evident in collective claims of villagers as early as the thirteenth century that they were rightfully tenants of ancient demesne, that is the king's tenants and thereby free to sue in the king's courts.

Relatively few historians other than Hilton have explored the issue of class in the medieval village in the same way and certainly not to the same extent. In a later chapter we will consider some of the ways in which historians have conceived of other kinds of social, economic and political organisation within the medieval English countryside; other attempts to identify features of class and class action amongst the medieval peasantry have mostly been confined to Hilton's own students or those associated with him and the Birmingham 'school' of historians who adopted and developed his approach.[52] These have though not always been presented in ways so evidently directed at the issue of class or formulated in terms of class conflict; instead a generation of medieval historians writing after Hilton, including Christopher Dyer, Rosamund Faith, Ralph Evans, Zvi Razi and Peter Franklin, tended to deal with issues of conflict and lord–tenant dispute, themes consistent with and no doubt informed or often encouraged by an earlier Marxist programme but not necessarily framed in terms of a Marxist dialectic.[53] In other words, these historians have recognised tension and dispute between lords and tenants but, to a degree less than that sometimes – but certainly not always – exhibited in Hilton's own work, have often couched it less in terms of class struggle or expressly identified in it the machinery of transition from feudalism to capitalism.

In an approach that is generally consistent with Hilton's theoretical stance, Robert Brenner, chiefly in two articles published in *Past and Present* in the 1970s and 1980s, offered a more polemical thrust at the historical analysis of the relationship between lord and tenant, but one also aimed at establishing the motive force in the later medieval economy.[54] Brenner's use of a range of secondary literature in relation to the medieval English economy serves as a useful index of the earlier debate regarding rent and its movement and development in the middle ages. Thus, to review Brenner's citations is to return to work by Postan and by Kosminsky in the 1930s but not to proceed beyond them into an earlier historiographical tradition. In this respect, the early publications of Postan and Kosminsky stand as a watershed moment, their articulation of a changing incidence of rent and its application to wider developments in the agrarian economy providing Brenner with an intellectual starting point from which to engage and against which to test his own propositions. Postan's and Kosminsky's main arguments, and especially those set out in Postan's work on the chronology of labour services, are employed by Brenner as illustrations of the ways in which previous historians, in opposition to an earlier teleological tradition of economic change, had identified economic development with an expansion of lordship and feudal rent rather than with its contraction.[55] For Brenner, though, Postan's examination of rent and its extraction had not been carried to its logical conclusion. While Postan and, in France, le Roy Ladurie, had been correct to reject a simple chronology of change they had, according to Brenner, failed to recognise that, even with some development in the form of rent, including commutation of labour rent, it was the lord's capacity to restrict the peasantry's mobility, to make particular and excessive demands of their tenants, and generally to coerce them that was of paramount importance. In other words, Brenner argued that the extraction of feudal rent, and the capacity of lordship to extract it, was at the very heart of the movement and development of the medieval economy. For Brenner, the opportunity for lords to extract rent and to adjust it to their needs was a significant impediment to the economy and its development. Feudal rent, to follow Marx, was the usable surplus extracted from the peasant economy, thereby rendering the economy of peasant tenants illiquid and removing any major opportunity for investment. Lords, for their part, re-employed the capital from this rent, extracted from the agrarian labour force, not in economic development but in military endeavour and in consumption. Such an economy, again according to Brenner, could not develop without some significant adjustment of the relationship between lords and their tenants, and this could occur only through class conflict.[56] In reviewing socio-economic change across parts of late medieval and early modern Europe, Brenner was able to argue that other potentially determinative factors, such as population or commerce, were inconsistent in their incidence and that historical argument for their primacy was unsustainable. However, as commentators on the 'Brenner debate' have since noted, the pursuit of a mono-causal explanation inevitably founders when confronted with the variety of potentially significant causative mechanisms that might be deemed to explain change.[57] This has encouraged a more varied reading of the later medieval to early modern economy in recent decades, one that has often eschewed the pursuit of single explanatory causes in favour of an often detailed investigation of the form and function of rural society. In this, as Rigby points out, a Marxist approach was not fundamentally incompatible with other analyses favouring other primary causes. Indeed, Brenner's own work implicitly invoked a multiplicity of such causes and it was more a question of emphasis than of a fundamental difference of approach and conception.[58] Historians writing in the decades after Brenner's articles appeared have tended to argue for a different kind of medieval agrarian economy than that envisaged by Brenner: an economy in which the activities of lords were not so fundamentally determinative of the agrarian economy, where the peasantry enjoyed wider socio-economic relations, and where greater investment in the economy was at least evident.[59] We will consider, towards the end of this chapter, the ways in which this important theme has persisted, even if, in more recent years, its overall significance within the historiography has reduced and the position adopted by Marxist historians has been subject to significant challenge.

Before we turn to examples of that challenge, we should stay a little longer with the Marxist historiography and examine the ways in which historical investigation of lord–tenant relations extended beyond the regular, day-to-day transactions into the irregular and in particular resistance to lordship, both on the manor and beyond it. Of no doubt, Rodney Hilton's most famous contribution to the study of medieval history, in terms at least of international recognition, was his work on peasant resistance and revolt. Beginning with Hilton's own contribution, which sits at the heart of this topic and illustrates an important shift in perspective, we can take the opportunity to review other work on peasant resistance and its expression in the medieval English countryside. Hilton was, from the outset of his publishing career, deeply interested in the nature of revolt and resistance, including peasant resistance prior to the later middle ages.[60] In 1950, with H. Fagan, he co-authored a highly politicised study of the English rising (or Peasants' Revolt) of 1381; intended 'to redress the balance' of historical discussion of the rising, the authors set out to reconstruct 'the inadequately recorded motives and aims, not of the oppressors but of the oppressed'.[61] The discussion is couched in terms entirely consistent with a Marxist agenda of class struggle and the authors present their account as an important instance of the British people's struggle for liberty.[62] While not written as a detailed historical investigation, the *English rising* does display, in the opening chapters where Hilton sets out the socio-economic context of revolt, the fruits of his research to date, not least in his awareness of the changing economic condition of the post-plague peasantry and a persistence of seigneurial demands and of the general condition of serfdom which served to foment revolt, not least amongst the wealthier peasants who saw their advantage curtailed by lordship.[63]

Hilton's detailed discussion of peasant resistance had its fullest expression in his later seminal discussion of the 'English rising', *Bond men made free*, published in 1973, a work that has remained the single most important study of the Revolt and its comparative European context.[64] Hilton's study is an important one for a number of reasons. Firstly, it is a nuanced discussion of the events, social composition, ambition and consequences of the Revolt, juxtaposed with a wider contextual commentary, setting the English events of the later fourteenth century within a much broader timeframe and geographical range. As importantly, from a historiographical point of view, Hilton's discussion really stands alone as the most important contribution by a Marxist historian of the middle ages to our understanding of peasant agency in effecting political change. Thus, whilst there have been more recent attempts to place peasants within the 'politics' of the period and to recognise a peasant capacity for social, economic and political agency, as we will consider a little later in this chapter and more fully in the discussion of peasants and culture in a subsequent chapter, Hilton's direct and deliberate engagement with the issue of a politicised peasantry directly effecting change stands alone. As such, *Bond men made free* has some claim to be the only major example of a medievalist in this subject area employing, in strict terms, 'history from below' where that can be taken to mean the deliberate organisation of groups or 'classes' in order to bring about long-term change through their own direct action.[65]

Both from long before Hilton wrote and also in more recent years, there have been a number of other, chiefly narrative, studies of the events of the Peasants' Revolt, beginning, in the modern era, with Réville's posthumously published study of 'the rising of the English labourers' which offers both a preliminary narrative and, above all, an introduction to relevant primary materials.[66] At about the same time as the publication of Réville's work, studies by Sir Charles Oman and Edgar Powell, founded upon new research and tending to offer comment on the causes and progress of the Revolt in particular locales as well as to provide important transcripts of associated documents, were also published.[67] These works, to which Fagan and Hilton were explicitly responding in their later work, had most to say on the issue of taxation and of its contribution to the causes of the Revolt but there is also some comment on the condition of peasant society. Powell briefly discusses conditions on particular manors prior to and immediately after the Revolt and suggests that lords had learned to be mindful of the newly acquired power of 'the great working class of England'.[68] Oman offers a fuller consideration of the causes of the Revolt and engages in comment on earlier work on such issues as the post-plague seigneurial reaction by landlords and pre-Revolt incidences of resistance on the part of customary tenants.[69]

A number of other accounts of the Revolt have been published in the century and more since Réville's, including some generalised discussions which have offered surprisingly little in the way of new insight.[70] There have also been, and especially in the years around 1981 and the six-hundredth anniversary of the Revolt, a number of close investigations of aspects of the Revolt which have been intended to examine the peasantry's motive for Revolt in this period. We will reserve, for later in this volume, discussion of historical work on the wider culture of complaint associated with the Peasants' Revolt, but for now we can note that historians, writing in the years after the appearance of *Bond men made free* and to various degrees guided or at least informed by Hilton's agenda, were directed to study of peasant resistance and its aims, as one potentially important feature of later medieval political society. In this respect, also, peasant resistance was identified as a potential cause of change in rural society, and one worthy of close examination.

Contemporary chroniclers had explained the Revolt as, in no small part, an attack upon the obligations of villeinage and an extreme expression of resentment by unfree tenants and their allies. Modern historians have, unsurprisingly, tended to follow suit. Rogers, at the end of the nineteenth century, had noted that 'the true cause [of the Revolt] was the incidents of villeinage, and the dissatisfaction felt at revived oppression'.[71] This is a perspective also strongly evident in Hilton's view of the Revolt. Hilton rejects the notion that the membership of the Revolt operated across classes and instead sees, at its core, the motive force that contemporaries themselves identified, a demand from tenants that lordship and villeinage be removed. For Hilton, the rebels' call for an end to villeinage was to be accepted at face value, as real rather than totemic, and reflected a common concern in later medieval England.[72] This stated position by the rebels in 1381, and the lack of inter-class participation in the Revolt, seemed to confirm again for Hilton the significance of the feudal mode of production and class struggle as a defining characteristic of the period.[73]

This emphasis has not been so clearly replicated in more recent studies, and historians writing in the last two or three decades have tended to be a little more circumspect, emphasising the complexity of issues which underlay the Revolt and to be chary of identifying primary causes for the Revolt.[74] The relation of lord and tenant, issues of tenure and the significance of rent and its variety in fomenting complaint and encouraging resistance on the part of landlords and of their tenants have though all remained signally important features in discussion of the antecedents to the Revolt. Most obviously, some historians, including Hilton, Dyer, Poos and Eiden, have sought to examine the composition of the rebel groups, as well as the social make-up of the victims, using manorial records other than relying on chronicle accounts so as to investigate the prosopography of revolt and, thereby, to glean some clearer sense of potential motive.[75] Dyer, for instance, argues that the Revolt in eastern England was often headed by members of the village elite, including unfree tenants, but that is not to suggest that lord–tenant dispute can be taken to explain the underlying tensions, which extended from a variety of motives, local and more general, into an attack on all kinds of lordship and governance.[76] Poos has noted similar targeting and a concerted action of violence by rural rebels in Essex; Eiden also identifies a shared and collective grievance in attacks on officials in Essex and Norfolk and rejects the notion, proposed for the Norfolk rebels by earlier historians such as Réville and Oman, that their actions was mindless and redolent of 'ruffianism'. Instead, he sees the rebels as dominated by village elites, as also identified by Dyer, and, in Norfolk, labourers and craftsmen.[77] Nicholas Brooks has also argued that the speed and the evident, from their actions, focus of those involved in the rising suggest a co-ordinated and planned assault on particular features of government.[78] Other historians, approaching the events and outcomes of the Revolt from different perspectives, have not entirely seen the Revolt in the same terms and have tended to eschew some of the more traditional 'economic' features. Margaret Aston has, for example, argued, in tackling 'an old problem from a new direction', that the feast of Corpus Christi, which coincided with the main events of the

Peasants' Revolt, helped to define those events and to provide a spiritual context for the Revolt, as well as to strengthen the view of orthodox clerics that the coincidence of the Revolt with the feast revealed God's anger at the eucharistic heresy associated with John Wycliffe.[79]

Developing work by Hilton as well as by earlier historians, there has also been considerable engagement with relatively low-level peasant resistance as well as evidence for heightened tension between lord and tenant. While certainly not concentrated upon the decades after the Black Death, an important tranche of this scholarship has been directed at the period between the first outbreak of the Black Death in 1348 and the Peasants' Revolt of 1381. During these three decades, it has often been claimed, the English countryside appears to have experienced a period of seigneurial reaction, an Indian summer of direct lordship; while this was soon to give way to a declining serfdom, a number of historians have argued that, in its last great flaring, English serfdom burned brightly. The concept of a post-plague period of seigneurial or feudal reaction was established fairly early in the historical literature, but was not embraced by all historians. In essence, the discussion of a period of feudal reaction by historians writing at the end of the nineteenth and the beginning of the twentieth century was closely aligned to a consideration of the rise of the money economy as well as the long-standing discussion of the chronology of labour services and the process of commutation. J.E.T. Rogers was one of the first historians to identify a feudal reaction in the decades after the Black Death, in particular suggesting that lords took the opportunity to re-impose labour services as part of a policy aimed at retaining control of their estates and demesnes in a period of severe dislocation and of rapidly rising wages.[80] His views were not immediately accepted and, instead, historians such as W.A. Cunningham, who argued for a relatively crude and inexorable progression towards a money economy and away from labour in kind, could not accept the sorts of fluctuation in lordly power consistent with a period of feudal reaction.[81] E.A. Lipson, writing in the second decade of the twentieth century, was also inclined to identify the growth of the money economy relative to an economy founded on labour and kind as the crucial context, and thereby to reduce, though not to dismiss, the notion of a feudal reaction in the period after the plague. However, Lipson subtly accommodates the earlier arguments of Rogers with the suggestion of Page *et al.* that a process of commutation was not reversed in the decades after 1348-9. He thereby recognises that some lords might seek to oblige their unfree tenants to labour for them in a period when it was far from in their tenants' best interests to do so, but suggests that this was as much manifested in the enforcement of surviving kinds of obligation, such as customary fines, and restrictions on mobility, as it was in the re-imposition of older tenurial forms.[82]

Work in the second half of the twentieth century on the feudal reaction reveals a change of intellectual emphasis, one associated with the influence of Rodney Hilton. Whereas an earlier generation of historians had associated the feudal reaction with an attempt by landlords to re-impose labour services and had discussed this development as part of an investigation of the growth of a money economy, medievalists writing after the Second World War were far more inclined to focus their attention upon the nature of the lord–tenant relationship and the relative calculation of the two discrete interest groups in a period of significant change. Thus, Hilton, argued that, given the general ubiquity of money rent relative to labour rent in medieval England, it was not the reintroduction of previously commuted labour services that was the fundamental issue in the mid- to later fourteenth-century countryside but rather the capacity and willingness of landlords to adjust their exactions and to make revised demands of their tenants. Rather than see this issue as a test-case for the development of a monetary economy, Hilton perceived the feudal reaction as an important instance in the conflict between lords and tenants over rights and power. Any continuance of an arbitrary lordly control over the surplus of the peasantry stood as illustration of the persistence of a feudal mode of production; its erosion in favour of a peasant economic independence suggested a diminution of seigneurial and feudal power in favour of new arrangements.[83] Other historians also writing on this period have identified similar issues though they have not all couched them in exactly the same terms. L.R. Poos's study of later medieval Essex also illustrates the chequered pattern of imposed or re-imposed labour services and argues that these were not a consistent index of villein discontent; he does however note a fair degree of consistency on the part of landlords who sought 'to exploit as fully as possible the traditional seigneurial incidents at their disposal'.[84] Importantly, in outlining a great deal of lordly imposition and collective and individual resistance, Poos also describes a transition from 'a more lord–villein to a more landlord–tenant pattern of confrontation'.[85] He also notes the apparently increased prevalence of non-seigneurial elements within Essex-based revolt, not least those engaged in religious dissent. In so doing Poos maintains a line of argument consistent with Hilton's own, namely that tension between lords and tenants was an important feature of the later medieval countryside and an agent for change, as well as describing a more fluid amalgam of resistance. R.H.

Britnell's account of the feudal reaction by lords within the Palatinate of Durham illustrates both the willingness of lords to attempt to impose significant demands upon their tenants in the period after the Black Death but also the relative weakness of their position; even such a major landlord as the bishop of Durham was ultimately unable to maintain his estates in their pre-plague condition; interestingly, as well, Durham did not experience a peasants' revolt in 1381, a reflection not so much of a restrained lordship as the absence in the north-east of those other contributory factors which, in the south, stirred revolt.[86] In fact, Britnell's analysis, while steeped in discussion of lord–tenant relations and feudal reaction, also has a great deal to say on the tension within village society more generally.[87] Recently, Peter Larson has argued, again for the Palatinate of Durham, that the reaction of the bishop and prior was conditioned by their tenants, and the capacity of tenants to respond, either positively or negatively. Distinctive in Larson's work is the limited focus on longer-term economic change or the underlying economic significance of tension between lord and tenant: here, instead, the emphasis is upon a more broadly sociological investigation of the nature and purpose of dispute, both between lord and tenant and also within rural society itself.[88] Most recently, and as part of a growing body of work which has sought to challenge the notion that serfdom was central to the functioning of the medieval agrarian economy, Mark Bailey has suggested that the post-plague incidence of serfdom went into an immediate, steep and inexorable decline, a reflection of the preparedness of lords to admit a changed environment needful of new forms of landholding and tenantry disinclined to accept established customary or villein tenures. Bailey's data certainly supports a post-plague decline in traditional unfree tenure and associated obligations but he also identifies instances of a persistent, often sporadic but potentially damaging (from a tenant's perspective) influence of a lordship which, even in retreat, could still find opportunities to impose its authority upon members of its tenantry.[89] Bailey's work offers a balance to a historiographical emphasis upon the ways in which lords continued to make demands upon their tenantry after the plague; it is likely to generate further test-cases intended to support or refute its central contention.

This wider interest in revolt and tension within rural society, acknowledging dispute between lord and tenant but discussing it as one significant element within a greater panoply of dispute, tension and complaint, is also evident in a number of recent studies, especially of the later fourteenth and fifteenth centuries. As in the case of Poos's study of rural Essex, it is not entirely surprising, or even inconsistent with a Marxist model of class struggle, that the boundaries between disputants became clouded in the fifteenth century; this may simply reflect the dwindling significance of lord–tenant dispute in an evolving economy and society. Those historians who, in the last decade or two, have discussed rural tension and revolt in the fifteenth and sixteenth centuries have certainly not lost sight of the economic foundation of these events. Thus, for instance, Jane Whittle's comparison of the events of 1381 and Kett's rebellion in 1549 in Norfolk reveals some consistencies in the stated aims of the rebels, including clear opposition to villeinage, which persisted in Norfolk into the sixteenth century. Nevertheless Whittle is wary of identifying this as a collective expression of class-consciousness and suspects instead that the manifold ambitions of those involved were hidden from view behind the stated aims and ambitions of the peasant elites who led the uprisings.[90] Examination of the mid-fifteenth-century Jack Cade's rebellion makes clear how various might be the parties in a later medieval rising as well as the variety of ambitions and motives of the rebels.[91] Earlier, in the thirteenth century, it has also been suggested in recent work, common aims in revolt could extend across the range of the political community and were conditioned by opposition to misrule rather than economic or class-bound associations and ambitions.[92] These are themes that will also be considered further in a later chapter in terms of historical discussion of peasant agency and of the political culture of the peasantry.

If studies of lordship and, by extension, of lord–tenant relationships have then persisted throughout the last century, some historians of the medieval peasantry, at least since the middle decades of the twentieth century, have sought to shift the historical focus from lordship and have sought to engage with the peasantry almost in isolation, in so far as that is ever possible.[93] This shift is now to be seen in the reduction of the role of the lord relative to that of markets in the lives of the peasantry, a theme to be discussed later in this volume. It is also important to observe here that, contrary to most of the preceding discussion in this chapter, not all historians of the medieval English peasantry have accorded significant space to discussion of lordship. Most obviously, Raftis and other historians of Ramsey Abbey and its estates, adopting a largely sociological interpretative approach, have found little place for discussion of lordship in their work on the peasantry. Thus, villagers on the Ramsey manors studied by Raftis, Britton and Edwin and Anne DeWindt have tended to be discussed in terms of their interactions within and beyond the village, but with relatively less attention given to their direct engagement with their lord.[94] Where they do explore relationships between with local lords, as for instance in the examination of the town of Ramsey and its local monastic lord, Ramsey Abbey, this tends to be seen in terms of neighbourliness rather than outright opposition, suggesting also that matters pertaining to lordship were not necessary to everyday dealing in the later middle ages.[95] Edwin DeWindt, in his study of Holywell-cum-Needingworth, is reluctant to identify the co-operation he identifies in the fourteenth-century village as '"class" solidarity', instead characterising it as 'a simple familiarity and closeness of experience'; in fact, there is little sense of outside influence or of the kinds of lordship against which the peasantry might combine in solidarity.[96] Undoubtedly a significant reason for this focus on the peasantry, without a similar emphasis on lordship, has been the methodological and theoretical approaches adopted by this team of researchers. We might also identify the range of sources, and especially a reliance on manorial court rolls rather than account rolls, as significant in determining the direction of research, the former directing researchers more obviously towards interaction within the village than would manorial accounts, with their focus on the demesne and the seigneurial obligations of the peasants, or more particularly the tenantry.

While, then, some studies of the medieval English peasantry, especially those associated with the new social historical approaches emanating from North America in the first decades after the Second World War, have tended to eschew the study of lordship, others have acknowledged its importance but have reinterpreted its significance, casting it far more as a benefit than as a significant disadvantage to tenants in the middle ages. In the first instance it would not be correct to suggest that all those historians whose focus was on the peasantry and its 'sociology' ignored the relationship of lord and peasantry in its entirety. When, within this particular historiographical context, lordship has been reintroduced into the discussion, as for instance in the later work of Ambrose Raftis, it has tended to serve to emphasise the relative placidity of the lord–tenant relationship.[97] In his last major contribution, Raftis argued that lords enjoyed reciprocal relations with their most substantial tenants and that, in so far as lordship impinged above the lives of the tenantry, it was chiefly in support of the economic stability and security of wealthier tenants. Raftis identifies recruitment and maintenance of highly capitalised customary tenants as a priority for lords, and considers this an economic decision of greater importance to lords than the preservation of villein tenures.[98]

Adopting an approach that shares a common assessment of the role of lordship if not a common methodology, a few other historians, chiefly British and operating outside of that same 'sociological/social structural' position, have sought to reduce the historical significance of lordship within the peasant economy, or rather to reinterpret it as a benefit and source of security for the tenantry. John Hatcher challenged the notion that serfdom in villeinage was a uniquely onerous condition; instead, as he argued, it offered tenants in villeinage by the later thirteenth century significant protection. As rents and other obligations were secured by custom, Hatcher argued that they were unresponsive to the inflationary trends of the middle ages and left wealthy villein tenants in positions of relative security.[99] Additional force for this argument has come from Junichi Kanzaka's reassessment of the later thirteenth-century Hundred Rolls; in ways that stand in contradiction to Kosminsky's conclusions discussed earlier in this chapter, Kanzaka argues that the evidence of the rolls generally supports Hatcher's earlier observations and follows Hatcher in suggesting that custom prevented landlords from wholly exploiting customary rents and that only some of the most powerful ecclesiastical and monastic estates were able to force significant impositions upon their tenants.[100]

More recently, Bruce Campbell has also added weight to Hatcher's conclusions; through an extensive analysis of early fourteenth-century inquisitions *post mortem*, Campbell, with Ken Bartley, has been able to show that the customary rent typically did not provide the greater component of seigneurial income and that money rents and free tenures dominated on most estates.[101] He has also shown that, contrary to what has always been supposed, lordship in medieval England was not dominated by large secular and ecclesiastical landlords and that the emphasis upon the large estates, with their demesnes supported by labour rent to a degree not evidenced elsewhere in the seigneurial economy, has led historians to misrepresent the typicality of lord–tenant relations in the pre-plague period.[102] Campbell drew upon these conclusions in later work, especially in arguing that peasants in eastern England enjoyed relative advantage over land, their rights as tenant of greater force often than those possessed by lords. If, as was the case, the tenantry faced difficulties in terms of generating an adequate surplus by the end of the thirteenth century, this was not, according to Campbell, because of the rapacity of landlords, as Brenner had originally claimed, but because of their weakness.[103] Allowing themselves to be coerced by adherence to custom and a tenantry accustomed not to paying a commercial rent, lords found their incomes weakened. To follow Campbell further, this seigneurial incapacity encouraged sub-division and the eventual pauperisation of large sections of the tenantry. In this process, Campbell also notes that the high proportion of money rents, including rents on free land as well as customary land, and the relatively low proportion of labour rent attached to large units of customary land, helps explain this development, with tenants seeking small plots of land and encouraging the partition of landholdings to a point that heightened population density left families and individuals highly vulnerable.[104] Most recently, Mark Bailey, initially through a series of publications on medieval Suffolk, has argued that villeinage was not especially prominent in that county and that its role as a cause of tenant distress was thereby insignificant as was the consequence of its disappearance in the later midde ages.[105] Bailey has extended his argument in a more general work on the decline of serfdom in which, through a series of case-studies, he proposes that serfdom was in full retreat from the mid-fourteenth century and that lords, by accepting new forms of landholding for their villein holdings, conceded their traditional tenurial position very quickly after the first outbreak of plague. This encourages Bailey in his view, discussed earlier, that a post-plague seigneurial reaction cannot have been as severe as had been previously supposed.

Partly in the light of this work, there has also been a considered reassessment of the burden of villeinage, even by those who are not so convinced of the hidden benefits or insignificance of serfdom. While it is clear that most historians now agree that the actual weight of customary rent could be relatively light, and certainly less onerous than was always supposed, there has been a renewed emphasis upon the burden of villeinage as perceived by the peasantry, and its limiting effects on opportunity and freedom of choice.[106] This is especially the case for discussion of post-plague resistance to villeinage during a period of enhanced opportunity for peasant landholders and wage labourers but it can also be extended to earlier periods, in which historians have identified peasant entrepreneurs straining against the confines of lordship and its demands.[107] There have also been considerations of the variety of ways in which the burden of villeinage might apply and the importance of regional distinctions in its incidence, especially in relation to the capacity of lords to control peasant engagement in a market for land.[108] That villeinage was perceived by aspiring peasants as an obstacle to progress and different kinds of economic engagement also chimes with the growing recognition by historians of the importance of the market and peasant engagement with the same in the middle ages, themes we will consider in the following chapter.

Notes

1 On this inclusive definition of 'peasant', see also above, pp. 21–3, and R.H. Hilton, *The English peasantry in the later middle ages. The Ford lectures for 1973 and related studies* (Oxford: Oxford University Press, 1975), p. 13.
2 M.M. Postan, 'The chronology of labour services', *Transactions of the Royal Historical Society*, 4th series, 20 (1937), reprinted in M.M. Postan, *Essays on medieval agriculture and general problems of the medieval economy* (Cambridge: Cambridge University Press, 1973), pp. 89–106, from which subsequent references are taken; E.A. Kosminsky, 'Services and money rents in the thirteenth century', *Economic History Review* 5 (1935), 24–45.
3 Postan, 'The chronology of labour services', pp. 89–91.
4 Postan, 'The chronology of labour services', pp. 100–2.
5 Postan, 'The chronology of labour services', pp. 103–6.
6 M.M. Postan, *The famulus. The estate labourer in the twelfth and thirteenth centuries* (Cambridge: Economic History Review Supplement, 2, 1954). In a subsequent review, Hilton noted that Postan's introduction of waged labour into the discussion challenged his own earlier argument on the extension of servile labour on the demesne, R. Hilton, Review of M.M. Postan, *The famulus. The estate labourer in the twelfth and thirteenth centuries* (Cambridge: Economic History Review Supplement, 2, 1954), *Economic History Review* 69 (1954), 63–5.
7 Hilton, Review of M.M. Postan, *The famulus*, 64–5.
8 Kosminsky, 'Services and money rents', 24–8, for a thorough review of the earlier literature.
9 Kosminsky, 'Services and money rents', 27; for recent comment on this discussion, see also P.R. Schofield, 'Conversion of rents in kind and in labour into cash in eastern England (c.1050–c.1300)' in L. Feller, ed., *Calculs et rationalités dans la seigneurie médiévales: les conversions et redevances entre xie et xve siècles* (Paris: Publications de la Sorbonne, 2009), pp. 58–66.
10 See above, pp. 38–9; see also below, p. 107.
11 Kosminsky, 'Services and money rents', 37–40.
12 Kosminsky, 'Services and money rents', 40–5.
13 E.A. Kosminsky, *Studies in the agrarian history of England in the thirteenth century* (Oxford: Oxford University Press, 1956).
14 Kosminsky, 'Services and money rents', 44–5.
15 R.H. Hilton, 'Editor's introduction', in Kosminsky, *Studies in the agrarian history of England*, p. xix.
16 Hilton, 'Editor's introduction', pp. xx–xxi.
17 Kosminsky, *Agrarian history*, pp. 172–8.
18 The theme is taken up again in Postan's later work on the *famulus*, for which see above [this chapter].
19 Kosminsky, *Agrarian history*, pp. 178, 180–96, 326–8.
20 R. Lennard, *Rural England, 1086–1135. A study of social and agrarian conditions* (Oxford: Oxford University Press, 1959).
21 Lennard, *Rural England*, pp. 364–87 (quote at p. 375).

22 M.M. Postan, 'Glastonbury Abbey estates in the twelfth century', *Economic History Review* 8 (1953) ; R.V. Lennard, 'The demesnes of Glastonbury Abbey in the eleventh and twelfth centuries', *Economic History Review* 8 (1955–56), 355–63; R.V. Lennard, 'The Glastonbury estates: a rejoinder', with an introduction by B.F. Harvey and E. Stone, *Economic History Review* 28 (1975), 517–23. For a brief comment on this, see J. Hatcher and M. Bailey, *Modelling the middle ages. The history and theory of England's economic development* (Oxford: Oxford University Press, 2001), pp. 14–15, and for a more detailed return to the issues which tends to locate changes in rent in terms of local adjustments more than more general economic factors, N. Stacy, 'The state of the demesne manors of Glastonbury Abbey in the twelfth century', in R. Evans, ed., *Lordship and learning. Studies in memory of Trevor Aston* (Woodbridge: Boydell, 2004), pp. 109–23.

23 E. Miller, *The abbey and bishopric of Ely. The social history of an ecclesiastical estate from the tenth to the early fourteenth century* (Cambridge: Cambridge University Press, 1951), pp. 89–90, 103.

24 See, for instance, E.M. Halcrow, 'The decline of demesne farming on the estates of Durham Cathedral Priory', *Economic History Review* 7 (1955), 345–56.

25 See, for instance, R.A.L. Smith, *Canterbury Cathedral Priory. A study in monastic administration* (Cambridge: Cambridge University Press, 1969), pp. 113–27; I. Kershaw, *Bolton Priory. The economy of a northern monastery, 1286–1325* (Oxford: Oxford University Press, 1973), pp. 47–52; B.F. Harvey, *Westminster Abbey and its estates in the middle ages* (Oxford: Oxford University Press, 1977), pp. 202–43; J.A. Raftis, *The estates of Ramsey Abbey. A study in economic growth and organization* (Toronto: Pontifical Institute of Mediaeval Studies, 1957), *passim*, and, for a fuller list of relevant studies, see also above, pp. 23–4, n. 4 and below, pp. 265–6.

26 R. Faith, 'Demesne resources and labour rent on the manors of St Paul's Cathedral, 1066–1222', *Economic History Review* 47 (1994), 657–76.

27 Faith, 'Demesne resources and labour rent', 671–5

28 Faith, 'Demesne resources and labour rent', 657, 675–6.

29 On earlier Marxist and non-Marxist discussion of villeinage in medieval England by Russian authors, see P. Gattrell, 'Historians and peasants: studies of medieval English society in a Russian context', *Past and Present* 96 (1982), 22–50, reprinted in T.H. Aston, ed., *Landlords, peasants and politics in medieval England* (Cambridge: Cambridge University Press, 1987), pp. 394–422, and especially 400–10 [subsequent references taken from this reprint]; Kosminsky also discussed Russian historians working on medieval English material in the first issue of the *Economic History Review*: E.A. Kosminsky, 'Russian work on English economic history', *Economic History Review* 1 (1928), 208–33.

30 R.H. Hilton, ed., *The transition from feudalism to capitalism* (London: Verso edition, 1978). For further discussion of the transition debate, see S.H. Rigby, *Marxism and history. A critical introduction* (Manchester: Manchester University Press, 2nd edition, 1998), pp. 160–70.

31 M. Dobb, 'From feudalism to capitalism', in Hilton, ed., *The transition from feudalism to capitalism*, pp. 165–9, and further essays in the same collection.

32 R.H. Hilton, 'Capitalism – what's in a name?', in R.H. Hilton, ed., *Transition from feudalism to capitalism*, pp. 145–58. For comment on the same, see P.R. Schofield, 'Lordship and the peasant economy, c.1250–c.1400: Robert Kyng and the Abbot of Bury St Edmunds', in C. Dyer, P. Coss and C. Wickham, eds, *Rodney Hilton's Middle Ages. An exploration of historical themes* (Past and Present Supplement, 2007), pp. 54–5.
33 For instance, Hilton, 'Capitalism – what's in a name?', pp. 148–50; Hilton, *English peasantry*, pp. 11–12. For an earlier and important Marxist framing of an investigation of the medieval agrarian economy, see Kosminsky, *Agrarian history*, pp. 319–20.
34 R. Brenner, 'Agrarian class structure and economic development in pre-industrial Europe', *Past and Present* 70 (1976), reprinted in T.H. Aston and C.H.E. Philpin, eds, *The Brenner debate. Agrarian class structure and economic development in pre-industrial Europe* (Cambridge: Cambridge University Press, 1985), pp. 10–63, from which this and subsequent citations taken: pp. 26–7, with quote at p. 26.
35 For recent considerations of Hilton's contribution, including a full bibliography of his work, see C. Dyer, P. Coss and C. Wickham, eds, *Rodney Hilton's Middle Ages. An exploration of historical themes* (Past and Present Supplement, 2007); on Hilton, his career and his contribution, see also H.J. Kaye, *The British Marxist historians. An introductory analysis* (Basingstoke: Macmillan, 1995), pp. 70–98.
36 R.H. Hilton, *The economic development of some Leicestershire estates in the fourteenth and fifteenth centuries* (Oxford: Oxford University Press, 1947).
37 Hilton, 'Peasant movements', pp. 123–4; R.H. Hilton, *A medieval society. The west Midlands at the end of the thirteenth century* (Cambridge: Cambridge University Press, 1983; first published London: Weidenfeld and Nicolson, 1966), pp. 123, 145.
38 See, for instance, Hilton, *English peasantry*, pp. 58–60; Hilton, 'Reasons for inequality' and below.
39 See below, Chapter 4, pp. 118–20.
40 Hilton, *A medieval society*, pp. 147–8.
41 For instance, P. Vinogradoff, *Villainage in England. Essays in English Mediaeval History* (Oxford: Oxford University Press, 1892), pp. 140–1, 153, 185, 211, 220, 223; P. Vinogradoff, *English society in the eleventh century. Essays in English medieval history* (Oxford: Oxford University Press, 1908), pp. 431–70.
42 F.W. Maitland, *Domesday Book and beyond. Three essays in the early history of England* (1897; republished Cambridge: Cambridge University Press, 1987), p. 24.
43 T.W. Page, *The end of villeinage in England* (New York: Macmillan, 1900), p. 67.
44 R.H. Tawney, *The agrarian problem in the sixteenth century* (London: Longmans, 1912), pp. 55–6.
45 Tawney, *Agrarian problem*, p. 82.
46 Lennard, *Rural England*, pp. 390–1.
47 Hilton, *Economic development*, pp. 94–105.

48 Hilton, *Economic development*, pp. 1-2; Kaye, *British Marxist historians*, p. 72, notes that Hilton describes his doctorate as 'researched and written under the inspiration of Marxism'.
49 Rodney H. Hilton, *Bond Men Made Free. Medieval Peasant Movements and the English Rising of 1381* (London: Maurice Temple Smith, 1973; republished, London: Routledge, 2003), pp. 34-5.
50 Historians writing after Hilton have tended to see economic stratification less in terms of class structures. See below, pp. 207-8, 211-16.
51 See especially in this respect Hilton's discussion of 'the peasantry as a class' in Hilton, *English peasantry*, pp. 14-15.
52 See, for reference to the Birmingham 'school', C. Dyer. 'Obituary: Rodney Hilton', *The Guardian*, 10 June 2002, available on-line at www.theguardian.com/news/2002/jun/10/guardianobituaries.humanities (accessed 8 September 2015).
53 See below, pp. 101-5; also Chapter 8, pp. 233-6, for further discussion of this work. This is not to say that some historians have not held on to what might be termed a 'vulgar Marxist' interpretation, as illustrated in some of the fairly recent contributions to Dyer *et al.*, eds, *Rodney Hilton's Middle Ages*; essays there by M. Müller, 'A divided class? Peasants and peasant communities in later medieval England', pp. 115-31, and S. Dimmock, 'English towns and the transition, c.1450-1550', pp. 270-85 (especially pp. 270-2).
54 R. Brenner, 'Agrarian class structure and economic development in pre-industrial Europe', *Past and Present* 70 (1976), 30-75; R. Brenner, 'Agrarian class structure and economic development in pre-industrial Europe: the agrarian roots of European capitalism', *Past and Present* 97 (1982), 16-113; both articles reprinted in T.H. Aston and C.H.E. Philpin, eds, *The Brenner debate. Agrarian class structure and economic development in pre-industrial Europe* (Cambridge: Cambridge University Press, 1985), pp. 10-63 and 213-327 (from which citations are taken).
55 Brenner, 'Agrarian class structure and economic development', p. 25, with reference to Postan, 'Chronology of labour services'.
56 Brenner, 'Agrarian class structure and economic development', pp. 25-7; 33-4.
57 See especially S.H. Rigby, 'Historical causation: is one thing more important than another?', *History* 259 (1995), 227-42.
58 See, for instance, S.H. Rigby, 'Historical materialism, social structure, and social change in the middle ages', *Journal of Medieval and Early Modern Studies* 34 (2004), 510-13.
59 See below, pp. 105-6 and Chapter 4, pp. 125-39.
60 R.H. Hilton, 'Peasant movements in medieval England', *Economic History Review*, 2nd series, 2 (1949), reprinted in E.M. Carus-Wilson, ed., *Essays in economic history*, ii (London: Arnold, 1962), pp. 73-90 (from which subsequent references are taken).
61 H. Fagan and R.H. Hilton, *The English rising of 1381* (London: Lawrence and Wishart, 1950), p. 9.
62 Fagan and Hilton, *English rising*, p. 10.
63 Fagan and Hilton, *English rising*, pp. 13-36.

64 Hilton, *Bond men made free*; the volume has been translated into Spanish and French.
65 On 'history from below', see, for example, P. Burke, *New perspectives on historical writing* (Cambridge: Polity, 1991); for brief comment on Hilton and 'history from below', see J. Whittle and S.H. Rigby, 'England: popular politics and social conflict', in S.H. Rigby, ed., *A companion to Britain in the later middle ages* (Oxford: Blackwell, 2002), p. 67.
66 A. Réville, *Le soulèvement des travailleurs d'Angleterres en 1381: études et documents publiés avec un introduction historique* (Paris: Picard, 1898); Réville died at a very young age and long before he could bring his work on the Revolt to completion, Sir C. Oman, *The Great Revolt of 1381* (Oxford: Oxford University Press, 1906), p. v; for a recent summary of the main historiography, see H. Eiden, '*In der Knechtschaft werdet ihr verharren ...*' *Ursachen und Verlauf des englischen Bauernaufstandes von 1381* (Trier: Trier Historische Forschungen, 1995), pp. 37-45. I am most grateful to Nikolas Helm for kindly providing me with a copy of this work. In reviewing the documentary evidence for the Revolt and encouraging historians and literary scholars to a multi-faceted approach, A. Prescott, 'Writing about rebellion: using the records of the Peasants' Revolt of 1381', *History Workshop Journal* 45 (1998), 1-25, also has much useful comment on developments in the historiography.
67 Oman, *Great Revolt of 1381*; E. Powell, *The rising in East Anglia in 1381 with an appendix containing the Suffolk poll tax lists for that year* (Cambridge: Cambridge University Press, 1896).
68 Powell, *Rising in East Anglia*, pp. 64-6 (quote at p. 66).
69 Oman, *Great Revolt of 1381*, pp. 5-13.
70 For instance, A. Dunn, *The great rising of 1381. The Peasants' Revolt and England's failed revolution* (Stroud: Tempus, 2002); P. Lindsay and R. Groves, *The Peasants' Revolt, 1381* (London: Hutchinson, 1950).
71 Rogers, *Six centuries*, p. 256.
72 Hilton, *Bond men made free*, pp. 224-5.
73 Hilton, *Bond men made free*, pp. 233-6.
74 See, for instance, E.B. Fryde and N. Fryde, 'Peasant rebellion and peasant discontents', in E. Miller, ed., *The agrarian history of England and Wales, vol. iii, 1350-1500* (Cambridge: Cambridge University Press, 1991), pp. 760-1; Dyer, 'Social and economic background to the Revolt', pp. 214-19; see also Rigby, *English Society*, pp. 110-24, for a useful survey of the Revolt and its potential causes.
75 Hilton, *Bond men made free*, pp. 176-85; C. Dyer, 'The causes of the Revolt in rural Essex', in W.H. Liddell and R.G. Wood, eds, *Essex and the Great Revolt of 1381* (Essex Record Office Publication 84, Chelmsford, 1982), pp. 21-36; C. Dyer, 'The social and economic background to the Revolt of 1381', in R. Hilton and T.H. Aston, eds, *The English rising of 1381* (Cambridge: Cambridge University Press, 1984), pp. 9-42 (reprinted in C. Dyer, *Everyday life in medieval England* (London: Hambledon, 1994), pp. 191-219, from which subsequent references are taken); C. Dyer, 'The rising of 1381 in Suffolk: its origins

and participants', *Proceedings of the Suffolk Institute of Archaeology and History* 36 (1986), (reprinted in Dyer, *Everyday life in medieval England*, pp. 221–39, from which subsequent references are taken); H. Eiden, 'Joint action against bad lordship. The Peasants' Revolt in Essex and Norfolk', *History* 83 (1998), 5–30.
76 Dyer, 'Social and economic background to the Revolt'.
77 L.R. Poos, *A rural society after the Black Death: Essex 1350–1525* (Cambridge: Cambridge University Press, 1991), pp. 232–40; Eiden, 'Joint action against bad lordship', pp. 16, 26.
78 N. Brooks, 'The organization and achievements of the peasants of Kent and Essex in 1381', in H. Mayr-Harting and R.I. Moore, eds, *Studies in medieval history: presented to R.H.C. Davis* (London: Hambledon, 1985), pp. 247–70.
79 M. Aston, 'Corpus Christi and Corpus Regni: heresy and the Peasants' Revolt', *Past and Present* 143 (1994), 3–47.
80 J.E.T. Rogers, *Six centuries of work and wages. The history of English labour* (London: Sonnenschein, 1908), pp. 253–4.
81 W.A. Cunningham, *The growth of English industry and commerce during the early and middle ages* (Cambridge, 5th edn, 1910), i, p. 397.
82 E. Lipson, *An introduction to the economic history of England. I. The middle ages* (London: Adam and Charles Black, 1915), pp. 124–5.
83 Hilton, *Bond men made free*, p. 156.
84 Poos, *A rural society*, pp. 242–6 (quotation at p. 246).
85 Poos, *A rural society*, p. 252.
86 R.H. Britnell, 'Feudal reaction after the Black Death in the palatinate of Durham', *Past and Present* 128 (1990), 28–47.
87 Britnell, 'Feudal reaction after the Black Death', pp. 39–40: 'At a time when the rebels in London were murdering the archbishop of Canterbury, the bishop of Durham's men were more anxious to stop the people from killing each other.'
88 P.L. Larson, *Conflict and compromise in the late medieval countryside: lords and peasants in Durham, 1349–1400* (New York: Routledge, 2006).
89 M. Bailey, *The decline of serfdom in late medieval England. From bondage to freedom* (Woodbridge: Boydell, 2014), pp. 307–11.
90 J. Whittle, 'Peasant politics and class consciousness: the Norfolk rebellions of 1381 and 1549 compared', in Dyer *et al.*, eds, *Rodney Hilton's Middle Ages*, pp. 233–47.
91 I.M.W. Harvey, *Jack Cade's rebellion of 1450* (Oxford: Oxford University Press, 1991); Poos, *A rural society*, pp. 255–60.
92 C. Valente, *The theory and practice of revolt in medieval England* (Aldershot: Ashgate, 2003), pp. 95–7.
93 See, above, for instance, for both Bennett's lament on the utter lack of sources generated from the peasantry and the relative glut of seigneurial records, as well as his reviewer's angry riposte, p. 5.
94 For instance, J.A. Raftis, *Peasant economic development within the English manorial system* (Stroud, 1996); E. Britton, *The community of the vill: a study in the history of the family and village life in fourteenth century England* (Toronto: Pontifical Institute of Mediaeval Studies, 1977); E.B. DeWindt, *Land and*

people in Holywell-cum-Needingworth (Toronto: Pontifical Institute of Mediaeval Studies, 1972); A.R. DeWindt, 'Redefining the peasant community in medieval England: the regional perspective', *Journal of British Studies* 26 (1987), 163-207.

95 A.R and E.B. DeWindt, *Ramsey. The lives of an English fenland town, 1200-1600* (Washington, D.C.: Catholic University of America Press, 2006), pp. 47-67.
96 DeWindt, *Land and people*, p. 247.
97 Raftis, *Peasant economic development*.
98 Raftis, *Peasant economic development*, pp. 24-5, 135, and, for further discussion of this work, below, pp. 123-4. For a critique of this position, see Z. Razi, 'The Toronto School's reconstitution of medieval peasant society: a critical view', *Past and Present* 85 (1979), 152-5.
99 J. Hatcher, 'English serfdom and villeinage. Towards a reassessment', *Past and Present* 90 (1981), 3-39; John Hatcher has also offered his own assessment of the relevant historiography, J. Hatcher, 'Lordship and villeinage before the Black Death: from Karl Marx to the Marxists and back again', in M. Kowaleski, J. Langdon and P.R. Schofield, eds, *Peasants and lords in the medieval English economy* (Turnhout: Brepols, 2015), 113-45.
100 J. Kanzaka, 'Villein rents in thirteenth-century England: an analysis of the Hundred Rolls of 1279-1280', *Economic History Review* 55 (2002), 593-618.
101 B.M.S. Campbell and K. Bartley, *England on the eve of the Black Death. An atlas of lay lordship, land and wealth, 1300-49* (Manchester: Manchester University Press, 2006), pp. 251-68.
102 Campbell and Bartley, *England on the eve of the Black Death*, pp. 68-79.
103 In a more recent statement Brenner reflects upon a developing commercialisation amongst the peasantry and concludes, in a manner quite consistent with parts of Campbell's argument, that peasant involvement in the market reflected a retreat by peasants from a position of advantage as they lost the means of subsistence in a period of growing population, land hunger and limited urban expansion. In other words, the move towards the market was not a deliberate best-opportunity choice but a consequence of the diminution of their means of subsistence, R. Brenner, 'Property and progress: where Adam Smith went wrong', in C. Wickham, ed., *Marxist history writing for the twenty-first century* (Oxford: Oxford University Press, 2007), pp. 49-111, and especially, pp. 66-8, 78-80. I am most grateful to Professor Rigby for drawing this work to my attention.
104 B.M.S. Campbell, 'The agrarian problem in the early fourteenth century', *Past and Present* 188 (2005), 3-70.
105 M. Bailey, 'Villeinage in England: a regional case study, c.1250-c.1349', *Economic History Review* 62 (2009), 430-57; Bailey has recently extended this discussion in Bailey, *Decline of serfdom*, in which he offers case-studies in order especially to refine and help explain the chronology of change as regards unfree tenure in the later middle ages.
106 See, for instance, C. Dyer, 'The ineffectiveness of lordship in England, 1200-1400', in Dyer *et al.*, eds, *Rodney Hilton's Middle Ages;* also Schofield, 'Lordship and the peasant economy'.
107 C. Dyer, 'Memories of freedom: attitudes towards serfdom in England,

1200–1350', in M.L. Bush, ed., *Serfdom and slavery. Studies in legal bondage* (Harlow: Longman, 1996); Schofield, 'Lordship and the peasant economy', pp. 53–68. Though set in a different historiographical context, earlier work by Hilton and Razi addresses similar issues: R.H. Hilton, 'Peasant movements in medieval England', *Economic History Review*, 2nd series, 2 (1949), reprinted in E.M. Carus-Wilson, ed., *Essays in economic history*, ii (London, 1962), pp. 73–90; Z. Razi, 'The struggles between the Abbots of Halesowen and their tenants in the thirteenth and fourteenth centuries', in T.H. Aston, P.R. Coss, C. Dyer and J. Thirsk, eds, *Social relations and ideas. Essays in honour of R.H. Hilton* (Cambridge: Cambridge University Press, 1983), pp. 151–67.

108 J. Whittle, 'Individualism and the family-land bond: a reassessment of land transfer patterns among the English peasantry c.1270–1580', *Past and Present* 160 (1998), 25–63; P.R. Schofield, '*Extranei* and the tenure of customary land on a Westminster Abbey manor in the fifteenth century', *Agricultural History Review* 49 (2001), 1–16; P.R. Schofield, 'Lordship and the early history of peasant land transfer on the estates of the abbey of Bury St Edmunds', in Kowaleski, Langdon and Schofield, eds, *Peasants and lords*, pp. 201–24. On regional distinctions more generally and the variety of tenurial regimes that could operate within a region and a large estate, see J. Mullan and R. Britnell, *Land and family. Trends and local variations in the peasant land market on the Winchester bishopric estates, 1263–1415* (Hatfield: University of Hertfordshire, 2010).

4

Peasants and markets

In the last quarter-century the importance of the market as a driving force for the medieval economy has emerged to take centre stage in the historiography of the middle ages. The role of peasants as participants in markets and as distinctive players in the medieval English economy has been emphasised by a number of historians. In this chapter we will examine the ways in which the last generation or two of historians have emphasised anew this mercantile aspect of the medieval English peasantry and also set out the ways in which, in earlier strands of the historiography, the market has often tended to be set aside in discussion of the medieval peasant.

No subject illustrates more effectively the changing attitude of historians to the medieval English peasantry than does the study of peasants in relation to the wider economy. Early economic theorists, such as Adam Smith, as we have had cause to mention in an earlier chapter, had encouraged those medievalists, such as Ashley, Cunningham and Lispon, who first came to examine the medieval economy to conceive of its development in terms of the growth of a money economy and as being dependent upon an extension of markets.[1] This interest in the market and its impact in the medieval countryside is also to be found in the writings of Thorold Rogers, Tawney, Gras and others writing in the later nineteenth and early twentieth centuries.[2] It is also evident in analyses in subsequent decades suggestive of a reasonably persistent thread, if a rather thin one. So, for example, William Hudson's discussion of land transfer at Hindolveston in the early fourteenth century, published around 1920, recognises the potential influence of market forces and the pragmatic economics of entrepreneurialism.[3] A generation later, Edward Miller also identified evidence for peasant investment in the mid-thirteenth-century land market that moved beyond the dictates of family form and the immediate expectations of lordship. Miller attributes this to 'a quickening of economic life in England' which reduced the significance of the manorial economy in favour of the peasant economy.[4] Yet if there were already some historians in the later nineteenth and early to mid-twentieth century who were prepared to recognise and to investigate the more market-orientated and loosely commercialised aspects of the medieval village, their influence in the historical literature tended to diminish. In the following decades, as we saw in Chapters 2 and 3, other views and emphases would come to dominate the study of the medieval agrarian economy, and the study of peasant economic exchange and market involvement was subsumed within other over-arching approaches to the medieval rural economy for many decades in the twentieth century. Here we will first examine the most important alternative discussions of medieval rural society and economy (models of change based upon class struggle, population and a social structural view of village society and economy) in each of which the importance of the market, as we will see, was reduced in favour of other explanations for either long-term change or social organisation and dealing.

Marxists and the peasant economy

Marxist historians writing either side of the Second World War argued for a peasant economy that was, in its development, principally influenced by lordship and which was certainly not determined in the greater part by the market or commerce. This certainly did not mean that Marxists were blind to the existence and role of markets – in fact, markets were often of critical importance to their models of economic change – but rather that the focus of these historians was directed elsewhere and that the close investigation of market structures and market activity was not, typically, central to their research and writing. Thus, as was discussed in the previous chapter, Rodney Hilton, described a peasantry in many respects defined by the expectations of lordship but one that was certainly not hermetically sealed from a wider world and economy.[5] Yet within Hilton's work on the medieval rural economy we can detect a fairly consistent tension between an explicit position, which places the struggle between lords and tenants at the heart of rural society in this period, and an implicit one which, while identifying lord–tenant relations, has also to engage with evidence for the influence of the market. In Hilton's earliest work on the development of estates in Leicestershire in the fourteenth and fifteenth centuries he discusses the division and consolidation of peasant holdings, as well as the acquisition of the lords' demesnes by peasants in the later middle ages. In explaining these changes, Hilton notes that the changing velocity of a market for land in this period was driven by the 'general market for agricultural produce' but that it was also encouraged by the weakening tenurial ties of this period:

> But once the customary framework of agrarian society had begun to crumble, the process of division of the peasantry into a richer and richer section and a more and more landless section went on, even during the early fifteenth century economic stagnation.[6]

Hilton appears to be suggesting here that, while the market may have helped to encourage initial change, it did not continue to drive or to control it; instead it was the reduction of seigneurial control that had freed the rural economy in this period. In so far as Hilton discusses the nature of exchange amongst the peasantry, and he certainly does, his main focus, not unlike other contemporary historians of the medieval rural economy, was upon land. In particular he, like a number of his other contemporaries, was interested in a range of matters associated with the tenure and the transfer of customary land, including such issues as the alienability of land, the fragmentation of holdings and their engrossment, as well as the changing chronology of peasant land-holding and land transfer in this period. Hilton also includes a chapter on 'the peasants' economy' as one of the published lectures from his 1973 series of Ford lectures.[7] The chapter is of interest for a number of reasons, not least for the historiographical context in which Hilton himself sets it, noting that his focus, is not upon estates and their economy but instead and, as he makes clear, atypically upon the 'village economy'. In seeking 'to get as far away as possible from the estate', Hilton makes a significant departure from much of the relevant literature associated with his contemporaries.[8] It is striking in this context that Hilton takes the opportunity to review what appear to be quite novel approaches to the economy of the medieval village. Thus, for instance, he discusses the types of goods exchanged in the medieval village as well as the ways in which they were exchanged; he considers the degree of social and economic polarisation within rural communities as well as the extent of monetarisation. Other relevant themes, also illustrative of a village and peasant economy, feature in his discussion: the extension of credit and of indebtedness, investment in cash crops, the transfer of land and so on. Also indicative of an attempt to set out a relatively new approach to the study of the peasantry and to direct researchers to the potential material available for such a study, Hilton's conclusion to this discussion reflects the ways in which his view of the medieval village was conditioned by his own conceptual framework of society and economy in the period. In reflecting upon the ways in which economic exchange within and beyond the village might generate differences in social structure and organisation, he rejects the notion that market exchange would be the decisive determinant; instead, he posits a rural society where 'mutual adjustment' and co-operation were the foundation to the lives of the peasantry and where the most important social distinction was between lord and tenant.[9]

In other respects Hilton does not offer a great deal of comment on the relative importance of the market compared to lordship and such tenurial obligations as rent; instead he proposes a fairly general picture dominated by an economy which, though monetarised and infused with mechanisms of exchange, was not wholly outward-looking or drawn extensively into networks of trade. Hilton's medieval village is dominated by an interdependent peasantry engaged in economic activity centred upon local and domestic consumption and where lordship and its demands are significant determinants of the direction of economic development. In discussing urban society in the same period, Hilton is also keen to stress similar features, noting the important of domestic economies in towns, especially the smaller, regional and market towns such as Thornbury in Gloucestershire. Here, unlike in the major towns and cities, the economic emphasis, according to Hilton, was upon production and consumption of foodstuffs and other basic products, such as everyday clothing. A great deal of this, as Hilton describes it, involved petty trade, though it might include proto-industrial activity such as textile production and could add to the process of urbanisation and thereby of commercial expansion, a point he is also keen to identify and explore.[10] Above all, however, it is the domestic and local economy, founded on the economic and political relation of lord and tenant that dominates Hilton's account of the medieval economy, rural and urban, and there is less to say about the commercial economy and the growth and nature of medieval markets.[11]

Robert Brenner also, in his challenging essays on the transition of feudalism to capitalism, recognised the potential importance of markets and commerce as the driving force of change in the medieval economy.[12] However, for Brenner in some of his earliest work at least, the pattern of commercial development in this period was ancillary to the relationship between lord and tenant; a changing engagement of peasants with the market was also conditional upon the lord–tenant relationship.[13] As such he has far less to say about market activity and involvement; he recognises its existence and importance and identifies ways in which the changing nature of the economy may be charted (for instance, the growth of a money economy) but tends to present the market as controlled by lords. Thus, the flow of capital into markets, the price of produce and the capacity of the peasantry to enter into market exchanges are presented by Brenner as constrained by lordship and the demands of the manorial economy.[14] It is the relative strength or weakness of lordships within regions that helps to explain, in fact is fundamental to our understanding of, the relative performance of commerce and market strength within medieval England, just as it is the changing strength of lordship and the force of its powers to extract surplus from the tenantry that dictates the degree to which lords engage with or distance themselves from commercial activity and the market.[15]

In challenging the earlier argument of Paul Sweezy, a contributor to the first phase of the debate regarding the transition from feudalism to capitalism, Brenner does not accept that a growth in the market may have also encouraged lords to impose greater demands and inflict more severe restrictions on their own tenants as lords sought to maximise opportunities presented by the market. He doubts that lords enjoyed significant freedom of manoeuvre in this respect and they, rather like their tenants, were constrained by the feudal relationship in ways that hampered significant innovation and a leap toward commerce and capitalism. Their mindset was, in effect, attuned to feudal property relations and not capitalist ones: 'for the serf-lords' survival simply did not depend on their relationship to the market'.[16] It would take a major rupture of this system, such as ongoing peasant resistance and revolt issuing from within the inherently 'contradictory character of pre-capitalist social relations'[17] to enable such a change but, for Brenner, it is unlikely that the pull of the market was capable of generating such a rupture. Only once such a rupture had occurred could capitalism replace feudalism and, for Brenner, this occurred in England in the later fifteenth and sixteenth centuries when landlords were able to take full control of the landed property of their tenants and to adopt new profit-maximising agricultural practices.[18] Brenner has much less to say about the nature of those markets, their qualities and the actual involvement of the peasantry within them and, in truth, he had, in the 1970s when his first key statements were published, relatively little secondary literature to which he could turn for detailed accounts of peasant market involvement in this period.

Brenner has, in more recent work, developed his views on the role and importance of the market. This is especially evident in an assessment of the state of the historiography published in 2007 and which returns to his 1977 discussion of 'Neo-Smithian Marxism' and the historical understanding of the role of the market in the transition from feudalism to capitalism. Brenner, in this later essay, challenged the good sense of the most recent generation of historians in embracing anew the views of Adam Smith, identifying almost wherever they look the expansion of the market and growth of output *per capita*.[19] Brenner detects a rejection of pre-existing models, especially the Malthusian model associated for medieval England with M.M. Postan, in favour of this leap to accept market expansion as the corner-stone of economic change. While, in fact and as we will consider in more detail later in this chapter, historians of medieval England have been more willing to describe the market and its activity than to locate it in models of long-term economic change, Brenner is right to note this significant change in focus. In seeking to locate the market within his own explanatory model of the changing economy where the presiding relation of production (or what Brenner prefers to call 'social-property relations') was feudalism, Brenner argues that, throughout the medieval period, a transition to capitalism, in which the market came to dominate and individuals elected to direct their economic activity towards the market (above all because they lacked the means of subsistence and were thereby obliged to engage with the market in order to survive) did not take place. Instead, feudal social-property relations encouraged a considerable degree of separation from the market in that economic agents, both peasants and lords, identified their best advantage in peasant subsistence and production for consumption. Market opportunities certainly existed but none of the relevant parties considered it sensible or attractive to seek to engage more fully with these opportunities and to an extent that would rupture pre-existing social-property relations. Brenner contends that peasants chose this route so long as they could do so. However, once they could not do so – because, most obviously, population increase and the morcellisation of landholding reduced their capacity to subsist – they were thrown on to the market, 'a second choice, made under duress'.[20] While few if any medieval historians would disagree with Brenner that the market was insufficiently developed to afford extensive protection and drive growth in the high and late middle ages, there are plentiful indications of a peasant-level immersion in the market which may at least suggest that feudal social-property relations were at risk of abandonment by some peasants in this period. As already noted, it is the relative significance of such developments that is likely to foster disagreement amongst historians seeking to explain economic change and the role of the peasantry in this process. Whilst, as we shall see later in this chapter, a number of medieval historians since Brenner have addressed the issue of economic exchange and its development in this period, it is striking that relatively few have done so with direct reference to the intellectual framework employed by Brenner and earlier established by historians engaged in the transition debate. Before we turn to this more detailed work on peasant involvement in the market, we can look at one further instance of a historiographical approach which tended to downplay the role of the market.

Neo-Malthusians, sociologists and the peasant economy

As we have seen, the work of Postan has dominated much modern study of the medieval economy. Yet, Postan's explanatory model of economic change left little room for the role of market-driven exchange; instead, as we have seen, Postan's view of change was founded upon a relationship between population and available resources. So, for Postan, the main indices of economic change, especially wages and prices, were influenced above all by movement of population, prices responding positively to population increase and wages negatively (and vice versa).[21] Pressure on land, its availability and its relative 'value' were also influenced by population change; colonisation of poorer-quality land during the period of population growth before the early to mid-fourteenth century, for instance, evidenced the heightened worth of land, as did a retreat from marginal land in the subsequent period of population decline.[22] This overarching conception of the motor of economic development tended to restrict Postan's view of the nature of the rural economy and of the nature of exchange within the medieval village. Importantly also it strongly influenced a generation and more of historians writing in his wake.[23]

Economic exchange and elements of rudimentary commercial activity also feature in passing in the body of work undertaken by those historians keen to chart the social cohesion and changing social dynamic of the medieval village. Most typically associated with the so-called 'Toronto School', and focused upon an extensive corpus of material issuing from the archive of the Ramsey Abbey estates, historians such as J. Ambrose Raftis, Edwin DeWindt, Anne DeWindt and Edward Britton have concentrated their attention upon the ways in which social interaction was effected in the medieval village. As such, they pay close attention to possible indices of economic change but are inclined to interpret these more in terms of their significance for our understanding of changing social relations and structure in the later middle ages than in terms of a changing peasant economy *per se*.[24] In one of the last significant statements by the main contributors to this 'school', Raftis addressed the theme of the peasant economy directly. The tone of this work, written at the end of a half century of research on the topic by the author, is striking, not least because it seems to be chiefly one of surprise. Raftis's thesis, that tenants' capital was of crucial importance to lords and that the peasant economy was of great influence to the seigneurial economy, is, as the author notes, a significant departure from earlier positions and one that effectively turns the tables on a good deal of earlier interpretation. However, it is also noteworthy that Raftis's assessment leaves little or no room for direct discussion of how peasants generated their capital, and certainly includes only sparse comment on the potential for economic dealing within and beyond the village to increase the peasants' access to capital and the means of generating capital. In fact, while Raftis makes it clear that he is certainly aware of this potential influence he describes work in this area as in its infancy and he suggests he can only assume that peasant entrepreneurs bought and sold in markets.[25] He suggested that much additional work needed to be done in order 'to obtain a proper grasp of the actual available capital resources of the English countryside by the thirteenth century'. While this was certainly true, Raftis, in overlooking quite a range of directly relevant literature published by the time his own book appeared in print in 1996, was able to characterise the historiographical positions as rather more polarised, and his own contribution as rather more ground-breaking, than was in fact the case.[26] Yet he does recognise features of a commercialising economy, identify some comparative material, such as the investigation of the Peterborough Abbey peasant land market by Edmund King, and point the way towards further potential research in this area. Illustrative of his own methodological and theoretical position, however, is Raftis's disinclination to see the peasant economy as essentially competitive and aggressive, and he rejects the idea of peasant entrepreneurs preying upon the misfortune of their less fortunate neighbours.[27]

If then Raftis, writing at the end of a research campaign that had begun in the 1950s, was able to countenance but not entirely to embrace or to describe a competitive peasant economy, earlier contributors within the same 'campaign' had shied away from, or not evidently contemplated, the role of commerce and commercial activity within the medieval village. Edwin DeWindt's discussion of peasant interaction within the medieval village, based upon a close analysis of court rolls for the Ramsey Abbey manor of Holywell-cum-Needingworth, includes a great deal on exchange within and beyond the manor but it tends not to be couched in economic terms.[28] DeWindt, in his discussion, clearly and purposefully acknowledges the potential for economic exchange within and beyond the medieval village.[29]

His research also itemises a number of potentially significant indices of economic exchange but he tends to employ these as measures more of social interaction than of economic exchange. Thus, for instance, DeWindt explores the brewing of ale in the medieval village and, while evidently alive to the economic significance of such interaction, he focuses his attention instead upon the importance of such exchange as a measure of social cohesiveness; the same is also true for his discussion of indebtedness and of personal pledging.[30] There is then little here that engages directly with the detail of economic exchange, something in fact that the author is inclined to shun as representing an outmoded view of the medieval peasantry; and yet, at the same time, DeWindt laments the lack of detailed research into market structures and inter-peasant economic exchange, features of peasant life which he considers to have been neglected by historians in favour of a manorially focused view of the peasantry.[31]

Historians and markets

In two or three key works published in the later 1980s and early 1990s, notably by Christopher Dyer and by Richard Britnell, the direction of historical study certainly shifted towards a greater investigation of economic exchange; the cumulative influence of such work has produced a significant adjustment in the historical investigation and perception of the rural economy and society of the middle ages, initially at least for England and then, in some cases, further afield.[32] The recent market-focused development in the historiography of the medieval English economy and of the peasantry has been above all one of shifting emphasis. As we have seen, historians have for more than a century recognised the existence of markets with which peasants engaged in medieval England but have not seen commerce or economic engagement with the market as determinative of economic change. While there has been a much greater focus upon the medieval market and a testing of its significance and durability since the later 1980s, medievalists would still tend to the view that the market and commerce did not drive medieval society and economy. So, for instance, in the first of Christopher Dyer's University of Oxford Ford lectures, delivered in 2001, Dyer emphasises the strength of the high and late medieval market but rejects the notion that medieval England was already a capitalist country by this period, he describes a continued process of change, of 'transition', but one in which, most importantly for this discussion, a greater degree of peasant autonomy and commercial activity existed than was once supposed.[33]

Dyer's view of the economy in his Ford lectures was a drawing together of a great deal of earlier research and writing and, as a key-note statement, reflects an important trend in historical writing on the peasantry. In his earlier study of standards of living, published in 1989, Dyer quite deliberately distinguishes his approach from earlier discussions of the medieval rural economy, in terms of his intention to examine consumption rather than production as well as his desire to examine social status and the role of the market in helping to define such differences.[34] In separate chapters, Dyer attempts a detailed modelling of the peasant economy, distinguishing between the domestic economies of the relatively wealthy and the relatively poor peasantry; he also examines the consumption of the medieval peasantry. In both respects, and even in the case of wealthier villein tenants of substantial holdings, where by far the largest elements of the family economy are explicable in terms of the unit of landholding, Dyer places considerable store upon the role and importance of the market; he also notes the greater degree of market dependency, especially in terms of employment, amongst poorer tenants and small-holders.[35] In other published work Dyer developed his ideas regarding the significance of the market and commercial and non-agrarian sectors within the medieval English rural economy and, in a series of articles, he has illustrated the ways in which villages and small towns interacted extensively with wider economies, including national and international trade in raw and finished products. This is particularly the case in his discussion of small-town trade and of consumption.[36] Dyer also emphasises that, while the importance of the market has been recognised and reasonably well understood by historians, the role of consumption, relative to production, in driving the economy has been little investigated. Dyer makes the point that the small-scale petty consumption of rural dwellers was pervasive and, cumulatively, of great significance to the medieval English economy.[37] In recent work he has looked in detail at various aspects of consumption, including the ways in which peasants consumed a range of goods, including high-quality goods purchased through local markets as well as markets operating on an international level.[38] We will return in fuller detail to this work and related issues in terms of consumption later in this chapter, and also in the final chapter on peasant culture.[39]

Britnell's study of commercialisation in medieval English society details the interaction of markets, trade, commerce and lordship across three sub-periods between the beginning of the eleventh and the end of the fifteenth centuries. He argues for the need to recognise the importance of marketing structures and commercial interaction throughout the period while at the same time describing and discussing the rise of commercial interaction and the changing degree of market orientation.[40] The main thrust of Britnell's discussion, which has certainly encouraged some further careful reflection on the nature of the medieval English economy, as we shall see, is to emphasise the potential for the market to influence the choices individuals and institutions were capable of making in order to bring about changes in their lives and the lives of others. In this respect, Britnell contrasts this approach directly with both a population-driven model of the medieval economy and also, to a lesser extent, a Marxist model. As to the former, Britnell suggests that a population-driven view of the economy precludes consideration of the capacity of the populace both to innovate in order to escape the hegemony of population over resources and by extension to improve the general quality of life over time, through technological advancement for instance; this model, he contends, is not consistent with the information on market orientation available for the medieval period. While also, and more by implication, challenging an overtly Marxist view of the medieval economy, Britnell also suggests that the social inequalities occasioned, in part, by the market, were also both product of and accentuated by such structures as lordship, monarchy and the burgeoning state; in this respect, he accommodates both a perception of the economy as partially market-driven and one that is conditioned by institutions such as lordship. In this latter respect, and while it is difficult to pin down his work in theoretical terms, Britnell's analysis may be said to fall within the broad sphere of institutional economics.[41] It is striking that, while Britnell engages directly with the pre-existing historiographical conventions only occasionally in his account, he does identify the much earlier historiographical tradition that placed the market closer to the heart of the medieval economy, a 'rehabilitation' of an earlier tradition, founded initially in the early twentieth-century writings of Lipson, Gras and Salzmann on trade, markets and commercial expansion.[42] While Britnell's focus is not upon the peasantry *per se*, though he does offer some comment on peasant involvement in the market, the contribution of his work in furthering the formulation of the research agenda in this areas was clearly important. Alongside the work of Dyer, his investigation of commercialisation in medieval England served to direct and encourage new approaches to the study of the medieval English economy.

We can explore the influence of this 'commercialisation' thesis from more than one direction, examining the development of new directions in this area of research as well as the adoption of new approaches to familiar sources, previously investigated with other research agendas in mind.

Central features of this approach are: a reassessment of the importance of other key institutions of medieval rural society, notably lordship and the family, relative to the role of the individual and the market, an approach especially but not uniquely evident in the investigation of the peasant land market; an awareness of the potentially significant impact of peasant economic endeavour on medieval gross domestic product (GDP); and, finally, a reconsideration of the role of commerce, including rural trade and peasant economic activity, in effecting and indeed driving change in the medieval English economy.

Markets, lordship and family

A renewed emphasis upon commercial and market-orientated exchange within medieval peasant society has not seen historical study abandon all reference to previous discussions of economic activity in the medieval economy. Thus, the role of such institutions as lordship and the family, at certain times perceived by historians as fundamental to explanations of peasant interaction and economic exchange, has been reduced in recent decades by historians keen to stress more market-driven factors. This is most evident in discussion of the peasant land market but, as we shall see, the themes identified in discussion of the peasant land market have subsequently informed investigation of other features of the peasant economy, notably relations between creditors and debtors as well as the buying and selling of everyday goods.

It would not be too great an exaggeration to suggest that discussion of the peasant land market in medieval England has been central to, indeed a microcosm of, wider debates concerning medieval peasants. In terms of a chronological development of the relevant historiography, description and analysis of the peasant land market, here taken to mean the buying and selling of land, and especially villein or customary land, for money or money's worth (goods or services of equivalent monetary value),[43] has moved apace with general themes and approaches directed at this subject. Thus a preoccupation with institutional forms in the late nineteenth century passed into discussion of the societal consequences of a land market and, in the middle years of the twentieth century, of the explanations of that market, expressed in terms of a dynamic that was either Marxist or demographic. In the last quarter-century, since the mid- to late 1980s, the land market has been explained in quite different terms, and chiefly in relation to commercial developments in the medieval economy. This last shift returns us, in certain respects at least, to the position of early twentieth-century analysts of the peasant land market, such as Tawney.[44]

This transformation of approach is especially evident in two major works on the peasant land market, both published in 1984. P.D.A. Harvey's edited collection on the peasant land market, the arguments of which were discussed in Chapter 2 as evidence for the take-up of Postan's view of a peasant land market, drew together the published versions of four PhD theses on the peasant land market, one of which was completed in the early 1960s and the other three in the mid-1970s.[45] The other work published in 1984, Richard Smith's edition of essays on land, kinship and life-cycle, also combined earlier doctoral research with the results of current and ongoing research involving a number of key contributors to medieval and to early modern social and economic history.[46] Together, the two volumes reveal a moment, or at least a decade, of change in the interpretation of the peasant land market and an insight into the preconceptions that those working on the subject brought to their research. The difference between these works, one which has become increasingly evident since the early 1980s, is that Harvey's discussion and the doctoral work published there were reflective of significant trends and themes operating within this area of study in the 1960s and early 1970s; by the time the works were published the terms of the debate were beginning to change.

This is particularly evident when we explore the identified motive for peasant engagement in the transfer of land. Harvey, in reviewing the body of work on the peasant land market including the doctoral work reproduced in his collection, recognised, as we saw in Chapter 2, that 'sheer economic ambition' was not the only significant factor in defining the medieval market in land.[47] Instead, making direct reference to the work of A.V. Chayanov, who had argued that Russian peasant farms expanded and contracted in size according to the size of the peasant family, he stressed the potential importance of adjustments by the peasant family aimed at accommodating the increased or reduced needs of that family. Harvey also discussed in some detail the capacity of lords to contain the excesses of that market, but recognised that such seigneurial control could be limited at best.[48] Finally, and in a tone that is suitably circumspect and reflective, Harvey recognises that familial concerns over the transfer of land could have been significant in influencing the tenor and velocity of land transfer but that such constraints were not inimical to a market in land.[49]

Smith, in a far-reaching and extensive introduction to his edited volume, also engages closely with the work of Chayanov and seeks to discuss the nature of the peasant land market as well as to review the contribution, by the early 1980s, of medieval historians in this area.[50] Smith's introductory essay offered a novel statement on the potential implications of *inter-vivos* exchange in the medieval village and was instrumental in establishing the historiographical *status quo ante* as well as pointing towards new approaches to and conceptions of the peasant land market. In the 1960s, as Harvey's conclusion makes clear, it was the work of A.V. Chayanov that had come to dominate thinking in discussion of the peasant land market. Postan's far-reaching overview of the peasant land market, published in 1961, makes no mention of Chayanov's theory of peasant economy but it is difficult to think that he was not incorporating its chief tenets.[51] By contrast Smith's overall analysis emphasises the contrasts within manors and between regions in the high and later middle ages. Importantly, he describes and examines the sorts of distinctions evident between the manors and peasant landholding of central England and a model of landholding and land transfer illustrated by research on eastern England, and East Anglia in particular.[52] While earlier commentators on the land market in East Anglia had been slightly more circumspect or uncertain in their analysis, pondering perhaps the lack of evident consonance with an anticipated Chayanovian model of land transfer dominated by changing family structure and size, Smith argues for patterns of land transfer inconsistent with family form.[53] In particular he stresses the alternative explanations for the existence of and engagement with a peasant land market and, in a telling consideration of the financial systems which might have permitted the expansion of a family holding and the acquisition of additional units of land, Smith notes that 'the main problem with the application of Chayanov's model to late thirteenth- and early fourteenth-century England remains not what is in the model itself but what has been excluded from it'.[54] He has in mind access to capital, and rejects, on the basis of his and the observations of others, an equal distribution and redistribution of capital; instead he posits the existence of and explores the dynamics of a labour force not generated entirely from within the family farm but one that encompassed waged and non-family labour created by inequalities of land-holding, variety of economic opportunity and a varying degree of market dependency.

Smith's analysis of the peasant land market in medieval England, which modifies and in some contexts replaces an earlier view of that market, allowed for and indeed encouraged a fuller reflection on the role of the market and of commercial forces within the peasant land market. As we have seen, earlier commentators and notably Postan, were not dismissive of the notion that the market had an influence upon land transfer but this was considered of secondary or even tertiary importance.[55] Hyams, in an important contribution which challenged that earlier position, had already, before Smith, argued that the land market, such as it was, must have been dependent on external sources of capital.[56] Developing and, in key respects, challenging Postan's analysis of the market in free land on the Peterborough Abbey estates, Edmund King, writing in the early 1970s, had also stressed the important role of village 'kulaks' in the buying and selling of free holdings. King identified such activity as entrepreneurial, and described the ways in which a relatively wealthy villein elite operated in a market in free land which provided far greater access to land than did villein land, the latter much more constrained and controlled by lords and, as King, notes, possibly by families as well. In fact, in his final analysis King does not altogether abandon some of the prevailing standards of peasant life, identifying the motive force for the buying and selling of land as rooted in the family, and identifies the market in free land as piecemeal in comparison to the solid and unyielding customary holdings of the villeins, which were not subjected to the market.[57] We can detect in King's work a testing of the theoretical and conceptual boundaries of peasant exchange; however, such testing seems still to be conditioned by the expectation that peasant engagement with the market was founded upon the claims and needs of the family and its constituent members as well as the dictates of lordship. This is evident in other work on the buying and selling of land also produced at about the same time. In her discussion of the transactions of the tenants of Westminster Abbey, Barbara Harvey is cautious in her identification of anything akin to a true market throughout the later middle ages, recognising both the strong resistance of the abbey up until the later fifteenth century to alienation of substantial units of land and what she perceives as a lack of available capital which prevented extensive investment in all but small piecemeal plots.[58] It is striking that Harvey characterises the market as largely unsupportive of land transactions on the abbey's estates and really of only negative influence: it was the lack of available capital that allowed the demands of lordship to outweigh the influence of a relatively weak market.

In the 1980s and 1990s historians took further steps in exploring this association between the land market and capital, and often headed in rather different directions. While the important line of enquiry suggested initially by Smith, that the waged labour force and the labour market were important determinants of the market in land, has been pursued less vigorously by historians, there has been rather more work undertaken in exploring the relationship between land markets and the extension of capital. A more general discussion of credit in the medieval village has included examination of the mechanisms that facilitated and recorded credit and indebtedness in the medieval village as well as the social and economic structures that encouraged, supported and, conversely, restrained it. In terms of the peasant land market, a few historians have attempted to relate discussion of an emerging credit market, or at least mechanisms which permitted some levels of lending and borrowing, to the land market. In the last decade in particular, Briggs and Schofield have sought to establish the ways in which security might be attached to peasant-held land and its transfer in the thirteenth and fourteenth centuries.[59] In work published since the 1990s, Schofield has also illustrated the ways in which, during periods of crisis and harvest failure, credit might be withdrawn from village society with consequences for a peasant land market in terms of both the preparedness of needy tenants to sell or release their land and the willingness of the relatively advantaged to expand their landholding 'portfolio'.[60]

This approach to the peasant land market builds upon the earlier suggestion of historians such as Smith and Hyams that the market could only operate in this way if it were financed or facilitated in some way other than from within the immediate family. In earlier work, Smith and Bruce Campbell, in particular, had not investigated the sorts of mechanisms that might provide evidence for that financing or facilitation but they had provided robust dissections of an aggressive and volatile land market in parts of eastern England, c.1300, and sought to offer a wider, contextualising explanation for the patterns they were observing.[61] Striking in their description of the peasant land market is the extent of turnover of holdings and the small size of these holdings, as well as the preparedness of some peasants to engage actively in the market for land, accumulating significant, though not always long-lasting, units of landholding.

If historians working mostly on eastern England identified and described different patterns of landholding and land transfer from those that had always been considered emblematic of the medieval village, their researches also seemed to challenge two of the main tenets of the orthodoxy of peasant landholding in this period: namely that both lords and peasant families, keen to preserve the integrity of holdings either as a rent-generating unit of account (lords) or as a holding capable of sustaining individual families and one that could be transferred across generations through inheritance within the family (peasant families), were both generally resistant to an active and impersonal market in land. The resistance of lords to a market in peasant-held land is discussed in a number of studies and has remained an important theme in the modern historiography. The same is also true of familial intervention in land transfer; writing at the end of the 1970s, and drawing especially upon the researches of Richard Smith on peasant families, inheritance and the land market on manors of the estates of Bury St Edmunds, Alan Macfarlane challenged the notion that families constrained individual engagement in a land market. Instead, he detected an individualistic and entrepreneurial spirit pervading economic dealing at the village level and so rejected the notion that medieval rural England was, indeed, a 'peasant' society at all.[62] With some modification of the parameters of the debate (few have questioned the 'peasantness' of medieval rural society, for instance),[63] much research undertaken on the peasant land market since the early 1980s has been conducted with such questions in mind, not least the degree to which peasant land transfer operated with or without the constraints of family and lordship; in fact, and as we have seen, some of the emphasis has shifted to the mechanisms which encouraged and supported a market in land rather than restricting it.[64]

Peasant economic activity and GDP

Relative to the involved and long-standing investigation of the factors that might have influenced patterns of exchange in the high and late middle ages, discussion of peasant contribution to gross domestic product (GDP – the sum of the money value of the all final goods and services produced in a single year; this has been taken by at least one medievalist to mean 'the total income in cash and consumed produce in a normal year, without deduction for rents or other expenses')[65] has been recent and slight. Calculation of GDP in the middle ages is dependent upon detailed quantitative investigation allied to a good deal of informed estimation and guesswork. Mayhew has recently argued that historians' focus upon such potentially significant and traditional measures of GDP as the extent of exports risks ignoring the importance of domestic production for local consumption as a key feature of GDP.[66] Discussion of GDP has been subjected to a number of studies in recent years and these have tended to stress the importance of the peasant sector in helping to define GDP. Even in the generally pessimistic analysis of Bruce Campbell, who emphasises the inherent problems in terms of standard of living and economic stability and growth associated with a dense population unable adequately to sustain itself, the contribution of various elements of those who may be counted within the ranks of the peasantry, broadly defined (identified as yardlanders, small-holders, cottagers, labourers, rural craftsmen, paupers and vagrants) contributed over sixty per cent of England and Wales's GDP (c.1290).[67] Nicholas Mayhew's earlier and pioneering estimate of GDP for England, using similar categories and upon which Campbell based his own initial approach to this subject, also suggests that the peasant sector accounted for in excess of sixty per cent of GDP; Graeme Snooks's own comment on GDP, c.1300, reflects a far less positive view of the economic strength of the peasant sector as well as the capacity of the sources to permit any reasonable estimate. He proposes that, using a simulated model of GDP growth by c.1300, real GDP per capita had increased by a factor of 1.9 and suggests that this was driven by especially dynamic growth in the late eleventh and early twelfth centuries which took place during a period of investment in technology and economic organisation; thereafter GDP per capita is likely to have declined as population increased to unsustainable levels.[68] In reflecting upon the likely reduction in GDP by the end of the thirteenth century, he argues that Mayhew, in his own more positive estimates of GDP by the end of the thirteenth century, failed to take sufficient account of 'the very long tail in the income distribution for peasant and urban wage-earning households'.[69]

Most recently, a research team including Stephen Broadberry and Bruce Campbell has constructed higher still figures for GDP c.1300; these estimates of GDP are based on a different measure of GDP, namely the sum of agricultural, industrial and service industry outputs. While GDP in this estimate has not been not disaggregated by socio-economic sector, the assumption must be that the peasant sector provided a high proportion of the overall GDP, especially as, in the middle ages, agricultural output predominated.[70] Their observation, that GDP was low in the thirteenth century, and falling in the later middle ages, does not prevent them from drawing the conclusion that, relatively speaking, GDP per head, even in the most difficult years of the middle ages, was double that of the poorest countries in the world today and that GDP helped support conspicuous cultural expression, architectural campaigns and significant expenditure on luxury goods, especially of course amongst the elite.[71]

As will be evident, the pursuit of GDP estimates has directed historical investigation of GDP in the direction of the peasantry and, at least in its earliest interventions, closely informed work carried out in the 1990s by James Masschaele aimed at exploring the extent of peasant involvement in agrarian production.[72] Building upon the calculations and observations of Mayhew in particular and applying them especially to investigation of the medieval wool trade, Masschaele notes that, as previous historians of the wool trade had also identified, the most familiar suppliers of wool for export and domestic consumption, namely the great monastic houses, could not have met all the demands of the market. Instead, as he argues, it was, for example, wool from flocks owned by fourteenth-century peasants that accounted for at least half of all exports in that century.[73] Furthermore, investigation of thirteenth- and fourteenth-century tax assessments of movable goods (lay subsidies) indicates that two-thirds of saleable surplus was held by medieval peasants.[74] These are quite extraordinary sums that have served to illustrate the cumulative economic significance of the medieval peasantry and which have reinforced historians' conception of the peasantry as economically significant not only in terms of their labour and rent but also in terms of their market engagement, in terms of production and consumption.

Trade, towns and the medieval peasant

Historical discussion of production and consumption has also directed historians towards, and been informed by, investigation of the interaction of peasants with towns and trade. Estimates of GDP, to varying degrees dependent upon the base-line data and the method employed for a calculation of GDP of the kinds discussed above, recognise that peasants contributed to outputs and surpluses that extended beyond subsistence needs and could be sold at market within and beyond medieval England and that peasants were also active and extensive consumers of domestic, as well as in some instances imported, produce. As we have seen in earlier sections of this chapter, investigation of buying and selling amongst the medieval peasantry has been dominated by discussion of transactions in land. There has been relatively less study of movable goods and their buying and selling. Some of the earliest investigation of movement of goods within the ranks of the peasantry had tended to conceive of such as exchange of basic foodstuffs and other simple necessities. Undoubtedly, as more recent work has also shown, this kind of transaction must have been important; however, historians and archaeologists, while not denying the relevance, ubiquity and general mass of such piecemeal exchange, have also recognised that production and consumption of a different order might also be exercised by the peasantry in this period. Again, there has been a dramatic shift of emphasis in this respect since the 1970s and early 1980s. In conceiving of a peasantry that was engaged in buying and selling at more than the most rudimentary of levels, historians have set out to investigate a number of potential avenues illustrative of this enhanced economic dealing.

We can return to these themes later in the volume, especially as they relate to issues of peasant culture.[75] For now we should note the new historiographical emphasis as illustrated through a recent series of investigations of various kinds of production and consumption. To conceive of a peasantry as significantly engaged in market-led production and consumption is to place discussion of the peasantry within a rather different context from that earlier explored by historians. As has already been discussed in this chapter, historians have in recent years recognised the likely major – indeed, overwhelmingly significant – contribution that peasants made to GDP. To itemise that a little more, and thereby to set out some of the ways in which historians have expanded their research agendas, we can see that historians have directed a new focus upon, for instance, foodstuffs and animal products, and not just in terms of their own consumption needs. Bailey's investigation of the medieval Breckland, for example, has illustrated the ways in which peasants were able to exploit the less-than-propitious cereal-growing conditions by developing other opportunities for food production. Directed at the prevailing Postanian orthodoxy, namely that the condition of the peasantry is directly and uniquely related to the capacity for arable husbandry, Bailey's account reveals the ways in which peasants developed alternative routes to agrarian production, including the development of rabbit warrens, pastoral husbandry (particularly of sheep) and a considered investment in certain grains, as well as flax and hemp.[76] Judith Bennett has also illustrated, with a particular emphasis upon the economic experience of women in this period, the ways in which brewing, a staple requirement of consumption throughout medieval society, provided outlets for economic specialisation and a degree of economic independence.[77] In addition, historians, recognising the productive capacity of the peasantry and its potential to intersect with a market more active than had always been supposed, have considered other points of intersection other than those in relation to basic foodstuffs and the more essential consumer goods. Finished goods and pottery, produced from within a rural context, have also been the subject of study within this growing historiographical focus upon commerce.[78] The link between rural living in the middle ages and other kinds of by-employment is also evident on work on mining and rural society in the last thirty or forty years, as for instance in the investigation of Derbyshire lead-mining by Blanchard or Hatcher's research into tin mining in Cornwall.[79] More recently, historians have also examined the ways in which the countryside, and not just the great landlords of the countryside, provisioned towns and institutions, such as monastic houses. Kowaleski's detailed discussion of medieval Exeter, for example, illustrates the important links between town and countryside and the opportunities which towns afforded rural dwellers, a point also illustrated in the ground-breaking 'Feeding the city' project, a detailed attempt to chart the ways in which London in the middle ages drew upon its hinterland and those resident within it, allowing peasant producers to adjust their activity in order to meet the expectations of urban dwellers.[80] This project also illustrated the ways in which arable land within the London region was farmed relatively intensively in order to meet the demands of the city.[81] As well as towns, historians have also turned to institutions, such as monastic houses, to explore the ways in which these entities were provisioned, a question which in its answer also sheds much light upon the significance of peasant producers. Threlfall-Thompson's study of Durham Cathedral Priory, for instance, has illustrated the variety of suppliers which clearly included local tenantry, especially for the less specialised consumables; John Lee has studied medieval Cambridge and its hinterland in similar terms.[82] Furthermore, a fuller discussion of credit within rural society, especially during the last two decades or more, has prompted medievalists to consider the capacity of rural dwellers, including peasants, to share capital and to extend loans, in the form of money, goods and services, or as deferred payment.[83] As well as goods, a greater focus upon the economic exchanges within and beyond medieval rural society has also encouraged historians to reflect upon capital and labour as saleable resources within the control of the peasantry.

Labour as a resource extended by the peasant family has long attracted interest even if its implications for market integration of peasant labour beyond the peasant family holding and labour on the lord's demesne have not always been extensively explored. The recognition that labour was generated by the peasant family and was employed beyond the peasant family is dependent on a number of historical assumptions or observations: namely, that some peasant families enjoyed surpluses of labour, explicable in terms either of their inability to absorb that labour or their exploitation of that labour indirectly through labour markets; that there were opportunities for exploitation of that labour indirectly through labour markets; that there were opportunities for peasant labour to be absorbed into external labour markets, including urban markets and more local by-employments. In addition, as a number of models of economic change in the middle ages have made clear, the potential for such a labour market to absorb peasant labour, and for a surplus of peasant labour to exist at all, was heavily dependent upon major external factors, including population change, the expansion of the urban economy and the weakening of institutions, such as lordship, that may have served to constrain peasant mobility and access to labour markets. These are themes that will also be discussed in later chapters, especially in terms of the demographic and historical investigation of family and household formation, marriage patterns and life-cycle service.[84] Here we need only note that labour and its availability have for long been employed by historians as a potential index of the capacity of the peasantry to cope; early discussion of wages, in town and countryside, revealed a preoccupation with the relationship between labour, its availability and population movement which has persisted until the present.[85] In more recent years historians have also considered the ways in which peasants may have rather more deliberately offered their services as waged or live-in labourers, not just in order to reduce risk and in response to exogenous variables but to maximise the benefits of their available labour.[86] So, for instance, in the period after the Black Death, as John Hatcher has described, labourers were able to circumvent attempts to control rising wage rates in a period of major population loss by pressurising their employers to pay *de facto* higher wages, including the additional benefits of goods in kind (especially food and drink), in what was 'a seller's market'.[87] These new wages also allowed labourers the opportunity to choose when to work and to enjoy greater amounts of leisure time.[88]

Historical interest in the peasantry as consumers has also grown apace in recent years. This is not say that historians had not reflected earlier upon the consumption patterns of peasants; such consideration was however typically couched in terms of the limited consumption practices of peasants. Basic consumption of foodstuffs was explored by Rogers in the nineteenth century. For instance, in the introductory sections to his monumental gathering of price data, he offers some comment on foodstuffs and domestic accommodation, tending strongly to the view that most rural dwellers consumed according to necessity rather than from choice occasioned by surplus and 'lived in chilly dark huts, where glass was unknown, fuel comparatively dear, and cleanliness all but impossible'.[89] An informed description of a variety of forms of consumption in the medieval midlands is also offered by Hilton more than half a century later; striking in his detailed investigation of peasant buildings and chattels, which includes plentiful evidence of the investment on the part of the peasantry, is his reluctance to suggest that such consumption was ever extravagant or indicative of a significant surplus. Thus, for Hilton, household furnishings in the west midlands of the thirteenth century were 'very simple'; he suggests that 'the poorer and richer households probably differed in the possession of these goods only as to quantity rather than as to quality', and that peasants were left 'underequipped' in terms of livestock and enjoyed only a poor diet.[90]

Such an emphasis is not as evident in more recent writing on peasant consumption, be that a discussion of consumption in the difficult years of the thirteenth century, or in the later fourteenth or fifteenth centuries when it is generally held that the standard of living rose. The move towards a history of peasant consumption in the middle ages has been led in the last thirty years by Christopher Dyer, whose earliest work on harvest worker diets extended into fuller considerations of standard of living, as well as a sustained attempt to draw together archaeology and history in ways intended to improve our understanding of features of peasant life not easily observed in the written record alone.[91] Thus, most obviously, work on housing, foodstuffs, animal products, clothing and other finished goods, as well as consumption of other kinds of consumable 'goods' including credit, law and legal advice, and learning, including religious learning both orthodox and heretical, have all been discussed in terms of peasant consumption. These are considered in greater detail in the final chapter of this book when we consider historical approaches to peasant culture.[92]

As Hatcher and Bailey note in their assessment of the key debates regarding change in the medieval economy, few historians working on the market and commerce in medieval England have offered 'tightly argued and empirical expositions comparable to those which have been written from the demographic and the Marxist perspectives'.[93] Rather than engaging with the significance of markets and commerce as factors in the development and transition of the medieval or feudal economy, most medievalists working on such topics in the last thirty or so years have tended to examine markets and exchange in their own terms, and above all to explore and to describe the range, depth and integrity of markets, peasant commercial activity and the nature of the rural economy. All such issues have potential application to the debates encouraged by Marxist historians, for instance, just as they also have great relevance for the earlier debates concerning the nature and condition of villeinage, but they have not been approached in such terms; this is not of course to say that historians working in the last generation have not been encouraged by these earlier debates to reflect anew upon the quality and history of commerce, trade and exchange in the medieval rural economy.

If few historians have as yet applied a commercial model of the kind outlined above to explanations of long-term change in the medieval economy, there have been some attempts to do so.[94] Richard Britnell, in concluding his study of commercialisation, noted that, while it was accepted that changing population levels had inevitable consequences for standards of living and social exchange in the middle ages, 'nevertheless, the scope of an historical model that simply relates population to resources, assuming static technology and a static institutional setting, is bound to be limited'.[95] As we also had cause to mention in Chapter 2, Langdon and Masschaele argue, in a recent article, that 'entrepreneurship' and the 'income-generating power of families' were defining criteria in explaining the potential significance of commerce as a driver of the medieval economy and population growth in the thirteenth century.[96] It is also sometimes assumed, and there are again some recent attempts to test the principle which were discussed more fully in Chapter 2, that the kind of limited technological advances that historians have begun to describe for the demesne sector may, to varying degrees, have also been applied amongst the peasantry.[97] Further to this discussion of limited economic advancement and its potential impact on longer-term economic and demographic change, Bruce Campbell has also made the observation that commercial expansion in an era of fragile markets generated vulnerability of a kind that made populations, both rural and urban, susceptible to crises in food availability. For the period before the Black Death, therefore, Campbell associates economic expansion with population expansion, as well as reflecting that any significant growth brought with it the risk of eventual collapse. Clark also draws similar conclusions from his analysis of wages relative to prices, as we have also discussed in an earlier chapter.[98] Campbell's recent discussion of the importance of factor markets (in labour, land and capital) also offers a new assessment of the potential importance of key elements of economic exchange in town and countryside and their possible significance in driving forward the medieval economy. His own conclusion, which is consistent with most relevant work in this area, is however that the respective factor markets were insufficiently developed in the period before the Black Death to offer more than a limited or 'sub-optimal' benefit to the developing medieval economy.[99] In ways that also associate demographic and economic factors in making sense of long-term change, a small group of historians have sought to associate declining fertility with changing labouring opportunities for young men and, especially, women.[100] In the following chapters, these themes will re-emerge, and will be considered in greater detail, as we turn to more particular aspects of the historiography of the medieval English peasantry. As we will see, even in their particularity of approach and their sometimes seemingly discrete agendas, study of demography, family structure, community and culture all respond to the broader discussions set out in these initial chapters.

Notes

1 See above, Chapter 2, pp. 60–1.
2 See above, Chapter 1, pp. 39–42.
3 W. Hudson, 'The prior of Norwich's manor of Hindolveston: its early organisation and the right of the customary tenants to alienate their strips of land', *Norfolk Archaeology* 20 (1919–20), 179–84.
4 E. Miller, *The abbey and bishopric of Ely. The social history of an ecclesiastical estate from the tenth to the early fourteenth century* (Cambridge: Cambridge University Press, 1951), pp. 148–53. See also, for instance, W.G. Hoskins, *The Midland Peasant. The economic and social history of a Leicestershire Village* (London: Macmillan, 2nd ed., 1965), pp. 52–3.
5 In fact, the extent to which market structures are capable of being admitted into a Marxist analysis is far from consistent; see, for instance, S.H. Rigby, 'Historical materialism, social structure, and social change in the middle ages', *Journal of Medieval and Early Modern Studies* 34 (2004), 493–8.
6 R.H. Hilton, *The economic development of some Leicestershire estates in the fourteenth and fifteenth centuries* (Oxford: Oxford University Press, 1947), p. 105.
7 R.H. Hilton, *The English peasantry in the later middle ages. The Ford lectures for 1973 and related studies* (Oxford: Oxford University Press, 1975), pp. 37–53.
8 Hilton, *English peasantry*, p. 37.
9 Hilton, *English peasantry*, p. 53.
10 R.H. Hilton, 'Low-level urbanization: the seigneurial borough of Thornbury in the middle ages', in Z. Razi and R. Smith, eds, *Medieval society and the manor court* (Oxford: Oxford University Press, 1996), pp. 482–517, and especially pp. 504, 515–16.
11 See, for instance, R.H. Hilton, *English and French towns in feudal society* (Cambridge: Cambridge University Press, 1992); also R.H. Hilton, 'Towns in English feudal society', in R.H. Hilton, *Class conflict and the crisis of feudalism. Essays in medieval social history* (London: Hambledon, 1985), pp. 175–86.
12 R. Brenner, 'Agrarian class structure and economic development in pre-industrial Europe', *Past and Present* 70 (1976), and 'Agrarian roots of European capitalism', *Past and Present* 97 (1982), both reprinted in T.H. Aston and

C.H.E. Philpin, eds, *The Brenner debate. Agrarian class structure and economic development in pre-industrial Europe* (Cambridge: Cambridge University Press, 1985), pp. 10–63; 213–327, from which subsequent citations are taken.
13 Brenner, 'Agrarian class structure', pp. 25–7.
14 Brenner, 'Agrarian roots of European capitalism', pp. 246–53.
15 Brenner, 'Agrarian roots of European capitalism', pp. 265–6, 293, 297.
16 R. Brenner, 'The origins of capitalist development: a critique of Neo-Smithian Marxism', *New Left Review* I (1977), 25–92 (quote at p. 45).
17 Brenner, 'Origins of capitalist development', p. 53.
18 See, for example, Brenner, 'Origins of capitalist development', pp. 78, 83.
19 R. Brenner, 'Property and progress: where Adam Smith went wrong', in C. Wickham, ed., *Marxist history writing for the twenty-first century* (Oxford: Oxford University Press, 2007), pp. 49–111.
20 Brenner, 'Property and progress', p. 79.
21 See above, Chapter 2, pp. 61–3.
22 See, for instance, M.M. Postan, 'Some agrarian evidence of declining population in the later middle ages', *Economic History Review* 2 (1950), reprinted in M.M. Postan, *Essays on medieval agriculture and general problems of the medieval economy* (Cambridge: Cambridge University Press, 1973), pp. 186–213.
23 See above, Chapter 2, pp. 63–77.
24 See, most obviously, J.A. Raftis, *Peasant economic development within the English manorial system* (Stroud: Sutton, 1997; first published Montreal: McGill-Queen's University Press, 1996); E. Britton, *The community of the vill: a study in the history of the family and village life in fourteenth century England* (Toronto: Pontifical Institute of Mediaeval Studies, 1977); E.B. DeWindt, *Land and people in Holywell-cum-Needingworth* (Toronto: Pontifical Institute of Mediaeval Studies, 1972); A.R. DeWindt, 'Redefining the peasant community in medieval England: the regional perspective', *Journal of British Studies* 26 (1987), 163–207.
25 Raftis, *Peasant economic development*, pp. 123–6.
26 Raftis, *Peasant economic development*, p. 123. See below, for instance, for discussion of a more commercial and market-orientated historiography dating from the 1980s and early 1990s, pp. 128–39.
27 Raftis, *Peasant economic development*, pp. 128–9.
28 DeWindt, *Land and people*.
29 DeWindt, *Land and people*, pp. 203, 277, 278.
30 DeWindt, *Land and people*, pp. 235–41; 244–50; 250–4, respectively.
31 DeWindt, *Land and people*, pp. 277–8.
32 See especially R.H. Britnell, *The commercialisation of English society, 1000–1500* (Cambridge: Cambridge University Press, 1993; republished by Manchester University Press, 1996), all subsequent references are taken from the 1993 edition; C. Dyer, *Standards of living in the later Middle Ages: social change in England c.1200–1520* (Cambridge: Cambridge University Press, 1989 and later edition); C. Dyer, 'The consumer and the market in the later middle ages', *Economic History Review*, 2nd series, 42 (1989), 305–27, reprinted in C. Dyer, *Everyday life*

in medieval England (London: Hambledon, 1994), pp. 257-81; C. Dyer, *An age of transition? Economy and society in England in the later middle ages* (Oxford: Oxford University Press, 2005), pp. 126-72. The response to such developments was slower elsewhere but has since evidently come to influence historical accounts of the medieval rural economy in other parts of Western Europe, as for instance in current investigation of consumption for medieval Spain; see the collection of papers on consumption at www.uv.es/consum/textos.htm, and the historiographical introduction which references the wider impact of the study of commercialisation for medieval England, www.uv.es/consum/historiographic.htm (last accessed 8 September 2014); relevant work has also been translated into Spanish: C. Dyer, *Niveles de vida en la Baja Edad Media. Cambios sociales en Inglaterra* (Barcelona: Primera, 1991). For a series of case-studies that illustrate differences in the perception of the nature of the medieval rural economy, see, for example, L. Feller and C. Wickham, eds, *Le marché de la terre au Moyen Âge* (Rome: École Française de Rome, 2005).

33 Dyer, *Age of transition?*, pp. 7-45, and especially pp. 40-5.
34 Dyer, *Standards of living*, pp. 6-8.
35 Dyer, *Standards of living*, pp. 109-18; 151-87.
36 Dyer, 'Consumer and the market'.
37 Dyer, 'Consumer and the market', pp. 280-1. On the non-agrarian presence in the countryside, see C. Dyer, 'L'industrie rurale en Angleterre des années 1200 à 1550: géographie, sociologie et organisation de la production et des marchés', in J.-M. Minovez, G. Verna and L. Hilaire-Pérez, eds, *Les industries rurales dans l'Europe médiévale et modern* (Toulouse: Presses Universitaires du Mirail, 2013), pp. 43-61. These are themes taken up by other historians in more recent years, as we shall see below.
38 See, for instance, C. Dyer, 'Furnishings of medieval English peasant houses: investment, consumption and life style', presently available on-line at www.uv.es/consum/dyer.pdf (accessed 10 September 2014).
39 See below, pp. 227-31; Chapter 8, pp. 138-9.
40 Britnell, *Commercialisation of English society*.
41 See, for instance, the reviews of Britnell, *Commercialisation of English society*, by L.R. Poos, *Journal of Historical Geography* 19 (1993), 345-6; also J.L. Bolton, *English Historical Review* 108 (1993), 971-3.
42 Britnell, *Commercialisation of English society*, p. 230; R.H. Britnell, 'Commercialisation and economic development in England, 1000-1300', in R.H. Britnell and B.M.S. Campbell, eds, *A commercialising economy. England, 1086 to c.1300* (Manchester: Manchester University Press, 1995), pp. 7-8.
43 P.R. Hyams, 'The origins of a peasant land market in England', *Economic History Review* 23 (1970), 19. It is tempting and indeed would be appropriate to include free land, held by peasants, within this categorisation. Some reference will be made to the market in peasant-held free land but it should be noted that the bulk of historical discussion of a peasant land market has been directed at a market in customary or villein land, the main source for which is the record of the manor court, the manor court roll.

44 See above, pp. 41–2, 117–18.
45 P.D.A. Harvey, ed., *The peasant land market in medieval England* (Oxford: Oxford University Press, 1984).
46 R.M. Smith, ed., *Land, kinship and life-cycle* (Cambridge: Cambridge University Press, 1984).
47 P.D.A. Harvey, 'Conclusion', in Harvey, ed., *Peasant land market*, pp. 352–3; for a fuller discussion of this work, see above, Chapter 2, pp. 75–6.
48 Harvey, 'Conclusion', pp. 344–7; 352–3.
49 Harvey, 'Conclusion', pp. 353–6.
50 R.M. Smith, 'Some issues concerning families and their property in rural England 1250–1800', in Smith, ed., *Land, kinship and life-cycle*, pp. 6–21.
51 See above, pp. 64–5, 74–5.
52 Smith, 'Families and their property', pp. 18–21.
53 See, for instance, Smith, 'Families and their property', p. 21; compare, for instance, Williamson, 'Norfolk: thirteenth century', in Harvey, ed., *Peasant land market*, pp. 104–5, where an accelerated market in land is explained in terms largely consistent with a population-driven view of the medieval economy, and above p. 76.
54 Smith, 'Families and their property', p. 22.
55 See above, pp. 65–6.
56 Hyams, 'Origins of a peasant land market', 20.
57 E. King, *Peterborough Abbey. 1086–1310. A study in the land market* (Cambridge: Cambridge University Press, 1973), pp. 110, 120–5, and especially p. 124 for discussion of the possible motive for peasant engagement in a land market: 'that their younger sons should have some small independent position; that their daughter should have a dowry'. These are points also noted by Smith in his own overview of the relevant historiography, Smith, 'Families and their property', pp. 13–16, who feels that King's discussion, along with some few others presented in the later 1960s and 1970s, had left 'Professor Postan's arguments basically unscathed' (p. 16).
58 B.F. Harvey, *Westminster Abbey and its estates in the middle ages* (Oxford: Oxford University Press, 1977), pp. 316–17.
59 C.D. Briggs, *Credit and village society in fourteenth-century England*, (Oxford: Oxford University Press, 2009), pp. 79–99; P.R. Schofield, 'Peasants and contract in the thirteenth century: village elites and the land market in eastern England', in P.R. Schofield and T. Lambrecht, *Credit and the rural economy in north-western Europe, c.1200–c.1800* (Turnhout: Brepols, 2009), pp. 129–52. For an earlier consideration of mortgages and landholding in the peasant land market, see also P.R. Schofield, 'Credit and debt in the medieval english countryside', in, Simonetta Cavaciocchi, ed., *Il Mercato della Terra. Secc. xiii–xviii* (Prato: Monash University, 2004), pp. 785–96; see also especially C. Briggs, 'Mortgages and the English peasantry c.1250–c.1350' available at www.hss.caltech.edu/~jlr/events/Briggs-EMGV.pdf (last accessed 7 July 2015).
60 P.R. Schofield, 'Dearth, debt and the local land market in a late thirteenth century Suffolk village', *Agricultural History Review* 45 (1997), 1–17; P.R. Schofield, 'The

social economy of the medieval village', *Economic History Review* 61 S1 (2008), 38-63.
61 B.M.S. Campbell, 'Inheritance and the land market in a fourteenth century peasant community" in Smith, ed., *Land, kinship and life-cycle*, pp. 87-134; R.M. Smith, 'Families and their land in an area of partible inheritance: Redgrave, Suffolk 1260-1320', in Smith, ed., *Land, kinship and life-cycle*, pp. 135-95.
62 A. Macfarlane, *The origins of English individualism* (Oxford: Blackwell, 1978).
63 For fuller discussion of which, see above, pp. 21-3.
64 See, for instance, J. Whittle, 'Individualism and the family-land bond: a reassessment of land transfer patterns among the English peasantry c.1270-1580', *Past and Present* 160 (1998), 25-63; P.R. Schofield, '*Extranei* and the tenure of customary land on a Westminster Abbey manor in the fifteenth century', *Agricultural History Review* 49 (2001), 1 16; Briggs, *Credit and village society*; Schofield, 'Peasants and contract'.
65 For which definition see N.J. Mayhew, 'Modelling medieval monetisation', in R.H. Britnell and B.M.S. Campbell, eds, *A commercialising economy. England 1086 to c.1300* (Manchester: Manchester University Press, 1995), p. 59.
66 See, for instance, N.J. Mayhew, 'Scotland: economy and society', in S.H. Rigby, ed., *Blackwell companion to later medieval Britain* (Oxford: Blackwell, 2002), p. 120.
67 B.M.S. Campbell, 'Benchmarking medieval economic development: England, Wales, Scotland, and Ireland, c.1290', *Economic History Review* 61 (2008), 940.
68 G.D. Snooks, 'The dynamic role of the market in the Anglo-Norman economy and beyond, 1086-1300', in Britnell and Campbell, eds, *A commercialising economy*, pp. 51-3.
69 Mayhew, 'Modelling medieval monetisation', p. 58; G.D. Snooks, 'Appendix 1: a note on the calculation of GDP and GDP per capita in 1086 and c.1300', in R.H. Britnell and B.M.S. Campbell, eds, *A commercialising economy. England, 1086 to c.1300* (Manchester: Manchester University Press, 1995), p. 195.
70 S. Broadberry, B. Campbell, A. Klein, M. Overton and B. van Leeuwen, 'British economic growth: 1270-1870' , available at www.lse.ac.uk/economicHistory/seminars/ModernAndComparative/papers2011-12/Papers/Broadberry.pdf (last accessed 20 September 2014), and for comment on the same, as well as a useful summary of current GDP estimates, N.J. Mayhew, 'Prices in England, 1170-1750', *Past and Present* 219 (2013), 34-5. See also now S. Broadberry, B.M.S. Campbell, A. Klein, M. Overton and B. van Leeuwen, *British economic growth, 1270-1870* (Cambridge: Cambridge University Press, 2015), p. 194, and for discussion of GDP and approaches to its measurement, pp. xxxii-xxxiv.
71 Broadberry *et al.*, *British economic growth*, pp. 197-208.
72 J. Masschaele, *Peasants, merchants and markets. Inland trade in medieval England, 1150-1350* (Basingstoke: Macmillan, 1997).
73 Masschaele, *Peasants, merchants and markets*, pp. 51-3.
74 Masschaele, *Peasants, merchants and markets*, pp. 53-4.
75 See below, Chapter 8, pp. 227-31.

76 M. Bailey, *A marginal economy? East Anglian Breckland in the later middle ages* (Cambridge: Cambridge University Press, 1989), pp. 115–42.

77 J. Bennett, *Ale, beer and brewsters in England. Women's work in a changing world, 1300–1600* (Oxford: Oxford University Press, 1996), and below, Chapter 5, pp. 187–8, 190–1.

78 See, for instance, Dyer, *Age of transition?*, pp. 91–2 and references there. See also H.E.J. Le Patourel, 'Documentary evidence of the medieval pottery industry', *Medieval Archaeology* 12 (1968), 101–26; also J. Birrell, 'Peasant craftsmen in the medieval forest', *Agricultural History Review* 17 (1969), 91–107.

79 I. Blanchard, 'The miner and the agricultural community in late medieval England" *Agricultural History Review* 20 (1972); J. Hatcher, *The English tin industry and trade before 1550* (Oxford: Oxford University Press, 1973), pp. 47, 58; there is a significant difference between Hatcher and Blanchard in their interpretation of the potential of industrial activity to generate engagement with wider economies, and the extent to which mining was at the core of an individual's economic activity: J. Hatcher, 'Myths, miners and agricultural communities', *Agricultural History Review* 22 (1974), 54–61; I. Blanchard, 'Rejoinder: Stannator fabulosus', *Agricultural History Review* 22 (1974), 62--4; see, also most recently, Dyer, 'L'industrie rurale en Angleterre'.

80 M. Kowaleski, *Local markets and regional trade in medieval Exeter* (Cambridge: Cambridge University Press, 1995); B.M.S. Campbell, J.A. Galloway, D. Keene and M. Murphy, *A medieval capital and its grain supply: agrarian production and distribution in the London region, c.1300* (London: Institute of British Geographers, 1993).

81 Campbell *et al.*, *A medieval capital and its grain supply*, pp. 139–44.

82 M. Threlfall-Holmes, *Monks and markets. Durham Cathedral Priory, 1460–1520* (Oxford: Oxford University Press, 2005), pp. 192–219; J.S. Lee, *Cambridge and its economic region, 1450–1560* (Hatfield: University of Hertfordshire Press, 2005).

83 See, in particular, P.R. Schofield, 'L'endettement et le crédit dans la campagne anglaise au moyen âge', in M. Berthe, ed., *Endettement paysan et crédit rural dans l'Europe médiévale et moderne. Actes des XVIIes journées internationales d'histoire de l'abbaye de Flaran, Septembre 1995* (Toulouse: Presses Universitaires du Mirail, 1998), pp. 69–97; Briggs, *Credit and village society*.

84 See below, pp. 156–67, 172–82.

85 Most obviously, M.M. Postan, 'Some agrarian evidence of declining population in the later middle ages', *Economic History Review* ii (1950), reprinted in M.M. Postan, *Essays on medieval agriculture and general problems of the medieval economy* (Cambridge, 1973), pp. 188–213; G. Clark, 'The long march of history: farm wages, population, and economic growth, England 1209–1869', *Economic History Review* 60 (2007), 97–135; for a recent summary, see P.R. Schofield, 'Salaires et salariés dans l'Angleterre médiévale: historiographie', in P. Beck, P. Bernardi and L. Feller, eds, *Rémunérer le travail au Moyen Âge, Pour une histoire sociale du salariat* (Paris: Picard, 2014), pp. 107–24.

86 For instance, J.P. Goldberg, *Women, work, and life-cycle in a medieval economy.*

Women in York and Yorkshire, c.1300–1520 (Oxford: Oxford University Press, 1992); H.S.A. Fox 'Exploitation of the landless by lords and tenants in early medieval England' in Razi and Smith, eds, *Medieval society and the manor court*, pp. 518–68.
87 J. Hatcher, 'England in the aftermath of the Black Death', *Past and Present* 144 (1994), 24.
88 Hatcher, 'England in the aftermath of the Black Death', 27–8.
89 J.E.T. Rogers, *A history of agriculture and prices in England* (Oxford, 7 volumes, 1866–1902), i, p. 66.
90 Hilton, *A medieval society*, pp. 94–113; quote at p. 105. The same is also true, unsurprisingly given the tenor of his comments on consumption, of Hilton's assessment of production, which he characterises as often a reduction in peasant family subsistence in order to meet obligations to 'lords and others', production for middle-ranking peasants essentially only a means to raise funds in order to pay for such basics as rent and taxes, *A medieval society*, p. 123.
91 Dyer, *Standards of living*.
92 See below, Chapter 8, pp. 227–31, 239–45.
93 M. Bailey and J. Hatcher, *Modelling the middle ages. The history and theory of England's economic development* (Oxford: Oxford University Press, 2001), p. 248.
94 For general discussion of commerce and the development of the medieval economy, see Brenner, 'Agrarian class structure', pp. 25–9; also J. Hatcher and M. Bailey, *Modelling the medieval economy. The history and theory of England's economic development* (Oxford: Oxford University Press, 2001), pp. 120–73.
95 Britnell, *Commercialisation*, p. 230.
96 J. Langdon and J. Masschaele, 'Commercial activity and population growth in medieval England', *Past and Present* 190 (2006), 35–81.
97 See above, Chapter 2, pp. 70–4.
98 Campbell, 'Agrarian problem'; Clark, 'Long march of history'; see also above, p. 74.
99 B.M.S. Campbell, 'Factor markets in England before the Black Death', *Continuity and Change* 24 (2009), 79–106.
100 See below, pp. 165–6.

PART II

Debates

In the following chapters, we will examine the ways in which debates or particular avenues of research have emerged from three main strands of research identified in the previous chapters. These chapters identify features of the relevant historiography that often relate to or respond to the major shifts in our understanding of the medieval peasantry. Some of these developments reflect an intensification or a deepening of research in relation to more general theories regarding the functioning of medieval rural society and economy. In these instances, it is reasonable to identify such development often as responses, both positive and negative, to prevailing themes within the historiography, either reinforcing a core thesis by adding depth and sophistication to their argument or challenging some major tenet through a more particular study. So, for example, a heightened focus on issues of demography and, most especially, social structure has encouraged greater scrutiny of such issues as household size and the relative significance of fertility and mortality within the medieval village. Similarly, much of the discussion of medieval peasant culture, in so far as that has been informed by one of the prevailing main historiographical themes, has emerged in relation to discussion of peasant agency, be that in terms of politics and the political engagement of the peasantry, in or beyond the manor, or in commercial exchanges involving peasants, as producers and consumers.

In other respects, some of the topics discussed in the chapters below have a history that predates any of the significant themes of the relevant historiography. Thus, the nineteenth-century study of the nature of the village community, conducted at a date much earlier than the flourishing of historical discussion of population, lord–tenant dispute or the role of the market in the medieval economy, was informed by other prevailing intellectual agendas, in this instance the chronology and process of emergent communities and the organisation of society over time. That said, and despite these antecedents, themes such as the nature of the village community re-emerge from time to time in relation to more current debates. For instance, the question of the nature and integrity of the village community has been examined in terms of disputes between lords and tenants as well as in relation to the discussion of the importance of the impersonal market within the medieval village and the preparedness of villagers to set aside a sense of communal obligation in favour of their own best interests.

Finally, it is also important to recognise that not all of the discussion as set out in the following chapters is dependent upon any of the three main defining agendas discussed in Part I of this volume. As we have already noted, some debates (as for instance that concerning the village community) predate these discussions. In other respects, historical investigation of themes relevant to our understanding of the medieval peasantry has been conducted by historians working, for the greater part, in other areas and often responding to other agendas. This is especially evident in the discussion of 'culture' and the peasantry, in the final chapter of this volume, in which consideration of both a wider political awareness and of religious activity and spirituality, themes highly germane to our understanding of the medieval peasantry, have mostly been undertaken by historians of politics and political society and of religion as part of their examination of such themes as the nature of the political community in the thirteenth century or the reception of orthodoxy and heresy in the later middle ages. In addition, it is also the case that some of the work outlined in the following chapters was undertaken by historians of the medieval peasantry and of rural society and economy without any or great regard for the prevailing orthodoxies regarding the nature and function of medieval economy and society. For instance, a good deal of the discussion of social structure, especially that carried out by Raftis and his colleagues and students in the 1960s and 1970s, was aimed more at illustrating the potential for a sociological investigation of the medieval village than it was to engage with the two significant and countervailing features of medieval social and economic history at that point, namely relations between lord and tenant and the importance of population change.

5

Demography and the medieval peasantry

The study of the medieval peasantry in demographic terms is new relative to other kinds of historical approach in this area. The history of population emerged as an academic subject in the second half of the twentieth century. It was, mostly, with the expansion of the subject range of the discipline of history in the 1960s that systematic demographic investigation of past societies was undertaken, and this was as true for the study of the medieval English countryside as for other research areas. Themes central to demography, most obviously identification and explanations of long-term change in population, were embraced by historians of medieval and, even more evidently, early modern society and applied, with various levels of success to sources from these periods. It is especially the case that sources from the early modern period, and notably parish registers for England, have sustained some of the most rigorous and demanding levels of analysis, particularly in terms of techniques such as family reconstitution and reconstruction of populations using 'back projection'.[1] In addition, explanations of long- and short-term change in population and in social structure, gleaned from population studies, as well as from early and significant demographic studies of later periods, have been reapplied in discussions of medieval society and have been applied to ongoing debates regarding economic change, its causes and its consequences.

As we shall discuss in what follows, a consequence of this demographically charged research and publication has been to shift, or at least to adjust, the more general agenda of historians. After c.1970 few medieval economic and social historians approaching the topic of the medieval peasantry could do so without including some discussion of the demography of their object of investigation. Furthermore, any such attempt needed to be couched in terms capable of being assimilated within the main parameters of debates regarding the relative importance of population and of key demographic variables upon the behaviour of the medieval economy. As such population estimates, mortality rates, life expectancy, sex ratios, the relative significance of fertility and mortality became staples of historical discussion of medieval society including the peasantry. While the introduction of new approaches to the study of medieval rural society reflects the significant input of techniques gleaned from population studies, a good deal of this more nuanced discussion of demographic and social structural themes in relation to medieval peasantries was not conducted *ab initio*: it would not be correct either to suggest that previous generations of historians had shown no interest in such matters or that the race into population history was conducted on new terms. Rather, almost all of the demographic and social structural study of the medieval English peasantry, while quite new in certain, largely methodological, respects, has been carried out within a pre-existing intellectual agenda focused upon the description and explanation of long-term change in the medieval English economy and society.

The introduction of subtle and involved demographic technique into the research of medievalists was dependent upon the development of the subject of demography and of an overlap between historians and demographers. The first stirrings of research relevant to the study of the medieval peasantry occurred, therefore, in the middle decades of the twentieth century when both demography as a subject took hold in the universities and history as a discipline widened its intellectual base, especially through the development of 'new social history'.[2] J.C. Russell, one of the most important exponents of historical demography in the middle decades of the twentieth century, had begun to consider the sources and approaches to the population history of the middle ages in the 1920s and 1930s while teaching relevant university courses in New Mexico. It is clear from references in his *British medieval population*, published in 1948 and the first survey of the topic, and the historiographical and broader intellectual context in which he sets his work that he was closely influenced by a variety of demographic work on past populations which was circulating, especially in the 1930s.[3] Russell's statements on the contemporary, that is the mid-twentieth-century, demographic history of the middle ages are instructive in the sense that he sets out what he considers to be the key issues confronting those studying, or yet to study, in this area. It is also evident that Russell was operating in what was largely virgin territory and that he approached his topic with great optimism, quite clearly placing some unreasonable expectations upon the relatively unresponsive medieval data at his disposal.[4] The main aim of this early research, as might be expected of all such work on past populations, was to chart population change and to explain that change in so far as it was possible so to do. In such an endeavour, there was a clear emphasis upon identifying the sorts of source material capable of supporting such an analysis.[5] Russell's own discussion of medieval demography, while certainly not confined to the sources of the social elites in this period, offers little comment on the rural population *per se* or the demography of the medieval English peasantry in particular. He does investigate sources issuing from rural communities, not least annual tithing payments by males over the age of twelve arising from the lord's jurisdiction over so-called frankpledge, but this is not discussed in the context of a rural-focused or peasant-focused demography.[6] While there is also implicit argument in Russell's main research, notably in his attempts to quantify change over time, the greater ambition in his work is to set out the available data and to establish the demographic foundations of the subject in this period.

A good deal of the 'demographic' discussion in studies of medieval rural society, even those completed after demographic history was a well-established sub-discipline, remained incidental to other established themes. Thus, for instance, some of the most significant estate and manorial studies of the 1960s, 1970s and 1980s admitted discussion of themes relevant to demographic history without losing a focus upon some of the more well-established issues already closely associated with the study of the medieval English peasantry, especially the interaction of lords and tenants. So, for instance, as part of a consideration of the importance of partibility on the Kentish estates of the lordship of Canterbury, F.R.H. DuBoulay attempts some estimates of childhood survival rates, suggesting that a sample of late medieval wills from Kent illustrate the relatively small number of potential heirs surviving at the time of testators made their wills.[7] John Hatcher's study of the Duchy of Cornwall estates in the later middle ages details fluctuation in the institution of parish priests as a proxy for movement in population over time and offers cautious comment and detail on both monthly mortality rates during the first onset of plague (which confirms the plague's presence in the Duchy in the middle of 1349) and longer-term mortality trends.[8] These discussions are however quite clearly set within a framework dominated by discussion of tenurial change and the movement of rent and of land; matters relevant to demographic themes, such as tenant death, inheritance and mobility, almost inevitably appear in such discussions though they do not dominate.[9]

It is also evidently the case that a growing number of authors of estate and local studies completed from the 1950s and, especially the 1970s and 1980s onwards, whilst continuing to locate discussion of demographic themes within the wider social and economic history of the period, subjected the main corpus of available material, especially but exclusively manorial documentation, to a greater level of investigation. If we take Christopher Dyer's study of the bishopric of Worcester as an example, we can see that he incorporates detailed discussion of population movement, as well as the annual behaviour of mortality and life-expectancy, into a study which has, at its core, a study of lord–tenant relations in the high and late middle ages. In fact, Dyer devotes significant portions of his text to discussion of population change and, in ways that reflect the broader themes of demographic discussion, consideration of the demographic variables that explain the trends in tenant numbers he describes.[10] The same is also the case for L.R. Poos's study of the county of Essex in the later middle ages which has at its heart discussion of demographic themes, including the relative significance of mortality and fertility in ordering medieval society as well as mobility and novel approaches to the identification of long- and short-term population change.[11] If then, by the later twentieth century, historians of the medieval village and rural society had certainly not lost contact with such established themes as the organisation of the estates, rent and the changing relationship of lord and tenant, and continued to write within a long-standing tradition founded upon local, manorial, estate or regional studies, it is also the case that in the last decades of the twentieth century the study of mortality, population movement and other important features associated with medieval demography was conducted more clearly upon its own terms and demanded its own place within the research agenda of those setting out to study the medieval village.

The intrusion of this agenda into more general studies of medieval rural society was encouraged initially by detailed and rather more particular studies of an intensely demographic kind. Central to this development was the research and writing of M.M. Postan. As we have already considered in an earlier chapter, M.M. Postan offered what was a relatively early foray into the discussion of medieval rural population, employing an explanation of population change and its significance as both an index and an explanation of changes in the high and later medieval English economy. While work previous to that of Postan, including discussion of medieval economy and society undertaken in the second half of the nineteenth century, had also considered the role and significance of population change and of key demographic events, especially the Black Death of the mid-fourteenth century, there was, of course, little in the way of close engagement with strictly demographic themes.[12] Here we will concentrate our attention on the emergence of a demographic study of the peasant which was coincident with the development of the modern study of past populations. Postan's main empirical work on medieval population was an investigation, in an article published with Jan Titow in 1959, of heriots (death-duty payments) of tenants of the bishop of Winchester; published at the outset of modern work on historical demography and drawing upon the expertise of a statistician, J. Longden, the article presents loosely demographic data and subjects it to 'demographical argument'.[13] Postan and Titow, in suggesting that the numbers of deaths rose and fell in accord with changing grain prices in the later thirteenth and early fourteenth century, compare their results with work on modern populations and engage with some of the structural concepts associated with demography, including the mortality rate and the age structure of the population. In this sense then, their work reflects a new engagement with medieval demography and the techniques associated with it.[14] It also reveals a desire to use medieval material in order to generate the sorts of evidence capable of sustaining particular lines of argument, in this case the ebbs and flows of population in relation to changing food prices in ways consistent with a population-resources model of the kind which Postan had already espoused.[15]

The analysis undertaken by Postan and Titow in the late 1950s lacks much in the way of direct engagement with other work on medieval demography and for the best of reasons: there really was very little comparable work with which to engage at that point.[16] However, within a relatively short period of time, fuller work on aspects of medieval demography, with considerable relevance to the study of the medieval English peasantry, had begun to emerge and in these later writings historians found opportunity to build upon and to respond to the earliest initiatives. As well as the particular historical arguments promoted by these historians, which we examine below, there are one or two features of this development which are especially worthy of note and reflect reasonably well-established patterns in the emergence and growth of disciplines and sub-disciplines. In the first place, detailed demographic study of the medieval peasantry has been confined to a relatively small number of practitioners, operating often within certain institutions, especially, though certainly not exclusively, the University of Cambridge and the Cambridge Group for the History of Population and Social

Structure, wherein there have developed certain intellectual traditions and approaches. There is therefore also a tendency, as with any subject area, for some demographic projects to be associated with certain individuals and their students, and for the development of methodological approaches and historical explanations to proceed hand-in-hand. In what follows, we can both chart some of these historiographical traditions and explore two distinct themes in the demographic investigation of the medieval countryside and of the peasantry. The first relates to attempts to describe the rural population of the middle ages in terms of absolute numbers, to set out change over time and to explain that change within demographic terms. Consideration of historical explanation 'within demographic terms' draws us into a second theme, namely the investigation of family and household, and the constituent elements of that investigation, namely as household structure, marriage and household formation. More correctly identified with research into social structure rather than with demography *per se*, discussion of this latter theme is admitted here in part because the practitioners of both the demography and social structure of the peasantry are often closely associated and, in no small way consequentially, study of either demography or social structure has clear significance for the study of the other.

It is the latter of these two broad themes, the investigation of social structure, which has attracted the greater investigation of historians interested in the medieval peasantry. The kinds of source material available for a detailed study of aspects of household formation, points to which we return below, are more abundant than are those sources which encourage detailed assessments of actual population. That said, and to begin with discussion of population estimates and attempts to quantify the population of the medieval English countryside, there have been some significant attempts to bring us closer to the population history of the medieval village.

Rural populations

In concluding his research into monastic populations and their mortality in the fifteenth century, John Hatcher concluded that the great challenge remained a similar investigation of the contemporary peasantry.[17] He suggested that, while a general investigation of the medieval peasantry would almost certainly remain beyond the reach of historians, it remains possible that detailed study of the wealthier peasant families, whose lives are better represented in our records, might come to furnish some relevant material.

To date, however, such studies remain few indeed while our ability to quantify larger populations remains highly limited.

Estimates of total population for a locale, region, or even medieval England in its entirety, remain relatively small in number. In what follows we will focus our attention on some of the more recent attempts to estimate populations, attempts which are, to varying degrees, couched in terms of modern demographic technique. The modern pursuit of total population figures is not without its antecedents and, while there has been a shift in terms of technique and certain parameters of the discussion, the broadest question – how many? – was explored by economic and social historians writing a century and more earlier.[18] More particularly, there was, near the very outset of the modern era of historical enquiry into society and economy, some quite involved discussion of medieval population, the nature of population change and its impact upon, amongst other things, the rural economy. In the nineteenth century, both Rogers and Seebohm had expressed the firm conviction that the mid-fourteenth-century plague outbreak and its consequent excessive mortality had caused a revolution in English agrarian organisation; for the purposes of the present discussion, however, especially striking in Rogers's discussion of the extent of the medieval population was his attempt to base his estimate upon another necessary element, that is, the overall extent of food available to feed the population. In this respect Rogers's work offers an unusually early attempt to calculate population figures for the middle ages in relation to estimates of resources, a theme, as we have already discussed, which was highly relevant to later considerations of medieval population.[19] Rogers argued that any estimation of total population figures and an explanation of its change were necessarily to be based upon a close consideration of the changing context of the medieval countryside. This was true in a number of respects: for instance, in terms of the resources which could sustain the population, the significant proportion of the total population which lived in the countryside in the middle ages, and the degree to which that population was dependent upon local or regional agrarian output. In recent years, one historian, Bruce Campbell, has returned to this same approach and, using evidence for agrarian output gleaned for the greater part from manorial accounts, has offered his own estimates of the English population c.1300 and c.1375.[20] Campbell stresses the importance of the yield data, rather than extrapolation from taxation data, for estimating population and concludes that population in England in the fourteenth century was, at least c.1300, significantly lower than a number of previous estimates have suggested. While Campbell's initial estimate for a population of 4 to 4.25 million c.1300, which he has recently adjusted upwards as discussed below, was greater than J.C. Russell's estimate of 3.7 million, it was substantially lower than the possibility of a population of or greater than 6 million proposed by most other commentators including M.M. Postan, John Hatcher and Richard Smith.[21] Important for the present discussion, Campbell's calculations rest upon a large amount of data extracted from accounts and subjected to close statistical analysis in ways largely distinctive from other, earlier and more regionally focused studies. In this sense at least Campbell's discussion of the extent of a general population offers a departure in terms of its sophistication. Yet, in other respects, Campbell's analysis remained highly dependent upon an earlier historiography not least in his employment of estimates of, or lack of clarity as regards, yield on land held by peasants.[22] The difficulty of identifying with any degree of accuracy such totals is perhaps best illustrated by the degree of honing which Campbell has himself applied to his figures and, most recently, he has recognised that new and higher estimates of the total arable acreage in the later thirteenth century argue against his own lower population estimates. So, rather than 4.25 million hectares feeding a maximum of 4.5 million persons, as Campbell originally suggested, Campbell and Barry now propose that, c.1290, 5.3 million hectares may have fed 4.75 million people, assuming 'a daily diet of around 1,400 grain-based kilocalories'.[23] Campbell's estimates have in any case been subjected to challenge from bases other than arable acreage alone, notably by David Stone, who has proposed revised figures for national grain acreage allied to estimates of peasant productivity and, thereby, a higher population total c.1300. Stone argues, from his own extrapolations, for a population c.1300 of 5.46 million, a figure closer to traditional estimates of the medieval English population maximum set out above.[24]

Despite these few exercises in estimation, only a small number of historians writing since the nineteenth century have in fact ventured into discussion of national population trends or offered estimates of the total population in the medieval English countryside. Instead, for manors and villages there have been estimates based upon estate documentation and, most especially, head counts drawn from the appearance of identified individuals in manorial court records.[25] H.E. Hallam, notably, attempted population estimates for individual manors in thirteenth-century Lincolnshire. Using what the author terms 'censuses' of some of the unfree tenants of the Prior of Spalding, as well as surveys of local townships, Hallam is, *inter alia*, prepared to offer quite detailed estimates of the total population and, from there, to consider the explanations for differing patterns of population on neighbouring manors, as well as the significance of the population densities he detects.[26] Hallam's work illustrates the potential of medieval sources to shed light on medieval populations and overall numbers but his research is also illustrative of the pitfalls associated with extrapolation from what remain highly limited sources.[27] Hallam's techniques also reveal his research, conducted in the 1950s and early 1960s, to be of its time rather than ahead of it, not least in the fairly basic analysis to which his data was subjected, chiefly counting individuals by defined groups within the original source, and the strong sense he encourages that the goal of identifying an average household size is realisable. Above all, the particular contextual assumptions in which Hallam's work is located is revealed in his uncertainty as regards a whole series of potentially significant variables, including the availability of different grain types, cropping practices and peasant consumption patterns. While not all of these matters have been resolved in the decades since Hallam wrote, historians are now more fully aware of such issues and their applicability to the rural society at the heart of Hallam's research.

It is only in the last generation or so, and especially since the 1980s, that some historians have attempted more thorough estimates of total populations for the medieval village. Most obviously, Zvi Razi has pursued the possibility of using court records to calculate the total population of a manor and, by extension, of a village. Razi's argument in short is that excellent court roll series, of the kind that have survived for the west midlands manor of Halesowen or the Norfolk manor of Gressenhall, both subjects of his own study, permit reasonably solid estimates of total populations within a locale, or at least estimates of cohorts within the same location.[28] By sampling names over fixed periods of time, Razi was encouraged to the view that virtually all adult villagers were likely to be identified as a result of their all but inevitable appearance in the court rolls in some or other context.[29] His initial method of recording all individuals in the rolls, cross-referencing names in order to establish a prosopographical listing and thereby to identify individuals and reconstitute families, relied on little more in the way of technique than would have been available to historians engaged in similar work at the beginning of the twentieth century; in fact, as he makes clear, his initial sifting of tens of thousands of entries for Halesowen, undertaken in the 1970s, was completed without the use of a computer.[30] What was distinctive about Razi's work, in comparison with those earlier works which had included estimates of populations, was both the scale of his enterprise and his deliberate focus upon demographic themes. This latter point certainly reflects the rise of historical demography, as does Razi's interest in such methods as family reconstitution. We will return to other elements of Razi's demographic analysis later in this chapter; for now we can note that Razi was able to propose total population figures for Halesown by treating the main source for the manor, a series of manorial court rolls, as a census-type document. This allowed him to estimate total populations on the basis of counts of those attending the court from the later thirteenth century to the end of the fourteenth century, and to describe long-term trends in population.[31] His estimates suggest that, contrary to Postan's prediction of a Malthusian pre-plague slump following the famines of the first decades of the fourteenth century, population continued to grow into the early to mid-fourteenth century, that it was significantly reduced by plague (with approximately 40 per cent mortality), recovered slightly thereafter but was in a further decline by the end of the fourteenth century.[32] A decade or more later, Ray Lock also attempted some limited prosopographical reconstruction and simple counting of individuals recorded in manorial court rolls in order to offer estimates of manorial population for the manor of Walsham-le-Willows (Suffolk), as well as the proposed age structure of the population and its potential mortality rates. His population estimates were constructed from extrapolations based upon identified tenant numbers and, as he notes, reflect a considerable potential range.[33] The same kind of difficulties of extrapolation are also noted by Martin Ecclestone who uses lists of landless tenants, *garciones*, on the estates of Glastonbury Abbey to estimate life expectancy for adult males in the decades immediately before the arrival of plague in the mid-fourteenth century and to identify the kinds of variable mortality rates identifiable in other case-studies of manors.[34] One of these, and also one of the last significant attempts to estimate local population totals, was undertaken in the 1980s by Poos, who, adopting quite a different approach from those of Razi and Lock, drew upon data drawn from the records of frankpledge jurisdictions, and in particular tithing lists and tithing penny payments, to extract broad figures of local population totals as well as evidence for their change over time. As well as employing quite different and relatively rare source material, Poos's research illustrates the ways in which recent work in this area has adopted some of the techniques of modern population studies, in particular in this case the use of life-tables in order to 'model' total populations.[35] Using both data from tithing lists and payments allied to taxation records and the 1377 poll-tax as well as information from Tudor lay subsidy and muster rolls, Poos was able to use the basic count of tax-payers and tithing members in relation to model life-tables both to construct total population estimates and to compare the capacity of different source types to deliver such information.³⁶ His broad conclusion is that, for Essex at least, most of the previously assumed general patterns of population movement hold firm, namely population growth into the fourteenth century, severe mortality in the famine of the early fourteenth century and especially as a result of the Black Death, and, despite hints at post-plague recovery, general stagnation in the later fourteenth and fifteenth centuries.³⁷

It is also clear that few historians have been drawn into detailed work on local population history of this kind. In fact, an important refrain in this more recent discussion of the demography of the medieval peasant, and no doubt one of the reasons why few have headed in this direction of research, has been the weaknesses of the relevant sources, and especially manorial court rolls, relative to the ambitions of the intellectual agenda. While Razi's discussion of the population history of medieval Halesowen was an important and pioneering study it did not generate a major body of further research in the same area; instead it prompted a methodological debate over the capacity of manorial court rolls to accommodate medieval demographers' research designs. The rather involved discussion, initially conducted in the journal *Law and History Review*, took place between Razi, who argued the case for manorial court rolls as a prime source for population estimates of medieval rural society, and Poos and Smith, who cautioned against too great a trust in their demographic usefulness. Poos and Smith suggested that comparison of the court roll evidence with ancillary material, such as rentals, and recognition that the material recorded in manorial courts lacked consistency over time, served at least to illustrate the potential pitfalls of this area of research; it also served to engage the readership in consideration of the legal and administrative development of local court records.³⁸ Reflection on the technicalities and intricacies of the discussion has, in the end, replaced and indeed subverted the original ambition, namely to quantify such populations; the earlier optimistic attempts of historians such as Hallam, Russell and, latterly, Razi have been curtailed by those historical demographers who have, in pointing out the significant shortfalls of the relevant material, served to direct the researcher elsewhere. Instead, historians of the medieval village, while not entirely eschewing the hunt for estimates of total population, have been more inclined to discuss population movement within identifiable cohorts, those cohorts defined by the available sources and, by extension, the institutional structures which determined them. In doing so, they have thereby presented themselves with opportunities both to describe demographic developments, which may or may not apply to a wider population, and also to consider the reasons for such movements.

Rural population: change and its causes

Most obvious in this respect has been discussion of peasant mortality. Postan and Titow's study of mortality on the estates of the bishop of Winchester in the decades either side of 1300, already briefly considered in this chapter, was one of the first, but certainly not the first, attempt to quantify mortality in the medieval countryside and to examine changing mortality levels over time. Earlier work, including late nineteenth-century writing on the Black Death and its impact, had already identified the potential for investigation of the mortality of rural dwellers.[39] Research by M.M. Postan and Jan Titow and, separately, by Sylvia Thrupp, in the 1950s and 1960s, introduced the discussion of a more technical and demographic kind, including examination of crude annual death rates, replacement rates and life expectancy, into historical investigation of medieval rural society.[40] We have already had cause to note the pioneering role of Postan and Titow's work on mortality on the estates of the bishop of Winchester in the thirteenth and early fourteenth centuries. Here we can also recognise that their study of death-duty payments by tenants (heriots) introduced a level of technical discussion which brought the study of the medieval peasantry to the attention of social scientists. So, for instance, the research of Postan and Titow, as well as the contribution of the statistician, Longden, who worked with the authors on this material, was subjected to further statistical analysis in 1966 by Goran Ohlin, who in particular questioned some of the data selection choices made; in Ohlin's opinion these may have led to weak or unsubstantiated assumptions regarding the mortality experience of the poorer tenants.[41] In turn, Ohlin's own comments were subsequently explored by Loschky and Childers in 1993, in ways that moved further beyond close examination of the raw data or the period itself but closer to a technical discussion of the crude death rates, which, using comparative data, they identify as high for the period before plague and in comparison to the lower early modern death rate.[42] Sylvia Thrupp's analysis of replacement rates and the construction of limited peasant biographies, both of which provide certain limited views into mortality patterns, offered a similarly pioneering attempt to exploit manorial court rolls in order to chart the behaviour of local populations in this period. Including as it does, some direct reference to other work on the same issues in later populations, including that on early modern France, Thrupp's work is essentially a counting exercise, identifying and enumerating heirs across generations, allied to some extrapolation from that data. While there is little in the way of statistical sophistication and some clear concern that the data cannot sustain the kind of research questions aimed at it, and quite possibly there is little call for greater sophistication given the size of the samples and the problems of suitability and robustness of the sources for an exercise of this kind,[43] Thrupp's discussion does introduce the study of replacement rates into the relevant corpus of study and, as she explains, allows her to set some more loosely demographic data against the more established economic models of change in this period. In famously concluding that the later middle ages were, if anything, a 'golden age of bacteria' she also called for further research in this area which she hoped would test her own conclusions.

It was Zvi Razi who most obviously responded to that call.[44] As we have already had cause to mention, Razi has attempted what remains the most detailed demographic investigation of manorial court rolls to be published.[45] While a significant amount of his discussion does not concern mortality, but covers such themes as household formation and marriage (to which return will be made below), he does have a good deal to say about mortality, its measurement and its significance in the medieval village. Couching his discussion, for the period before the Black Death, in terms of the behaviour of population and directly engaging with Postan's assertion that population growth would, irrespective of the arrival of plague, have inevitably been reversed through lack of sufficient resource, Razi argues that localised, empirically based studies, such as his own of Halesowen, offer a means of testing the broader assertions which, according to him, were typically applied to the population history of the period. In his analysis of population movement before, during and after the Black Death, Razi makes use of a series of fairly straightforward statistical devices in order to examine his material and to assert that mortality was, throughout the period a key determinant, though not the only determinant, of local population movement. As in earlier work, such as that by Postan and Titow discussed above, as well as the earlier article of Sylvia Thrupp, Razi employs an arrangement of argument and of themes partly drawn from the social sciences.[46] In his discussion of mortality, Razi offers a calculation of a crude average mortality rate, based upon observable tenant deaths, and also presents data on mortality crises, especially those associated with harvest failures of the late thirteenth and early fourteenth centuries and plague and its recurrence from the mid-fourteenth century onwards.[47] In analysing evidence for mortality, Razi makes use of records of tenant deaths, heriot payments, and in doing so tends to record total numbers of deaths by year, or by slightly longer period, in order to 'smooth' the data and thereby reduce problems of interpretation related to the original recording of the data.⁴⁸ Razi draws attention to the years of, what he deems to be, crisis mortality, especially periods associated with significant food shortage in the later thirteenth and early fourteenth centuries as well as the first outbreak and recurrence of epidemic disease in the middle years of the fourteenth century.

In addition to his consideration of such crisis mortality, Razi also offers some more general comment on what might be referred to as background mortality, the average or 'constant' mortality regime within which context the extent of the crises can be measured. One such potential measure, the calculation of the male replacement rate, is used by Razi in his study of general and crisis mortality at Halesowen in this period. Employing a method also used by Thrupp in her own earlier work on replacement rates in medieval rural society, Razi, by counting the number of male heirs who succeeded their fathers, sought to establish the changing capacity of families to reproduce their membership. In doing so he detected a significant difference either side of the Black Death of the mid-fourteenth century in the proportion of sons who came to replace their fathers.⁴⁹ As Razi notes and also seeks to explain within his broader thesis, the decline in the replacement rate across the century – a reduction in the number of available male heirs in the second half of the fourteenth century – may be as much a consequence of changed patterns of geographical mobility as of mortality, a point to which we will return later in this chapter. For now, we should note that Razi's attempt to calculate replacement rates is one of only a very few undertaken by historians of medieval rural society to estimate the level of mortality relative to fertility. Intriguingly, Razi also seeks to illustrate mortality in relation to life expectancy; his estimates of life expectancy are also based upon close investigation of movement of property through inheritance allied to estimates of age at inheritance and of the relative life expectancy of differing socio-economic cohorts within the manor. His estimates of life expectancy, based though they are upon some potentially problematic inferences, indicate that the crude annual death rate at Halesowen in the later thirteenth and early fourteenth centuries was typically at a level consistent with endemic crisis (his estimate stands at 36 to 40 deaths per thousand members of the population).⁵⁰

While, as we have seen, Razi was able to offer a depth and detail of analysis hitherto unknown in the demographic study of the medieval peasantry, it was other historians, especially Razi's near contemporary, Richard Smith, and Smith's student, L.R. Poos, who brought a new methodological rigour and sophistication to this area of study. As already noted in this chapter, Smith and Poos challenged the methodological underpinnings to some of Razi's work in reconstructing population estimates from manorial court rolls and in a quite vigorous debate both sides sought to show the durability (Razi) and the relative fluidity (Smith and Poos) of court rolls as a foundation for demographic work of this kind.[51] Poos also, in his study of early fourteenth-century mortality employed demographic modelling techniques, including the use of model life-tables in order to establish the general demographic patterns in this period of study and to confirm the basic trends evident from contemporary sources.[52] Using tithing lists and associated tithing penny payments,[53] Poos's findings suggest significant surges of mortality in the famine years of the early fourteenth century and mortality in the region of 45 per cent during the Black Death in the mid-fourteenth century. While not inconsistent with other crisis mortality estimates for the period, both in terms of the particular sources he has located and the employment of comparative techniques in establishing their usefulness, Poos's study adds to our understanding of the general chronology of crisis mortality as well as the variety of experience of local communities especially in non-crisis years.[54]

By contrast, sources for the study of the medieval economy and society provide relatively little insight into fertility, in comparison to evidence available for discussion of mortality. Unlike the examination by historians of peasant deaths, which is fairly abundant even in relevant research from the later nineteenth and early twentieth centuries, there is little or no reference to fertility, birth-rates and such proxies as nuptiality in the same works. Instead, it was only, in the second half of the twentieth century, with the introduction of an agenda established beyond the 'normal' research range of medievalists working in this area that a topic such as fertility came to be an object of discussion for historians working on the medieval English peasantry. Above all, it was the work of historians at the Cambridge Group for the History of Population and Social Structure which defined the terms of debate for historians working on the medieval rural population. Wrigley and Schofield's investigation of the population history of England and Wales from the sixteenth century through to the nineteenth century had illustrated the significance of birth-rate relative to death-rate for the behaviour of the post-medieval population.[55] Historians working on the demography of medieval society were encouraged by such work to seek similar evidence, especially for the later middle ages, in order both to map population movement in the fifteenth century against the more robust evidence of the sixteenth century and, more generally, to examine changing fertility patterns in this period. Thus, for instance, L.R. Poos has tried to identify fertility rates by using the few surviving churching records from fifteenth-century Essex while P.J.P. Goldberg has employed church court litigation in relation to female life-cycle service to suggest patterns of delayed nuptiality and fertility.[56] Richard Smith also, through investigation of marriage and the reception of the canon law of marriage within an English context, has sought to emphasise the close association of nuptiality with fertility, and thereby the relative insignificance of extra-marital births; thus, while marital registration data do not exist for medieval England, reference to age at marriage might be taken as an approximate index of a fertility-rate, with marriage perceived as or near the onset of individual fertility.[57]

The historical focus upon fertility as a theme capable of study in this period is in part a product of research upon women and the nature of female employment in this period. Most obviously, some of the main contributors to discussion of fertility as a demographic determinant in this period have also been closely involved in the study of women in the middle ages more generally. Goldberg has, chiefly through his study of women in and around medieval York, examined the changing female employment patterns in this period. Goldberg's study is important in that it defines the development of female employment in the later middle ages and illustrates the gendered distinctions evident in the economic relationship between town and countryside. He identifies important shifts in the chronology of such developments, in the later fourteenth and fifteenth centuries, as well as recognising their regional distinctiveness, and argues for a significant degree of female choice in terms of employment and marriage in the later middle ages, a factor that had important implications for fertility as women worked longer, for better pay and, as a consequence and in a manner contrary to the 'logic' of a post-plague recovery in which improved opportunity might be expected to encourage early marriage and child-rearing, delayed marriage and first pregnancy.[58] Poos's discussion of rural Essex in the later middle ages also encourages him to the view that a combination of employment structures, including a high prevalence of life-cycle service and a significant degree of mobility consistent with such kinds of employment, added to perceived neolocality (i.e. a coincidence of marriage and the establishment of new households through marriage followed by, rather than preceded by, childbirth), supported a fertility-led demographic regime in this period.[59]

Such attempts have certainly not been without their critics; both Bailey and Hatcher have chastised historians for their eagerness to 'back-project' the proposed demographic regime of the early modern period into the middle ages and have questioned the capacity of the medieval sources to admit any such investigation.[60] In fact, while historians have been inventive in their pursuit of material which might permit some purchase on fertility, it is evident that no medieval source for the study of the peasantry will permit the kinds of investigative techniques, including statistical modelling based on extensive census-type data, including parish registers recording births, marriages and deaths utilised by demographic historians working on later periods, or indeed on particular cohorts for the middle ages.[61] If the net effect of this assault upon the demographic potential of court roll series and ancillary documentation has not been to close discussion of this area, it has at least encouraged would-be researchers to exercise extreme caution in venturing into this terrain. Allied to some or all of the external pressures which have come to bear upon research agendas and which were discussed at the outset of this volume, changes in historiographical fashion have seen a diminution in the number of such specialist studies. It remains highly probable, however, that new approaches, especially the bringing together of various source types in order to confront particular research questions, and a melding of pre-existing work will see further, if perhaps often occasional, developments in the population history of the peasantry. More extensive to date has been work in the often allied subjects, sometimes undertaken by the same groups of researchers and with approaches also issuing from the social sciences; this is especially the case for examination and discussion of social and familial structure, topics to be considered in the next chapter.

Notes

1 R.M. Smith, 'Demography and medicine', in W.F. Bynum and R. Porter, eds, *Companion encyclopedia of the history of medicine* (2 vols, London: Routledge, 1993), ii, pp. 1663–92; also E.A. Wrigley and R. Schofield, *The population history of England, 1541–1871: a reconstruction* (Cambridge: Cambridge University Press, 1981).
2 R. Harrison, 'The "new social history" in America', in P. Lambert and P.R. Schofield, eds, *Making history: an introduction to the history and practices of a discipline* (London: Routledge, 2004), pp. 109–20.
3 J.C. Russell, *British medieval population* (Albuquerque: The University of New Mexico Press, 1948).
4 See, for instance, Russell's detailed estimates of infant mortality; extrapolated for the total population, they draw almost exclusively upon a small sample of proof of age inquests, Russell, *British medieval population*, pp. 208–14. Cf. T.H. Hollingsworth, *Historical demography* (Cambridge: Cambridge University Press, 1969), p. 58, who notes that 'Russell's chief virtue ... is that he gives others something to refute'.

5   See, generally, on this point, Hollingsworth, *Historical demography*, passim.
6   Russell, *British medieval population*.
7   F.R.H. DuBoulay, *The lordship of Canterbury. An essay on medieval society* (London: Nelson, 1966), pp. 159–60.
8   J. Hatcher, *Rural economy and society in the duchy of Cornwall, 1300–1500* (Cambridge: Cambridge University Press, 1970), pp. 102–3, 292–4.
9   See also, for instance, B.F. Harvey, *Westminster Abbey and its estates in the middle ages* (Oxford: Oxford University Press, 1977); P.D. Harvey, *A medieval Oxfordshire village. Cuxham, 1240–1400* (Oxford: Oxford University Press, 1965), pp. 113–40.
10 C.C. Dyer, *Lords and peasants in a changing society: the estates of the bishopric of Worcester, 680–1540* (Cambridge: Cambridge University Press, 1980), pp. 218–35.
11 L.R. Poos, *A rural society after the Black Death: Essex 1350–1525* (Cambridge: Cambridge University Press, 1991), pp. 89–179.
12 See above, Chapter 1, pp. 42–4.
13 M.M. Postan and J.Z. Titow, 'Heriots and prices on Winchester manors', *Economic History Review* 11 (1959); reprinted in .M. Postan, *Essays on medieval agriculture and general problems of the medieval economy* (Cambridge: Cambridge University Press, 1973), p. 151.
14 For a criticism of aspects of their technique from within the demographic community, see G. Ohlin, 'No safety in numbers: some pitfalls of historical statistics', in R. Floud, ed., *Essays in quantitative economic history* (Oxford: Oxford University Press, 1974), pp. 68–90, and below, p. 162.
15 See above, Chapter 2, pp. 61–3.
16 The work of G.C. Homans, conducted in the 1930s and 1940s, includes, in a discussion that is essentially sociological, themes of great relevance to demographers, especially marriage, inheritance and family structure. Homans had, however, little direct research interest in the demographic implications of his research. For discussion of Homans, see above, pp. 5–6, 11, 75, and below, Chapter 6, pp. 174–5, 178–80, and Chapter 7, pp. 205–6.
17 J. Hatcher, 'Mortality in the fifteenth century: some new evidence', *Economic History Review* 39 (1986), 38.
18 See above, Chapter 1, pp. 43–4.
19 See Chapter 2, pp. 61–3. There was also some investigation of total and local populations conducted much earlier, as Russell points out in reflecting on seventeenth- and eighteenth-century estimates of medieval population, Russell, *British medieval population*, pp. 7–8. See also the same for further discussion of efforts to calculate total populations using the poll-taxes of the later fourteenth century, *British medieval population*, pp. 9–10.
20 B.M.S. Campbell, *English seigniorial agriculture 1250–1450* (Cambridge: Cambridge University Press, 2000), pp. 386–410.
21 Campbell, *English seigniorial agriculture*, p. 402; and see especially table 8.06 (p. 403) and references there to previous population estimates.
22 Campbell, *English seigniorial agriculture*, p. 404.

23 B.M.S. Campbell and L. Barry, 'The population geography of Great Britain c.1290: a provisional reconstruction', in C. Briggs, P.M. Kitson and S.J. Thompson, eds, *Population, welfare and economic change in Britain, 1290-1834* (Woodbridge: Boydell, 2014), pp. 51-2; see also S. Broadberry, B.M.S. Campbell, A. Klein, M. Overton and B. van Leeuwen, *British economic growth, 1270-1870* (Cambridge: Cambridge University Press, 2015), pp. 20-1.
24 D. Stone, 'The consumption of field crops in late medieval England', in C. Woolgar, D. Serjeantson and T. Waldron, eds, *Food in medieval England: diet and nutrition* (Oxford: Oxford University Press, 2006), pp. 19-21. See also the discussion above, Chapter 2, pp. 72-4, and the brief but highly relevant discussion in S.H. Rigby, 'Introduction. Social structure and economic change in late medieval England', in R. Horrox and W.M. Ormrod, eds, *A social history of England, 1200-1500* (Cambridge: Cambridge University Press, 2006), pp. 25-7.
25 The first such attempts, again, predate the introduction of modern demographic technique into the study of the medieval peasantry, for discussion of which see above, Chapter 1, pp. 43-4.
26 H.E. Hallam, 'Some thirteenth-century censuses', *Economic History Review* 10 (1957-58), 340-1; H.E. Hallam, 'Population density in medieval Fenland', *Economic History Review* 14 (1961), 71-81.
27 Hallam's analysis has been criticised from more than one quarter: J.C. Russell, 'Demographic limitations of the Spalding serf lists', *Economic History Review* 15 (1962), 138-44; R.M. Smith, 'Hypothèses sur la nuptialité en Angleterre aux xiiie-xive siècles', *Annales: Economies, Sociétés, Civilisations* 38 (1983), 107-36, suggests that rather than listings of family members the Spalding lists are genealogies and not therefore an accurate index of actual family size.
28 Z. Razi, *Life, marriage and death in a medieval parish. Economy, society and demography in Halesowen, 1270-1400* (Cambridge: Cambridge University Press, 1980), pp. 2-3; Z. Razi, 'Manorial court rolls and local population: an East Anglian case study', *Economic History Review* 49 (1996), 758-63.
29 A conclusion which was soon subjected to vigorous challenge by Poos and Smith; see below.
30 Razi, *Life, marriage and death*, pp. 23-4; Razi calculated that he reconstituted 1,041 families using more than forty thousand separate pieces of information, *Life, marriage and death*, p. 83.
31 Razi, *Life, marriage and death*, pp. 24-6. Razi made similar efforts with material for the Norfolk manor of Gressenhall: Razi, 'Manorial court rolls and local population', and see especially, p. 762, 'periodic counts of males appearing in Gressenhall court rolls, and in other similar high-quality court records, can provide crude but nonetheless reliable data for estimating population'.
32 Razi, *Life, marriage and death*, pp. 30-2, 106, 116-17.
33 R. Lock, 'The Black Death in Walsham-le-Willows', *Proceedings of the Suffolk Institute of Archaeology and History* 37 (1992), 316-37.
34 M. Ecclestone, 'Mortality of rural landless men before the Black Death: the Glastonbury head-tax lists', *Local Population Studies* 63 (1999), 6-29.

35 L.R. Poos, 'The rural population of Essex in the later middle ages', *Economic History Review* 38 (1985), 515–30.
36 For other attempts to calculate local populations, or at least fluctuations in population numbers, using tithing data, see, for example M. Mate, 'The occupation of the land. H. Kent and Sussex', in E. Miller, ed., *The agrarian history of England and Wales*, vol. iii *1350–1500* (Cambridge: Cambridge University Press, 1991), pp. 127–8; Russell, *British medieval population*, pp. 226–7.
37 Poos, 'Rural population', 526–30.
38 A debate republished as L.R. Poos, Z. Razi and R.M. Smith, 'The population history of medieval English villages: a debate on the use of manor court records', in Z. Razi and R. Smith, eds, *Medieval society and the manor court* (Oxford: Oxford University Press, 1996), pp. 298–368.
39 See above, Chapter 1, pp. 42–4.
40 Postan and Titow, 'Heriots and prices'; S. Thrupp, 'The problem of replacement rates in late medieval English population', *Economic History Review*, 2nd series, 18 (1965).
41 Ohlin, '"No safety in numbers"', 68–90.
42 D. Loschky and B.D. Childers, 'Early English mortality', *Journal of Interdisciplinary History* 24 (1993), 85–97, especially pp. 86, 89.
43 For critical comment, see J. Hatcher, *Plague, population and the English economy, 1348–1530* (London and Basingstoke: Macmillan, 1977), p. 28.
44 Thrupp, 'Problem of replacement rates', 101–19, and especially 117–18.
45 Razi, *Life, marriage and death*. Other, unpublished studies also offered highly sophisticated demographic analyses of the medieval village, and were clearly reflective of the same broad trend in historiographical development. See, for instance, R.M. Smith, 'English peasant life-cycles and socio-economic networks: a quantitative geographical case study' (unpublished PhD thesis, University of Cambridge, 1975). Some of Smith's students also completed doctoral theses with the same emphasis upon a strongly quantitative analysis and a demographic investigation of the material, as, for instance, L.R. Poos, 'Population and mortality in two fourteenth-century Essex communities' (unpublished PhD thesis, University of Cambridge, 1984), and J.L. Phillips, 'Collaboration and litigation in two Suffolk manor courts, 1289–1364' (unpublished PhD thesis, University of Cambridge, 2005). For the continuity and development of doctoral research at Cambridge under Richard Smith and others at the Cambridge Group for the History of Population and Social Structure, see the list of completed PhDs at www.geog.cam.ac.uk/research/centres/campop/graduate/theses.html (last accessed 19 August 2014).
46 Postan and Titow, 'Heriots and prices'; Thrupp, 'Problem of replacement rates'.
47 See, for example, Razi, *Life, marriage and death*, pp. 38–42.
48 Razi, *Life, marriage and death*, pp. 36–7.
49 Razi, *Life, marriage and death*, pp. 32–4, 115, 119.
50 Razi, *Life, marriage and death*, pp. 43–5.
51 See above, p. 161.
52 Poos, 'Rural population of Essex', 515–30.

53 Poos, 'Rural population of Essex'.
54 Poos, 'Rural population of Essex'; see also Russell, *British medieval population*, pp. 226-7, for a similar mortality estimate, also using Essex tithing data; P.R. Schofield, 'Frankpledge lists as indices of migration and mortality', *Local Population Studies* 52 (1994), 23-9.
55 Wrigley and Schofield, *Population history of England*.
56 Poos, *A rural society after the Black Death*, pp. 120-7; P.J.P. Goldberg, *Women, work, and life-cycle in a medieval economy. Women in York and Yorkshire c.1300-1520* (Oxford: Oxford University Press, 1992), pp. 345-50.
57 Smith, 'Hypothèses sur la nuptialité en Angleterre'.
58 Goldberg, *Women, work and lifecycle*, pp. 339-40; see also P.J.P. Goldberg, 'Female labour, service and marriage in the late medieval urban north', *Northern History* 22 (1986), 18-38. For further comment on the same, see also S.H. Rigby, 'Gendering the Black Death: women in later medieval England', *Gender and History* 12 (2000), 745-54, and especially, pp. 747-8.
59 Poos, *A rural society*, pp. 133-79.
60 M. Bailey, 'Demographic decline in late medieval England: some thoughts on recent research', *Economic History Review* 49 (1996), 1-19, which argues that evidence for low fertility is limited and that the existing case-studies cannot stand as representative of the national demographic experience; J. Hatcher, 'Understanding the population history of England 1450-1750', *Past and Present* 180 (2003), 83-130, and especially, pp. 91-5.
61 For discussion of fertility and its examination in an early modern context, using parish register data, see Wrigley and Schofield, *Population history of England*, pp. 228-36, 363-8, and *passim*. The study of medieval monastic communities, also undertaken in the last quarter century or so, has furnished by far and away the most robust demographic data for the later middle ages in England. Studies by Hatcher and by Harvey have illustrated the ways in which a combination of different types of monastic sources, including lists of novices, obituary and infirmary records, have permitted relatively close and robust investigation of mortality, morbidity and life expectancy, and to a degree that cannot be replicated through investigation of the secular sources. See, for instance, Hatcher, 'Mortality in the fifteenth century'; B.F. Harvey, *Living and dying in England 1100-1540. The monastic experience* (Oxford: Oxford University Press, 1995). Hatcher stresses the relative strength of the mortality data in his discussion of the relative claims of mortality and fertility in explanatory models of later medieval population change, Hatcher, 'Understanding the population history of England', pp. 95-8.

6

Family, household and gender

Alongside investigation of the demographic study of peasant populations there has been closely related work on social and familial structure. The two strands have often been closely associated both in their mutual relevance and also, almost inevitably, in the identity of historians engaged in research in these areas. Thus, discussion of total populations has been dependent upon estimates of average family size whilst almost all attempts to explore changing fertility rates have been informed by investigation of changing family form and the average age at marriage of both spouses. As a result, historians have tended to move between these two areas of investigation in order to find support in formulating their interpretations. This has especially been the case in the relatively recent work on the demographic history of the medieval peasantry where historians have looked to treat all such aspects as part of a general schema of investigation, an association less evident in earlier work on the topic. However, one distinctive element within this research area has been discussion of family structure. Alongside a demographically driven investigation of the family, there has existed research into the peasant family which has owed more, in its origins, methods and approaches, to sociology and anthropology.[1] Since much relevant work on gender has also emerged in relation of consideration of family, household and social structure and has often been set within the same research parameters, we will also discuss, in the second half of this chapter, historical work on gender and, especially, the condition and role of women in peasant society. We will though begin by examining the peasant family and household in demographic terms and by looking at household formation, age at marriage and the size and structure of the peasant household, as well as the evolution of the peasant household in the high and late middle ages.

Household formation

Historical interest in household formation owes a great deal to work on post-medieval populations. L.R. Poos, in his discussion of household formation in later medieval Essex, offers one of the more theoretically informed considerations of this issue, at least for the middle ages. Drawing upon the comparative analysis of Jan Hajnal and early modern demographers, who identified north-western Europe in the early modern period, and perhaps earlier, as a society dominated by relatively late marriage, a significant proportion of individuals who never married and a household formation system influenced far less by biology (i.e. the physical ability to procreate) than by economy (i.e. having sufficient resources to marry and establish a household), Poos has set out the foundations for household formation in the late medieval English countryside and the most plausible hypotheses for household formation.[2] While contending that household formation was dependent upon the acquisition of resources necessary to allow a couple to marry, or what is termed 'neolocality', Poos also distinguishes between the ways in which this neolocality could operate. More particularly, Poos identifies for the later middle ages both a 'peasant' or 'niche' model of neolocality and a 'proletarian' or 'real wages' model. The former is the model most typically associated with household formation in the medieval countryside, where the establishment of a household was dependent upon the acquisition of land and, in turn, that acquisition was determined by key events in the life-cycle, most obviously marriage and the receipt of dowry and the transfer of property through inheritance. In other words, a couple intending to marry and establish a household of their own were dependent upon the creation of an opportunity or a 'niche' arising. This model also tends to assume a fairly stationary economy, with a limited circulation of any significant landed and/or movable goods. Restrictions in the movement of such property and, as a consequence, the limited access to opportunities were determined by institutional structures, including familial conventions, communal pressures and the strictures of lordship. By contrast, a 'proletarian' model involves the possibility that a couple planning to marry and to establish a household of their own might accumulate their own resource, through paid employment (or 'real wages'); in this respect they were not dependent upon resources access to which might be contained by such vital events as the death of parents or other kin but, instead, they could, over time, establish sufficient resource through their own labour.

As Poos noted, given that both forms of household could co-exist, it was the relative significance of each in any period that was especially important; historians of early modern England have argued for a 'proletarian' model in operation as the dominant form of household formation from the mid-sixteenth century and Poos, through his analysis of Essex employment and taxation material, including the later fourteenth century poll-taxes, is inclined to the view that a proletarian or real wages model was not only also in existence but was the predominant model by the second half of the fourteenth century. This, he points out and as we discussed in the previous chapter, has implications for our understanding of the demographic and economic landscape of later medieval England, the lowered fertility occasioned by later marriage, itself a consequence of forms of employment, such as servanthood in adolescence and early adulthood, potentially fundamental to our understanding of the population history of later medieval England.[3]

While neither as theoretically charged nor so focused on the broader population history of the period as is the discussion by Poos, other historians of the medieval rural family have also engaged with this distinction or have focused upon particular aspects of it. A generation and more before Poos, historians, operating within a rather particular view of the medieval rural economy, had implicitly tended to focus their attention upon the 'peasant' or 'niche' model even if they did not explicitly describe it as such. G.C. Homans's investigation of impartible inheritance in midland or champion England in the thirteenth century encouraged him to the view that most offspring who did not inherit or receive dowry appear to have been destined for a life without marriage and household formation or perhaps one of relative poverty and insecurity as they wandered the world in search of new opportunity.[4] In a chapter entitled 'The marriage of the heir', Homans remarked that, if we turn our attention to the inheriting rather than the non-inheriting offspring, we find 'evidence that the heir's marriage was often dependent on, or even coincident with, his acquiring the whole or part of a family tenement'.[5] While Homans identified exceptions to this rule, he located these exceptions within the same broad framework of neolocality dependent upon land acquisition (i.e. individuals marrying in anticipation of the inheritance of land or settled in some dependent property prior to a parent's death). Importantly for this discussion, Homans explained the neolocality within his established view of the rural economy and society of the period:

> In an age when nearly everyone made his living by tilling the soil and raising crops, and these not for the most part to be sold in a market but

to be consumed directly, land was a possession which had an importance all its own. Only if he had land was a man sure of his livelihood.[6]

While, as we have seen, Homans could conceive of non-inheriting heirs seeking their fortune elsewhere, his focus was not upon such activity; instead his attention was concentrated upon the large holdings of central England and their single heirs. While Homans did not employ the terminology of neolocality and household formation systems he had clearly concentrated his view upon a 'peasant' or 'niche' model of household formation and had little or nothing to say about what were effectively 'proletarian' or 'real wages' models. Clearly, as the above quotation also suggests, an important reason for this was his view that such tenurial and familial regimes operated at the very heart of the high and late medieval rural economy in England. Writing a couple of decades later, Postan, while acknowledging the potential of the market to influence the distribution of resources, also concluded that it was the family and its own natural adjustments in size that determined the fundamental distributions of property, and especially land.[7]

Given the conclusions of more recent research on the market and the more overtly commercial aspects of life within the medieval English countryside, Homan's conceptualisation of the wider economy no longer stands up to close scrutiny. Historical discussion of the market and rural commerce is discussed in an earlier chapter in this volume[8] but this approach also has important implications for how we understand changes in family structure and household formation. For example, Razi, who in other respects argued against the significant role of a market economy within the social structure of the village, set out the varied experience of the relatively wealthy and the relatively poor in terms of household formation.[9] While he in fact followed Homans in arguing for a close association of land acquisition, marriage and household formation, Razi also, in differing from Homans, stressed an important distinction in the apparent tendency for peasant couples to marry whether or not their landholding was capable of supporting them.[10] As importantly, Razi, in his case study of the manor of Halesowen in the thirteenth and fourteenth centuries, also identified differences existing not so much between family members in terms of household formation but in relation to inter-familial distinctions occasioned by relativities of wealth: in short, wealthier families might distribute resources to kin in order to enable them to establish families and households within the manor ('functionally extended kin', as Razi termed them) while poorer families, unable to support their members in such a way, could do nothing but send them into the world in search of opportunity.[11] While Razi offers little in the way of speculation regarding the life-cycle and careers of such poorer out-migrants, he acknowledges the potential capacity of the medieval economy and society to absorb at least some such individuals.[12]

By contrast, for other historians it is the fortune of this group of poorer villagers and non-inheriting kin, as well as the capacity of the medieval society and economy to present them with opportunities and to permit them to establish households of their own, which is of central importance. In ways that neatly illustrate the association of demographic and social structural themes, both Poos and Goldberg offer detailed comment on the possibilities which were presented to rural dwellers through limited migration including movement into towns in search of employment.[13] Finally, historians, particularly those writing in recent years, have also recognised that out-migration and life-cycle service are not necessarily the preserve of the relatively poor: apprenticeships of sons of wealthier tenants, including non-inheriting sons, and the opportunities afforded daughters of the relatively wealthy through exogamy and employment beyond the family hearth have also been themes of interest to those historians exploring the impact of demographic and social structural change on rural society.[14]

Age at marriage

Despite its clear importance for many of the issues already explored in this chapter – the fertility-rate, replacement rates, household formation and so on – a paucity of potentially relevant sources means there has been relatively little work on age at marriage. Historical demographers working on later periods have recognised in age at marriage a crucial index for understanding the demographic regime operating in their period of study. Most famously, Jan Hajnal identified age at marriage and the married proportion of the population as being both closely associated and determinative of the social structure and the population history of particular societies. Thus, for Hajnal, early marriage and a high or all but universal proportion of the population entering into marriage were characteristic of southern European societies in the early modern and modern period, in contrast with the later marriage and the relatively low proportion of those who married to be found in northern, and more particularly north-western, Europe.[15] Again we turn to Razi's study of Halesowen for one of the few estimates of age at marriage amongst the medieval English peasantry.[16] In the first instance,

Razi made some estimates of age at marriage on the basis of information also associated with the individual life-course, including age at inheritance and the first appearance of inheriting offspring; from such extrapolations, Razi argues that his sample suggests that age at marriage tended to be early (i.e. 18 to 22 years of age) in pre-plague Halesowen, but that for a sample of the relatively poor and the non-inheriting marriage may have been postponed until a later age or delayed indefinitely.[17] In the post-plague period, again according to Razi, with land in greater supply, it appears that both young men and women were able to acquire land and to establish households at similarly young, and sometimes even younger, ages; it is possible also that this opportunity, for land acquisition and household formation, was afforded to a wider section of rural society, with such chances extended to the relatively poor as well as non-inheriting siblings in a system of impartible inheritance.[18] In a late restatement and partial reassessment of his earlier views, Razi suggested that, while age at marriage remained low throughout the period and may have been even lower in the decades after the Black Death, there were clear distinctions between the experience of the wealthier and poorer villagers, with the poorer villagers thrown more towards the labour market and potentially delayed marriage. Interestingly, Razi has also argued that fertility may not have been constrained by neolocality; instead, as he argued, poorer women were far more likely to have had illegitimate births, and presumably to have done so at a young age.[19] Importantly also, Razi suggested that, in a number of respects, the situation he described for Halesowen may have been regionally specific, noting evident distinctions between the west midlands manors of the kind he had studied, where primogeniture and relatively large holdings dominated, and the areas of partibility and of smaller holdings in the eastern counties. Interestingly, then, one of the few other attempts to calculate age at marriage using manorial documents, Hallam's study of age at marriage for the Lincolnshire fenland from the mid-thirteenth to the mid-fifteenth century offers a view of age at marriage which contrasts quite markedly with that presented by Razi for Halesowen.[20] Hallam identifies relatively late marriage and what he identifies as the early stirrings of a north-west European marriage pattern, suggesting that the average age at marriage across the entire study period was 22.4 for women and 25.9 for men, with some increase in the age at marriage for women after the Black Death.[21] Overall, Hallam detects, from before the Black Death, a household formation system with the characteristics of Hajnal's model of later marriage and delayed household formation, and he also identifies the continuation and entrenchment of such a system in the post-plague period.[22]

Poos, in research that stands in some contrast to the work of both Razi and Hallam, questioned the value of the pursuit of explicit data on age at marriage for this period, suggesting instead that it was the implicit information on household formation that offered the best guide to the likely relative age at marriage, that is whether marriage came relatively early in the life-cycle or relatively late.[23] For Poos, the conditions which helped facilitate neolocality, the association of marriage with household formation, are a better indication of the relative age of marriage in this period; if we assume that family and household formation and marriage were closely associated in this period and that they were activated by the attainment of resources sufficient to allow marriage and family formation to occur, then a close consideration of employment patterns of men and women might also allow some access to estimates of relative age at marriage. Above all, for Poos, the less individuals were reliant upon inheritance or gifts from their parents but upon their own labours, the more likely it would be that marriage was delayed. In this model, which rejects a wholesale commitment to a 'peasant' or 'niche' model of household formation of the kind envisaged by historians such as Homans and Postan, in favour of a 'proletarian' or 'real wages' model, the potential for a market, including an active market in labour, to have a far greater impact on household formation patterns and fertility is identified, as we have also already discussed.[24] For Poos, then, in a manner consistent in part with the analysis attempted by Hallam, it is the relatively late marriage of a significant proportion of the relatively poor which should dominate our view of the marriage regime operating at least in later medieval England.

The size and structure of the peasant household

Clearly, discussion of age at marriage and the process of family and household formation are closely associated with discussion of the size and structure of the peasant household as well as any regional and temporal differences. G.C. Homans, writing in the early 1940s as a sociologist with more than a passing interest in these matters, addresses these themes directly and usefully describes the distinction between family and household, the latter including not only relatives but also those who fall within the sphere of the house, including resident servants and other domestic employees. Writing in a generation before significant historical research in this particular area was under way, Homans was though not armed with the range of secondary material necessary to analyse the structure of the family and household directly; instead he offered some limited comparative reference, implied a general ubiquity of familial form and, for the greater extent, proposed that, as amongst the modern German peasantry which shared the same Anglo-Saxon stock as medieval English peasants, 'families were large'.[25]

Historians, while recognising some of the features identified by Homans, would now tend to the view that his depiction of a peasant family, as large, fairly static over time and, in many respects, self-sufficient, would fail to accord with the sorts of distinction, including poorer, nuclear families holding small plots of land, for instance, more recently identified. Since Homans wrote there have been only a few attempts to describe the extent and structure of the peasant family in this period; while we are thrown back again in particular on the familiar names of Hallam and Razi, a few other historians have ventured their own estimates.[26] Most obviously, and prior to the efforts of Hallam, Russell had sought to use the poll-taxes of the later fourteenth century, during a post-plague period of recurrent epidemics, to provide a quantitative foundation for estimates of household size and calculated that the average household size (at 3.5 persons) was really quite small, smaller he suggested than had been previously supposed.[27] Hallam's use of the Spalding serf lists, from a pre-plague period, suggested, in accordance with Homans's earlier views, that family size could be large, larger on average than Russell had identified for the later fourteenth century when different demographic conditions almost certainly pertained, but he also stressed the variety of structure and extent. He also, as Russell, emphasised the significant proportion of small, two-generational households and, in some contrast to Homans, identified the larger, multi-generational as relatively atypical.[28] While, as we also considered in discussing population estimates in the previous chapter, Richard Smith has subsequently and convincingly questioned the value of the lists as snapshots of peasant family form and has argued that Hallam's analysis of such sources tended to exaggerate the size of peasant families, the tendency in the relevant literature, including the early studies of Russell and of Hallam, has also been to shift the historical focus from the more established, extensive and larger peasant households, of which there were undoubtedly examples throughout this period, towards the ubiquitous small, nuclear families.[29] Cecily Howell's detailed discussion of household structure for the midlands manor of Kibworth Harcourt, one of the few such discussions to grapple closely with such issues and to compare medieval and early modern demographic structures, reflects these developments. Published in the early 1980s and reflecting a strong demographic and social structural strand in the then current historiography, Howell employed court rolls, tithing lists and poll-taxes in order to extract some usable data for her reconstruction of family and household form for the middle ages and identified a possible diminution in the average size of families (from 4.84 members over the age of five in the pre-plague period to 3.72 in the later fourteenth century) as well as the relative reduction in the proportion of complex family and household structures.[30] Razi also, writing only a few years earlier, explored available evidence for the size of the peasant family and concluded that, while families in medieval Halesowen could be large, there were considerable differences in size between the wealthier and the poorer peasant families in this period.[31]

Historians' explanations for such differences in family and household size and structure are themselves instructive as to the prevailing historiographical view, not least in the tendency for historians to associate any such difference with either purely or largely demographic factors or with external influences, such as the impact of markets in labour or in goods. Historians writing in the middle years of the twentieth century were inclined to emphasise the internal dynamic of the medieval family as self-determining in terms of size and structure; thus, for Postan, it was the natural evolution of family size and structure, with some families increasing whilst others declined, which influenced the local rural economy, rather than the reverse.[32] While Postan had little to say on the actual size and structure of the peasant family and household, other historians writing in the mid-twentieth century did both discuss size and structure and seek to examine them. Thus, Homans tended to the view that, within the villages of 'champion' England in an area of open fields and large labour-service-owing holdings, a consistency of tenurial arrangement, itself the consequence of settled long usage, helped to influence family and household form, in terms both of keeping heirs close to the family hearth and of predetermining the life-chances of the non-inheriting siblings.[33] Hallam also describes the variety of family and household size in the medieval Fenland and suggests that family and household structures were a consequence of inheritance practices, monogeniture forcing the non-inheriting to seek their fortunes elsewhere whilst partible inheritance encouraged young men and women to stay and take up opportunities closer to home. Hallam's conception of the motive force of medieval peasant society is evidently tied quite closely to issues of landholding and inheritance, standard themes within the historiography, and he gives much less weight to other features of the medieval economy, such as the draw of regional and urban economies, the significance of local proto-industries and so on.³⁴ By contrast, writing a decade and more later and reflecting a growing interest in the impact of markets on the medieval peasant, Cicely Howell, in her discussion of the Kibworth Harcourt peasantry, recognises the importance of labour markets and the availability of outside labour as key determinants in family and household form; also writing initially in the late 1970s and early 1980s, Razi stresses the significance of relative wealth in influencing the formation and durability of peasant households. For Razi, who explicitly contrasts his approach with the work of earlier historians, the economic opportunity available to some villagers but not to others was the main factor in establishing such distinctions in family size and structure.³⁵

The evolution of the peasant household

In certain respects, then, the study of the peasant family and household, just as the study of the demography of the medieval peasantry, was dependent upon the introduction of approaches from social sciences and the agendas and methodologies of historians working essentially in other periods. Without the historical adoption of these external agendas, no such study of the medieval peasantry would have been undertaken. However, discussion of the medieval family has also been influenced by changing views of the medieval economy; where once the peasant family was most typically perceived as timeless, historians writing in the last generation have tended instead to emphasise the ways in which structural forms were driven by external factors, and especially economic ones. Given this shift in interpretation, discussion of the peasant family has, in the more recent work on the subject, been accommodated within the history of a changing demographic and economic landscape. While it is impossible to quantify the varying proportion of complex households within rural society in this period, historians writing since the 1980s have proposed some likely shifts in the proportion of household types. Though it is now generally acknowledged that nuclear households predominated throughout the period, historians writing on this topic in the 1980s and 1990s considered the sorts of factors that might encourage change in the relative proportions of family and household types. Most importantly, dramatic population decline in the second half of the fourteenth century allied to new economic opportunity for those who survived the recurrent epidemics of the period helped encourage mobility, itself a motor for the establishment of nuclear households as individuals moved away from their place of birth in order to settle elsewhere.³⁶ Furthermore, the potential for upward social mobility in the later middle ages and the greater availability of landed resources also helped generate new complex domestic units, especially the households of a new wealthy peasant elite in the fifteenth century.[37] Interestingly, both those historians who have favoured a fertility-based argument in order to explain demographic change in this period and those who have promoted a mortality-driven demographic regime have, explicitly or implicitly, recognised that household formation systems were far from static in this period. This is especially evident in Razi's final significant contribution to the discussion; while arguing for the continuity of established family and household forms he also recognises the likely adjustments to household formation systems and plausibly suggests ways in which the larger, wealthier households might persist in this period whilst other, weaker, units might dissipate. In this thesis both of continuity and of change of the peasant family and household, there is accommodation of an established view of the medieval peasantry, as a relative constant, its cycle determined by its membership in relation to inheritance practice, custom and the dictates of lordship, as well as an acknowledgement that other significant external factors, including epidemic disease and the lure of labour markets and towns, also had vital roles to play.[38]

Gender and the study of peasant women

As will be evident from the preceding discussion, historical discussion of social structure and family history has, inevitably, a good deal to say about matters pertaining to gender, including most obviously household formation, household structure and marriage. That said, we might suggest that, some significant contributions notwithstanding, there has not been very much in the way of close study of gender and especially the study of women in the medieval village.[39] A case could certainly be made for this if we simply counted works directed exclusively at the study of female peasants in this period, a point to which we will return when we attempt to review that work. However, as again will be evident from previous discussion, women have featured significantly in the study of the medieval village, as wives and widows, as family members, labourers, tenants and servants, and so forth. If medieval peasant women have not always or often been examined as the main and direct objects of study *per se*, this also does not mean that they have been dismissed to a significantly greater degree than have their male counterparts who have also seldom been the subject of direct or individual, as opposed to indirect or collective and group, study.

Just as in the 1960s the social scientific turn in history opened up new areas of study relevant to the medieval peasantry so, in the 1980s, the turn to gender also encouraged the emergence of a more gendered study of medieval peasants. Thus, for instance, Barbara Hanawalt's work on the peasant family and on women and children within the family is informed by a social science agenda current in the 1980s and already discussed earlier in this chapter. Consideration of topics such as age at marriage, household formation and child-rearing also necessarily involved Hanawalt in discussion founded upon aspects of gender division.[40] In particular, making use of coroners' inquests alongside other more typical sources, such as manorial court rolls, Hanawalt describes family and household, the domestic economy and the life-cycle of the peasant family. An important and recurrent theme in her study is the distinctive role of men and women, and of children. She distinguishes between the labouring opportunities of adult males and females, their respective roles within their families and households, and also, and unusually for studies of the medieval English peasantry, offers comment on the gendered roles of children, revealed to us, grimly enough, in consistent patterns of accidental deaths.[41] Hanawalt also contends that, while roles within and beyond the peasant household were conditioned by gender, wives enjoyed a significant role in managing and securing the success of the domestic unit.[42] Also writing in the mid-1980s, Judith Bennett could with complete justification claim that her study of gender in pre-plague Brigstock was a radical departure in the historiography of medieval peasantry.[43] Certainly her work still provides the only book-length study of gender and the English peasantry published to date. Bennett's exploration of gender and household is both a study aimed at elucidating the lives of women and an investigation of social structure of a kind consistent with other contemporary research on the demography of the peasant family and household.[44] Such topics as the nature and structure of the household and the respective roles of women and men, daughters and sons, wives and husbands dominate. Bennett's book is though distinguished from other studies of similar date in that issues more directly informed by gender theory and gender politics are central to her discussion. Thus, she emphasises the ways in which female choices were conditioned by prevailing cultural constraints, notably a society that was avowedly patriarchal, that is, one in which authority resides with men, and in which peasant women tended only to experience social and/or economic independence in adolescence and widowhood.[45]

We can identify a number of related themes which illustrate the absorption of issues of gender, and especially women's studies, into historical discussion of the medieval English peasantry. In the first instance, we can detect a continuation allied to a more detailed investigation of matters pertaining to rent, obligation and the nature of tenure that address issues of gender and especially the rights of women or their lack of them.[46] It is though through the changes in the direction of historical research in this area that we can see a further adoption of newer historiographical issues. So, for instance, Richard Smith's work, written in the 1980s and 1990s, on the opportunities for women to hold customary land reflects a development in this area of study encouraged by his intellectual interests rooted in demography and the social sciences. Smith's thesis also owes a great deal to his interest in the development of the customary law of the manor court in relation to the common law of the king's court; as part of that research, he argues persuasively that developments in the recording of land transfer in the manor court responded to changes at common law and that women, as wives as much as and more than widows, were supported in landholding through the introduction of devices such as jointure (essentially the holding of title to land by both husband and wife).[47] Similarly, Peter Franklin's discussion of widowhood and the transfer of customary land offers an attempt to examine gendered distinctions in landholding and tenure in the medieval village, and to move away from earlier historical treatments of widows in the medieval village which Franklin considered to be 'inadequate and patronizing'.[48] Instead of perceiving widows as constrained by structures beyond their control, such as the instruments of seigneurial policy and the prey of often-younger males and aspiring tenants, Franklin, using court records from Thornbury (Gloucestershire) from the fourteenth century, argues that widows showed evidence of their own agency, displaying tactical awareness and economic savvy in retaining tenancies after the deaths of their husbands and managing them directly.

The same can also be said for recent discussion of female economic activity in the medieval village, which is both reflective of developing themes at the core of medieval peasant studies and studies of the wider medieval economy, notably the development of commercial activity in and beyond the medieval village, and responsive to an agenda that insists upon the importance of locating gender and women's studies within the relevant historiography. Hilton, in his Ford lectures in the early 1970s, was in the vanguard of such work and identifies some of the ways in which women could be drawn into the village economy, as for instance litigants, brewers and conceivably money-lenders.[49] He also pondered the wage parity of women in the medieval countryside and noted some similarities in rates for men and women by the later fourteenth century.[50] Reflective of the limited work in this area by the early 1970s, Hilton's tentative suggestions have been explored in greater depth in more recent studies. A number of studies have sought to test the extent to which women operated and were able to operate within the medieval economy, including the rural economy. Beginning in the 1970s and 1980s, studies by Bennett, McIntosh, Hanawalt, and Briggs amongst others have illustrated the ways in which women could be perceived as active agents in the medieval economy, though perspectives on the depth and quality of this agency vary considerably, a point to which we will return in what follows.[51] As with much else in the historical discussion of the medieval peasantry, study of peasant women and their economic activity and development is necessarily conditioned by the defining themes of the historiography. Thus, it was highly unlikely that women would be considered active economic agents at a point in the historical discussion when the economy of peasants more generally was held to be relatively limited and conditioned by lordship and domestic constraints rather than by the market and more commercial activity. Christopher Middleton, in significant and trenchant statements on class and gender, offered the view that female employment on the demesne was more constrained by custom and seigneurial policy than it was likely to be in the open market; his suggestion that women's exclusion from surplus production and, thereby, from the 'front-line of class struggle' is conditioned by a particular and now rather dated view of a medieval peasant economy built upon domestic economies largely confined by the manor and the household. Middleton recognises the presence and importance of female roles beyond the domestic sphere and identifies opportunities of some significance for women in these roles; he reflects, though, that women were prevented from wholly accepting such opportunity by the demands of lordship and the gendered roles afforded within the medieval village. In particular, Middleton argues that a village patriarchy and the subordination of women were not just consistent but products of seigneurial demands, the latter encouraging peasants to organise their household economies and female roles in order to meet the expectations of lordship.[52] Rigby has argued against such an explanatory framework, suggesting, for instance, that it is far from easy to identify a causal link between features of female subordination in medieval England, such as exclusion from full legal and political identities, and the demands of lordship; in other words, while there is plentiful evidence for the kind of patriarchal society that reduced opportunity for women, it is not at all evident that, for peasant women in particular, this sprang from the manor and lordship.[53] In ways that accord with Rigby's argument, an adjusted view of the medieval peasant economy in the last three decades, and one which has tended to admit a greater role for individual peasant agency in the market and to reduce the defining role of lords in the lives of peasants, so features of economic behaviour identified by Middleton have been explored more fully and directly for women as well as for men of the medieval village and countryside.

While historians have debated the relative economic position of medieval women in more than one context, a number of historians have recently proposed significant economic roles for women in the medieval countryside. As Hilton and Middleton, writing in the 1970s on women in the medieval village, had both recognised, the potential for women to enjoy some economic engagement that extended beyond the domestic sphere was evident from the sources. For both historians, any such activity was likely to be constrained by institutional factors, notably lordship, custom and the perceived limits of the medieval economy. Writing more recently and often within the context of a revised view of the medieval economy, other historians have tended to see female activity as a potentially important extension of a shifting but sometimes vibrant rural economy; where they detect the constraint of such female involvement, these historians have been inclined to ascribe that less to lordship but instead to an overriding patriarchal system and/or the dictates of the economy *per se*.

So, for instance, in his examination of female lending patterns in the later thirteenth- and fourteenth-century village, Chris Briggs describes and discusses features of credit agreements involving women on two manors in Buckinghamshire and Cambridgeshire; he identifies female economic activity, with women acting both as lenders and borrowers, within and outside of marriage, but concludes that such opportunities were relatively few and that it was the application of law in manorial courts that served to disadvantage women. Where women were married, rules of so-called 'coverture', which placed married women under the protection and authority of their husbands, meant that their credit relations were subsumed within the dealings of their husbands; the more extensive activity of single women tended to be most evident where widows and long-term unmarried women also enjoyed control over substantial landholdings.[54] Implicit in Briggs's discussion is the defining influence of institutions, including the manor court and its constituents, as well as lordship and the limited opportunities for landholding and capital accumulation, and what may be taken as underlying assumptions regarding norms of behaviour in economic dealing. There is though only a subtle association between these factors and the limited opportunities afforded to women in this period. Miriam Müller offers reasonably complementary conclusions, which arise from her comparative work on thirteenth- and fourteenth-century manors in Wiltshire and Suffolk, in so far as she finds that the extent and visibility of female peasant agency were significantly influenced by the kinds of seigneurial policy that may, for instance, have facilitated particular kinds of reporting structures (such as the recording of hue and cry in leet courts) as well as customary conventions relating to the holding and transfer of land.[55] Marjorie McIntosh, in work on medieval women and their economic roles that has tended to focus more on urban than rural society in the later middle ages, has also tested at least one way in which women could enjoy some kind of economic independence and self-regulation, if though conditioned by law and pervading business practices.[56] At Havering-atte-Bower (Essex), a royal manor and a rural setting, McIntosh also noted a good deal of confident economic activity on the part of women in the later middle ages and concluded that the particular tenurial conditions pertaining on the manor, allied to a 'commercialised but not deeply capitalised' economy in the later fourteenth and fifteenth centuries, created the kind of conducive economic environment in which women could operate effectively, if in particular niches.[57]

One such niche, for at least part of the middle ages, was brewing, and more than one historian has sought to identify the socio-economic structure as well as the gendered dimensions to this kind of employment. In this respect, a major contribution has been made by Judith Bennett, who has analysed both the social-economic and gender constituency of later medieval and early modern brewers and its change over time. Bennett notes how brewing, whilst still a by-employment intended to service highly localised markets and involving relatively modest investment in terms of capital and labour, was well suited to the medieval peasant household and to the oversight of married women in particular. While, as we shall see, Bennett argues strongly that such advantages did not last and could not be counted upon as symptomatic, it is also evident that there were moments of relative economic independence and strength for some rural women involved in brewing.[58] Matthew Stevens, taking some issue with Bennett's assessment, focuses on the evident capacity of women to engage in local markets and economic activity such as brewing in his study of male and female activity in the Welsh marcher lordship of Dyffryn Clwyd in the late thirteenth and early fourteenth centuries. In reality, Stevens's assessment, which has as its focus the small town of Ruthin as much as or more than the surrounding countryside and its commotes, does not sit at significant variance with Bennett's own in that implicit in his assessment is the view that women took opportunity to the extent that this was available to them; where opportunity, in the form of available capital for instance, was not forthcoming, then their hold on their place within the economy weakened.[59] Similar observations are made by Helena Graham in her study of women's work at Alrewas (Staffordshire) in the fourteenth century: she tends to the view that women, while active economically, were often subsumed within the identities of their male relatives, especially husbands. This, she contends, may have been more particularly the case where the family was wealthier and, presumably, the capital outlay in any commercial activity likely to have been greater.[60]

Important in these discussions has been consideration of the changing economic condition of women. In this respect, exploration of female economic activity has been integrated with a wider discussion of change in the medieval economy. Thus, for instance, it has been suggested that the changed social, economic and demographic landscape of the post-plague medieval countryside presented new opportunities for women, with new inroads into labouring, including harvest work, and some apparent increase in wage-earning capacity. In fact, some historians, such as Caroline Barron and P.J.P. Goldberg, the former reflecting particularly on women in town and city, have inclined to the view that the later middle ages was a 'golden age' for women, a shortage in male labour supply and a generally enhanced standard of living presenting new and significantly improved opportunities for women.[61] This has generated some discussion in the last three two or three decades about the extent and the longevity of female earning patterns in the later middle ages. Sandy Bardsley, in responding to an earlier debate on the 'golden age' of female employment and wage earning, has suggested that, while female wage-earning opportunities may have improved in the later middle ages, and especially in the period after the Black Death, any improvement was slight relative to the advantages enjoyed by men in the same period. Bardsley's argument, which she suggested had helped counter a long-standing commitment to the idea that women's wage-parity had tended to improve in the post-plague era, was not greeted with universal approval.[62] John Hatcher rejected the core of Bardsley's findings on the basis that the evidence could not support such conclusions; he suggests instead that the variety of small but significant adjustments in calculating piece-rate wages would militate against any easy comparison of male and female wages in this period and that physiology and convention determined that certain tasks, such as mowing with a long-handled scythe, were customarily performed by the most able, skilled and efficient workers, typically men, or a particular sub-set of men.⁶³ Hatcher's position is similar to that adopted by one or two other researchers in this area who have tended to reject or reduce cultural and gendered explanations for differences in male and female labouring experience in favour of the needs of employers. Hatcher's argument that 'farmers employed labourers to get work done, and the cost of accomplishing that work was uppermost in their minds when they made decisions about which particular labourer to hire and what wage to pay him or her' accords with other work that places primacy upon the economic rationale of male and female employment in this period.⁶⁴ Simon Penn's use of inquests under the Statute of Labourers presents one such instance of this approach; by moving away from the demesne and seigneurial records and by looking instead at cases brought through the agency of government as regards piecemeal violations of labour legislation, Penn seeks to examine evidence for a more flexible and mobile female labour force. He suggests that women faced no significant barriers to employment in the kinds of work, for instance harvest work such as reaping (but not mowing with scythes), where such work was consistent with the needs of employers and the capacity of female employees to deliver.⁶⁵ The same also appears to be the case in John Langdon's discussion of the marginal work of women and children at Woodstock (Oxfordshire) in the later thirteenth and fourteenth centuries, where fluctuations in the extent of available building work seem either to have helped generate or to have reduced employment opportunities for women involved in such work.⁶⁶ In addition, and as we have already discussed in an earlier chapter, both Goldberg and Poos have suggested that female employment opportunities, especially in towns, improved in particular ways in the later fourteenth and fifteenth centuries; young rural women, as well as young men, could find work in neighbouring communities and towns as live-in servants.⁶⁷ It is also likely that an improved standard of living and a heightened polarisation of landholding in the medieval countryside by the mid-fifteenth century created disparities in household structure of a kind that also presented niches for life-cycle service in the houses of the relatively wealthy.⁶⁸

As noted above, the extension of such an argument has been to identify some moments or sub-periods in the later middle ages when women enjoyed a 'golden age' of employment, their employment opportunities enhanced by population decline and intensification of productivity in some areas of the economy, to the extent that female employment was sought out by employers. Much of this discussion has been fed by work on urban society and the role of women within towns, but it also reflects upon the general condition of women in the later middle ages and, by extension, relates to opportunities available to women in and beyond the medieval countryside. Judith Bennett has been the most vocal critic of the 'golden age' thesis. Bennett notes on more than one occasion that evidence for women's work in the middle ages is not necessarily or indeed at all about affirming the strength and powerfulness of medieval women; even when women enjoyed moments of economic parity with women, as on occasion was the case for female wage earners in the later fourteenth century, for instance, such opportunities were piecemeal and contrary to the long-term trend.[69] As Bennett has sought to show, female success in the medieval economy was relative; as she notes, strikingly, in her assessment of female brewing in the later middle ages, successful female brewers were successful '... *for women* [her italics]'.[70] In particular, Bennett has shown how brewing opportunities for women contracted during the later middle ages: as the economic conditions associated with brewing altered, and its regulation and technologies changed so women moved out or were moved out in favour of men. This transformation which, as Bennett notes, looks to accord in some general ways with the more traditional historiographical assumptions which locate medieval women's economic experience in a golden age soon to be lost in the early modern period, is not accepted by Bennett.[71] Instead, as she proposes, the fact that women's opportunities reduced over time does not signify that they were, at any previous point, abundant and rich; instead, they were unable to take a next step into a period of economic growth and expansion of their 'sector': rather than 'history-as-change', Bennett views the varied female experience in brewing, in town and countryside, as 'history-in-continuity'.[72]

Bennett then identifies no more in the concept that women enjoyed a golden age of employment in the fifteenth century than the largely acritical application of an ill-conceived and weakly tested hypothesis, one based upon the assumption that, if women's work opportunities declined in the early modern and modern periods, they must have enjoyed an earlier high point from which to fall.[73] While of course any decline must suggest an original higher point from which the decline began, for Bennett the issue revolves around the actual extent of the advantage women enjoyed while they occupied those heights in the late middle ages. She notes that women's roles in the medieval economy, and especially in the domestic economy of the household and family, tended not to be chosen by the female participant but given according to the dictates of social norms. Even if, then, some women enjoyed a domestic equilibrium and some authority within the sphere of the household, their role remains one established by a custom that was, in essence, patriarchal.[74] As importantly, female roles tended to be multiple and low- or lower-skilled than those undertaken by males; the latter could also benefit from a higher level of specialisation in a single skill or craft and consequently enjoy greater remuneration.[75]

As already noted, Bennett's work is distinctive in its framing for its insistent focus upon core tenets of gender politics, notably the inherent disadvantage of women and the strength of patriarchy. No other historian researching the medieval English peasantry has adopted, so directly and consistently, this approach even if few if any would seek to dismiss it as irrelevant or inappropriate.[76] Here again, as more than once in this volume, we see a coming together of different historiographical strands in order to effect a progression in an area of study; Bennett's conception of the changing proto-industrial context of brewing is closely informed both by her view of gender politics and the adjusted opportunities for women but also by her awareness of long-term economic, demographic and social structural change of a kind consistent with other studies but not directed at issues pertaining to gender. This nuancing and extension of research agendas, as well as what may be perceived as a developing consensus on the likely analytical range and potential of the surviving material, is an important feature of work on the medieval peasantry since the last decades of the twentieth century and illustrates a significant inter-dependency of research topics, something that will also be evident in the next chapter in which we consider historical work on the so-called 'village community'.

Notes

1 See below, pp. 173-82; also, see Chapter 7, pp. 204-9.
2 L.R. Poos, *A rural society after the Black Death. Essex 1350-1525* (Cambridge: Cambridge University Press, 1991), pp. 141-2. For Hajnal, see below, pp. 176-7, and for a very useful recent summary of Hajnal's influence, E.A. Wrigley, 'European marriage patterns and their implications: John Hajnal's essay and historical demography during the last half-century', in C. Briggs, P.M. Kitson and S.J. Thompson, eds, *Population, welfare and economic change in Britain, 1290-1834* (Woodbridge: Boydell, 2014), pp. 15-41.
3 Poos, *A rural society*, pp. 156-8, and above, pp. 165-6.
4 G.C. Homans, *English villagers of the thirteenth century* (Cambridge, Mass.: Harvard University Press, 1941), pp. 139-43.
5 Homans, *English villagers of the thirteenth century*, p. 149.
6 Homans, *English villagers of the thirteenth century*, p. 158.

7   M.M. Postan, 'The charters of the villeins', in M.M. Postan, *Essays in medieval agriculture and general problems of the medieval economy* (Cambridge: Cambridge University Press, 1973), p. 114, and above, Chapter 2, p. 64-5.
8   See above, Chapter 4, pp. 117-41.
9   For Razi's comments on the economy of the medieval village and its impact on village solidarity, see Z. Razi, 'Family, land and the village community in later medieval England', in T.H. Aston, ed., *Landlords, peasants and politics in medieval England* (Cambridge: Cambridge University Press, 1987), p. 368.
10 Razi, *Life, marriage and death*, pp. 50-7.
11 Z. Razi, 'The myth of the immutable English family', *Past and Present* 140 (1993), pp. 3-44.
12 Razi, 'Myth of the immutable English family', 23-44.
13 Poos, *A rural society*; Goldberg, *Women, work and lifecycle*, and above, Chapter 5, pp. 165-6, for discussion of the same.
14 See pp. 177, 181-2.
15 J. Hajnal, 'European marriage patterns in perspective', in D.V. Glass and D.E.C. Evesley, eds, *Population in history. Essays in historical demography* (London: Edward Arnold, 1965), pp. 101-43; J. Hajnal, 'Two kinds of pre-industrial household formation system', in R. Wall, ed., *Family forms in historic Europe* (Cambridge: Cambridge University Press, 1983), pp. 65-104.
16 Razi, *Life, marriage and death*, pp. 60-4, 136-7; Z. Razi, 'Myth of the immutable English family'. See also H.E. Hallam, 'Age at first marriage and age at death in the Lincolnshire Fenland, 1252-1478', *Population Studies* 39 (1985), 55-69.
17 Razi, *Life, marriage and death*, pp. 63-4.
18 Razi, *Life, marriage and death*, pp. 135-7.
19 Razi, *Life, marriage and death*, pp. 64-71.
20 Hallam identifies Razi's work and recognises, in the most oblique way, the differences in age at marriage set out by Razi for Halesowen, but he neither challenges them nor seeks to explain them, Hallam, 'Age at first marriage and age at death', n. 16, pp. 62-3.
21 Hallam, 'Age at first marriage and age at death', p. 59. A similar male age at first marriage is identified by C. Howell, *Land, family and inheritance in transition. Kibworth Harcourt 1280-1700* (Cambridge: Cambridge University Press, 1983), p. 225.
22 Hallam, 'Age at first marriage and age at death', pp. 68-9.
23 Poos, *A rural society*, pp. 145-6.
24 Poos, *A rural society*, p. 146.
25 Homans, *English villagers*, pp. 208-19, and especially 214.
26 For reference to the detailed studies on family form, see P.R. Schofield, *Peasant and community in medieval England* (Basingstoke: Palgrave, 2003), pp. 82-7.
27 J.C. Russell, *British medieval population* (Albuquerque: The University of New Mexico Press, 1948), pp. 30-1.
28 H.E. Hallam, 'Some thirteenth-century censuses', *Economic History Review* 10 (1957-58), 340, 352-3.
29 R.M. Smith, 'Hypothèses sur la nuptialité en Angleterre aux xiiie-xive siècles',

Annales: Economies, Sociétés, Civilisations 38 (1983), 107–36; on factors that helped determine range in family and household form, including a significant proportion of smaller family and household forms, see, for example, Poos, *A rural society*, pp. 133–58.

30 Howell, *Land, family and inheritance*, pp. 232–5.
31 Razi, *Life, marriage and death*, pp. 74–5, 83–6, 142–4.
32 Postan, 'Charters of the villeins', p. 114.
33 Homans, *English villagers*, pp. 214–15.
34 Hallam, 'Some thirteenth-century censuses', 360–1.
35 Howell, *Land, family and inheritance*, p. 235; Razi, *Life, marriage and death*, pp. 86–93, 144.
36 Razi, 'Myth of the immutable English family'.
37 See, for instance, Howell, *Land, family and inheritance*, p. 236; Schofield, *Peasant and community*, pp. 85–6.
38 Razi, 'Myth of the immutable English family'.
39 As Bennett points out, the study of women's history and of gender history are not easily separable and often in reality, gender history and women's history occupy the same ground; this is true of the study of the medieval peasantry, where by far the greater part of a deliberately gendered discussion is aimed at the study of women. See J.M. Bennett, *History matters. Patriarchy and the challenge of feminism* (Philadelphia: University of Pennsylvania Press, 2006), pp. 16–19.
40 B.A. Hanawalt, *The ties that bound. Peasant families in medieval England* (Oxford: Oxford University Press, 1986).
41 Hanawalt, *Ties that bound*, pp. 156–87.
42 Hanawalt, *Ties that bound*, pp. 141–55.
43 J.M. Bennett, *Women in the medieval English countryside. Gender and household in Brigstock before the plague* (Oxford: Oxford University Press, 1987), pp. 4, 9.
44 Bennett, *Women in the medieval English countryside*.
45 Bennett, *Women in the medieval English countryside*, pp. 175–6; on this point, see also Hanawalt, *Ties that bound*, pp. 222–6.
46 See, for instance, historical discussion of merchet, Schofield, *Peasant and Community*, pp. 110–11.
47 R.M. Smith, 'Women's property rights under customary law: some developments in the thirteenth and fourteenth centuries', *Transactions of the Royal Historical Society* 36 (1986), 165–94; R.M. Smith, 'Coping with uncertainty: women's tenure of customary land in England, c.1370–1430', in J. Kermode, ed., *Enterprise and individuals in fifteenth-century England* (Gloucester: Sutton, 1992), pp. 43–67.
48 P. Franklin, 'Peasant widows' "liberation" and remarriage before the Black Death', *Economic History Review* 39 (1986), 186–204 (quote at p. 186).
49 R.H. Hilton, *The English peasantry in the later middle ages. The Ford lectures for 1973 and related studies* (Oxford: Oxford University Press, 1975), pp. 103–5.
50 Hilton, *English peasantry*, pp. 102–3.
51 See below for references to the work of these authors.

52 C. Middleton, 'The sexual division of labour in feudal England', *New Left Review* 1 (1979), 147–68. See also C. Middleton, 'Peasants, patriarchy, and the feudal mode of production in England: a Marxist appraisal: 1. Property and patriarchal relations within the peasantry' and 'Peasants, patriarchy and the feudal mode of production in England: 2. Feudal lords and the subordination of peasant women', both in *Sociological Review* 29 (1981), 105–54.
53 S.H. Rigby, *English society in the later middle ages. Class, status and gender* (Basingstoke: Macmillan, 1995), pp. 244, 257–62, and especially p. 261.
54 C. Briggs, 'Empowered or marginalized? Rural women and credit in later thirteenth- and fourteenth-century England', *Continuity and Change* 19 (2004), 13–43. Contrast M. Stevens, *Urban assimilation in post-Conquest Wales. Ethnicity, gender and economy in Ruthin, 1282–1348* (Cardiff: University of Wales Press, 2010), p. 134, n. 34.
55 M. Müller, 'Peasant women, agency and status in mid-thirteenth to late-fourteenth century England: some reconsiderations', in C. Beattie and M.F. Stevens (eds), *Married women and the law in premodern northwest Europe* (Woodbridge: Boydell, 2013), pp. 91–113; Müller, 'Social control and the hue and cry in two fourteenth-century villages', *Journal of Medieval History* 31 (2005), 29–53.
56 M.K. McIntosh, 'The benefits and drawbacks of *femme sole* status in England, 1300–1630', *Journal of British Studies* 44 (2005), 410–38; McIntosh, 'Women, credit, and family relationships in England, 1300–1620', *Journal of Family History* 30 (2005), 143–63.
57 M.K. McIntosh, *Autonomy and community. The royal manor of Havering, 1200–1500* (Cambridge: Cambridge University Press, 1986), pp. 170–6 (quote at p. 175).
58 J. Bennett, *Ale, beer and brewsters in England. Women's work in a changing world, 1300–1600* (Oxford: Oxford University Press, 1996), pp. 34–5, 40–3.
59 Stevens, *Urban assimilation*, pp. 152–3; 171–2, 215–19.
60 H. Graham, '"A woman's work ...": labour and gender in the late medieval countryside', in P.J.P. Goldberg, ed., *Women in medieval English society* (Stroud: Sutton, 1997), pp. 126–48.
61 For a useful summary of these issues and reflection upon the key contributions, see S.H. Rigby, 'Gendering the Black Death: women in later medieval England', *Gender and History* 12 (2000), 745–54, and especially, pp. 747–8.
62 S. Bardsley, 'Women's work reconsidered: gender and wage differentiation in late medieval England', *Past and Present* 165 (1999), 5–11.
63 J. Hatcher, 'Debate: women's work reconsidered: gender and wage differentiation in late medieval England', *Past and Present* 173 (2001), 191–8; see also the short reply by Bardsley, 199–202 in the same issue.
64 Hatcher, 'Debate: women's work reconsidered', 193.
65 S.A.C. Penn, 'Female wage earners in late-fourteenth century England', *Agricultural History Review* 35 (1987), 1–14.
66 J. Langdon, 'Minimum wages and unemployment rates in medieval England: the case of Old Woodstock, Oxfordshire, 1256–1357', in B. Dodds and C.D. Liddy (ed.), *Commercial activity, markets and entrepreneurs in the middle ages* (Woodbridge: Boydell, 2011), pp. 25–44.

67 Poos, *A rural society*, pp. 175-9; Goldberg, *Women, work and lifecycle*, pp. 280-304; see also above, Chapter 5, pp. 165-6.
68 Razi, 'Myth of the immutable English family'; Schofield, *Peasant and community*, pp. 86-7.
69 J.M. Bennett, 'Medieval women, modern women: across the great divide', in D. Aers, ed., *Culture and History 1350-1600. Essays on English communities, identities and writing* (London: Harvester Wheatsheaf, 1992), pp. 147-75, and especially p. 162.
70 Bennett, *Ale, beer and brewsters*, p. 15.
71 Bennett, *Ale, beer and brewsters*, pp. 145-7.
72 Bennett, *Ale, beer and brewsters*, pp. 147-57.
73 See, for instance, Bennett, 'Medieval women, modern women', pp. 149-51, 163-4; also Bennett, *Ale, beer and brewsters*, p. 147.
74 As Bennett also makes clear, in ways that raise issue consonant with the present discussion, male and female employment could also be imposed upon individuals by the state, a point which seems to challenge some of the assumptions regarding the motive force for entry into service in the later middle ages, J.M. Bennett, 'Compulsory service in late medieval England', *Past and Present* 209 (2010), 20-1.
75 Bennett, 'Medieval women, modern women', pp. 152-5, 158.
76 See, for instance, the highly appreciative review by Elaine Clark of Bennett, *Women in the medieval English countryside*, in *Speculum* 65 (1990), 119-21.

7

The village community and the nature of peasant society in medieval England

For much more than a century historians, often with different approaches and agendas, have pondered the nature of peasant society and, more precisely, the bonds that held that society together. A main focus of that historical investigation has been directed at the nature of community and its persistence or decline. In what follows we can approach discussion of peasant society in the high and late middle ages through a consideration of changing conceptions of community and of the varying ways in which the subject of 'community' has been treated from the second half of the nineteenth century through until the present. We will also consider the ways in which discussion of certain important aspects of peasant society, for instance the transfer of land, are sometimes examined by historians as explicable in terms of their significance for society and community.

Study of the village community in this period has encouraged exploration of a number of different themes. Highly relevant in this respect, not least because of its impact upon other themes, most obviously the nature of peasant society and the form of interaction within that society, is discussion of the structures associated with community, including judicial and fiscal 'communities', such as the various points of intersection with jurisdiction of lords and the medieval state. A further important element in discussion of the village community and of peasant society has been consideration of change over time. In what follows we will not address closely the historical discussion of the causes of that change, in so far as these have been explored elsewhere in this volume,[1] but instead we will seek to describe the ways in which historians have discussed change within the village community, notably in the pre- and post-Black Death village communities.

Lastly, historians have also been prompted by research in this area to question the main premises upon which study has been based; this is especially and most obviously the case in terms of the nature of 'community' and its usefulness as a concept applied to the medieval village and its inhabitants. Christine Carpenter, in a relatively recent discussion which, though not focused upon the medieval English peasantry, is certainly highly relevant, is strongly critical of the employment of the concept of 'community'. Its use, she argues, supposes, or at least suggests, the kinds of bonds and ties which may not have existed in, for instance, the medieval village but are almost transposed there by the very presence of the term in our thinking. 'Community', at least for Carpenter, assumes the kinds of cosy reciprocities that did not necessarily exist in the medieval village. Certainly, Richard Smith, in his forceful analysis of the literature relating to the 'corporate medieval village' noted that early modern historians, writing in the 1960s and most especially in the 1970s, tended to identify, or rather to assume, a relatively supportive, pre-commercialised, village community in the middle ages which stood in marked contrast to the more aggressively individualistic communities of the sixteenth and seventeenth centuries.[2] Carpenter's own conception of the 'community of the medieval village' is also framed by a response to an earlier historiography which had, in her view, established a false but also pervasive conception of the medieval community. While Carpenter posits, only circumspectly, that the term might have some potential referential worth for the medieval village (which, though noting evidence to the contrary, she identifies as capable of being perceived as 'isolated' and with 'clearly defined borders, both geographical and social'), she suggests that the concept of community as applied to the county community or the village community has been overly influenced by structural-functionalist anthropology and the kinds of investigation that saw in modern, underdeveloped communities 'harmonious social organisms, free from conflict, from history, and from links from the outside world'.[3]

There is no doubt that historians of the medieval village have projected, if not always a timelessness upon the medieval village, then at least an entrenched persistence of certain values and customary practices which challenge any notions of flexibility, mobility and general transience. While, as we shall discuss below, the rejection of a 'histoire immobile' for the medieval English village has gathered force in the last fifty years, earlier discussion tended to suppose certain 'abiding features'. This is, as will already be evident from earlier chapters, a feature of M.M. Postan's work upon the medieval village and its inhabitants. While it would be wholly wrong to suggest that Postan argued for a society or economy without change in the middle ages, he did not embrace a view of rural society undergoing, or capable of undergoing, significant change. Postan, in apparent contradiction to his more general portrayal of an economy changing in line with the rise and fall of population, was able to conceive of a village society that, above all, responded to the internal dynamic of the changing needs of peasant families and where evidence for change in the pattern of landholding was more apparent (a fiction of the surviving sources) than real.[4] It is, in part, against such description of and emphasis upon the constants of peasant life and of communal structures that a later historiography has reacted.

Since the end of the nineteenth century, the extent to which groupings beyond the level of the individual maintained a corporate or communal body consistent with the assumed identity of a village community has exercised considerable interest for historians approaching the subject from quite discrete directions. We can identify four main historical approaches which, with differing motives, have explored the nature, and changing nature, of the medieval village community and the durability of the bonds which sustained it. These are: *institutionalists*, that is, those historians, such as Helen M. Cam, who have emphasised the importance of legal and quasi-legal structures in defining the village community and its relative strengths and weaknesses; if we broaden this category it can also be taken to include other kinds of institutional structure such as systems of land management, especially field systems, and the structural development of the manor and village; *social structuralists*, especially J. Ambrose Raftis and his students, who have tended to define the village community according to the activities of its constituents, and especially in terms of co-operation; *Marxists*, notably Rodney Hilton, who have seen the village community as essentially defined by its opposition to external agents, most obviously, but certainly not exclusively, lords; and, finally, *individualists*, an approach associated with Alan Macfarlane but one that also admits a nuanced discussion of individual enterprise and entrepreneurship. We will consider each group in turn.

Institutionalists and the medieval village

In one strand of literature historians have tended to identify the village community in relation to its institutions and operating structures; this institutional approach has been applied to the legal and administrative organisation of the manor and the vill as well as to the ways in which land was distributed and utilised, most especially through shared activity in open fields. This has been a persistent and persisting feature of studies of the medieval village, not least in discussion of the manor, and has deep roots in constitutional and administrative history. Indeed, the history of the early, pre-Conquest development of the manor has, for instance, remained a standard of the literature, even if it has struggled, save in the work of archaeologists, to move forward from the work of nineteenth- and early twentieth-century historians, notably Maitland, Vinogradoff, Seebohm and Stenton.[5] Trevor Aston's important and much later contribution to this discussion envisages a variety of ways in which manors might form before the eleventh century – as outgrowths from pre-existing settlements, as new establishments and as extensions of smaller units, such as farmsteads – and, importantly for the discussion here of the potential impact of institutional development on communal organisation, identifies these developments as consistent with the growth of Anglo-Saxon society itself.[6]

Discussion of the open-field system within champion England has also tended to stress the impact of a closely regulated farming system upon the organisation of the community.[7] The Orwins, writing in the 1930s, described the origins of the open-field system as 'lost in the days of prehistory' but identified in its origin an attempt by early settlers and colonists of pre-Anglo-Saxon Britain to organise their communities to their best advantage, using the resources available to them. This necessarily involved collective organisation of available labour as well as management of sub-divided fields and was identified as a consequence of those resources and the management choices associated with them, not least in the use of the mould-board plough and the need to sustain a community gathered about the open fields.[8] In this respect, it might appear that fields held in common helped determine the organisation of communities but it is also evident that the organisation of agriculture was modified and adjusted by other than the field systems themselves.

Historians and archaeologists in the second half of the twentieth century have examined the early development of the open fields and have attempted to add complexity and variety to the more general patterns described by earlier commentators.[9] This had led to an enormous range of case-studies and a variety of explanatory models, including the suggestion by Joan Thirsk that common-field organisation was a relatively late development of the twelfth and thirteenth centuries intended to enhance land use.[10] C.C. Taylor has also suggested, in adding definition to the general development of open fields set out by the Orwins, that while open fields organised by communal gatherings of one kind or another were likely to

199

have been quite ancient, the medieval common field system of, say, the thirteenth century was also dependent upon the development of nucleated villages and that such a development was unlikely to have occurred until between the ninth and eleventh centuries.[11] Not all of this is, of course, relevant to the discussion of different kinds of communal organisation, though the coming together to establish a structure of nuclear villages that was at that point or subsequently surrounded by open fields, of a kind that then persisted into the later middle ages, presupposes some kind of communal organisation, even if the imposition from lords, or some other external factor, such as the pull of the market, also had an important role to play.[12] As almost all commentators on the open fields note, not only was the original organisation of open fields, whatever the general chronology, needful of some shared and communal initiative, its subsequent organisation from season to season was also wholly dependent upon mutual support and co-operation. This is a theme that emerges, by extension, in most of the work intended to pinpoint changing development of the open fields in surviving sources and is discussed more directly by Warren Ault in his examination and publication of high and later medieval by-laws associated with open-field agriculture.[13]

Economists and non-medievalists have also paid considerable attention to the organisation of the open fields, principally as a means of examining the ways in which individuals and/or communities might seek to spread risk.[14] As such the open fields are examined as an institutional form and often perceived as a drag upon economic development, the assumption being that management of risk and maintenance of collective security were given primacy over innovation and risk-taking in agriculture.[15] Deirdre McCloskey also makes the point, refined and developed in a number of publications on the open fields from the 1970s to the 1990s, that peasants, for reasons of prudence, spread their asset across open fields; this, for her, has less to do with collective responsibility and the sharing of resources ('these medieval folk were not saints or socialists') but instead a rational economic choice reflective of the prevailing conditions.[16] Relatively recently that position has been challenged by Gary Richardson, who has attempted to show that co-operative activity – identified by him in the form of fraternities and grain storage, as well as a labour, land and credit market, all operating within the medieval village – helped to reduce the inherent risks of the medieval economy and to smooth out some of its idiosyncrasies and, in other words, was shared activity of a kind consistent with a considered economic choice.[17]

By the same token, different forms of landholding and land-use organisation have also been taken by historians as instances of and explanations for varied activity and communal solidarities within the medieval English countryside. In the early twentieth century Gray outlined and sought to classify the main regional differences in terms of land-use and its organisation.[18] In his work he both set out a variety of distinct regional features, founded on the distinction between the large open fields of central England and a range of more irregular field types outside of the central-England band, and, with reference to the earlier discussion of Seebohm *et al.* on the origins of village communities, sought to explain them in terms of early patterns of settlement. As has since been noted, Gray's identification of regional difference has stood the test of time far more successfully than has his explanation of the origins of that difference.[19] Since Gray wrote, the distinctions he identified have been further studied and a good deal of research has been undertaken on the differences as well as the similarities. While it is most likely correct to say that the midlands-type, two- or three-field, system arranged about a nucleated settlement remains central to most discussion of communal organisation associated with medieval peasant agriculture, historians have also recognised the possibilities for quite discrete forms of land management and associated communal organisation. Most recently, David Hall has reviewed and extended the discussion of open fields throughout medieval England; he describes in some detail the arrangement of open fields and other kinds of field-type beyond the classic midland model, and associates different settlement types with discrete field patterns.[20] He notes that the organisation of the open field was more evident and, indeed, more necessary in the midland and central England areas of dispersed strips and communal arrangements; beyond the central belt of open fields, in East Anglia, the southwest and Kent, where field patterns were often more irregular and strips were not distributed throughout large open fields, communal organisation of management of the fields was confined often to issues of drainage and regulation of access to the common.[21]

Relative to discussion of management of cropping in the open field, there has been far less discussion of the commons in medieval England and the fifteenth-century victory of sheep over men than there has been discussion of eighteenth- and nineteenth-century enclosure and its consequences for rural society and its cohesion. Christopher Dyer has offered the fullest reflection on the medieval commons and disputes over rights of access and control. He has shown that, in the century before the Black Death, there was already an assault on common grazing land by landlords and by smaller but wealthy landholders. Importantly, in the context of discussion of communal organisation and collective responsiveness, while some enclosure could not be resisted, there is also plenty of evidence that villagers could combine either to defeat such attempts through open resistance and acts of violence and disruption or to organise legal defence against any such initiative.[22] That said, it is also clear that evidence for such associations against enclosure does not necessarily imply the existence of a village community, its resolve cemented in opposition to a rapacious outsider; rather, as Dyer describes, collective responses were often forged between members of neighbouring villages in order to protect shared grazing and inter-commoning rights while the enclosers could include groups of tenants and neighbours of those campaigning against such developments.[23]

Of relevance also in terms of a structural approach to the issue of village community is discussion of the administrative organisation of the manor and vill, both from within and from without. Helen Cam, writing in the 1940s, set out the ways in which the vill, as an administrative unit of central government as well as a focus for agrarian activity and as a defender of its own privileges and rights, might be defined in the middle ages.[24] In this Cam also drew upon the work of Maitland, who, in his study of *Township and borough* had reflected upon some of the elements which bound men and women together in rural communities which were, in his words, other than 'corporate'.[25] In other words, Maitland's community was one in which its members enjoyed rights and responsibilities but their role, as a collective, was not a determining one; as members of the village community, the responsibility of Maitland's rustics was to maintain the *status quo ante* rather than to impose a new order, an important distinction for Maitland which separated the medieval village from the modern town.[26]

Only a few historians before or since Cam have discussed the village community chiefly in terms of its administrative and legal organisation. Writing in the early 1960s, Paul Harvey offers one such instance in his discussion of the village community of medieval Cuxham (Oxfordshire), which he elects to describe in terms largely defined by manorial offices and the organisation of the vill.[27] There have been though certain continuities between the themes identified by Cam and historians writing more recently. Thus, for instance, research into demesne leasing by collectives of villagers has illustrated one of the ways in which historians might identify communal solidarities and shared agendas.[28] Here the motive for combined or communal action is established through the decision of landlords, namely the decision to lease their demesnes. In other instances, as for example, the combining of villagers in order to gather their resources or manpower to resist the demands of lordship, for example, the impetus is one of peasant resistance.[29]

To keep, though, for the moment with the kinds of administrative and institutional imperatives that encouraged collective action, we might also consider the expectations that both central government and local lords placed upon villagers as part of the regular and irregular management of state and estate. In terms of the former, there has been relatively little discussion, post-Cam, on the impact of the two main thrusts of medieval government – law and taxation – within the medieval village and upon the organisation of the local community. To begin with law, most discussion of law and the peasantry has been confined to customary law (essentially private law as employed in the manorial and other seigneurial courts of lords and with a particular but not unique focus upon the management of land held by the unfree tenants of those lords) and matters observable through the manor court. There has been some suggestion, seldom explored in any great detail, that the legal and quasi-legal structures of the manor, in particular the manor court, was, to a greater or lesser extent, a product of and foundation to the village community. Henry Maine, writing at the end of the nineteenth century, considered the manorial court, in its more ancient elements such as the view of frankpledge and the court leet, to be a product of earlier assemblies and to be at the heart of communal organisation.[30] Writing over a century later and identifying the manorial court as the 'village court', Sherri Olson makes a similar argument, suggesting that communal policing through the hue and cry and systems of pledging and mutual surety helped 'school' the individual as a member of village society.[31] The frankpledge system – a system of mutual surety and policing through tithing groups of males over the age of twelve – as an organising principle of medieval rural society and its administration through the manorial court has also been the subject of a few studies, though these have been aimed more at describing and explaining the processes of change in the system than at discussing the role of the system in helping to mould the village community.[32]

The law of the king's court has featured less, though it has appeared in some work. In one slightly anomalous context, that of local studies of the king's own manors (ancient demesne), we can say that central law has informed discussion of the rural and local community. McIntosh's investigation of the Essex vill and royal manor of Havering-atte-Bower in the later middle ages uses local court records to examine the social and economic activity of a community that, as a manor of the king's personal estate, fell within royal jurisdiction. Striking in her analysis, which chimes with earlier studies, such as that of Cam, is the view she offers of the manor court: as an important factor in the operation of the manor, helping to maintain social order, as a forum for the communication of social norms, and also as the organising body responsible for ensuring the good order of the manorial landscape, its hedges, ditches and roadways.[33] Some few historians have addressed the local or village community from the perspective of central law. Notably, John Maddicott, in influential articles both on the county court and, as we shall see below, on taxation, has identified some of the ways in which villagers might, collectively or as representatives of their communities, be identified as vills or communities, and drawn into the machinery of central government, their involvement in community in this instance imposed from above.[34] While Maddicott's aim was not to explore the peasantry or the rural community *per se*, his work did examine themes consistent with such an investigation, not least in his identification of peasant representatives within the county court. In such instances, though, individuals were there not so much as representatives of their communities but as proxies (mainpernors) for their lords.[35] Masschaele's fairly recent examination of jurors and juries in medieval England has rather more to say on the direct association between the village community and the state, and also makes clear the ways in which jury membership reached into village communities and located villagers in different fora, involving villagers, as individuals and as representatives of their communities, in dialogues with institutions of government and their social superiors.[36]

Sociological approaches to the medieval village

As Smith notes, in his discussion of the legacy of the nineteenth-century interest in the medieval village, one illustration of its persistence is what might be identified as a sociological or social structural focus upon the village community. An abiding interest of early social historians was the family and its significance as a foundation of social and communal organisation. Historians and social theorists at the end of the nineteenth and the beginning of the twentieth century developed, either more generally or within particular historical contexts, theories of social organisation and structure. Most famously, Tönnies, in his discussion of communal organisation in the middle ages, forced a distinction between *Gemeinschaft* and *Gesellschaft*, respectively communal organisations of an essentially organic kind, based for instance upon the family or the village, in contrast to such deliberately established *ad hoc* associations as guilds and other 'artificial' combinations of individuals.[37] While, as Reynolds points out, the chronology of development for the middle ages which is assumed in Tönnies's model and which proposes a succession from *Gemeinschaft* to *Gesellschaft* fails to survive close scrutiny,[38] the suggestion of a fundamental communal association based upon 'natural' or familial ties is an enduring one. Historians of the medieval English village, inspired also by early sociological work by, for example, Frederic le Play and, to a less evident degree by early sociological and anthropological study of village communities in past and present societies, have founded much of their study on the ties of the family.[39]

Most obviously, G.C. Homans, in a largely theoretical final chapter of his work on the English villager of the thirteenth century in which he discusses the 'anatomy' of medieval rural society, returns to his sociological training and sets out what, for him, appear to be the determining factors in communal organisation, essentially the interaction of common purpose and shared sentiment. He suggests that as one element in the structure of society varied, so did others in order to compensate and to allow a system of mutual support and dependency to function. Thus, for Homans, differences in, say, inheritance practice between eastern and central England reflected other differences between these differing regions.[40] The fundamental features of this difference included landholding and its organisation, family structures, lordship and communal or cultural ties, such as the influence of the church, of feasts and holy days.[41] A quarter of Homans's book on the villager in the thirteenth century relates to discussion of the family and of inheritance; in his discussion of the family, he appears to echo Tönnies in his suggestion that, by the thirteenth century and especially in champion or open-field England, the rule of primogeniture in inheritance had brought medieval society a step closer to 'the social isolation in which many families live in the great urban agglomerations of today'.[42] While Homans detects, in place-name evidence for instance, indication of communities once all but defined by shared kinship, he sees in high and late medieval England a different kind of social organisation, and one which, through inheritance regimes, maintained a close familial link with communities while at the same jettisoning the non-inheriting members of the community.[43] The net effect within village communities in champion England, to follow Homans, was to generate stability and a general consistency of landholding and of familial continuities.[44] This was especially notable in the link between families and their land – the so-called 'family-land bond' – in which familial attachment to particular units of land is maintained over generations, the family name closely associated with discrete landholding. Such close association was identified as inimical to alienation of landholdings, and Homans offered examples which indicate that, beyond the family, village communities reflected the same resistance to piecemeal alienation of land. In this respect, familial and communal expectations were shared at the village level, and were generally intended to maintain the *status quo*.[45]

Homans's work had a significant impact upon later study of the medieval village and its peasantry. His claims about the peasant family's close ties to the land took firm hold for a generation and were, as we have also considered in earlier chapters, consistent with historical assessments of a generally sluggish market in land.[46] Homans's work also helped, in the promotion of a sociological approach, to establish the agenda for the next generation of historians, one which focused upon family and kinship, social structure, patterns of inheritance and the transfer of land. In this respect, as we shall see, the establishment of these research areas stood in contrast to other countervailing approaches, notably a Marxist investigation of the medieval village with its focus upon lord–tenant relations and class solidarities.[47] Fuelled also by the approaches of new social history in the 1960s and 1970s, historians writing a generation after Homans also turned to his work for inspiration while, at the same moment, they also developed new routes into the medieval village. Thus, J.A. Raftis acknowledged his significant debt, identifying Homans as a 'pioneer' and one occupying pride of place in his own historiographical pantheon.[48] He also suggested that Homans's agenda needed a response, not least in the call for close study of particular manors and communities.

Raftis's work, especially in his study of *Tenure and mobility* on the manors of the abbey of Ramsey's estate, established a new direction in the study of medieval communities. While much of Raftis's study was grounded in the traditional historiography of lordship and the obligations of tenants, Raftis also devoted considerable space in his study to the analysis of 'group activity' in the village. Drawing inspiration from sociological literature, most notably Redfield's *The little community*, Raftis discusses the regulation of the 'village', rather than the manor, as a feature of 'self-government', and a reflection of 'corporate responsibility', terms that take the medieval village closer to Tönnies's *Gesellschaft* than to *Gemeinschaft* and suggest that some distance existed between Raftis's conception of the village community and that presented by Maitland.[49] For Raftis, the capacity for self-organisation, not so much in opposition to lordship but more as a means of mediating lordship as one facet of village life, is an important index of communal organisation, as illustrated by his discussion of village by-laws and the ways in which contemporaries made frequent and informed reference to the same.[50]

Rather less evident in Raftis's early work on manor and village is the peasant family. While Raftis does indeed discuss the peasant family in some of his earliest work, especially in terms of distribution of landholding and inheritance, he offers little comment on the relative importance and role of peasant families within the village community.[51] In this Raftis's work stands in some contrast to those other historians who, adopting similar approaches and, like Raftis, focusing their research upon the Ramsey Abbey estates, wrote in the two or more decades after the publication of *Tenure and mobility*. Making use of court rolls for the manors of Ramsey Abbey, historians at the Pontifical Institute in Toronto, the so-called 'Toronto School', explored the structure of the medieval village communities under their observation as well as changes in the nature of 'community' across the high and late middle ages.[52] Adopting a sociological approach of the kind already noted, and drawing extensively upon fairly simple identifiers, Raftis and in particular his colleagues from the following generation distinguished between three sub-sets of the manor, or village as they chose to term it: rich, middling and poor villagers. The Toronto historians have tended to identify such distinctions by types of activity recorded in the manorial court rolls, especially the propensity of male members to hold office (identified as an activity of the relatively wealthy);[53] from this, other kinds of activity, such as taking on further office, having children out of wedlock or engaging in a variety of misdemeanours and trespasses, also then tend to be explained in terms of one's membership of a particular social group.[54]

The approach of the 'Toronto School' is distinctive in that it has at its core a focus upon a perceived community, founded upon its villager membership and where the significant activity of that membership was intra-communal interaction. In this discussion of community a good deal of the analysis is directed at the internal dynamic of the village, with the main areas of discussion dominated by inter-villager exchange, as well as some additional discussion of movement, permanent and temporary, of individuals and families to and from the village or manor. Thus, important themes for this analysis include mutual reciprocity, as evidenced by small-scale exchange, and patterns of neighbourliness. In this historiographical tradition, the community is subjected to analysis in terms of the sub-groups within particular villages and manors and also as regards change over time. In the first place, most historians working within this tradition have tended to stress distinctions between sub-groups and to have identified certain kinds of activity as either exclusive to certain groups or tending to transfer between groups. In this the historians of the Pontifical Institute were effectively, though certainly not explicitly, adopting an approach that was structurationist, in that, by their account, peasants' own activity helped to mould the kinds of social structures that regulated village society, and through which, in turn, they were also defined.[55] Thus, for instance, by taking on office and important roles within the village, the more powerful and affluent villagers were able to secure their position and to extend their control over the village community.[56] Secondly, historians working within this tradition have tended to observe change in the nature of the village community and to have characterised such change mostly in terms of a decline in the force of the bonds which held together the medieval village community.[57] For these historians, the strength of the village community is defined by a number of significant indicators, including the willingness of individuals to support each other, as for instance in standing as surety for one another, to take on responsibilities, such as office-holding, and to cooperate in everyday life, and thereby not to inflict misdemeanours and acts of petty violence or theft upon each other. Analysis of the Ramsey court rolls suggested to the historians working in this tradition that, in fact, such communal bonds were loosened in the later fourteenth century. Increases in criminal and tortious behaviour are matched, in their analysis, only by declines in the rate of mutual support and reciprocity, measured through, for instance, the preparedness of villagers to involve themselves in such activity as personal pledging, standing surety for their neighbours and/or family members. While, as already noted, such an analysis has not been without its critics and there is certainly a justifiable sense that the changing content of the court rolls does not wholly or even closely reflect an absolute measure of the kinds of activity under observation, it is clear that historians working outside of this 'Toronto School' tradition have also identified at least familiar features of change in manors and villages subjected to their own analysis. Their interpretation of long-term change has however been quite distinctive. Christopher Dyer, for instance, identifies change within the medieval village over the later middle ages but suggests that the concept of 'decline' is not helpful when applied to that process. He argues that pre-plague villagers were not evidently harmonious but instead 'a practical and functional organization, not a cozy association of neighbors'; post-plague developments, including what appears to have been a greater role for village elites in managing moral behaviour and the social integrity of the village, do not speak to decline but a vigorous response to a changing social and economic landscape.[58]

In this respect, therefore, we can also note that North American historians working within this broad Toronto framework helped to establish a new approach to the study of the medieval peasant and his or her community, and thereby managed to encourage the development of an important area of study. In so doing, however, the shift of emphasis was such that long-established agenda items in the investigation of the medieval peasantry were, at least partially and sometimes only temporarily, set to one side. Thus, most obviously, lordship and matters pertaining to the manor rather than the village feature far less prominently in this approach than they did in earlier traditions of writing on the medieval peasant and the medieval village, something their critics were not slow to point out.

Marxism and the village community

One of the most strongly critical attacks upon the sociological view of the medieval village community came from Zvi Razi, who, in a trenchant article in the journal *Past and Present*, demanded that historians employ a nuanced investigation of manorial court rolls when attempting to analyse relations within the village community. Strikingly, Razi, a postgraduate student of the University of Birmingham and supervised by Rodney Hilton, the doyen of Marxist studies of the medieval English peasantry, concentrated his attack upon the historical analysis and the reading of the sources. Though he did not offer a detailed alternative to the sociological analysis of the working of the medieval community, there are more than just tell-tales hints of his sympathies, notably in his insistence that, while distinctions between rich and poor tenants existed in the medieval village, a chief threat to both rich and poor was the oppression and exploitation of the seigneurial regime. Razi also notes, significantly, that despite inevitable communal tension and competition between members of the same village community, the defining characteristic of the medieval peasantry, at a point when he contends the village community was at its zenith, was its preparedness to combine against the demands of lordship. Razi refines this point by suggesting that, as well as a shared resistance to lordship, wealthier medieval villagers co-operated with their poorer neighbours in order to maintain the degree of harmony necessary for their own socio-economic benefit, especially in terms of their ability to make use of the labour provided by lowlier village households.[59] As he notes, Razi was also, in general terms, reflecting the arguments of Rodney Hilton. As we have discussed earlier in this volume, Hilton contended that the medieval peasantry was a class, defined by its resistance to lordship. While, as we have seen, Hilton also detected intra-village tensions, he contended that the main communal thrust was towards collective organisation and a shared agenda of resistance to lordship.[60] These are themes that have also been explored in an earlier chapter, as part of the consideration of historical discussion of lords and tenants, and we will not make a detailed return to the same points here.

Historians such as Hilton have also identified the ways in which tenants might combine their actions in defiance of their lord. In the following chapter – as part of a discussion of political culture – we will consider the ways in which medieval historians have often identified such shared grievance and its expression as an instance of collective action and communal solidarity. This could take the form of open revolt and violent resistance, but could also include such action as non-cooperation towards lords, especially as regards the payment of rent and, particularly in this respect, labour services.[61] Discussion of resistance is also used by historians to define the medieval village community in terms of its combined activity in endeavours other than violence and revolt. Thus, and again most of this work has been produced by historians operating from within or by association with a Marxist school even if they were not necessarily Marxists themselves, historians in the last half-century have studied, *en passant*, the ways in which villagers combined their finances in order to employ lawyers or to pursue in other ways actions against their lords in the central courts. Hilton first drew attention to the potential of the records of central government, including *curia regis* and chancery rolls, to shed light on this kind of activity in the thirteenth century and a next generation of his students, Rosamund Faith and Christopher Dyer, have also shown how 'communities' of peasants might combine their energies in similar pursuits in the central courts.[62] As an approach this stands in some contrast, but one chiefly of emphasis, to the earlier work of Cam, already discussed in this chapter. Cam, as we have seen, had also identified the potential of central government to help define and draw together the village community but in her work there was rather less room for peasant agency; that said, she did, alongside the identification of a series of ways in which central government gave shape and purpose to the community of the vill, also recognise that the community might act as an entity in law.[63] Despite this considerable degree of consonance, evidence for a distinct approach between the institutional and Marxist traditions is evident as, for instance, in the historical discussion of manorial officers. For historians with a focus upon class struggle, local manorial officers, such as the reeve and bailiff, who worked for the lord in securing the function of the manorial economy but were also of the peasantry and were members of that community, were ultimately and necessarily to be associated with their class and not their institutional role.[64]

Individualists and the medieval village community

Few if any medieval historians have ever been inclined to suggest that the medieval village was constructed around the individual rather than some broader grouping. Indeed for most historians of the medieval village the individual seldom features prominently, if at all, in their construction of medieval society. Whole monographs have been written on the medieval English agrarian economy without reference to the name of a single peasant; instead, and this is a feature consistent with an earlier focus on institutions and especially lordship rather than peasants and/ or tenants, rural dwellers have more often been identified by their socio-economic or tenurial status, that is as collectives: as family members, tenants, peasants, small-holders, cottars, virgaters, villeins, free tenants and so on.

There has of course also been occasional and clear focus on the individual and on the detailed case study, both for its own sake and as an example of some wider trend, experience or development. Thus, most obviously, Judith Bennett's account of one peasant women, Cecilia Penifader of Brigstock, illustrates the ways in which a detailed prosopographical analysis can be employed to illustrate a range of features of the medieval economy and society.[65] Bennett's discussion, which reveals the possibility of extracting some few but pertinent features of individual peasant lives, is also a product of her desire to place medieval women in the foreground of historical study, themes also considered in the previous chapter.[66] Earlier studies might also have included similar ambitions, as for instance Eileen Power's biographical exploration of 'medieval people' which brings a verve and sense of mission to 'reconstructing the life of some quite ordinary person'.[67] Power's famous discussion of medieval lives does not include a history of a medieval English peasant though she does offer a chapter on a French peasant, Bodo, from the late eighth or early ninth century, and a French townswoman of the later middle ages. More recently, there has been some return to a more immediately biographical investigation of medieval peasants and their associates, most obviously in Dyer's close examination of John Heritage, a Cotswold wool merchant, grazier and farmer operating in the later fifteenth and early sixteenth centuries and whose account book permits a variety of insights into his own business dealings but also a particular view of a more general world of rural trading at the end of the middle ages. Dyer had earlier also adopted a quasi-biographical approach in discussing the career of the Suffolk farmer Robert Parman, the fifteenth-century lessee of substantial units of land from the abbey of Bury St Edmunds at Chevington (Suffolk). Dyer sets Parman's life within the context of later medieval agrarian change and employs him as an exemplar of the upwardly mobile peasant, able to use his position, reputation and capital to promote his own advancement and that of his family.[68] Investigation of particular events, of legal tussles and of small- and larger-scale conflicts has also thrown up relatively detailed commentaries of individual peasants, their actions and their motives, as have case-studies of economic activity, including buying and selling on the peasant land market.[69] There is also a light tradition of imagined, or partly imagined, lives, reconstructed from the generality of recorded experience.[70] Despite these occasional and sometimes piecemeal attempts at reconstructing lives or aspects of the lives of medieval peasants, the individual peasant as a subject for investigation remains quite remote from traditional writing in this area. The *Oxford Dictionary of National Biography*, to quote one obvious example, does not include biographies of medieval peasants, even as exemplars, say, of a social or economic type, and reference there to 'peasants' or to 'peasantry' tends to be confined to reference to the origins of those who had risen to new social levels (for instance, the wife of William Paston (I)) or to events in which peasants, again identified *en masse*, participated (such as the beheading of 315 'peasant archers' by Henry III in May 1264).[71]

While undoubtedly the main reason for the lack of detailed biographies of medieval peasants is practical and wholly evident, namely a lack of sources of a kind that might allow such a detailed and individual reconstruction,[72] it is also the case that our expectation of biography is largely predicated on a sense of the unusual and rare, with more than a hint of the spectacular or exceptional. Such criteria seem to be more evidently generated within political, religious, intellectual or cultural history than they are, say, in economic or perhaps even social history, where historians are often thrown back upon the wider social or economic unit and where the individual is introduced by the historian into the discussion in order to exemplify the greater unit rather than to be identified as separate from it or in some other way discrete.

This is not however to say that the concept of the individual and the view that the peasant might operate as an individualist rather than wholly and always as a member of a larger unit – family, tenantry, village community, guild, peasantry and so on – does not operate within the relevant literature. We find relatively little discussion of the individual peasant as economic agent and player, as kulak and village leader, as an individual in his or her own right before the last decades of the twentieth century. That said, references by R.H. Tawney to village usurers as 'the bugbear' of the medieval village certainly stand out as representative of a view that not all peasants shared a common notion of collective good and shared endeavour.[73] W.H. Hudson, writing also in the first decades of the twentieth century was regretful of the competitive and other than altruistic zeal with which some villagers entered in to the land market.[74] It is though most evidently in the 1970s and 1980s, with the shift towards a history of the medieval countryside more closely focused upon the market, exchange for money's worth and a commercialised economy operating both within and beyond the medieval village, that we can detect what is in fact a very strong theme of individual economic endeavour.[75]

Writing in the mid-1990s, Raftis challenged the use of the term 'kulak' in describing the wealthier villagers of medieval England. Quoting Solzhenitsyn's particularly charged definition of a kulak as 'a miserly, dishonest rural trader who grows rich not by his own labor but through someone else's, through usury and operating as a middleman', he defied historians of the medieval village to apply the term to the relatively well-to-do of the medieval English peasantry.[76] This is not to suggest that Raftis rejected the notion of social and economic differentiation within the village; much indeed of his work was based upon the identification and dissection of such differences and he recognised the willingness of peasants to engage in individual activity. It is though also evident that he, along with many other historians such as Marxist historians whose perspective we have already had cause to discuss in this chapter, was not especially comfortable with the notion of an aggressively acquisitive peasantry, an environment in which neighbour might routinely prey upon neighbour. Such a perspective was however increasingly subject to challenge. In terms of empirical research on the medieval peasant and individual economic activity, the major development came through the investigations of Richard Smith. Smith's research on the Bury St Edmunds manor of Redgrave illustrated, as has already been discussed, the vitality and volatility of land transfer on the manor. While recording the patterns within the land market, Smith also offered some substantial comment on the individual activity within that market and set out instances of the campaigns of buying and selling by individual peasants.[77] At Redgrave, some of the more active purchasers of land behaved in ways that were focused neither, as it seemed, upon the expectations of a supposed wider community nor on those of their own families and kin groups. Smith identifies acquisitive behaviour on the part of some families, such as the Jops and the Pistors in the later thirteenth and early fourteenth centuries, as well as piecemeal sale of land by a number of families. In fact Smith detects extensive evidence for inter-familial sales, to an extent that forces him to question 'any notion of the sanctity of the family holding'.[78] He also notes, however, evidence for adjustment of landholding from within the family, the net effect of which, in an area of partible inheritance, was to lead to fragmentation and polarisation of landholding as small parcels of land found their way on to a market in land.[79]

Smith's work attracted interest both from other medievalists working in the same area and from those eager to draw broader conclusions from his research. Most notably and as we have discussed in more detail in the introduction to this book, Alan Macfarlane made use of Smith's doctoral thesis as the basis of a forthright denunciation of the very concept of a medieval English peasantry.[80] Macfarlane argued that rural dwellers in the middle ages did not meet such accepted criteria as would allow them to be identified as 'peasants'; contending that peasants were defined by a set of characteristics inconsistent with the evidence emerging for medieval England, he suggested that medieval rural dwellers in England 'were rampant individualists, highly mobile both geographically and socially, economically "rational", market-oriented and acquisitive, ego-centred in kinship and social life'.[81] In attempting such an argument he identified Richard Smith's research on Redgrave as central to his own interpretation of society and social structure in medieval England. At various points in his own survey Macfarlane draws attention to the ways in which Smith's work on medieval rural society had identified a high proportion of nucleated households relative to co-residencies, an extensive market in small plots of land for money or money's worth, and widespread recourse to life-cycle service.[82] Macfarlane especially embraced Smith's own challenge to the assumption that a family-land bond was prevalent in medieval England. Reviewing the work of earlier generations of historians – Homans, Raftis, Postan, Hilton – Macfarlane also suggested that the historical perception of a familial attachment to land was founded upon an assumption on the part of medieval historians and not something evidently supported by the sources. He contended that such views of rural dwellers and their motive forces were predicated upon underlying preconceptions of the nature of an imagined 'peasant' society and economy.[83] In this, as will be evident, Macfarlane's discussion also reflects much earlier historiographical themes, most especially the later nineteenth-century debate, encouraged by the work of Henry Maine, regarding the perceived emergence of individualism from communalism. In this respect, Macfarlane appears to share a position adopted much earlier by Maitland that the rights of the individual are more in evidence in the medieval and pre-medieval rural settlement than are the rights of the community.[84]

While Smith himself had never offered such a stringent assessment of the distance between his work and that of previous discussions of the medieval English peasantry, there is no doubt that his investigation of quite discrete manorial conditions in eastern England played a significant part in helping to revise historians' perceptions of the nature of what, despite Macfarlane, most historians were still prepared to identify as medieval peasant society. The collection of essays edited by Smith in 1984 addressed themes that grappled with the seemingly alternative views of describing and accounting for medieval and early modern rural society.[85] For instance, Ian Blanchard's study of Derbyshire proto-industrial society in the later middle ages presents a revealing case study of the ways in which the complex regional and quasi-commercialised economy of a lead-mining community in medieval Derbyshire might, conceivably at least, accommodate both entrepreneurialism and long-standing and deep-rooted commitment to retaining familial holdings.[86] Blanchard's own involved argument, intended to illustrate the cross-generational persistence of communal and familial commitments to the retention of family holdings even where evidence appears to point towards disruption of a family-land bond, was treated with some scepticism by Smith who questioned the inherent difficulty of identifying the sorts of collective memory inherent in Blanchard's characterisation of the tenurial histories of peasant holdings in the later middle ages. Smith is however more convinced by Blanchard's discussion of the varying socio-economic contexts that may have allowed some groups of individuals in rural society to gather holdings while condemning others to a 'precarious hold on land'.[87] Other contributions in the same collection, and notably those by Razi and Dyer, also teased out such themes and both addressed the issue of familial links to land in the later middle ages. Razi, returning to his research on the manor of Halesowen, took a not wholly dissimilar line to that propounded by Blanchard. In his essay he argues that it was the nature of the family-land bond that shifted and that, rather than it being eroded, it was re-established through more indirect kin associations in the post-Black Death period.[88] Both Razi and Blanchard sought then not to question the assumption that a family-land bond existed in the middle ages but instead to challenge the suggestion that it was significantly eroded in the later middle ages, a point already discussed earlier in this chapter. Christopher Dyer, by contrast, argues that the socio-economic conditions, distinctions between tenurial forms and changes in the same, as well as the varying demand for land between places and over time, argue against consistent familial continuity in landholding; even, as he notes, in those instances where distant kin, beyond the original nuclear family, took up holdings upon the death of more immediate kin, a close link to the land had effectively been lost.[89]

As we have seen, some historians returned to the discussion of the family-land bond in the years after the publication of the essays in *Land, kinship and life-cycle*, most notably Razi, who developed his ideas more fully in an article published in *Past and Present* in 1993. The overall significance, in historiographical terms, of the arguments expressed in this collection and in the more general discussion of such themes as individuality, acquisitiveness and engagement with a market in land, was that these issues not so much led historians back to a reassessment of the familial nature of the peasant land market but instead directed them to examine other features of peasant interaction, not ones determined wholly or largely by family or tenure.[90] In this respect, then, more recent work, while focusing less upon such themes as the family-land bond and indeed upon the peasant family at all, has tended to pursue the individual, though not necessarily as the 'rampant individualist' of Macfarlane's characterisation. Instead, historians have explored such themes as quasi-entrepreneurialism in the medieval village, the use of law in manorial courts, litigation over debt and the establishment of credit relations.[91] This has inevitably directed historians' attentions towards the individual, as for instance in discussion of inter-personal litigation, but there is no strong sense that the identified individual has been altogether recast as other than a member of his or her own family or community.[92] Rather more, the consequence of this deeper investigation of the world of the medieval peasant has been to develop a more multi-faceted view of the individual, as someone capable of operating within more than a single sphere and not necessarily being so constrained or dominated by community, family and lordship as had previously seemed to be the case.[93] That multi-faceted view, as we will discuss in the final chapter, has also encouraged a fuller exploration of such themes as peasant agency and, to a certain degree, the cultural history of the medieval English peasantry.

Notes

1 See above, Chapter 2, pp. 59-77, Chapter 3, pp. 84-108, and Chapter 4, pp. 117-41.
2 C. Carpenter, 'Gentry and community in medieval England', *Journal of British Studies* 33 (1994), 340-80; see also R.M. Smith, '"Modernization" and the corporate medieval village in England: some sceptical reflections', in A.R.H. Baker and D. Gregory, eds, *Explorations in historical geography. Interpretative essays* (Cambridge: Cambridge University Press, 1984), pp. 140-79.
3 Carpenter, 'Gentry and community', p. 343.
4 See, for instance, M.M. Postan, 'The charters of the villeins', in M.M. Postan, *Essays in medieval agriculture and general problems of the medieval economy* (Cambridge: Cambridge University Press, 1973), pp. 114-15, 144-5, and discussion of the same above, Chapter 2, pp. 63-6, and Chapter 4, p. 123.
5 For a summary of relevant developments in the changing theory of manorial origins, C. Dyer, 'The past, present and the future in medieval rural history', *Rural History* 1 (1990), 37-49.
6 T.H. Aston, 'The origins of the manor in England', *Transactions of the Royal Historical Society* 8 (1958), reprinted in T.H. Aston, P.R. Coss, C. Dyer and J, Thirsk, eds, *Social relations and ideas. Essays in honour of R.H. Hilton* (Cambridge: Cambridge University Press, 1983), pp. 1-25, and T.H. Aston, 'The origins of the manor in England: a postscript', in Aston *et al.*, eds, *Social relations and ideas*, pp. 26-43.
7 For earlier discussion in this respect, see above, Chapter 1, pp. 44-7.
8 C.S. and C.S. Orwin, *The open fields* (2nd ed., Oxford: Oxford University Press, 1954), pp. 36-42, 61-2.
9 For discussion of which, see above, Chapter 1, pp. 44-5.
10 J. Thirsk, 'The common fields', *Past and Present* 29 (1964), and the subsequent debate: J.Z. Titow, 'Medieval England and the open-field system', *Past and Present* 32 (1965), and J. Thirsk, 'The origin of the common fields', *Past and Present* 33 (1966), all of which are reprinted in R.H. Hilton, ed., *Peasants, knights and heretics. Studies in medieval English social history* (Cambridge: Cambridge University Press, 1976), pp. 10-56. These and relevant themes are usefully discussed in H.S.A. Fox, 'Approaches to the adoption of the Midland system', in T. Rowley, ed., *The origins of open-field agriculture* (London: Croom Helm, 1981), pp. 64-111; Fox also concludes that the system was fully developed by the end of the twelfth century, p. 88.
11 C.C. Taylor, 'Archaeology and the origins of open-field agriculture', in Rowley, ed., *Origins of open-field agriculture* , p. 21.
12 On the variety of interpretations applied to the issue of how common field agriculture developed, see, for instance, Dyer, 'Past, present and the future in medieval rural history', 41-2.
13 W.O. Ault, 'Village by-laws by common consent', *Speculum* 29 (1954); W.O. Ault, *Open-field farming in medieval England* (London, 1972).
14 D.N. McCloskey, 'The persistence of English Common Fields', in W.N.

Parker and E.L. Jones, eds, *European peasants and their markets* (Princeton, N.J.: Princeton University Press, 1975), pp. 73–119; D.N. McCloskey, 'English open fields as a behaviour towards risk', in P. Uselding, ed., *Research in Economic History, I* (Greenwich, Conn.: JAI Press, 1976), pp. 124–70; C.J. Dahlman, *The open field system and beyond* (Cambridge: Cambridge University Press, 1980).

15 Contrast, though the discussion of R.C. Allen, 'Community and market in England: open fields and enclosures revisited', in M. Aoki and Y. Hayami, eds, *Communities and markets in economic development* (Oxford: Oxford University Press, 2001), pp. 42–69, for the view that pre-enclosure open fields were sites of innovation and agricultural development.

16 D. McCloskey, 'The prudent peasant: new findings on open fields', *Journal of Economic History* 51 (1991), 343–55 (quote at p. 355). McCloskey's work in this respect is summarised in D.N. McCloskey, 'The open fields of England: rent, risk, and the rate of interest, 1300–1815', in D.W. Gallenson, ed., *Markets in history. Economic studies of the past* (Cambridge: Cambridge University Press, 1980), pp. 5–51.

17 G. Richardson, 'The prudent villager: risk pooling institutions in medieval English agriculture', *Journal of Economic History* 65 (2005), 386–413; also G. Richardson, 'What protected peasants best? Markets, risk, efficiency, and medieval English agriculture', *Research in Economic History* 2003.

18 H.L. Gray, *The English field systems* (Cambridge, Mass.: Harvard University Press, 1915).

19 For instance, B. Campbell, 'Commonfield origins – the regional dimension', in Rowley, ed., *Origins of open-field agriculture*, p. 112.

20 D. Hall, *The open fields of England* (Oxford: Oxford University Press, 2014), pp. 7–10.

21 Hall, *Open fields*, p. 128.

22 C. Dyer, 'Conflict in the landscape: the enclosure movement in England, 1220–1349', *Landscape History* 28 (2006), 21–33; also, C. Dyer, *An age of transition? Economy and society in England in the later middle ages* (Oxford: Oxford University Press, 2005), pp. 58–66.

23 Dyer, 'Conflict in the landscape', 22–5, 31.

24 H. Cam, 'The community of the vill', in H. Cam, *Law-finders and law-makers in medieval England* (London: The Merlin Press, 1962), pp. 71–84.

25 F.W. Maitland, *Township and borough* (Cambridge: Cambridge University Press, 1898), pp. 25–6; also Maitland, 'The survival of archaic communities', pp. 313–65.

26 Maitland, *Township and borough*, pp. 33–6; this suggests some association with the *Gemeinschaften* of Tönnies's bi-partite model, namely that the influence of 'rustics' issued from pre-existing and essentially organic institutions, such as family, rather than new and more progressive bodies, such as guilds or urban governments, for fuller discussion of which see below, pp. 241, 242, 244.

27 P.D.A. Harvey, *A medieval Oxfordshire village. Cuxham, 1240 to 1400* (Oxford: Oxford University Press, 1965), pp. 140–8.

28 B.F. Harvey, 'The leasing of the abbot of Westminster's demesnes in the later

middle ages', *Economic History Review* 22 (1969), 17–27; F.R.H. Du Boulay, 'Who were farming the English demesnes at the end of the middle ages?', *Economic History Review* 17 (1964), 443–55.

29 For which, see below, pp. 209–11.

30 H.S. Maine, *Village communities in the east and west* (London: John Murray; 4th ed., 1881), pp. 139–40.

31 S. Olson, *A chronicle of all that happens. Voices from the village court in medieval England* (Toronto: Pontifical Institute, 1996), pp. 45–6.

32 D.A. Crowley, 'The later history of frankpledge', *Bulletin of the Institute of Historical Research* 48 (1975), 1–25; P.R. Schofield, 'The late medieval frankpledge system: an Essex case study', in Z. Razi and R.M. Smith, eds, *Medieval society and the manor court* (Oxford: Oxford University Press, 1996), pp. 408–49.

33 M.K. McIntosh, *Autonomy and community. The royal manor of Havering, 1200–1500* (Cambridge: Cambridge University Press, 1986), pp. 201–15.

34 J.R. Maddicott, 'The county community and the making of public opinion in fourteenth century England', *Transactions of the Royal Historical Society*, 5th series, 28 (1978), 27–43; J.R. Maddicott, 'Magna Carta and the local community', *Past and Present* 102 (1984), 25–65; J.R. Maddicott, 'Politics and the people in thirteenth-century England', in J. Burton, P.R. Schofield and B. Weiler, eds, *Thirteenth century England* XIV (Woodbridge: Boydell and Brewer, 2013), pp. 1–13.

35 See, for instance, Maddicott, 'County community', 32–3.

36 J. Masschaele, *Jury, state and society in medieval England* (Basingstoke: Palgrave, 2008).

37 F. Tönnies, *Gemeinschaft und Gesellschaft. Grundbegriffe der reinen Soziologie* (Berlin: K. Curtius, 1922). For a recent English edition, F. Tönnies, *Community and civil society*, ed. J. Harris; trans. M. Hollis (Cambridge: Cambridge University Press, 2001).

38 S. Reynolds, *Kingdoms and communities in western Europe, 900–1300* (Oxford: Oxford University Press, 1984), pp. 332–9.

39 For discussion of which see Smith, 'Modernization', p. 155. On le Play and his significance for the study of medieval English peasant families, see, for instance, G.C. Homans, *English villagers of the thirteenth century* (Cambridge, Mass.: Harvard University Press, 1941), p. 215.

40 Homans, *English villagers*, pp. 413–15.

41 Homans, *English villagers, passim*.

42 Homans, *English villagers*, p. 217.

43 Homans, *English villagers*, p. 215.

44 Homans, *English villagers*, p. 215.

45 Homans, *English villagers*, pp. 194–200.

46 See, for example, R. Faith, 'Peasant families and inheritance customs in medieval England', *Agricultural History Review* 14 (1966), 86–92, and also above, Chapter 2, pp. 64–6, 74–7, and Chapter 4, pp. 128–33.

47 See below, this chapter, and also above, Chapter 3, pp. 91–108.

48 J.A. Raftis, *Tenure and mobility: studies in the social history of the medieval English village* (Toronto: Pontifical Institute of Mediaeval Studies, 1964), p. 13.

49 Raftis, *Tenure and mobility*, pp. 93, 105; for Maitland's rejection of the argument for a corporate village community, see above, pp. 47, 202.
50 Raftis, *Tenure and mobility*, pp. 111-27.
51 Raftis, *Tenure and mobility*, pp. 33-62; 208-9.
52 Raftis, *Tenure and mobility*; J.A. Raftis, *Warboys: two hundred years in the life of an English medieval village* (Toronto: Pontifical Institute of Mediaeval Studies, 1974); J.A. Raftis, 'Changes in an English village after the Black Death', *Medieval Studies* 29 (1967), 158-77; E.B. DeWindt, *Land and people in Holywell-cum-Needingworth* (Toronto: Pontifical Institute of Mediaeval Studies, 1972); A. DeWindt, 'Peasant power structures in fourteenth-century King's Ripton', *Medieval Studies* 38 (1976), 236-67; E. Britton, 'The peasant family in fourteenth-century England', *Journal of Peasant Studies* 5 (1976), 2-7; E. Britton, *The community of the vill: a study in the history of the family and village life in fourteenth-century England* (Toronto: Pontifical Institute of Mediaeval Studies, 1977).
53 For a critique of this particular point, see S.H. Rigby, *English society in the later middle ages. Class, status and gender* (Basingstoke: Macmillan, 1995), pp. 47-8
54 See, for instance, DeWindt, *Land and people*, pp. 206-41; Britton, *Community of the vill*, pp. 12-15; such an approach has not been without its critics, Z. Razi, 'The Toronto School's reconstitution of medieval peasant society: a critical view', *Past and Present* 85 (1979), 141-57.
55 See, for example, Raftis, *Tenure and mobility*, p. 206: 'these villagers were capable of adapting all types of institutions to their own use'. On structurationist approaches more generally and their potential applicability for this period, see Rigby, *English society*, p. 59.
56 For instance, Britton, *Community of the vill*, pp. 94-102.
57 See, for example, DeWindt, *Land and people*, pp. 263-75.
58 C. Dyer, 'The English medieval village community and its decline', *Journal of British Studies* 33 (1994), 407-29 (quote at p. 429).
59 Razi, 'Toronto School', p. 156. Elsewhere, Razi was far more direct in espousing a more obviously Marxist line, as for instance, Z. Razi, 'The struggles between the abbots of Halesowen and their tenants in the thirteenth and fourteenth centuries', in Aston *et al.*, eds, *Social relations and ideas*, pp. 151-67; Z. Razi, 'Family, land and the village community in later medieval England', *Past and Present* 93 (1981), reprinted in T.H. Aston, ed., *Landlords, peasants and politics in medieval England* (Cambridge: Cambridge University Press, 1987), pp. 360-93, and especially pp. 372-3, 390-3, from which this and subsequent references are taken.
60 See above, Chapter 3, pp. 91-105.
61 See below, Chapter 8, pp. 233-4.
62 R. Faith, 'The "Great Rumour" of 1377 and peasant ideology', in R.H. Hilton and T.H. Aston, eds, *The English Rising of 1381* (Cambridge: Cambridge University Press, 1984); C. Dyer, 'Memories of freedom: attitudes towards serfdom in England, 1200-1350', in M.L. Bush, ed., *Serfdom and slavery. Studies in legal bondage* (Harlow: Longman, 1996).
63 Cam, 'Community of the vill', pp. 80-1.

64 For a more neutral assessment of the reeve, which focuses on the origins of the office and role but also identifies the office in relation to the longer-term historical development of the manor and vill and sees him as an agent of both the vill and the lord, see P.D.A. Harvey, 'The manorial reeve in twelfth-century England', in R. Evans, ed., *Lordship and learning. Studies in memory of Trevor Aston* (Woodbridge: Boydell, 2004), pp. 125-38; see also the comments in S. Justice, *Writing and rebellion. England in 1381* (Berkeley: University of California Press, 1994), pp. 229-30.
65 J.M. Bennett, *A medieval life. Cecilia Penifader of Brigstock, c.1295-1344* (Boston: McGraw-Hill College, 1999).
66 See above, Chapter 5, pp. 182-91.
67 E. Power, *Medieval people* (Harmondsworth: Penguin, 1937), p. vii.
68 C. Dyer, 'A Suffolk farmer in the fifteenth century', *Agricultural History Review* 55 (2007); C. Dyer, *A country merchant, 1495-1520: trading and farming at the end of the middle ages* (Oxford: Oxford University Press, 2012).
69 See, for instance, P.R. Schofield, 'Peasants and the manor court: gossip and litigation in a Suffolk village at the close of the thirteenth century', *Past and Present* 159 (1998), 3-42.
70 J. Hatcher, *The Black Death. The intimate story of a village in crisis, 1345-1350* (London: Phoenix, 2008). For earlier exercises in imagined village lives, see H.S. Bennett, *Life on the English manor. A study of peasant conditions 1150-1400* (Cambridge: Cambridge University Press, 1937; reprinted Stroud: Alan Sutton, 1987), pp. 4-25; P. Ziegler, *The Black Death* (London: Penguin, 1969), pp. 209-31.
71 For which see the following: C. Richmond, R. Virgoe, 'Paston, William (I) (1378-1444)', *Oxford Dictionary of National Biography* (Oxford: Oxford University Press, 2004, online edn, September 2010) [hereafter *ODNB*], available at www.oxforddnb.com/view/article/21514, accessed 24 September 2014; H. W. Ridgeway, 'Henry III (1207-1272)', *ODNB*, available at www.oxforddnb.com/view/article/12950, accessed 24 September 2014.
72 We might not quite agree with H.E. Hallam's assessment that 'a peasant diary from the thirteenth century or a peasant family's correspondence from the twelfth century would be worth all the Pipe Rolls and Curia Regis Rolls in the Public Record Office' but, of course, no such sources are available to the historian and herein lies Hallam's sense of frustration, H.E. Hallam, 'The life of the people', in H.E. Hallam, ed., *The agrarian history of England and Wales, vol. ii, 1042-1350* (Cambridge: Cambridge Universiy Press, 1988), p. 845.
73 R.H. Tawney, *Religion and the rise of capitalism* (London: John Murray, 1926), p. 40; see also R.H. Tawney, 'Historical introduction', in T. Wilson, *A discourse upon usury by way of dialogue and orations, for the better variety and more delight of all those that shall read this treatise* (1572) (London: G. Bell and Sons, 1925), p. 30.
74 W. Hudson, 'The prior of Norwich's manor of Hindolveston: its early organisation and the right of the customary tenants to alienate their strips of land', *Norfolk Archaeology* 20 (1919-20), 179-84.

75 On the market, its historiography and medieval peasants, see above, Chapter 4, pp. 125-39.
76 Raftis, *Peasant economic development*, p. 129, and above, Chapter 4, pp. 123-4.
77 Smith, 'Families and their land'.
78 Smith, 'Families and their land', p. 179; R.M. Smith, 'Kin and neighbors in a thirteenth-century Suffolk community', *Journal of Family History* 4 (1979), 219-56.
79 Smith, 'Families and their land', pp. 161-85.
80 A. Macfarlane, *The origins of English individualism* (Oxford: Blackwell, 1978).
81 Macfarlane, *English individualism*, p. 163.
82 See, for instance, Macfarlane, *English individualism*, pp. 127, 130, 140-1, 149, 158, 161.
83 Macfarlane, *English individualism*, pp. 131-64.
84 Maitland, *Township and borough*, pp. 20-1; F.W. Maitland, 'The survival of archaic communities', in H.A.L. Fisher, ed., *The collected papers of Frederic William Maitland* (Cambridge: Cambridge University Press, 2 vols, 1911), pp. 313-65; also Smith, 'Modernization', pp. 152-3, 160-1; Macfarlane, *English individualism*, pp. 102-30.
85 R.M. Smith, ed., *Land, kinship and life-cycle* (Cambridge: Cambridge University Press, 1984).
86 I. Blanchard, 'Industrial employment and the rural land market, 1380-1520', in Smith, ed., *Land, kinship and life-cycle*, pp. 241-8.
87 Smith, 'Families and their property', pp. 59-61.
88 Z. Razi, 'The erosion of the family-land bond in the fourteenth and fifteenth centuries: a methodological note', in Smith, ed., *Land, kinship and life-cycle*, pp. 295-304.
89 C. Dyer, 'Changes in the link between families and land in the west midlands in the fourteenth and fifteenth centuries', in Smith, ed., *Land, kinship and life-cycle*, pp. 305-11.
90 Z. Razi, 'The myth of the immutable English family', *Past and Present* 140 (1993), 3-44. See also above, pp. 205-6, for further discussion of the family-land bond, and for new directions in the study of the land market, see above, Chapter 4, pp. 128-33.
91 See above, Chapter 4, pp. 131-2.
92 See, for instance, Schofield, 'Peasants and the manor court'.
93 See, for instance, discussion of the peasant land market in Chapter 4, pp. 132-3, and of household formation systems and delayed marriage in Chapter 6, pp. 173-82.

8

Peasant culture

In this final chapter, we will explore one other element of the historiography of the medieval English peasantry – culture. Depending upon how we choose to define culture – and it is here taken to mean the ways in which a society or a sub-section of its members represent and distinguish themselves and are represented/distinguished through various kinds of self-selected behaviour, including types of dress, food and drink, speech, play, manners, as well as shared and often distinctive political, religious and social ideas or concepts – culture and historical approaches to its study might be considered to feature prominently in research on English peasants or, indeed, hardly to feature at all. To adopt the latter viewpoint in the first instance, we might suggest that investigation of culture, more often associated with the history of those of relatively high status and of elites in which a sophisticated and historically recoverable culture may sometimes be more easily assumed to reside, has been passed by in the study of the medieval peasants. How can we, it might be asked, study the cultural history of a society or section of a society that leaves little or no evidence of its culture in physical form? Yet, in answer and as will be evident from much that has been written earlier in this volume, we can show this would be a false assumption; there is evidence, as historians have come increasingly to exploit and not least as the defining boundaries of culture become ever more fluid, for peasant consumption and production, political action and so on, all of which suggest in certain measure the exercise of choice.[1] In that choice we can detect features akin to culture and its articulation, and we will examine other ways in which historians have sought to consider that, directly or indirectly, in this chapter.

To contemplate then a cultural history of the medieval peasantry is to acknowledge that there are manifold points of departure in considering a relevant cultural historiography, in fact more points of departure in exploring that potential historiography than there are points of arrival in what might pass for a fully developed field of study. That said, there are two important strands in the historiography of the medieval peasantry which, in terms of their core assumptions, have supposed the presence of a peasant culture at least capable of being posited and, in part at least, examined. The first of these is the examination of peasant engagement with the market, especially in terms of peasants as consumers, and the second is that aimed at exploring peasant agency, especially as regards politics, be that at the level of the manor and estate or on a national scale. We will consider each of these in turn before turning to some other, related, features of peasant culture, including relatively new initiatives, typically issuing from beyond studies directed at the medieval peasantry *per se*, and aimed at examining aspects of culture related to and encompassing the medieval peasantry.

To begin, though, we should note that the pursuit of the details – and even the very concept – of a peasant culture is something of an up-hill struggle. Contemporaries of medieval peasant society showed little or no inclination to recognise a peasant culture in any positive sense, a perspective often absorbed by later commentators. If, as some historians have suggested and as we shall discuss further below,[2] peasants identified themselves as a group or class, it is also evident that others also identified them in similar and cultural terms. Culture and the perception of that culture might then become part of that identification. Historians have certainly noted the ways in which peasants were themselves characterised and categorised in this period. Paul Freedman's thoughtful and illuminating exploration of late medieval and early modern perceptions of the medieval European peasantry illustrates the ways in which peasants were perceived, feared, mistrusted and misunderstood by their social superiors.[3] This 'top-down' view of the medieval peasant has been examined at closer quarters for medieval England, as for instance in Hilton's publication of and commentary upon Bodley MS. 57, a thirteenth-century poem written in celebration of the defeat of villeins by their lord, the abbot of Leicester.[4] Christopher Dyer also identifies similar attitudes in the caricature of a peasant-type employed in the capital of a demesne lease for the manor of Chevington (Suffolk) made in the mid-fifteenth century. The clerk of the abbey of Bury St Edmunds depicted a cunning, coarse figure, an image consistent with other contemporary imagery and description of the medieval peasant.[5] By contrast, literary and other artistic works from the period also on occasion present peasants as idealised types, such as Langland's and Chaucer's ploughmen who, it has been suggested, stand in contrast to and as a moral exemplar for, at least from the view of frustrated employers, the rather more coarse, rapacious and generally self-serving farm worker and rustic of real life in the later fourteenth century.[6] The images of peasants at work in the early to mid-fourteenth-century Luttrell Psalter also suggest an ordered estate, an idealised and elitist view of a society in which each section of society functions for the common good and knows its place.[7] In this idealisation there resides not a deep regard and sympathy for the late medieval peasant but rather an anxiety about the general condition, perceived failings and very real threat of the third estate.

As noted, such viewpoints are not entirely confined to commentators from the middle ages. Both Hilton and Dyer were sympathetic to the peasantry and also interested in the ways in which they were perceived and presented by their social superiors, chiefly as a further reflection of the political culture in which they operated. By contrast, other historians have been, directly or indirectly, less sympathetic and have, rather like their medieval forebears, not anticipated the possibility that a vibrant and identifiable peasant culture might have existed and be to some degree capable of recovery from the historical record. While, as we shall discuss further, a political culture of the peasantry might fit quite easily with a view of the peasant's lot as conditioned by the demands of law and lordship, the same overarching paradigm of obligation, limited opportunity and meagre surpluses exhausted by rent admitted less room in the historical mind-set for a culture of consumption founded upon surplus, be that in terms of money to spend or time to give to pursuits independent of labour, rent and the basic functions of everyday life.[8] Take for instance the debate over the 'origins of Robin Hood'. Some modern commentators have considered it quite plausible that the late medieval Robin Hood ballads, portraying Robin and his men as violent and merciless opponents of corrupt authority, were representative of peasant political culture; in particular Rodney Hilton and Maurice Keen have argued that, despite the lack of direct reference to oppressions of unfree tenants by landlords in the ballads, the plentiful references to the wrongdoing and eventual punishment of corrupt officials and officers of the law indicate that the ballads represent the anxieties and discontent of a peasant 'class'.[9] While Keen eventually conceded his position, accepting J.C. Holt's argument that the subversion expressed in the ballads was 'designed primarily for a gentle audience' and that its themes were consistent with the concerns of a gentry and knightly class in the thirteenth century, it is not evident that Hilton accepted any such view.[10] Holt was in particular adamant that, while it is quite conceivable that a peasant audience also enjoyed and responded to the ballads and may even have encouraged forms of the ballads more suited to their own concerns and appetites, the versions which have survived into the present day were not evidently part of their political culture. As such, historical discussion of the ballads reveals a tension over the conception and accessibility of peasant culture relative to cultures of those of a higher social status. In this it is striking that all commentators noted and, depending upon their argument, tried either to explain away or to use as evidence the lack of reference to landlord–tenant dispute at the heart of the ballads. More recently, historians commentating on the reception of Robin Hood have inclined to the view that a fifteenth-century yeoman or prosperous local landholder of peasant stock may well have constituted the most likely audience. This is a position also consistent with recent research work in that it identifies yeomen as consumers of tales and entertainments, activity at least consistent with the new-found wealth, upward mobility and leisure-time in a later medieval countryside that, by the early fifteenth century at least, was witnessing the retreat of lordship from direct management of demesnes and the emergence of successful peasant lessees and graziers.[11] In all of these variant hypotheses what is also revealing is the way in which a prevailing historical view of the medieval peasantry helped influence historians' expectations of the likely content of the peasantry's political culture.[12]

This potential for the dominant currents in the relevant historiography to squeeze out other possible avenues for examination is noted by Edwin DeWindt. DeWindt, in his detailed study of familial structures on the Ramsey manor of Holywell-cum-Needingworth and reflecting upon services in the medieval village performed by a range of families, interacting one with the other in some form of mutual support, identified such exchange as one possible inroad into the study of medieval peasant culture.[13] In making this suggestion for future research he acknowledged that 'it is a subject that has yet to receive the attention it demands from historians, being still largely left to the anthropologist'. DeWindt recognised in this seeming neglect of a cultural approach a fundamental distortion of the historical view of the medieval village and its society, dominated as that view was by 'economics and law'.[14] That historians have not tended to pursue 'peasant culture' with the same energy they have sought cultural expression elsewhere seems evident in other contexts as well. To take one possibly insightful instance of the kind of approach possibly envisaged by DeWindt, recent advances in medieval sigillography, the study of seals, suggest that there are tens of thousands of lower-status seals, including the seals of peasant sigillants (those who used seals and, as is often clear, owned them), which survive from medieval Britain; these are capable of shedding considerable light upon the choices sigillants made in terms of design, expression of personal identity, trade, faith and so on. In reviewing, in the late 1950s, Gloucester Abbey leases, which most likely involved peasant sigillants, Hilton noted, very much in passing, the potential of this source for revealing such aspects as choice of design and the visual representation of socio-economic interaction.[15] Until very recently however the vast majority of 'peasant' seals have been hardly examined at all, certainly relative to the extensive work on the comparatively very few instances of high-status seals.[16]

It is only since the mid-1980s that historians have begun to explore with any consistency features of a peasant culture that were not contained and conditioned by the demands of lordship or the perceived base nature of their condition. This displays, as has been set out in an earlier chapter, an important shift in the view of the medieval economy and the role of the peasantry within it. Particularly associated with the work of Christopher Dyer and Richard Britnell, this new strand in the historiography of the medieval economy, which has emphasised the commercialisation of the medieval economy and of the role of the peasantry itself within such an economy, has encouraged historians to pursue new approaches to peasant economy and society and to countenance the possibility that peasant investment choices, especially in terms of patterns of consumption, moved beyond basic foodstuffs and essentially functional items to display personal choice.[17] This choice has been seen as redolent of, *inter alia*, self-representation, investment and gratification, ambitions and desires not always associated with the condition or goals of the medieval English peasantry.

As discussed in a previous chapter, it is especially in the work of Christopher Dyer that patterns of consumption in the medieval countryside have been most fully and directly examined.[18] Allying historical investigation to archaeological record, Dyer has, throughout his career, sought to emphasise the capacity for medieval rural dwellers to generate a relative surplus and to employ that surplus in consumption, and production, capable of extending beyond the acquisition only of staples. In charting such patterns, especially in identifying change over time, Dyer has been especially keen to show that peasant consumption patterns responded to, above all, changing standards of living in a period of considerable economic and demographic change.[19] While rooted in a historiographical tradition founded upon discussion of economic transition and longer-term shifts in economy, Dyer's research has directed him to set out in detail the nature of this changing pattern of consumption and, by extension, to discuss more directly the actual nature of the consumption practices themselves. While much of such work is aimed at exploration of themes germane to economic history, and notably discussion of the relative advantage of different social groups in a period of economic change, Dyer is keen to emphasise that choices in terms of consumption reveal not only responses to external factors, such as the demands of lordship or the availability of particular resources, but could reveal the desires and expectations of individuals and peasant families. Early in his publishing career, Dyer had noted the capacity of some peasants to possess significant surpluses, which typically extended far beyond those required to meet the rental demands of their lords.[20] He developed these early observations more fully in his later work on standards of living, especially in his treatment of the relative economies of peasants and rural labourers. Beginning with models of the peasant economy of a kind that allowed him to identify significant surpluses in some peasant budgets, Dyer then also itemised some of the likely features of peasant consumption.[21] While much of the discussion of the consumption of foodstuffs illustrates the utilitarian quality of everyday peasant consumption, Dyer is also at pains to stress the centrality of the actual meal to peasant households, the evidence suggestive of some degree of ceremonial at mealtimes (aimed at reinforcing the role of the head of the household) as well as indication that wealthier peasants especially sought opportunities, including that obtained through purchases, to enliven and supplement a diet founded on grains, pulses and some protein.[22] In other words, while a considerable degree of observable variety in peasant consumption in the middle ages was dictated by geography, period and wealth, within particular sub-groups and particular periods some differences and/or patterns in consumption were explicable in terms of peasant choice dictated by fashion and a desire to enhance consumption for its own sake. This also emerges in Jean Birrell's thoughtful examination of negotiation over food and meals served to tenants by their lords during boon works, especially harvest work, which suggests that not only was negotiation over remuneration in the form of food a politicised exchange intended to test the relative strengths of lord and tenant but it was also a statement of peasant awareness not only of the amount of food but of its relative quality. Food was not only to be sufficient (*sufficienter*), it was to be honourable (*honorifice*), food, presumably, of a quality suitable to the estate of the tenants and that did not do them a dishonour in its serving.[23]

This choice in consumption, again as Dyer has been most consistent in illustrating, extended beyond foodstuffs. Evidence of peasant housing, for instance, also includes indication of consumer preferences.[24] While regional patterns of construction and general building trends were evidently conditioned by available materials and a generally prevailing sense of norms in construction, archaeological research, extracted by Dyer in his analysis of peasant consumption, reveals investment in, for example, carpentry that extended beyond a regard for the merely functional as well as in structures that allowed, in their form and organisation, wealthier peasants to display their social pretensions.[25] Thus, for instance, late medieval Wealden houses from Kent show plentiful evidence of investment in design, with central halls and upper storeys with overhanging jetties, and in execution, with decorative carpentry, developments also evident in contemporary rural housing in north Wales and the March.[26] Most recently, a detailed examination of 118 surviving peasant houses from the Midlands has illustrated the longevity of cruck houses (houses constructed from curved timbers to make a central timber A-frame) while the combination of the archaeological record with surviving inventories encourages a view of the late medieval house divided into hall, solar, chamber and kitchen, each room equipped with its requisite furnishings, some such as cushions and featherbed belying earlier characterisations of the mean peasant house.[27] As Dyer also notes in his discussion of medieval peasant housing, such buildings presented peasants with opportunities to express their distinctive qualities and their place within their communities, as for instance in the signs and symbols carved into doors or investment in bays and timber studs.[28]

Similarly, again as Dyer has identified and discussed, changes in fashion, for instance in clothing, houseware or the choice of particular pursuits, such as hunting or games, also cast some light on the choices peasants made and the potential for at least some members of rural society to invest available surpluses in goods and activities beyond the purely fundamental.[29] This has been extended to recent attempts to illustrate the ways in which peasant choice of clothing and accessory, evidenced by a limited cache of finds from manors in the north-eastern counties of England, may conceivably be interpreted as indicators of peasant self-expression and, rather more tendentiously given the available evidence, of peasant resistance.[30] While some such developments have been at least noted, and subjected to some analysis, there has however, save in the work of Dyer, been relatively little systematic analysis of changing patterns of consumption amongst the medieval peasantry.

As noted, much of the work to date has tended to locate consumption within a wider discussion of a changing later medieval economy and an adjusted standard of living which presented new consumption choices to peasants and rural labourers. In this respect, peasant consumption and, by extension, culture have remained adjuncts to consideration of the market, the economy and features of demographic change. As such, discussion of consumption as a manifestation of culture has been secondary to consideration of consumption as a reflection of adjusted economic conditions. This is the case, for instance, in terms of historical discussion of hunting and poaching. It is sometimes difficult for historians to distinguish between choices driven by need and those occasioned by preference. In the case of hunting and fishing, we can detect elements of both though it is also evident that historians are more or less likely to characterise such activity in ways conditioned by their own sense of the peasant's general condition. None the less historians have more recently tended to locate such activity, where it can be identified, within a context of changing economic conditions, and to see an increase in hunting and its censure as an index of generally improved socio-economic conditions with a consequent censure of such activity by the peasants' social superiors.[31] While detailed evidence for hunting, and a hunting and poaching culture amongst the peasantry, has been little pursued, and may well be difficult to pursue, such activity is one further example of a peasant (and, of course, non-peasant) culture which can be glimpsed but not always closely investigated.[32] That such activity may have existed has recently become a possibility of greater importance for historians as they seek ways to absorb such information within the defining historical orthodoxies: in this instance, the growing political, social and economic confidence of rural dwellers in the later fourteenth and fifteenth centuries.

This socio-economic contextualisation, itself often informed by the prevailing historiographical consensus, is also true of another aspect of peasant consumption practice: the investment in and use of law. The preparedness of the peasantry, from at least the thirteenth century, to invest in law, acquire some level of functional legal education and to employ lawyers has also become the subject of research in recent years. Inextricably linked with features of the economic assertiveness of sections of the peasantry, notably but not exclusively in terms of their dealing in local land markets, the use of law by the peasantry speaks at least to a culture that valued recourse to legal remedy, invested in some level of legal training, and was engaged in dealing with legal institutions and lawyers, often beyond the confines of the manor and the lord's manorial court. Both

Schofield and Briggs have explored the ways in which peasant litigants exhibited, from at least the later thirteenth-century, detailed awareness of legal practice at local level and, to a lesser extent, in central courts.[33] They, along with Clark, have also shown how peasants employed credit in supporting both consumption but also investment; the management of credit relations must also have placed some obligation on at least certain parties to maintain records of account and, in some relatively rare instances, written proof of debts owed or recovered. This in turn helped draw the relevant parties further into a world of literacy and numeracy, of proof and of public honesty.[34] Anthony Musson has reminded us that peasants were very much a part of a world of law, one that could not fail to pervade and define their existence; it was, as he also notes, incumbent upon members of medieval society to recognise their condition according to laws, as well as the advantages, disadvantages, securities and challenges such a condition might bring.[35] We have, in the previous chapter, discussed some of the ways in which historians have examined communal obligation and the institutions which underpinned 'community' in this period; Musson also emphasises the importance of such as factors in developing a working familiarity with law and its purpose in this period. As such, peasants were inevitably drawn into a legal culture of sorts, a point also noted by Paul Hyams, and to which we can return below.[36]

A further manifestation of such issues, and one that also speaks to issues of culture but of a kind not defined by consumption and offered only limited scrutiny in the relevant literature to date, is the light shed upon shared cultural norms as regards issues of public 'fame', neighbourliness, integrity and solvency; in short: creditworthiness. Early modern historians have explored credit as a cultural device and not only as a type of economic relationship;[37] while medievalists, and certainly those operating at the level of peasant credit, have not been so swift in following their lead, there is a recognition that investigation of economic relationships, a function, as we have seen, of one of the defining themes of medieval peasant study, also offers potential insight into peasant culture. This view of economic relationships as representative of one aspect of peasant culture brings us closer to the kind of investigation of peasant culture envisaged by DeWindt in 1971, when he wrote, that 'suretyship ... contractual relationships ... private economic practices' might all be deemed to be 'aspects of peasant culture', evidence for the elusive peasant voice.[38] As we have noted, since DeWindt wrote few historians have pursued such issues with peasant culture to the fore. Sherri Olson, like DeWindt a student of Ambrose Raftis, has been in the vanguard of such a pursuit; she has suggested that the local study founded upon manorial court rolls offers an effective means of recovering at least some of the shared culture of the medieval village. For Olson, the dealings of the manor court are imbued with cultural references, mediated through the legal language of the court but none the less revealing the purpose and concerns of the peasantry.[39] Insistent that the manorial court rolls are a 'running transcription of what was said in open court' and that the manor court was, in effect, the village court capable of capturing a 'village voice', Olson has sought to show that the court records offer inroads into local culture. Thus, for instance, the choice of words, the use of nicknames and popular epithets, and the comings and goings of participants in the court speak to the sounds and rhythms of medieval village life. Olson's view of the particular capacity of the manorial court rolls to offer a sense of the village voice stands in some direct and deliberate contrast with what Olson herself terms 'the older historiographical tradition, with its roots in legal history'.[40]

Other recent work in this area suggests a reluctance to embrace wholeheartedly the capacity of manorial court rolls to reveal a village culture though, as Schofield's discussion of an involved inter-personal plea between two Suffolk villagers illustrates, there is at least some cultural insight to be gleaned from legal records even if we choose not to reject the legal and seigneurial purpose of the record itself.[41] Wendy Scase's recent examination of judicial plaints c.1300 also raises similar issues and locates itself within relevant literature, especially that relating to political songs and venality satire.[42] Plaints were formal processes initiated by government, either the Crown or parliament, with inquests seeking responses to some or other perceived harm arising from activity related to governmental activity, such as the raising of taxation. These were in effect open invitations for individuals or groups to respond to some failure, typically a failure or breach of conduct on the part of local officers or administrators and, as Scase notes, their main purpose was not to remedy local grievances but to obtain recompense for the Crown.[43] Scase's purpose is not to use plaints as evidence for a peasant voice; she is instead as and more interested in the ways in which such forms of judicial complaint influenced the language of complaint and allowed other, higher-status groups to purloin the language of peasant-led plaint and villeinage within their own complaints. Thus, for instance, the 1297 *Monstraunces*, presented to the king by higher clergy and the baronage, uses the term 'tallage', a term at least associable with the arbitrariness of unfree obligation, to emphasise the severity of the obligations placed upon them by Edward I.[44] The original plaints, from which phrases and terms could be extracted and re-employed by other social groups, do provide evidence, in some form, for real peasant concerns but, again as Scase notes, this is likely to have been mediated and refined by the process as well as the language; peasant plaint, it is suggested, informs the political poetry and the language of complaint by other social groups, and that is often where we encounter it, at one and more remove from its source.

While it seems appropriate to suggest, as we have done in the previous paragraphs, that a new-found historiographical emphasis upon peasant agency and involvement in the wider economy of medieval England helped realign historical interests with at least some manifestation of peasant cultural choice and expression, historians had earlier still placed considerable store in other features of a shared culture. In fact, discussion of a political culture of the peasantry sits most comfortably with long-standing features of the relevant historiography, including tension between lord and tenant, the struggle over obligations and distinctions between freedom and unfreedom, all staples of historical writing on the topic since the nineteenth century. In terms of a political culture of the medieval peasantry, it is above all with a Marxist historiography, and one that promotes a strong sense of peasant agency, collective consciousness and self-determination, that we can see reflected at least some sense of 'culture'. Thus, to choose an early instance, Hilton's discussion of peasant resistance in the century or more before the Peasants' Revolt of 1381 is intended to illustrate the ways in which collective action, be it non-performance of labour services, the combining of resources to sue lords in central courts or acts of outright resistance, reveals a shared sense of disadvantage and a common will to do something about it.[45] In much subsequent work, Hilton was also keen, as discussed in an earlier chapter, to emphasise the ways in which, despite a number of other potential and real associations, peasants ultimately combined with their own, as a class.[46] In this respect, Hilton's Marxism defined and posited for the medieval English peasantry a culture of shared class and class boundaries, especially from the early thirteenth century when, as Hilton discusses, our sources allow a view of the peasantry engaged in opposition to their lords and at a time when greater pressure may have been employed by lords against their tenants.[47]

Historians writing in the early to mid-twentieth century and not so closely identified with a Marxist tradition also noted and discussed shared activity in resistance to the demands of lordship. Thus Elizabeth Levett, whose work in this respect is cited by Hilton and who, though writing before the establishment of a Marxist approach to medieval agrarian studies, may still reveal a socialist agenda, identifies evidence for what appear to be tactics of avoidance rather than random acts of disobedience.[48] Levett's examination of lordship on the estates of the abbey of St Albans describes consistent patterns of resistance to the performance of labour services, as does Marjorie Morgan in her discussion of peasant resistance on the estates of the abbey of Bec in the early fourteenth century. Morgan suggests that a shared concern over excessive levies of lordship, stimulated by a period of wider political upheaval, encouraged resistance to lords in this period; in all of this we find at least the suggestion of shared agendas and a common recognition of the limits of reasonableness, a partial sense at least of a political purpose, informed by a sense of grievance.[49]

One problem for those seeking to identify the existence of a class-consciousness of the medieval peasantry has been the isolation of its constituent elements and its durability. Identifying a consistent and persistent common political culture is no more straightforward than is identifying any other shared conviction or belief.[50] Historians, mostly those following Hilton's lead, have on occasion attempted to identify collective action in petty misdemeanour and apparent 'foot-dragging' in the performance of labour services and boon works. Thus, for instance, Franklin's investigation of poor performance of services on the Gloucestershire manor of Thornbury in the early fourteenth century or Larson's examination of post-plague tensions between lord and tenant in the Palatinate of Durham are often founded upon the assumption that particular actions were informed by grievance and that such grievance was shared.[51]

Historians might be inclined to suggest that shared agendas are most clearly illustrated in concerted political actions and expressions of collective grievance and action, such as combined litigation or petitioning against a lord or his official, local violent action and, in the most extreme instances, open revolt. We might indeed suggest that we come closest to hearing a shared voice in such expressions, most obviously in the utterances of rebels in 1381. Yet, in practice, few historians have sought to read into such statements and actions an over-arching sense of collective peasant culture; as Hilton noted, there are too many disaggregations (regionality, social, economic and tenurial distinctions within the body of rebels or complainants and so on) that serve to limit our confidence in ascribing to such actions a common agenda.[52] If we take the most obvious statement of collective peasant grievance, the demand that there be an end to villeinage, as relayed to Richard II in June 1381, we certainly find indication of a common voice.[53] We are though left uncertain as to the generality of the view and the extent to which it showed common concerns at that time; most importantly here, historians have either tended to assume that it did suggest a shared notion, a common cause, or that it at least reflected upon common grievances and, reducing them to a forceful slogan, served to promote them under a single banner.[54] To what extent though such views reproduced those of an unidentifiable mass remains a moot point.

Even when we observe concerted peasant action in opposition to the demands of lordship or the state, historians cannot always be entirely sure of the actual body represented or the motive force behind such activity and its expression. To take an important and instructive instance – joint litigation at common law against the landlord – a number of historians have explored the ways in which peasants combined their resources in pursuing their lords in court. Writing in the 1940s, Hilton explored some examples in detailing peasant resistance in the decades before 1381 and Dyer has also more recently addressed the same issues.[55] Rosamund Faith has also described the persistence of demands associated with claims of ancient demesne (land held by the king at the time of Domesday Book, the tenants of which enjoying, as a consequence, a level of security not shared by villein tenants of other estates) and a return to the free tenures which, by the later middle ages, some unfree tenants identified with a distant past which they imagined was enshrined in Domesday Book.[56] Much earlier still, in an article published in 1930 in the early days of the *Economic History Review*, Nichols had identified a formal complaint against the lord's official; while this did not result in litigation it again reflected a shared concern, according to Nichols, and one that allows us to observe 'the attitude of the masses of the English peasantry towards their masters and the institutions that determined the nature of their daily life'.[57] Nichols also obliquely suggests that it was only from the later fourteenth century ('the age of Wyclif and Langland') that we can expect, for the first time, to gain some sense of the articulation of the views of the peasantry. For Nichols, this complaint by the tenants is an example of an early expression by a body of villagers, 'conscious of their rights and of their common interests, and with a real very grasp of the legal niceties involved'.[58]

What Nichols does not really consider, though it is more evident in later work in the same area, is the possibility that this informed legal agenda, expressive of tenants' rights, was honed and, in its detail, more fully articulated by lawyers than by peasants. Both Hilton and Faith recognise that the voice of the dissenting peasant may have been refined and filtered by attorneys active in the medieval countryside, a potentially significant challenge to the view that such statements reveal only a peasant agenda and are rooted in a peasant political culture.[59] This is not to suggest that complaint and criticism were seldom present in the medieval

English countryside or that they were typically the product of external influence; rather more is it that most historians have come to recognise that peasant culture and expression, where they can be detected at all in our sources, were highly likely to be mediated in any number of ways.

In this respect also, where again we seem to observe views consistent with a general expression of grievance or complaint or even general political concern, historians have then from time to time pondered our actual potential to come close to an understanding of a popular peasant perception of politics, the state, ruling orders and so on.[60] It is also worth considering here that at least some of the supposed totems of a class consciousness, as set out by Hilton in his Ford lectures, actually embody ideas circulating more generally in high and later medieval England.[61] It remains, for instance, difficult to disassociate peasant conceptions of an idealised state, as discussed by Hilton, with theoretical statements regarding the nature of and ideal structure of the state current by the fourteenth century. Thus, for example, Hilton notes that a peasant conception of a popular monarchy in 1381 had apparently abandoned all of the fourteenth-century trappings of the state (nobles, churchmen, the common law), in favour of a government of king and peasant, the laws set by the peasants themselves. Hilton suggests that this was, potentially at least, an invention of the peasant rebels in 1381.[62] However, as Hilton also recognised, disassociating peasant invention from already circulating conceptions of a stripped-down medieval state is at best problematic. Thus, for instance, the anonymous author of the political tract *Modus Tenendi Parliamentum*, clause XXIII, written perhaps in the early fourteenth century, identifies an archetypal rule of king and commons, and one that also rejects the need for nobles and churchmen; far closer to the reality of political society in the high and late middle ages, the fourth clause of the coronation oath, as introduced in the early fourteenth century, recognised the need for the king to govern according to the laws identified by the commonalty (though contemporaries cannot have conceived of this last version of the commonalty or 'community of the realm' as including the peasantry).[63] In such instances it becomes very difficult to isolate a peasant political culture from wider, or narrower, cultures, one reason perhaps why relatively few historians have ventured in this direction. Hilton himself noted that 'the ruling ideas of medieval peasants seem to have been the ideas of the rulers of society as transmitted to them' and then subsequently re-employed by them, a point also noted in subsequent studies.[64]

Even in such absorption of externally generated conceptions and ideas, we do however detect, in their remoulding and re-employment often as the engines of complaint, evidence for a peasant political culture. In such instances, as a handful of historians have discussed, we also gain a sense of peasant action and of a peasant perception of the wider political world which has clearly been informed by more than a sense of shared grievance in the face of the immediate obligations occasioned by lordship. As we shall a little later in this chapter, in reviewing relevant historical discussions of faith and piety amongst the peasantry, much of this work has been conducted by a small handful of historians, mostly writing in the last thirty years or so and addressing themes which, in terms of their main research agendas, encourage some occasional reflection upon the medieval peasantry.

Instrumental in directing our attention towards peasant politics beyond the manor is John Maddicott; an important focus of Maddicott's work is political elites and the context of their activities within a thirteenth- and early fourteenth-century political community which extended some distance from the royal court and leading political figures. In a number of important contributions, Maddicott has explored the ways in which English royal government in the thirteenth century was dependent upon a relationship with the English peasantry. Arising from his research on the early fourteenth-century magnate and chief opponent of Edward II, Thomas of Lancaster, Maddicott's work has led him to discuss the ways in which lowlier members of society, including the peasantry, might be drawn into wider political processes as well as to reflect upon the kinds of institutional structures and governmental arrangements that established a form of partnership between the English government and rural dwellers, including more substantial peasants. This, in turn, may have helped shape their own engagement with 'politics' more generally, as in the widespread popular support for political 'saints' such as Thomas of Lancaster.[65] In his more recent biography of Simon de Montfort, Maddicott has briefly examined similar themes as part of his discussion of Montfort and has done so in greater detail in considering the ways by which political ideas might be transmitted to the wider public body, most notably peasants in the thirteenth century.[66] Maddicott identifies a variety of fora in which political ideas might circulate and discusses the kinds of institutional structures, such as markets, shire courts and churches, that facilitated the spread of political ideas.[67] Striking in Maddicott's developing analysis, the first expressions of which were published in the early 1970s, is the degree of separation from prevailing tendencies in a historiography more directly aimed at the study of rural society and economy and the English peasantry in particular. In fact, while undoubtedly influenced by those more common historiographical traits, the merit of Maddicott's examination is that it is informed at its core by a different perspective, one based upon a political and constitutional historiography. We can note the same bent in other, and typically intermittent, pieces informed as they are more by the author's research into high politics and political society than by a close consideration of society and economy. Most obvious in this regard is David Carpenter's article and occasional comment on peasants and politics in the thirteenth century.[68] Carpenter, a student of English high politics and especially of the reign of Henry III, is conscious in his research of the 'reach' of high political agendas during the baronial civil wars of the mid-thirteenth century. In particular, he is keen to emphasise the peasant-level awareness of the baronial aims during the civil wars.[69] In this his attention is directed more towards records of central government, especially the records of the special eyres that followed in the wake of the civil war and the Dictum of Kenilworth, allied to evidence of material and landed conditions of the peasantry contained in the late thirteenth-century Hundred Rolls.[70] While Carpenter does not seek to locate his work in an earlier historiography, he does offer some limited comment in contrasting his approach with that of historians of the medieval peasantry such as Rodney Hilton, the emphases of whom Carpenter identifies as directed at lord–tenant relations and tensions. Carpenter instead prefers to see lord–tenant struggles as relevant but part of a larger vista of political engagement on the part of the peasantry.[71] Important in this respect is Carpenter's suggestion that peasants involved themselves in national politics not only or even chiefly as agents of their lords but as politically informed participants, keen to take sides in a struggle which they deemed to be important for themselves.[72] Carpenter also recognises that peasants were able to do so because they were already well integrated into political society, through such institutions as the sheriff's tourn and the coroner's inquest, points that return us to Maddicott and discussion of the nature of the thirteenth-century political community.[73] Maddicott and Peter Coss have sought to explore that wider political consciousness in other ways as well, notably through investigation of political songs circulating in later thirteenth- and early fourteenth-century England.[74] Once again, this research emerges from an agenda directed at investigating the nature of political society in the long thirteenth century and one that admits the possibility of a politically aware and politically active peasantry. The political songs also raise the already familiar and potentially intractable questions of provenance and the nature of a truly peasant culture, themes that are suggested in discussion of later statements of resistance, such as the letters circulating in

1381 at the time of the Peasants' Revolt.[75] In historiographical terms, all of these last discussions are supported by the relatively recent notion that an engaged peasantry, or more likely wealthier and relatively powerful subsections of the peasantry, were sufficiently absorbed, through office and through the associated skills obtained through office (notably a degree of literacy) into the political and administrative culture of medieval England to engage in acts of meaningful and informed protest.

Where we might also expect to find some fuller engagement in peasant culture, expressed in terms other than consumption, would be in historical discussion of religion and pious expression. In most instances, historians of religion have tended not to focus directly upon medieval peasants, or certainly not medieval English peasants, but instead to draw generally on instances of piety amongst the lower social levels in town and countryside, but with some obvious reference to rural and peasant society. Peasants and other rural dwellers have certainly featured in broader consideration of the nature and extent of spirituality in the middle ages, as well as the extent of 'Christianization' of medieval society.[76] Conversely, a few historians of the medieval peasant have also, in exploring themes aimed more directly at the study of medieval peasants *per se*, directed some attention to issues of faith and the village-level reception of religious teaching. Richard Smith's study of the marriage process within the medieval peasant family is one instance of such work, Smith suggesting that choices in nuptiality and fertility were adjusted and constrained by orthodox teaching on marriage practices; by extension this reflected a shared culture of marital practice in medieval society.[77] As the discussion of the nature of the marriage fine, merchet, has also suggested *en passant*, a closer awareness of custom and cultural expression could furnish historians with a fuller understanding of the bases of relationships between lord and tenant, hitherto examined from a largely legal or socio-economic perspective; in this instance the nature of peasant marriage and the exchange of vows at the church door has left only occasional reference but speaks to a considered culture of marriage and betrothal involving more than the immediate parties to the marriage.[78] Schofield has also argued that, while the church's teachings on charitable obligation were absorbed at the level of the village and parish, there is some evidence that close regard for such teaching was limited and did not survive the strains of the most difficult harvest years. In crisis conditions, a culture founded more upon market opportunity than Christian charity may have been more to the fore.[79] Such work in the last thirty or so years, most often aimed at explicitly examining a highly particular feature of society, economy or demography in the medieval village, serves often to remind us that although moral codes of behaviour, societal norms and shared cultures most certainly operated in the medieval village, these are seldom recovered with ease and the surviving records are as likely to promote one layer of moral (or immoral) activity at the expense of another. The intractably of this is, for instance, illustrated in discussion of the peasant land market since at least the 1960s where, as we have already discussed, it has been relatively simple for historians to describe the activity of buying and selling but less easy to explain the underlying causes including the dominating moral compass of the land market.[80]

Peasant-level engagement with and absorption of a religious culture has been discussed more directly in terms of endowment of parish churches,[81] enthusiastic reception of certain of the sacraments (the eucharist and marriage, in particular)[82] and the developing incidence of anticlericalism and/or heresy in the later fourteenth- and fifteenth-century countryside,[83] as well as the celebration of local saints, shrines, the promotion of sabbatarianism and so on.[84] Much of this work has been conducted in relatively piecemeal fashion, and has seldom had as its main focus peasant faith and piety. That said, discussion of peasant faith and its articulation or, at best, religious expression at the rural and parish-level has at least gained significance in recent years. This gain has been driven less by discussion of peasants *per se* but by investigation of the vitality of the pre-Reformation church and faith in medieval England. It is especially evident in a revived interest in the nature of the pre-Reformation church and lay pious expression at the local level, notably in terms of the contention that lay faith at the eve of the Reformation was far more vibrant and engaged with orthodoxy and the teachings of the church than has previously been assumed. A good deal of work, the product of the last quarter century or so, has involved early modern historians as much as, if not more than, medievalists.[85] It has served to direct historians' attention towards aspects of local lay piety in order to test the nature of faith in the fifteenth and early sixteenth centuries. While not all such research has taken the village and rural dwellers as its focus, some historians have drawn upon the records of the parish, such as church wardens' accounts, which are far more available from the fifteenth century, in order so to do. Most obviously perhaps, Eamon Duffy's use of the unusually full accounts for Morebath in Devon during the middle decades of the sixteenth century illustrates the potential of this material to shed light on the everyday, and changing, piety of villagers.[86] In this context, pious expression offers a significant inroad into the religious culture of at least some later medieval and early modern villagers, mediated again as it is by the record, here compiled by the parish priest. One particularly striking, if unusual, instance of this is to be found in the redaction of a vision recorded by an Essex peasant, Thurkill, in the early thirteenth century. A testimony to a visionary episode experienced while the individual lay in a comatosed state, the details may speak to the depth of pious engagement of this apparently typical peasant but also hint at the ways in which a peasant voice was replaced by that of his clerical redactor. In fact, it was only the earliest redactions of the vision that included local references or any indication that the visionary was a peasant at all.[87]

The activity of guilds and fraternities, for which there is growing amounts of evidence from the later middle ages, has also attracted considerable attention since the 1990s. While discussion of craft and religious guilds has been a long-standing feature of medieval historical writing, as for instance Charles Gross's investigation of the guild merchant as well as Gasquet's survey of parish life in medieval England, recent years have seen a systematic attempt to analyse surviving parish and guild records from the later middle ages in order to identify trends in guild activity as well as the activity and aspirations of the guild participants, including rural guilds.[88] So, for instance, Virginia Bainbridge's study of Cambridgeshire rural guilds has illustrated the ways in which religious fraternities extended into the countryside and provided a significant impetus to communal organisation, local self-expression and collective solidarity. Similar issues are also noted by Beat Kümin, who illustrates the variety of ways, secular and spiritual, by which sub-parochial organisations such as guilds enabled local-level engagement in financial organisation and administration as well as a degree of influence in the provision of orthodox religious practice and the articulation of faith.[89]

In addition, while religious historians have, in general terms, recognised the competing spiritual agendas that undoubtedly operated in the medieval countryside, including the persistence of pre-Christian practice and of superstition, contemporary inroads into its detailed study have been few and in any case hardly pursued at all, a view summed up in Homans's engagingly eccentric assessment that 'we know so little of the mythology of elves, and what we know is of so late a date, that there is no good reason to talk about it in a description of countrymen in the thirteenth century'.[90] The combination of orthodox teaching and the more folkloric elements of rural society may also possibly be observed in relics of tales and superstitions, though identifying the provenance of these is far from straightforward and has not been subjected to detailed examination at the local level.[91] Where there have been attempts, historians have tended to the view that evidence for the persistence of actual pre-Christian, pagan worship had been swept away by and absorbed into Christian practice.[92]

As already noted, such investigations into matters of faith and piety tend, despite the few instances offered above relating to marriage and to charity in the medieval village, to be the product of a strand of historiography quite discrete from the usual approach of historians investigating the medieval English peasantry. The focus of historians such as Duffy is upon the nature of faith in the period of the Reformation rather, of course, than the peasantry or rural society *per se*; the same is also the case for a closely related avenue of research which also offers some insight into associated aspects of peasant religious culture, namely the examination of later medieval heresy. Work on Lollardy in the fifteenth century, ongoing in the second half of the twentieth century and especially vibrant since the 1980s, has also inevitably drawn historians' attention to the ways in which faith could be articulated in the medieval English countryside. Thus, for instance, the records of the Norwich heresy trials of the early fifteenth century indicate the transmission of Wycliffite teaching in the decades after 1400, which reached to the level of labourers in the countryside and informed the choices they made about everyday living and the articulation of faith, as for instance in the rejection of fasting or the election to work on the Sabbath or feast days.[93] In the bishops' registers and records of inquests in heretical activity, historians have noted and described the absorption of unorthodox teaching and the spread of Lollard teaching, processes that clearly involved rural dwellers, such as John Walcote, a shepherd from Hasleton, Gloucestershire, who was prosecuted in 1425 after years of heretical engagement across parts of central and southern England.[94] Thomson also speaks of pockets of unorthodoxy, spread throughout the country and only some of which are likely to have been identified by the church authorities; in such groupings we can anticipate adjustments of religious culture reflective of unorthodox teaching, including the rejection of such orthodoxies as sacerdotalism, the nature of the eucharist and existence of purgatory as well as the absorption of new teachings and a heightened regard for literacy in the vernacular.[95]

In certain respects, though often obliquely, this work has also effected an association between the changing economy of the later medieval countryside and the regionalised spread of heresy. Thomson, for instance, has linked the emergence of lollard cells in southern–eastern England with the growth of a rural and urban cloth industry there, much as work on orthodoxy and especially the development of guilds in the later medieval countryside has been set within its rural and economic setting.[96] In addition, and as we have also seen in discussion of the wider political engagement of the peasantry in the thirteenth century, 'lollards' loosely defined, including rural artisans, were drawn into seditious activity in the fifteenth century and associated by royal government with threats to its power. It has proved difficult for historians to separate out the constituent elements of these wide agglomerations of 'divers unknown rebels', though, as in the rising led by William Perkins (also known by the alias Jack Sharp of Wigmoreland) in 1431 and centred upon Abingdon, they certainly included rural dwellers and artisans, some of whom may have helped to drive the more radical of the lollard schemes in this period.[97]

It is also possible to note some of the admittedly few ways in which consideration of heresy has informed the historical discussion of economic and social historians working upon the medieval peasantry. Poos's work on rural Essex in the later fourteenth and fifteenth centuries has, for example, sought to associate indices of religious fervour and evidence for what may be a heightened regard for propriety and morality with features particular to Essex, including significant social stratification in the countryside and a volatile local economy. This context generated not only nonconformity but also ultra-zealous orthodoxy, the two not always easily distinguished in fifteenth-century religious expression. Important for this discussion, Poos notes that some of the more prosaic features of peasant life, including the stuff of social and demographic history such as marriage practice, were likely to have been mediated by local and regional religious convictions. In Essex, this may have included a significant tendency to adopt a marriage process that placed great store on the exchange of vows between the couple without the need for clerical approval.[98] In the fifteenth-century response to lollardy, a response organised and encouraged by episcopal visitations, the orthodox were also reminded of their responsibilities in resisting the deviance of unorthodoxy; Forrest notes how, in villages in the early fifteenth century, members of the trusted elites were tasked with overseeing the unfaithful and securing the compliance of those infected by lollardy.[99] Such insights into a collective peasant culture are often slight and fleeting but they serve to remind us that such a culture of shared, but undoubtedly also contested, values existed, even if historians have to date seldom pursued this as a subject of direct study and have yet to attempt any significant prosopographical analysis of lowlier heretics in the later medieval English countryside.

In ways that also point to attitudes to faith and shared moral norms at the level of the parish, we can also see aspects of peasant culture displayed in its censure; much of this is incidental in the historiographical discussion just as it was incidental in the historical record. It is however potentially revealing and comes closest to a full analysis in Marjorie McIntosh's investigation of later medieval and early modern behaviour and misbehaviour and its censure.[100] McIntosh's discussion also adds to our understanding of orthodoxy at the local level in the fifteenth century and the ways in which an informed orthodoxy could be applied in town and village in the later middle ages. Thus, such themes as harmony, neighbourliness, order and a regard for the welfare of others were, to follow McIntosh, applied in local communities in response to the instruction of 'intellectual, moral, and political leaders'.[101] How such broad injunctions were applied in a local context was, as McIntosh points out, largely dependent on the choices made by local leaders, as for instance in the establishment and management of guilds.[102] In her examination of a developing moral agenda from the later fourteenth century, McIntosh's study also sheds some light on the kinds of activity engaged in by country dwellers and those living in small towns. Thus we gain a sense of a growing culture of play in the later middle ages, with clear evidence of game-playing, gambling and the greater frequenting of public houses.[103] This has been couched very much in terms of the response of a changing society and a censorious one at that. Mark Bailey, in reviewing some of the same evidence, has also noted that most of our evidence for such expressions of play in town and countryside is a product of its censure. Notably, labour legislation from the second half of the fourteenth century has shed some light on the kinds of activity that lords and masters considered inconsistent with a compliant and diligent population, including hunting with dogs, tennis, football and new games such as 'Closh, Kails, Half Bowl...and Queckboard'.[104] As with other possible approaches to the investigation of aspects of peasant culture, this external perception of how peasants spent their time in activity other than labour has attracted relatively little attention from historians, a product perhaps of a persistent focus upon labour and rent as key indices of peasant economic and 'political' activity. Barbara Harvey, writing a generation before McIntosh and Bailey, had noted that the record of labour rent also included plentiful information on leisure, at least in terms of its measurement as leisure-time or time not worked.[105] By the thirteenth century villeins on some of the great monastic estates enjoyed extended holidays at Christmas, Easter and Whitsun, accounting for more than a month of holy days.[106] If we know that, typically, labour or at least certain kinds of labour were not carried out on holidays, we know less about what was done on those days. Harvey notes that, by the thirteenth century, the mass may not have sat at the centre of the day as once it may have; instead contemporaries complained of lewd behaviour and the frequenting of taverns outside of, and sometimes in place of, attendance at mass.[107] If we are left with uncertainties as to the kinds of activity in which peasants were engaged, that is in part then because these have tended not to dominate the research and writing of historians to date. The historiographical trend in studies of medieval peasants has, as this chapter has in part been intended to show, made the historical notion of 'peasant culture' more rather than less conceivable. This paves the way to further work in this area as, most likely, will a greater dialogue with those working in other and related disciplines, points we can now address in conclusion.

Notes

1 M. Rubin, 'What is cultural history now?' in D. Cannadine, ed., *What is history now?* (Basingstoke: Palgrave, 2002), p. 81; A. Arcangeli, *Cultural history. A concise introduction* (Abingdon: Routledge, 2012), p. 6.
2 See also Chapter 3, pp. 94–7.
3 P. Freedman, *Images of the medieval peasant* (Stanford: Stanford University Press, 1999).
4 R.H. Hilton, 'A thirteenth-century poem on disputed villein services', in Hilton (ed.), *Class conflict and the crisis of feudalism. Essays in medieval social history* (London: Hambledon, 1985), pp. 108–13.
5 C. Dyer, 'A Suffolk farmer in the fifteenth century', *Agricultural History Review* 55 (2007), 15. For a similar instance from the later fourteenth century, see F.R.H. DuBoulay, *The lordship of Canterbury. An essay on medieval society* (London, 1966), p. 189 and frontispiece, for a wonderful contemporary depiction of a villein at Wingham (Kent) in 1390, drawn in the margin of the Register of Archbishop Courtenay.
6 See, for example, M. Bailey, 'The ploughman', in S.H. Rigby, ed., with the assistance of A.J. Minnis, *Historians on Chaucer. The 'General Prologue' to the* Canterbury Tales (Oxford: Oxford University Press, 2014), pp. 360–4 and references there; see also C. Dyer, 'Work ethics in the fourteenth century', in J. Bothwell, J.P. Goldberg and W.M. Ormrod, eds, *The problem of labour in fourteenth-century England* (Woodbridge: York Medieval Press / Boydell, 2000), pp. 21–41; and D. Pearsall, '*Piers Plowman* and the problem of labour', in Bothwell *et al.*, eds, *The problem of labour*, pp. 123–32.
7 R.K. Emmerson and P.J.P. Goldberg, 'Lordship and labour in the Luttrell Psalter', in Bothwell *et al.*, eds, *The problem of labour*, pp. 60–3.
8 Historians writing on such topics in the later nineteenth and early twentieth century seem to have often come to such a conclusion, for which see above, Chapter 1, pp. 48–50. Writing in the mid-twentieth century, Reginald Lennard offers similar observations, and laments the lack of relevant sources: 'it is only the human nature which [the historian] shares with them that can inform his [*sic*] imagination in regard to the thoughts they tried to express when they

encountered one another, either at work or when work was done', Lennard, *Rural England*, pp. 387–8 (quote at p. 388).

9 R.H. Hilton, 'The origins of Robin Hood', *Past and Present* 14 (1958), reprinted in R.H. Hilton, ed., *Peasants, knights and heretics. Studies in medieval English social history* (Cambridge: Cambridge University Press, 1976), pp. 221–35 (from which this and subsequent references are taken); see also M. Keen, *The outlaws of medieval England* (London: Routledge and Kegan Paul, 1961), pp. 145–73, and M. Keen, 'Robin Hood – peasant or gentleman?', *Past and Present* 19 (1961), reprinted in Hilton, ed., *Peasants, knights and heretics*, pp. 258–66 (from which this and subsequent references are taken).

10 J.C. Holt, 'The origins and audience of the ballads of Robin Hood', *Past and Present* 18 (1960), reprinted in Hilton, ed., *Peasants, knights and heretics*, pp. 236–57 (from which this and subsequent references are taken); J.C. Holt, *Robin Hood* (London: Thames and Hudson, 1982), pp. 109–58; see also Keen, 'Robin Hood – peasant or gentleman?', p. 266 (Note, 1976). For Hilton's brief reflections on the debate, see R.H. Hilton, 'Introduction', in Hilton, ed., *Peasants, knights and heretics*, pp. 6–8, and, for a further expression of the view that the ballads did not represent a peasant voice, T.H. Aston, 'Robin Hood', *Past and Present* 20 (1961), reprinted in Hilton, ed., *Peasants, knights and heretics*, pp. 270–2 (from which this and subsequent references are taken). See also Hilton's review of Holt, *Robin Hood*, in *Times Literary Supplement*, 11 June 1982. I am most grateful to Professor Rigby for this reference.

11 A.J. Pollard, *Imagining Robin Hood* (London: Routledge, 2004), pp. 34–6.

12 See, for instance, Hilton, 'Origins of Robin Hood', pp. 232–4; Keen, *Outlaws of medieval England*, pp. 145–73 and Keen, 'Robin Hood – peasant or gentleman?', pp. 259–60; Holt, 'Origins and audience', pp. 243–4; Aston, 'Robin Hood', pp. 271–2.

13 E.B. DeWindt, *Land and people in Holywell-cum-Needingworth* (Toronto: Pontifical Institute of Mediaeval Studies, 1972), pp. 240–1.

14 DeWindt, *Land and people*, p. 241.

15 R.H. Hilton, 'Gloucester Abbey leases of the late thirteenth century', in R.H. Hilton, *The English peasantry in the later middle ages. The Ford lectures for 1973 and related studies* (Oxford: Oxford University Press, 1975), pp. 139–60, and especially pp. 154–5. For a review of the relevant literature and discussion of potential future research directions in this area, see P.R. Schofield, 'Seals and the peasant economy in England and Marcher Wales, ca.1300' in S. Solway, ed., *Medieval coins and seals: constructing identity, signifying power* (Brepols: Turnhout, 2015), pp. 347–58. See also P.D.A. Harvey, 'Personal seals in thirteenth-century England', in I. Wood and G.A. Loud, eds, *Church and chronicle in the middle ages. Essays presented to John Taylor* (London: The Hambledon Press, 1991), pp. 117–27; A.F. McGuiness, 'Non-armigerous seals and seal-usage in thirteenth-century England', in P.R. Coss and S.D. Lloyd, eds, *Thirteenth-century England, v* (Woodbridge: Boydell, 1995), pp. 165–77; also T.A. Heslop, 'Peasant seals', in E. King, ed., *Medieval England* (London: Guild Publishing, 1988), pp. 214–15.

16 See E. New, '(Un)conventional images. A case-study of radial motifs on personal seals', in P. Schofield, ed., *Seals and their contexts in the Middle Ages* (Oxford: Oxbow, 2015), pp. 151–60. See also, for observations on this apparent fixation on higher-status sealing, Harvey, 'Personal seals', 117–18.
17 See above, Chapter 4, pp. 138–9.
18 See above, Chapter 4, pp. 125–6, 139.
19 See, for instance, Dyer's work on the changing diet of harvest workers and other rural workers, C. Dyer, 'Changes in diet in the later middle ages: the case of harvest workers', *Agricultural History Review* 36 (1988), 21–37, reprinted in C. Dyer, *Everyday life in medieval England* (London: Hambledon, 1994), pp. 77–99, from which subsequent references are taken; also C. Dyer, *An age of transition? Economy and society in England in the later middle ages* (Oxford: Oxford University Press, 2005), pp. 126–72.
20 C. Dyer, 'A redistribution of incomes in fifteenth-century England', *Past and Present* 39 (1968), 21.
21 C. Dyer, *Standards of living in the later Middle Ages: social change in England c.1200–1520* (Cambridge: Cambridge University Press, 1989), pp. 110–18, 151–87.
22 Dyer, *Standards of living*, pp. 150–60; C. Dyer, *A country merchant, 1495–1520. Trading and farming at the end of the middle ages* (Oxford: Oxford University Press, 2012), pp. 27–9.
23 J. Birrell, 'Peasants eating and drinking', *Agricultural History Review* 63 (2015), 1–18, and especially p. 13.
24 It would though be incorrect to suggest that Dyer alone has directed historians' attention to such consumption. For instance, Hilton made some tentative comment on peasant housing, and other historians, mostly operating in the west midlands and linked to Dyer, Hilton and historians then at the University of Birmingham, have also explored the detail of peasant housing and other forms of consumption, Hilton, *A medieval society*, pp. 94ff; R.K. Field, 'Worcestershire peasant buildings, household goods and farming equipment in the later middle ages', *Medieval Archaeology* 9 (1965), 105–45.
25 Dyer, *An age of transition?*, pp. 135–9.
26 Dyer, *An age of transition?*, pp. 138–9.
27 N. Alcock and D. Miles, *The medieval peasant house in midland England* (Oxford: Oxbow, 2013), pp. 157–9. Similar points, as regards the range and quality of later medieval furnishings, are set out in C. Dyer, 'Furnishings of medieval English peasant houses: investment, consumption and life style', available at www.uv.es/consum/dyer.pdf (last accessed 12 July 2014).
28 Alcock and Miles, *Medieval peasant house*, p. 112.
29 See, for instance, Dyer, *A country merchant*, pp. 18–19. Here the emphasis is upon social aspiration amongst yeoman and rural merchants who were seeking, in the later fifteenth century, to move beyond the social level of the peasantry and to ape the county gentry.
30 S.V. Smith, 'Materializing resistant identities among the medieval peasantry. An examination of dress accessories from English rural settlement sites', *Journal of Material Culture* 14 (2009), 309–32.

31 For which, see especially J. Birrell, 'Who poached the King's deer?', *Midland History* vii (1982); Birrell, 'Peasant deer poachers in the medieval forest', in R. Britnell and J. Hatcher, eds, *Progress and problems in medieval England. Essays in honour of Edward Miller* (Cambridge: Cambridge University Press, 1996), pp. 68-88.

32 On which, see also I.M.W. Harvey, 'Poaching and sedition in fifteenth-century England', in R. Evans, ed., *Lordship and learning. Studies in memory of Trevor Aston* (Woodbridge: Boydell, 2004), pp.169-82.

33 For relevant work in this area, see, for instance, C.D. Briggs, 'Manor court procedures, debt litigation levels, and rural credit provision in England, c.1290-c.1380', *Law and History Review* 24 (2006); L. Bonfield, 'The nature of customary law in the manor courts of medieval England', *Comparative Studies in Society and History*, xxxi (1989); L. Bonfield, 'What did Edwardian villagers mean by "customary law"?', in Z. Razi and R.M. Smith, eds, *Medieval society and the manor court* (Oxford: Oxford University Press, 1996), pp. 103-16; J.S. Beckerman, 'Toward a theory of medieval manorial adjudication: the nature of communal judgements in a system of customary law', *Law and History Review* 13 (1995); P.R. Hyams, 'What did Edwardian villagers mean by "Law"?', in Razi and Smith, eds, *Medieval society and the manor court*, pp. 69-102; R.M. Smith, 'Some thoughts on "hereditary" and "proprietary" rights in land under customary law in thirteenth and early fourteenth century England', *Law and History Review* 1 (1983).

34 M.T. Clanchy, *From memory to written record: England, 1066-1307* (2nd ed., Oxford: Blackwell, 1992), pp. 44-80. C. Briggs, *Credit and village society in fourteenth-century England* (Oxford: Oxford University Press, 2009); P.R. Schofield, 'L'endettement et le crédit dans la campagne anglaise au moyen âge', in M. Berthe, ed., *Endettement paysan et crédit rural dans l'Europe médiévale et moderne. Actes des XVIIes journées internationales d'histoire de l'abbaye de Flaran, Septembre 1995* (Toulouse: Presses Universitaires du Mirail, 1998), pp. 69-97; P.R. Schofield, 'Access to credit in the medieval English countryside', in P.R. Schofield and N.J. Mayhew, eds, *Credit and debt in medieval England*, pp. 106-26; P.R. Schofield, 'Credit and debt in the medieval English countryside', in *Il Mercato della Terra. Secc. xiii-xviii* (Prato: Monash University, 2004), pp. 785-96; P.R. Schofield, 'The social economy of the medieval village', *Economic History Review* 61 S1 (2008), 38-63. On written record and peasant indebtedness, see P. R. Schofield, 'Credit and its record in the later medieval English countryside', in P.R. Rössner, ed., *Cities - Coins - Commerce. Essays presented to Ian Blanchard on the occasion of his 70th Birthday* (Stuttgart: Franz Steiner Verlag, 2012), pp. 77-88; also P.R. Schofield, 'Peasant debt in English manorial courts: form and nature', in Julie-Mayade Claustr, ed., *Endettement privé et justice au Moyen Age* (Paris: Publications de la Sorbonne, 2007), pp. 55-67.

35 A. Musson, *Medieval law in context. The growth of legal consciousness from Magna Carta to the Peasants' Revolt* (Manchester: Manchester University Press, 2001), pp. 84-134.

36 See above, Chapter 7, pp. 203-4. Hyams, 'What did Edwardian villagers mean by "Law"?', pp. 69-102, and below, pp. 232-9.

37 See especially C. Muldrew, *The economy of obligation: the culture of credit and social relations in early modern England* (New York: St Martin's Press, 1998).
38 DeWindt, *Land and people*, pp. 278, 283.
39 S. Olson, *A chronicle of all that happens. Voices from the village court in medieval England* (Toronto: Pontifical Institute of Mediaeval Studies, 1996), pp. 10–27.
40 Olson, *Chronicle of all that happens*, p. 21.
41 P.R. Schofield, 'Peasants and the manor court: gossip and litigation in a Suffolk village at the close of the thirteenth century', *Past and Present* 159 (1998), 3–42.
42 W. Scase, *Literature and complaint in England, 1272–1553* (Oxford: Oxford University Press, 2007), pp. 5–41. On the historical discussion of political songs and peasant culture, see also below, pp. 238–9.
43 Scase, *Literature and complaint*, p. 15
44 Scase, *Literature and complaint*, pp. 17–18.
45 See R.H. Hilton, 'Peasant movements in England before 1381', *Economic History Review*, 2nd series, ii (1949), pp. 117–36, reprinted in E.M. Carus-Wilson, ed., *Essays in economic history* ii (London: Arnold, 1962), pp. 73–91, and in R.H. Hilton, *Class conflict and the crisis of feudalism. Essays in medieval social history* (London: Hambledon, 1985), pp. 122–38 (from where subsequent references are taken), and especially, pp. 131–3.
46 See above, Chapter 3, pp. 91–101; Chapter 7, pp. 209–11; and especially the discussion of peasants as a 'class' outlined in Chapter 3, pp. 94–7.
47 Hilton, 'Peasant movements', p. 127.
48 A.E. Levett, *Studies in manorial history* (Oxford: Oxford University Press, 1938), pp. 203–5. See also 'Ada Elizabeth Levett, 10 August 1881–9 December 1932' by E.M. Jamison in the same book, pp. xiv–xv, on Levett's support for the Workers' Education Association and for prison reform.
49 M. Morgan, *The English lands of the Abbey of Bec* (Oxford: Oxford University Press, 1946), pp. 105–10.
50 See, for example, S. Reynolds, 'Social mentalities and the case of medieval scepticism', *Transactions of the Royal Historical Society*, 6th series, 1 (1991), 21–41.
51 P. Franklin, 'Politics in manorial court rolls. The tactics, social composition and aims of a pre-1381 peasant movement', in Razi and Smith, *Medieval society and the manor court*, pp. 162–98; P.L. Larson, *Conflict and compromise in the late medieval countryside: lords and peasants in Durham, 1349–1400* (New York: Routledge, 2006). Similar instances of later fourteenth-century resistance to seigneurial demands, in the years after the Peasants' Revolt of 1381, are set out in A. Réville, *Le soulèvement des travailleurs d'Angleterres en 1381: Études et documents publiés avec un introduction historique* (Paris: Picard, 1898), pp. cxxix–cxxxii.
52 R.H. Hilton, *Bond men made free. Medieval peasant movements and the English rising of 1381* (London: Routledge, 1973; republished with a new introduction by C. Dyer, London: Routledge, 2003), pp. 176–85, 220–30.
53 On which see for instance R.B. Dobson, *The Peasants' Revolt of 1381* (London: Macmillan, 1970), pp. 155ff.
54 For instance, Hilton, *Bond men made free*, pp. 224–8, 229–30.
55 Hilton, 'Peasant movements in medieval England', pp. 122–38; C. Dyer,

'memories of freedom: attitudes towards serfdom in England, 1200–1350', in M.L. Bush, ed., *Serfdom and slavery. Studies in legal bondage* (Harlow: Longman, 1996).

56 R. Faith, 'The "Great Rumour" of 1377 and peasant ideology', in R.H. Hilton and T.H. Aston, eds, *The English Rising of 1381* (Cambridge: Cambridge University Press, 1984), pp. 43–74; see also M. Müller, 'The aims and organisation of a peasant revolt in early fourteenth-century Wiltshire', *Rural History* 14 (2003), 1–20.

57 J.F. Nichols, 'An early fourteenth century petition from the tenants of Bocking to their manorial lord', *Economic History Review* 2 (1930), 300.

58 Nichols, 'Early fourteenth century petition', 300.

59 Faith, 'The "Great Rumour"', p. 62; R.H. Hilton, 'Social concepts in the English rising of 1381', in Hilton, *Class conflict and the crisis of feudalism*, pp. 221–2.

60 See again, most obviously, Hilton, *English peasantry*, pp. 14–15.

61 Hilton, *English peasantry*, p. 15.

62 Hilton, *English peasantry*, p. 15.

63 On the *modus tenendi parliamentum*, see V.H. Galbraith, 'The *Modus Tenendi Parliamentum*', *Journal of the Warburg and Courtauld Institutes* xvi (1953), and for text of the same, with specific reference to the cause mentioned above, see N. Pronay and J. Taylor, *Parliamentary texts of the later middle ages* (Oxford: Oxford University Press, 1982), pp. 89–90; for the coronation oath: H.G. Richardson, 'The English coronation oath', *Transactions of the Royal Historical Society*, 4th series, xxiii (1941), 137–40.

64 Hilton, *English peasantry*, p. 16. See also, for instance, the brief discussion of peasant agendas in J. Whittle and S.H. Rigby, 'England: popular politics and social conflict', in S.H. Rigby, ed., *A companion to Britain in the later middle ages* (Oxford: Blackwell, 2003), p. 70. See also see S.H. Rigby, *English society in the later middle ages. Class, status and gender* (Basingstoke: Macmillan, 1995), pp. 315–16.

65 J.R. Maddicott, *Thomas of Lancaster, 1307–1322* (Oxford: Oxford University Press, 1970), pp. 328–30; see also, for a brief case-study of this engagement as well as the questions it raises regarding explication of political allegiances, Schofield, *Peasant and community*, pp. 208, 213–14.

66 J.R. Maddicott, *Simon de Montfort* (Cambridge: Cambridge University Press), pp. 367–8; J.R. Maddicott, 'Politics and people in thirteenth-century England', in J. Burton, P. Schofield and B. Weiler, eds, *Thirteenth-century England xiv* (Woodbridge: Boydell, 2013), pp. 1–13.

67 Maddicott, 'Politics and people', pp. 6–9.

68 D.A. Carpenter, 'English peasants in politics, 1258–1267', *Past and Present* 136 (1992), reprinted in D.A. Carpenter, *The reign of Henry III* (London: Hambledon, 1996). All subsequent references are taken from the original 1992 article.

69 See also, for further reflections by Carpenter and a narrative account of material relevant to the story of thirteenth-century politicised peasantry, and one that draws upon central governmental records (Fine rolls), see www.finerollshenry3.org.uk/content/month/fm-09-2010.html (accessed 6 November 2012).

70 Carpenter, 'English peasants in politics', 6.
71 Carpenter, 'English peasants in politics', 4, 20.
72 Carpenter, 'English peasants in politics', 15–18.
73 Carpenter, 'English peasants in politics', 18–19.
74 J.R. Maddicott, 'Poems of social protest in early fourteenth century England', in W. Ormrod, ed., *England in the fourteenth century. Proceedings of the 1985 Harlaxton Symposium* (Woodbridge: Boydell, 1986), pp. 130–44; *The political songs of England, from the reign of John to that of Edward II*, ed. and trans. T. Wright (Camden Society, 1839; new edition by Peter Coss, with introduction, Cambridge: Cambridge University Press, 1996).
75 S. Justice, *Writing and rebellion. England in 1381* (Berkeley: University of California Press, 1994), pp. 13–66.
76 As well as the relevant literature as discussed below, see the important general discussions of religion and piety, R.N. Swanson, *Religion and Devotion in Europe c.1215–c.1515* (Cambridge: Cambridge University Press,1995); J. Bossy, *Christianity in the West 1400–1700* (Oxford: Oxford University Press, 1985); J. van Engen, 'The Christian middle ages as an historiographical problem', *American Historical Review* 91 (1986), 519–52; S. Reynolds, 'Social mentalities and the case of medieval scepticism', *Transactions of the Royal Historical Society*, 6th series, 1 (1991), 21–42.
77 R.M. Smith, 'Marriage processes in the English past: some continuities', in L. Bonfield, R. Smith and K. Wrightson, eds, *The world we have gained. Histories of population and social structure* (Oxford: Blackwell, 1986), pp. 43–99; see also above, Chapter 6, pp. 173–6.
78 See, for instance, R.J. Faith, 'Debate: seigneurial control of women's marriage', *Past and Present* 99 (1983), 137–8; E. Searle, 'Seigneurial control of women's marriage: the antecedents and function of merchet in England', *Past and Present* 82 (1979), 24–5.
79 Schofield, 'Social economy'.
80 See above, Chapter 4, pp. 129–33.
81 As, for instance, D. Postles, 'Lamps, lights and layfolk: "popular" devotion before the Black Death', *Journal of Medieval History* 25 (1999), 97–114.
82 M. Rubin, *Corpus Christi: the eucharist in late medieval culture* (Cambridge: Cambridge University Press, 1991); Smith, 'Marriage processes in the English past', pp. 43–99.
83 A. Hudson, 'The mouse in the pyx: popular heresy and the eucharist', in N. Crossley-Holland, ed., *Eternal values in medieval life* (Trivium, 26, 1991), pp. 40–53; D.M. Owen, *Church and society in medieval Lincolnshire* (History of Lincolnshire, 5, Lincoln, 1971); E. Mason, 'The role of the English parishioner, 1100–1500', *Journal of Ecclesiastical History* 27 (1976); M. Aston, 'Lollardy and literacy' in Aston, *Lollards and reformers. Images and literacy in late medieval religion* (London: Hambledon, 1984), pp. 193–217, and also below, pp. 242–3.
84 For instance, J. Crook, *English medieval shrines* (Woodbridge: Boydell, 2011); A. Reiss, *The Sunday Christ: sabbatarianism in English medieval wall painting* (British Archaeological Reports, 2000).

85 See, for instance, E. Duffy, *The stripping of the altars. Traditional religion in England, c.1400–c.1580* (New Haven and London: Yale University Press, 1992); E. Duffy, *The voices of Morebath: reformation and rebellion in an English village* (New Haven and London: Yale University Press, 2001); K.L. French, *The people of the parish: community life in a late medieval English Diocese* (Philadelphia: University of Pennsylvania Press, 2001).
86 Duffy, *Voices of Morebath*, pp. 65–83.
87 P.G. Schmidt, 'The vision of Thurkill', *Journal of the Warburg and Courtauld Institutes* 41 (1978), 50–64. I am most grateful to Professor Rigby for this reference; see also his comment on the same in his forthcoming review of D. Gray, *Simple forms: essays on medieval popular literature* (Oxford: Oxford University Press, 2015) in *English Historical Review* (forthcoming).
88 C. Gross, *The guild merchant. A contribution to British municipal history* (Oxford: Oxford University Press, 2 vols, 1890); F.A. Gasquet, *Parish life in mediaeval England* (London: Methuen, 1906).
89 V. Bainbridge, *Gilds in the medieval countryside: social and religious change in Cambridgeshire c.1350–1558* (Woodbridge: Boydell, 1997); B. Kumin, *The shaping of a community. The rise and reformation of the English parish* (Aldershot: Ashgate, 1996).
90 G.C. Homans, *English villagers of the thirteenth century* (Cambridge, Mass.: Harvard University Press, 1941), p. 398.
91 See, for instance, M.R. James, 'Twelve medieval ghost stories', *English Historical Review* (1922), 413–22. James notes that 'a study of local records, impossible to me, might not improbably throw light upon the persons mentioned in the stories', 414. See also A. Joynes, *Medieval ghost stories* (Woodbridge: Boydell, 2001), pp. 120–5.
92 R. Hutton, 'How pagan were medieval English peasants?', *Folklore* 122 (2011), 235–49.
93 See, for instance, M. Aston, 'William White's Lollard followers', in M. Aston, *Lollards and reformers. Images and literacy in late medieval religion* (London: Hambledon, 1984), pp. 93–5, previously published in *Catholic Historical Review* 68 (1982), 469–97.
94 J.A.F. Thomson, *The later Lollards, 1414–1520* (Oxford: Oxford University Press, 1965), pp. 28–9.
95 Thomson, *Later Lollards*, pp. 50–1, 63–6, 70, 125–6.
96 See, for instance, discussion of the weaver James Willis, a heresiarch in the Chilterns in the mid-fifteenth century, Thomson, *Later Lollards*, pp. 68–9.
97 M. Aston, 'Lollardy and sedition, 1381–1431', in Aston, *Lollards and reformers*, 31–8.
98 L.R. Poos, *A rural society after the Black Death. Essex, 1350–1525* (Cambridge: Cambridge University Press, 1991), pp. 132–41; 268.
99 I. Forrest, *The detection of heresy in late medieval England* (Oxford: Oxford University Press, 2005), pp. 207–30.
100 M.K. McIntosh, *Controlling misbehavior in England, 1370–1600* (Cambridge: Cambridge University Press, 1998).

101 McIntosh, *Controlling misbehaviour*, p. 187.
102 McIntosh, *Controlling misbehaviour*, pp. 187-95.
103 See, for instance, McIntosh, *Controlling misbehaviour*, pp. 96-107, 198-200.
104 M. Bailey, 'Rural society', in R. Horrox, ed., *Fifteenth-century attitudes. Perceptions of society in late medieval England* (Cambridge: Cambridge University Press, 1994), pp. 163-8 (quote at p. 164).
105 B.F. Harvey, 'Work and *festa ferianda* in medieval England', *Journal of Ecclesiastical History* 23 (1972), 289–308
106 Harvey, 'Work and *festa ferianda*', 295-7.
107 Harvey, 'Work and *festa ferianda*', 307.

Conclusion

The study of the medieval English peasantry began, in the nineteenth century, as an adjunct to the study of other themes. Thus, the history of the manor, of rent, of the early origins of the community, all included inevitable reference to the peasantry. There was however seldom a direct engagement with the peasantry, and the direction of enquiry was towards their social superiors, especially their lords. Where peasants featured in such discussions it was typically as tenants. Edward Miller, in reflecting upon the decline of villeinage and the manorial economy in the fourteenth century, succinctly noted that 'manorial England was rapidly becoming peasant England', but such a transition within the historiography did not take place until the middle years of the twentieth century.[1] It was with the emergence of a 'new social history' and the engagement with the social sciences that medieval historians directed more of their attention from the history of lords and tenants to the history of peasants.[2] Despite this newer element in the historical discussion, the persistence of research themes from the nineteenth century onwards is striking, as we have seen throughout this volume. The tenacity of long-standing research agendas, often modified in their emphases but seldom abandoned in their entirety, has had consequences for the range of study and the kinds of intellectual and cross-disciplinary engagement undertaken by students of the medieval English peasantry.

In the first instance, study of any historical period or theme is, of course, conditioned by the available sources. Historians have addressed rural society and the peasantry in particular through sources generated at the level of the manor and the estate. It is also noteworthy that there has been an important shift in emphasis in terms of sources, and especially a heightened focus upon manorial court rolls as the principal object of study for comprehending peasant society and economy in medieval England. Initially, as we have seen, a great deal of inferential comment on the medieval peasantry was the product of research in estate documents, often in particular accounts, custumals and surveys, and was aimed principally at understanding seigneurial economies or the legal institutions of freedom and villeinage. In the second half of the twentieth century, examination of peasant society encouraged a fuller, if not necessarily a systematic, investigation of manorial court rolls, seemingly the best source for a proximate study of the medieval peasantry.[3] Before, during and after this research phase, historians have continued to relate various ancillary sources to the study of the peasantry. At the level of the vill, manor and estate, for instance, rentals, custumals, manorial accounts, tithing listings have all been employed, as have, at the national level, chancery rolls, lay subsidy lists and so on. The choice of source material, and especially the preponderance of studies founded upon the study of estate records and in particular manorial court rolls, almost certainly has helped to cement agendas and research approaches, and to leave less room for other related areas of study. Furthermore, discussion of a wider peasant culture of engagement, including political, religious or legal culture and in terms of patterns of consumption, has often been explored not by historians of manorial court rolls and of peasant economy and society themselves but by historians whose primary research focus has typically been directed elsewhere: politics, religion, the law and so on. It remains the case that novel and exciting insights into the world of the medieval peasant may be gleaned from sources not as evidently directed at this area of study, a point noted by, for instance, E.B. Fryde, in his discussion of fourteenth-century Italian mercantile records and their records of payments and receipts relating to wool purchased in the Cotswolds, if more often through middlemen at local markets and fairs than directly at the farm gate.[4]

The persistence of historiographical themes and research questions as well as the concentrated attention offered to particular sources types, especially documentary sources generated at the manorial level, has also left little room for other elements to be absorbed into the historiographical framework employed to date. In the previous chapter, on culture and the medieval peasantry, it has been suggested that a significant range of topics, including discussion of political agency, forms of consumption, aspects of faith and peasant literacy, have tended to sit at one remove from the mainstream study in this area. So, for instance, historians of the medieval English peasantry have, with their predominant focus upon matters economic and structural, abandoned most opportunities for close engagement with literary and artistic sources potentially relevant to the study of medieval peasants.[5] This has, for instance, left little shared ground with literary scholars, and discussion of peasantry within a medievalism the focus of which has tended to be upon literary sources and culture remains muted. This is not to say that literary historians have not addressed matters pertaining to the medieval English peasantry, as is evident for example in Steven Justice's discussion of literacy and the Peasants' Revolt, which involves him in a close engagement with a wealth of relevant historical literature on the medieval peasantry.[6] From time to time historians have also contributed directly to what are more evidently literary studies of medieval rural life.[7] Where historians of the 'peasant-focused' sources, such as manorial court rolls, have sought to employ such records in ways more familiar to cultural historians, their efforts have as yet found little purchase with exponents of a more 'traditional' historiography.[8]

Similarly, while it will be quite clear that the works of the great economic theorists, including Smith, Marx and Ricardo, have all informed work on the medieval English peasantry and that their theoretical models have been central to the main conceptualisations of the medieval economy, it seems also reasonably evident that more general economic literature, issuing directly from the modern discipline of economics and of a kind intended to frame debate and to encourage case-studies, including historical case-studies, capable of testing its core propositions, has seldom found direct response from medievalists.[9] In the first instance, it would be far from correct to suggest that economists have not directed their attention to the study of the medieval peasantry, for they have indeed done so as we have seen in, for instance, discussion of the open fields and the management of risk; there is though little evidence that the majority of medievalists have absorbed, at least directly, the research and writings of modern economists and reapplied them in their own work. To take a classic instance of economic theorising linked to the medieval rural economy, North and Thomas's 1971 article 'The rise and fall of the manorial system: a theoretical model' has, according to Google Scholar, over 180 citations, but fewer than 1 per cent of these have evidently been authored by medievalists. Instead, development economists and historians of modern rural societies, including Mexico, Russia, Sweden, Africa and Cuba, have cited the work within their own research.[10] Part of the reason for this lack of 'take-up' must reside in the intended audiences for such work; North and Thomas, and other economists approaching the past, are not typically seeking to engage with period specialists or historians working in the particular subject area but rather more are seeking to employ research in that area to examine wider economic models and theories. This can often leave historians of the period perplexed and distrustful of their efforts, as reviews by medievalists of, for example, Dahlman's and Townsend's studies of the open-field system in medieval England seem to imply.[11] It is also the case, judging by citations, that more generally applicable, though non-specific, work on economics has been engaged with only indirectly by most medievalists. To take a fairly obvious instance, institutional economics, a familiar totem of economic history in recent decades, offers highly relevant insights into the economic history of medieval rural society. Thus, Douglas North's key statements on the importance of institutions in explaining economic change in past society and the rate of development have certainly not gone unheeded; indeed, they enjoy the highest of profiles, not least in the form of a Nobel Prize lecture.[12] It is though often only by inference that we can detect the influence of, for example, institutional economics in the study of the economy of the medieval English countryside.[13] Undoubtedly, disciplinary 'language' barriers inevitably hamper such engagement. The tools of econometric analysis are no more available to all medievalists than are the necessary palaeographic and linguistics skills accessible to economists.

We can pursue this point further, in considering disciplinary boundaries and areas of research that, while potentially offering a great deal to the future study of the peasantry, are not so evident in the relevant historiography. It is, in particular, surprising how small has been the role of archaeology in determining the nature and parameters of the debate concerning the medieval English peasantry in this period. It is emphatically not the case that archaeology has nothing to offer the student of the medieval English peasant and we can think of some startling and significant instances of the medieval archaeological study of the medieval peasantry. Some of these have been discussed already in this volume.[14] Important examples of archaeological engagement with medieval peasantry include, most obviously, showpiece investigation of deserted medieval settlements, such as Wharram Percy, Goltho and Barton Blount.[15] Examination of settlement patterns through field-walking and digs have helped to define the landscape and contours of the medieval peasant's world, while work on peasant diet and health has been invigorated by advances in palaeo-archaeology.[16] There are also clear examples of intersection between historical study of medieval peasants and the archaeological investigation of the same. The greatest exponent of that approach, as has been discussed on more than one occasion in this volume, has been Christopher

Dyer whose historical and documentary-based writing has been typically permeated by a close familiarity with archaeological material and reports. Thus, for instance, he has been instrumental in bringing together archaeologists and historians in order to discuss such issues as the circulation of coin in the medieval village, land use and management, and diet and standard of living.[17] It is striking that one of Dyer's most recent contributions in this respect is intended in part to make documentary-based historians familiar with a body of published archaeological work 'hidden in unfamiliar literature'.[18] Archaeologists also have been keen to remind historians of the limited nature of their documentary sources and the real need to absorb the results of archaeological investigation if they are to come closer to a fuller understanding of the material and cultural experience of medieval peasants.[19]

If such clear instances of interaction do exist, and they clearly do, it would be less easy to show, as Dyer's recent work also intimates, that most historians of the medieval English peasantry have embraced archaeological evidence and interpretations in their own work. The main debates and thematic approaches to this area of study, as set out in this volume, illustrate how bound historians of the medieval peasantry have been to the written record, as well as to their own interpretations.[20] This is neither surprising nor wholly inappropriate: there remains a vast corpus of written material as yet unexplored for the study of medieval rural society, and the research questions directed at it are often suited to, indeed formed by, the available written sources. That said, it seems at least possible that further engagement with archaeological material and commentaries by archaeologists might serve at least to test, sometimes to challenge but also to reinforce established historiographical positions. To date, this has been most evident in the last generation of research and writing where, in any case, pre-existing assumptions regarding the nature of the peasant economy have been generally set aside in favour of an assessment that graces a more positive and pro-active view of the medieval peasant.

If then there is an evident persistence of certain main themes in the study of the medieval English peasantry and one that risks a degree of isolation from at least some other disciplinary associations, it is also very clear that, within the examination of those themes, there has been much variety as well as nuance and the occasional departure. I have tried to suggest in the introduction to this volume that any such historiographical changes – from, say, a historical focus on lord–tenant relations to one on the peasant family and subsequently to the role of the market in defining peasant life – do not amount to paradigm shifts; instead, these largely thematic developments seldom lose sight of the same defining principles and core issues, the latter typically defined by the surviving written sources favoured by historians working in this area. In rereading the contributions of nineteenth-century historians such as W.J. Ashley or J.E.T. Rogers to the study of the medieval agrarian economy, it is possible to be struck both by the differences in interpretation on key points, such as perhaps the typicality of certain forms of manor and lordship, but also by the continuities and the 'modern' thrust of elements of their argument, for instance their interest in a changing countryside influenced by external factors. This is hardly surprising since historians such as these, as we have seen, helped to establish the core themes that continue to inform most debate in this area. This is also important because it speaks to a defining paradigm which exists beyond the themes studied here, namely the need to establish a compelling and testable argument according to the precepts of good historical practice.

This also does not mean, as should be evident from the discussion in this volume, that there has been no development in the study of the medieval English peasantry. This is true even where historians working in this area have not come to agree categorically. Debates, which often in mutated form have persisted for a century more (the nature and extent of medieval serfdom, for example), continue not necessarily because historians continue to hammer away at exactly the same questions. In fact, again as we have seen, particular debates may sometimes fade into the background as the protagonists exhaust their lines of enquiry or move on to other research topics or die but the general issue persists and even the particular may be resurrected many decades later.[21] On occasion, the discipline, or the particular area of study, is offered, through a restatement or nuancing of previous work, a reminder of this earlier tradition which, rather than initiating a further round of repetition, encourages a reassessment and the pursuit of new but relevant lines of enquiry. Further, the apparent exhaustion of one line of enquiry may generate other and new approaches and framings of relevant research. So, to return to a familiar instance, recent suggestions that the impact of serfdom upon the medieval peasant was less than has always been supposed demand a further reflection on the tenurial and seigneurial distinctions that applied across high and late medieval England as well as a careful consideration of 'impact' and how it is measurable, in terms not only of rent and tenure but in more subtle indices, such as economic freedom and self-perception.[22]

In these adjustments, nuances and new directions, the historical discussion has equally clearly responded to the changing environment in which historians have carried out their researches and framed their analyses. The imposition of certain norms and assumptions about how society worked and what caused it to change are all but unavoidable and all historians, directly or indirectly, consciously or subconsciously, employ models.[23] The declining interest in class structure in the medieval village coincided with a retreat from a more widespread support for Marxism in Western politics from the 1950s and 1960s; the growth of social science and feminist politics in the 1960s and 1970s also helped promote its own positive response in the historiography of the medieval English peasantry.[24] Further, it may not be entirely surprising to discover that medieval historians' fascination with the market, the consumptive and productive power of the peasantry, the extension of credit and the volatility of the land market has been at its greatest from the 1980s until the first decade of the twenty-first century, a period of unparalleled economic expansion. The shuddering halt to that growth which came in 2008 is beginning to see itself played out in an adjusted view of peasant economics.[25] None of this is to suggest that the study of the medieval peasantry is, like other areas of historical study, a plaything of historical fashion, subject only to the whims and musings of historians the views of whom are rooted only in the present. Rather, it reflects a nuancing and refining of questions that will lead to a fuller understanding of a topic and period of great and enduring interest.

Notes

1 E. Miller, *The abbey and bishopric of Ely. The social history of an ecclesiastical estate from the tenth to the early fourteenth century* (Cambridge: Cambridge University Press, 1951), pp. 152–3. We should however recognise that some nineteenth-century historians had already railed against this disregard, most obviously Thorold Rogers, who lamented the failure of historians 'to search into the life and doings of our forefathers, instead of skimming the froth of foreign policy, of wars, of royal marriages and successions, and the personal character of the puppets who have strutted on the stage of public life', J.E.T. Rogers, *Six centuries of work and wages. The history of English labour* (London: Sonnenschein, 1908), p. 178.

2 See, for instance, the view expressed in E.B. DeWindt, *Land and people in Holywell-cum-Needingworth* (Toronto: Pontifical Institute of Mediaeval Studies, 1972), p. 283, that 'the mediaeval peasant has been waiting long centuries to be heard ... How much longer must he [*sic*] wait?'

3 See, for instance, the itemisation of court rolls in J. Cripps, R. Hilton and J. Williamson, 'Appendix. A survey of medieval manorial courts in England', in Z. Razi and R. Smith, eds, *Medieval society and the manor court* (Oxford: Oxford University Press, 1996), pp. 569–637.

4 E.B. Fryde, *Peasants and landlords in later medieval England* (Stroud: Sutton, 1996), pp. 87–104.
5 Early twentieth-century explorations of village life and the manor did not neglect literary sources (see for instance, H.S. Bennett, *Life on the English manor. A study of peasant conditions 1150–1400* (Cambridge: Cambridge University Press, 1937)) but these have ceased to sit at the core of most subsequent work. For more recent reflections on the potential in literary sources as a counter-balance to the quantification of economic historians, see, for instance, J. Hatcher, 'England in the aftermath of the Black Death', *Past and Present* 144 (1994), 13–19.
6 S. Justice, *Writing and rebellion. England in 1381* (Berkeley: University of California Press, 1994); see also, for instance, A.J. Frantzen and D. Moffat, *The work of work: servitude, slavery and labor in medieval England* (Glasgow: Cruithne, 1994); Ellen K. Rentz, 'Half-acre bylaws: harvest-sharing in *Piers Plowman*', *Yearbook of Langland Studies* 25 (2011), 95–115.
7 J.M. Bennett, 'The curse of the Plowman', *Yearbook of Langland Studies* 20 (2006), 215–26; C. Dyer, 'Piers Plowman and Plowmen: a historical perspective', *Yearbook of Langland Studies* 8 (1994), 155–76.
8 Olson, *A mute gospel*, and above, Introduction, p. 15.
9 On engagement with the economics canon by medievalists working on the medieval economy more generally, see, for instance, M. Bailey and J. Hatcher, *Modelling the middle ages. The history and theory of England's economic development* (Oxford: Oxford University Press, 2001).
10 http://scholar.google.com/scholar?q=link:http://journals.cambridge.org/abstract_S0022050700074623 (accessed 27 November 2012). For the article itself, see D.C. North and R.P. Thomas, 'The rise and fall of the manorial system: a theoretical model', *Journal of Economic History* 31 (1971), 777–803.
11 See, for example, B.M.S. Campbell's review of R.M. Townsend, *The medieval village economy: a study of the Pareto mapping in general equilibrium* models (Princeton: Princeton University Press, 1993), in *Agricultural History Review* 43 (1995), 97–8; also the review of the same by J. Langdon, *Economic History Review* 47 (1994), 816.
12 For example, D.C. North and R.P. Thomas, 'An economic theory of the growth of the western world', *Economic History Review* 23 (1970), 1–17.
13 For an example of direct engagement, but at one remove from the study of the medieval English peasantry, J. Munro, 'The "new institutional economics" and the changing fortunes of fairs in medieval and early modern Europe: the textile trades, warfare and transaction costs', *Vierteljahrschrift für Sozial- und Wirtschaftsgeschichte* 88 (2001), 1–47.
14 See above, Chapter 8, p. 229.
15 For which, see, for instance, M.W. Beresford and J.G. Hunt, *Deserted medieval villages* (London: Lutterworth, 1971); G. Beresford, *Mediaeval clay-land village: excavations at Goltho and Barton Blount* (London: Society for Medieval Archaeology, 1975); M. Beresford and J. Hurst, *Wharram Percy. Deserted medieval village* (London: English Heritage, 1990); for a useful and fairly recent summary of relevant archaeological work, including exploration of village sites

and farmsteads, see D.A. Hinton, *Archaeology, economy and society. England from the fifth to the fifteenth century* (London: Routledge, 1998).
16 On landscape, M. Aston, D. Austin and C. Dyer, eds, *The rural settlements of medieval England. Studies dedicated to Maurice Beresford and John Hurst* (Oxford: Blackwell, 1989); C. Lewis, P, Mitchell-Fox and C. Dyer, *Village, hamlet and field. Changing medieval settlements in central England* (Macclesfield: Windgather Press, 2001); on diet, see, for instance, the essays in C. Woolgar, D. Serjeantson and T. Waldron, eds, *Food in medieval England: diet and nutrition* (Oxford: Oxford University Press, 2006).
17 See above, Chapter 4, p. 125-6, 139, Chapter 8, pp. 227-9.
18 C. Dyer, 'The material world of English peasants, 1200-1540: archaeological perspectives on rural economy and welfare', *Agricultural History Review* 62 (2014), 1-22.
19 See, for instance, R. Hodges, 'Parachutists and truffle-hunters: at the frontiers of archaeology and history', in M. Aston, D. Austin and C. Dyer, eds, *The rural settlements of medieval England*, pp. 287-305.
20 Dyer, 'Material world of English peasants', 1-2.
21 See, for instance, the comments on the reappearance of a commercial emphasis in R.H. Britnell, *The commercialisation of English society, 1000-1500* (Cambridge: Cambridge University Press, 1993; republished by Manchester University Press, 1996), p. 230.
22 For a recent statement on the perceived current position, see J. Hatcher, 'Lordship and villeinage before the Black Death: from Karl Marx to the Marxists and back again', in M. Kowaleski, J. Langdon and P.R. Schofield, eds, *Peasants and lords in the medieval English economy* (Turnhout: Brepols, 2015), pp. 113-45.
23 Compare, for instance, D. Cannadine, 'The present and the past in the English industrial revolution, 1880-1980', *Past and Present* 103 (1984), 131-72; also, on a similar point, J.M. Bennett, *History matters. Patriarchy and the challenge of feminism* (Philadelphia: University of Pennsylvania Press, 2006), p. 14.
24 See, for instance, Judith Bennett's reflections on the ways in which her view of women in the middle ages was moulded by her own experiences in the classroom and in feminist politics, J.M. Bennett, *Ale, beer and brewsters in England. Women's work in a changing world, 1300-1600* (Oxford: Oxford University Press, 1996), pp. 6-7.
25 It is worth noting that discussions of crisis, including famine and dearth, as areas of study have recently begun to appear with seemingly greater regularity as conference themes, with at least two dedicated groups of European medievalists exploring the topic. A recent series of meetings at Lleida, July 2011; Brussels, September 2012; Viterbo, October 2012, Stirling, November 2013, following, it has also to be noted, some pre-financial crisis gatherings in Seville, September 2005, and Paris, November 2007, have begun to bear fruit in publications: H.R. Oliva Herrer and P. Benito I Monclús, eds, *Crisis de Subsistencia y crisis agrarias en la edad media* (Seville: Universidad de Sevilla, 2007) and P. Benito I Monclus, ed., *Crisis alimentarias en la Edad Media. Modelos, explicaciones y representaciones* (Lleida: Universidad de Lleida, 2013). See also H. Kitsikopoulos, ed., *Agrarian*

change and crisis in Europe, 1200–1500 (London: Routledge, 2012); F. Menant, M. Bourin and Ll. To Figueras, eds, *Dynamiques du monde rural dans la conjoncture de 1300* (Rome: École Française de Rome, 2014); D.R. Curtis, *Coping with crisis. The resilience and vulnerability of pre-industrial settlements* (Farnham: Ashgate, 2014).

GUIDE TO FURTHER READING

Introduction

There are a number of works that touch on aspects of the relevant historiography and offer commentary on its development. See, for instance, M. Berg, 'The first women economic historians', *Economic History Review* 45 (1992), 308-29; P.R. Schofield, 'British economic history, c.1880-c.1930', in P. Lambert and P.R. Schofield, eds, *Making history: an introduction to the history and practices of a discipline* (London: Routledge, 2004), pp. 65-77; J. Hatcher and M. Bailey, *Modelling the medieval economy. The history and theory of England's economic development* (Oxford: Oxford University Press, 2001); Nils Hybel, *Crisis or change. The concept of crisis in the light of agrarian structural reorganization in late medieval England* (Aarhus: Aarhus University Press, 1989). P. Gattrell, 'Historians and peasants: studies of medieval English society in a Russian context', *Past and Present* 96 (1982), 22-50, reprinted in T.H. Aston, ed., *Landlords, peasants and politics in medieval England* (Cambridge: Cambridge University Press, 1987), pp. 394-422, offers an important view of the study of the medieval English peasantry from one international perspective.

Chapter 1 Early contributions

For a selection of indicative work in this area from the later nineteenth and early twentieth century, all of which offer some discussion of peasantry, though with a range of different emphases, see Sir W.J. Ashley, *An introduction to English economic history and theory. Part I. The middle ages* (London: Rivingtons, 1888); A. Jessop, 'Village life six hundred years ago', in *The coming of the friars* (London: Fisher Unwin, 1889); J.E.T. Rogers, *Six centuries of work and wages. The history of English labour* (London: Sonnenschein, 1908); F.W. Maitland, *Domesday Book and beyond. Three essays in the early history of England* (1897; republished Cambridge: Cambridge University Press, 1987); F.W. Maitland, 'The history of a Cambridgeshire manor', in H.M. Cam, ed., *Selected historical essays of F.W. Maitland* (Cambridge: Cambridge University Press, 1957), pp. 16-40; P. Vinogradoff, *Villainage in England. Essays in English mediaeval history* (Oxford: Oxford University Press, 1892); N. Neilson, 'Boon-services on the estates of Ramsey Abbey', *American Historical Review*, ii (1897), 213-24; T.W. Page, *The end of villeinage in England* (New York: Macmillan, 1900); F.G. Davenport, *The economic development of a Norfolk manor, 1086-1565* (Cambridge: Cambridge University Press, 1906; reprinted London: Frank Cass and Co., 1967); A.E. Levett, *The Black Death on the estates of the see of Winchester* (Oxford: Oxford University Press, 1916); H.L. Gray, 'The commutation of villein services in

England before the Black Death', *English Historical Review* 29 (1914), 625-56; R.H. Tawney, *The agrarian problem in the sixteenth century* (London: Longmans, 1912). H.S. Bennett, *Life on the English manor. A study of peasant conditions 1150-1400* (Cambridge: Cambridge University Press, 1937) and G.G. Coulton, *The medieval village* (Cambridge: Cambridge University Press, 1925) both offer surveys of village society but are grounded less in the kinds of issues (rent, tenure, commutation etc.) more evident in some of the earlier publications listed here.

Chapter 2 Population, resources and the medieval English peasantry

For a selection of key works by M.M. Postan, see the following: C.N.L. Brooke and M.M. Postan, *Carte Nativorum, a Peterborough Abbey cartulary of the fourteenth century* (Northants. Record Society, 1960); M.M. Postan, 'The chronology of labour services', *Transactions of the Royal Historical Society*, 4th series, 20 (1937); also published in M.M. Postan, *Essays on medieval agriculture and general problems of the medieval economy* (Cambridge: Cambridge University Press, 1973), pp. 89-106; M.M. Postan, 'The economic foundations of medieval society', in *Rapports, Libraire Armand Colin* (Paris: Libraire Armand Colin, 1950), reprinted in Postan, *Essays on medieval agriculture*, pp. 3-27; M.M. Postan, 'Village livestock in the thirteenth century', *Economic History Review*, 2nd series, 15 (1962); also published in Postan, *Essays on medieval agriculture*, pp. 214-48; M.M. Postan, 'Medieval agrarian society in its prime. England. F. The village rich', in M.M. Postan, ed., *The Cambridge economic history of Europe. I. The agrarian life of the middle ages* (Cambridge: Cambridge University Press, 2nd edn, 1966), pp. 548-632; M.M. Postan, *The medieval economy and society. An economic history of Britain in the middle ages* (Harmondsworth: Penguin, 1972). Postan's work has been tested and sometimes qualified in numerous studies, including some of the instances listed in the following chapters.

Chapter 3 Lords and peasants

There are numerous estate studies which include important commentary on peasants, especially as tenants of their lords. See, for instance, R.H. Hilton, *The economic development of some Leicestershire estates in the fourteenth and fifteenth centuries* (Oxford: Oxford University Press, 1947); E. Miller, *The abbey and bishopric of Ely. The social history of an ecclesiastical estate from the tenth to the early fourteenth century* (Cambridge: Cambridge University Press, 1951); J.A. Raftis, *The estates of Ramsey Abbey. A study in economic growth and organization* (Toronto: Pontifical Institute of Mediaeval Studies, 1957); R.A.L. Smith, *Canterbury Cathedral Priory. A study in monastic administration* (Cambridge: Cambridge University Press, 1969); I. Kershaw, *Bolton Priory. The economy of a northern monastery, 1286-1325* (Oxford: Oxford University Press, 1973); B.F. Harvey, *Westminster Abbey and its estates in the middle ages* (Oxford: Oxford University Press, 1977). An important gathering of research in this respect is to be found in the two relevant volumes of the agrarian history of England and Wales: H.E. Hallam, ed., The Agrarian History of England and Wales, volume ii, 1042-1350 (Cambridge: Cambridge University Press, 1988) and E. Miller, ed., *The Agrarian History of England and Wales, vol. iii, 1350-1500* (Cambridge: Cambridge University Press, 1991). The second of these two volumes, which was compiled over more than two decades, reveals changing approaches to this research area but also reflects a continued emphasis on landholding, land use and tenurial structures. Important discussions of rent include M.M. Postan, 'The chronology of labour services', *Transactions of the Royal Historical Society*, 4th series, 20 (1937), 169-93, reprinted in M.M. Postan, *Essays on medieval agriculture and general problems of the medieval economy* (Cambridge: Cambridge University Press, 1973), pp. 89-106; E.A. Kosminsky, 'Services and money rents in the thirteenth century', *Economic History Review* 5 (1935), 24-45; E.A. Kosminsky, *Studies in the agrarian history of England in the thirteenth century* (Oxford: Oxford University Press, 1956). Lord-tenant relations sit at the heart of discussion of economic change and the characterisation of the prevailing economic condition. This is especially evident in debate over the cause of transition from a medieval, 'feudal' economy to a modern, capitalist one. For key contributions to the 'transition debate', see R.H. Hilton, ed., *The transition from feudalism to capitalism* (London: Verso edition, 1978); R. Brenner, 'Agrarian class structure and economic development in pre-industrial Europe', *Past and Present* 70 (1976), 30-75; Brenner, 'Agrarian class structure and economic development in pre-industrial Europe: the agrarian roots of European capitalism', *Past and Present* 97 (1982), 16-113; both articles reprinted in T.H. Aston and C.H.E. Philpin, eds, *The Brenner debate. Agrarian class structure and economic development in pre-industrial Europe* (Cambridge: Cambridge University Press, 1985), pp. 10-63 and 213-327; R. Brenner, 'Property and progress: where Adam Smith went wrong', in C. Wickham, ed., *Marxist history writing for the twenty-first century* (Oxford: Oxford University Press, 2007), pp. 49-111. For more recent comments on this debate and its intellectual merits, see S.H. Rigby, 'Historical causation: is one thing more important than another?', *History* 259 (1995), 227-42. For discussion of lord-tenant relations framed in terms of class conflict, see especially R.H. Hilton, 'Peasant movements in medieval England', *Economic History Review*, 2nd series, 2 (1949), reprinted in E.M. Carus-Wilson, ed., *Essays in economic history*, ii (London: Arnold, 1962), pp. 73-90; H. Fagan and R.H. Hilton, *The English rising of 1381* (London: Lawrence and Wishart, 1950); R.H. Hilton, *Bond men made free. Medieval peasant movements and the English rising of 1381* (London: Routledge, 1973; republished with a new introduction by C. Dyer, London: Routledge, 2003). For reassessments of the lord-tenant relationship, see J.A. Raftis, *Peasant economic development within the English manorial system* (Stroud: Sutton, 1996); J. Hatcher, 'English serfdom and villeinage. Towards a reassessment', *Past and Present* 90 (1981), 3-39; M. Bailey, 'Villeinage in England: a regional case study, c.1250-c.1349', *Economic History Review* 62 (2009), 430-57; M. Bailey, *The decline of serfdom in late medieval England. From bondage to freedom* (Woodbridge: Boydell, 2014).

Chapter 4 Peasants and markets

For major statements on the medieval market and its place in the lives of peasants, see R.H. Britnell, *The commercialisation of English society, 1000-1500* (Cambridge:

Cambridge University Press, 1993; republished by Manchester University Press, 1996); C. Dyer, *Standards of living in the later Middle Ages: social change in England c.1200-1520* (Cambridge: Cambridge University Press, 1989 and later edition); C. Dyer, 'The consumer and the market in the later middle ages', *Economic History Review*, 2nd series, 42 (1989), 305-27, reprinted in C. Dyer, *Everyday life in medieval England* (London, 1994), pp. 257-81; C. Dyer, *An age of transition? Economy and society in England in the later middle ages* (Oxford: Oxford University Press, 2005), pp. 126-72. The market has been examined in different contexts by M. Bailey, *A marginal economy? East Anglian Breckland in the later middle ages* (Cambridge: Cambridge University Press, 1989), pp. 115-42; J. Masschaele, *Peasants, merchants and markets. Inland trade in medieval England, 1150-1350* (Basingstoke: Macmillan, 1997); M. Kowaleski, *Local markets and regional trade in medieval Exeter* (Cambridge: Cambridge University Press, 1995); B.M.S. Campbell, J.A. Galloway, D. Keene and M. Murphy, *A medieval capital and its grain supply: agrarian production and distribution in the London region, c.1300* (London: Institute of British Geographers, 1993). Discussion of the peasant land market, especially in unfree land, has provided an important testing ground in identifying the significance of the market in medieval rural society; see, most obviously, A. Macfarlane, *The origins of English individualism* (Oxford: Blackwell, 1978); P.D.A. Harvey, ed., *The peasant land market in medieval England* (Oxford: Oxford University Press, 1984); R.M. Smith, ed., *Land, kinship and life-cycle* (Cambridge: Cambridge University Press, 1984) and especially the opening chapter by Richard Smith. On the impact of credit and debt in rural society, see especially C.D. Briggs, *Credit and village society in fourteenth-century England* (Oxford: Oxford University Press, 2009); P.R. Schofield, 'L'endettement et le crédit dans la campagne anglaise au moyen âge', in M. Berthe, ed., *Endettement paysan et crédit rural dans l'Europe médiévale et moderne. Actes des XVIIes journées internationales d'histoire de l'abbaye de Flaran, Septembre 1995* (Toulouse: Presses Universitaires du Mirail, 1998), pp. 69-97.

Chapter 5 Demography and the medieval peasantry

Early investigations of demography include especially J.C. Russell, *British medieval population* (Albuquerque: The University of New Mexico Press, 1948), as well as more particular investigations such as H.E. Hallam, 'Some thirteenth-century censuses', *Economic History Review* 10 (1957-58), 340-61; Hallam, 'Population density in medieval Fenland', *Economic History Review* 14 (1961), 71-81; S. Thrupp, 'The problem of replacement rates in late medieval English population', *Economic History Review*, 2nd series, 18 (1965). One of the important initial discussion of peasant demography, and especially mortality, is M.M. Postan and J.Z. Titow, 'Heriots and prices on Winchester manors', *Economic History Review* 11 (1959); reprinted in M.M. Postan, *Essays on medieval agriculture and general problems of the medieval economy* (Cambridge: Cambridge University Press, 1973), pp. 150-85; see also M.M. Postan, 'Some agrarian evidence of declining population in the later middle ages', *Economic History Review*, 2 (1950), reprinted in Postan, *Essays on medieval agriculture*, pp. 188-213. The most important study with relevance to the peasantry and the potential for using relevant sources to trace its demography is Z. Razi, *Life, marriage and death in a medieval parish. Economy, society and demography in Halesowen, 1270-1400* (Cambridge: Cambridge University Press, 1980). Other discussions with relevance to this earlier work and aimed at refining our understanding of medieval demography and the demographic experience of the peasantry in particular include R.M. Smith, 'Hypothèses sur la nuptialité en Angleterre aux xiiie-xive siècles', *Annales: Economies, Sociétés, Civilisations* 38 (1983), 107-36; L.R. Poos, 'The rural population of Essex in the later middle ages', *Economic History Review* 38 (1985), 515-30; R. Lock, 'The Black Death in Walsham-le-Willows', *Proceedings of the Suffolk Institute of Archaeology and History* 37 (1992), 316-37; L.R. Poos, Z. Razi and R.M. Smith, 'The population history of medieval English villages: a debate on the use of manor court records', in Z. Razi and R. Smith, eds, *Medieval society and the manor court* (Oxford: Oxford University Press, 1996), pp. 298-368. Most of this work has been aimed at identifying total village or manorial populations or mortality estimates. There is discussion of rural fertility in P.J.P. Goldberg, *Women, work, and life-cycle in a medieval economy. Women in York and Yorkshire c.1300-1520* (Oxford: Oxford University Press, 1992), and L.R. Poos, *A rural society after the Black Death: Essex 1350-1525* (Cambridge: Cambridge University Press, 1991); this has been challenged in M. Bailey, 'Demographic decline in late medieval England: some thoughts on recent research', *Economic History Review* 49 (1996), 1-19.

Chapter 6 Family, household and gender

An important early statement on family and social structure in the middle ages is G.C. Homans, *English villagers of the thirteenth century* (Cambridge, Mass.: Harvard University Press, 1941). More particular studies of family and household formation include H.E. Hallam, 'Age at first marriage and age at death in the Lincolnshire Fenland, 1252-1478', *Population Studies* 39 (1985), 55-69, and later discussions by Razi, especially Z. Razi, 'The myth of the immutable English family', *Past and Present* 140 (1993), pp. 3-44. For other relevant studies, see, for instance, C. Howell, *Land, family and inheritance in transition. Kibworth Harcourt 1280-1700* (Cambridge: Cambridge University Press, 1983); B.A. Hanawalt, *The ties that bound. Peasant families in medieval England* (Oxford: Oxford University Press, 1986). On gender and, especially, the experience of women in the medieval village, see the important discussion in J.M. Bennett, *Women in the medieval English countryside. Gender and household in Brigstock before the plague* (Oxford: Oxford University Press, 1987). See also the case-study J.M. Bennett, *A medieval life. Cecilia Penifader of Brigstock, c.1295-1344* (Boston: McGraw-Hill College, 1999). The role of women in a patriarchal society is discussed in C. Middleton, 'The sexual division of labour in feudal England', *New Left Review* 1 (1979), 147-68; also Middleton, 'Peasants, patriarchy, and the feudal mode of production in England: a Marxist appraisal: 1. Property and patriarchal relations within the peasantry' and 'Peasants, patriarchy and the feudal mode of production in England: 2. Feudal lords and the subordination of peasant women', both in *Sociological Review* 29 (1981), 105-54. For relatively recent discussions that have sought to assess the extent of female economic agency in the medieval village, see

C. Briggs, 'Empowered or marginalized? Rural women and credit in later thirteenth- and fourteenth-century England', *Continuity and Change* 19 (2004), 13-43; J. Bennett, *Ale, beer and brewsters in England. Women's work in a changing world, 1300-1600* (Oxford: Oxford University Press, 1996); H. Graham, '"A woman's work ...": labour and gender in the late medieval countryside', in P.J.P. Goldberg, ed., *Women in medieval English society* (Stroud: Sutton, 1997), pp. 126-48; S.A.C. Penn, 'Female wage earners in late-fourteenth century England', *Agricultural History Review* 35 (1987), 1-14; S. Bardsley, 'Women's work reconsidered: gender and wage differentiation in late medieval England', *Past and Present* 165 (1999), 3-29; and the subsequent debate, J. Hatcher, 'Debate: women's work reconsidered: gender and wage differentiation in late medieval England', *Past and Present* 173 (2001), 191-8; reply by Bardsley, 199-202 in the same issue.

Chapter 7 The village community and the nature of peasant society in medieval England

For one of the more recent statements on the medieval community, see C. Carpenter, 'Gentry and community in medieval England', *Journal of British Studies* 33 (1994), pp. 340-80, and for a considered examination of an earlier historiography, see R.M. Smith, '"Modernization" and the corporate medieval village in England: some sceptical reflections', in A.R.H. Baker and D. Gregory, eds, *Explorations in historical geography. Interpretative essays* (Cambridge: Cambridge University Press, 1984), pp. 140-79. For important instances of early examination of the medieval village community, see F. Seebohm, *The English village community examined in its relation to the manorial and tribal systems and to the common or open field system of husbandry. An essay in economic history* (London: Longmans, 1883); G.L. Gomme, *The village community with special reference to the origin and form of its survival in Britain* (London: Walter Scott, 1890); see also F.W. Maitland, *Township and borough* (Cambridge: Cambridge University Press, 1898) for an interpretation of the potential influences upon the construction of community. H. Cam, 'The community of the vill', in H. Cam, *Law-finders and law-makers in medieval England* (London: The Merlin Press, 1962), pp. 71-84, offers a valuable statement on the kinds of institutional elements that may have encouraged communal organisation while G.C. Homans, *English villagers of the thirteenth century* (Cambridge, Mass.: Harvard University Press, 1941), presents a significant initial commentary on the nature of the village community. Other case-studies which touch on aspects of village community include P.D.A. Harvey, *A medieval Oxfordshire village. Cuxham, 1240 to 1400* (Oxford: Oxford University Press, 1965); M.K. McIntosh, *Autonomy and community. The royal manor of Havering, 1200-1500* (Cambridge: Cambridge University Press, 1986); Z. Razi, 'Family, land and the village community in later medieval England', *Past and Present* 93 (1981), reprinted in T.H. Aston, ed., *Landlords, peasants and politics in medieval England* (Cambridge: Cambridge University Press, 1987), pp. 360-93. A body of work associated with historians from the Pontifical Institute, Toronto (the so-called 'Toronto School') is exemplified in the following: J.A. Raftis, *Tenure and mobility: studies in the social history of the medieval English village* (Toronto: Pontifical Institute of Mediaeval Studies,

1964); J. A. Raftis, *Warboys: two hundred years in the life of an English medieval village* (Toronto: Pontifical Institute of Mediaeval Studies, 1974); J. A. Raftis, 'Changes in an English village after the Black Death', *Medieval Studies* 29 (1967), 158–77; E. Britton, *The community of the vill: a study in the history of the family and village life in fourteenth century England* (Toronto: Pontifical Institute of Mediaeval Studies, 1977); E.B. DeWindt, *Land and people in Holywell-cum-Needingworth* (Toronto: Pontifical Institute of Mediaeval Studies, 1972); A.R. DeWindt, 'Redefining the peasant community in medieval England: the regional perspective', *Journal of British Studies* 26 (1987), 163–207. One of the last products of that 'school' is S. Olson, *A chronicle of all that happens. Voices from the village court in medieval England* (Toronto: Pontifical Institute of Mediaeval Studies, 1996). See also Z. Razi, 'The Toronto School's reconstitution of medieval peasant society: a critical view', *Past and Present* 85 (1979), 141–57. For an innovative discussion of communal relations see R.M. Smith, 'Kin and neighbors in a thirteenth-century Suffolk community', *Journal of Family History* 4 (1979), 219–56, and for a review of the issue of communal decline, a theme associated with the Toronto historians, see C. Dyer, 'The English medieval village community and its decline', *Journal of British Studies* 33 (1994), 407–29. For discussion of individual peasants or those closely associable with peasants, see C. Dyer, 'A Suffolk farmer in the fifteenth century', *Agricultural History Review* 55 (2007), 1–22; C. Dyer, *A country merchant, 1495–1520: trading and farming at the end of the middle ages* (Oxford: Oxford University Press, 2012); J.M. Bennett, *A medieval life. Cecilia Penifader of Brigstock, c.1295–1344* (Boston: McGraw-Hill College, 1999).

Chapter 8 Peasant culture

There are a number of ways in which historians might seek to address the issue of peasant culture. One example of a literary culture conceivably directed at members of the later medieval peasantry relates to the ballads of Robin Hood. See, for instance, R.H. Hilton, 'The origins of Robin Hood', *Past and Present* 14 (1958), reprinted in R.H. Hilton, ed., *Peasants, knights and heretics. Studies in medieval English social history* (Cambridge: Cambridge University Press, 1976), pp. 221–35; see also M. Keen, *The outlaws of medieval England* (London: Routledge and Kegan Paul, 1961) and Keen, 'Robin Hood – peasant or gentleman?', *Past and Present* 19 (1961), reprinted in Hilton, ed., *Peasants, knights and heretics*, pp. 258–66; J.C. Holt, 'The origins and audience of the ballads of Robin Hood', *Past and Present* 18 (1960), reprinted in Hilton, ed., *Peasants, knights and heretics*, pp. 236–57; Holt, *Robin Hood* (London: Thames and Hudson, 1982); A.J. Pollard, *Imagining Robin Hood* (London: Routledge, 2004). Identifying peasants as consumers also helps recognise their cultural choices; see, for instance, C. Dyer, 'Changes in diet in the later middle ages: the case of harvest workers', *Agricultural History Review* 36 (1988), 21–37, reprinted in C. Dyer, *Everyday life in medieval England* (London: Hambledon, 1994), pp. 77–99; J. Birrell, 'Peasants eating and drinking', *Agricultural History Review* 63 (2015), 1–18; N. Alcock and D. Miles, *The medieval peasant house in midland England* (Oxford: Oxbow, 2013); A. Musson, *Medieval law in context. The growth of legal consciousness from Magna Carta to the Peasants' Revolt* (Manchester: Manchester University Press, 2001).

Political agency on the part of peasants also reflects a political culture as discussed in, for instance, R.H. Hilton, 'Peasant movements in England before 1381', *Economic History Review*, 2nd series, ii (1949), pp. 117-36, reprinted in E.M. Carus-Wilson, ed., *Essays in economic history*, ii (London, 1962), pp. 73-91 and in R.H. Hilton, *Class conflict and the crisis of feudalism. Essays in medieval social history* (London: Hambledon, 1985), pp. 122-38; J. Whittle and S.H. Rigby, 'England: popular politics and social conflict' in S.H. Rigby (ed.), *A companion to Britain in the later middle ages* (Oxford: Blackwell, 2003), pp. 65-86; D.A. Carpenter, 'English peasants in politics, 1258-1267', *Past and Present* 136 (1992), 3-42; J.R. Maddicott, 'Poems of social protest in early fourteenth century England', W. Ormrod, ed., *England in the fourteenth century. Proceedings of the 1985 Harlaxton Symposium* (Woodbridge: Boydell, 1986), pp. 130-44; S. Justice, *Writing and rebellion. England in 1381* (Berkeley: University of California Press, 1994). Religious practice and pious expression, both orthodox and unorthodox or heretical on the part of the peasantry also speak to one further aspect of peasant culture as, for instance, discussed in R.N. Swanson, *Religion and devotion in Europe c.1215-c.1515* (Cambridge: Cambridge University Press, 1995); D. Postles, 'Lamps, lights and layfolk: "popular" devotion before the Black Death', *Journal of Medieval History* 25 (1999), pp. 97-114; A. Hudson, 'The mouse in the pyx: popular heresy and the eucharist', in N. Crossley-Holland, ed., *Eternal values in medieval life* (Trivium, 26, 1991), pp. 40-53; D.M. Owen, *Church and society in medieval Lincolnshire* (History of Lincolnshire, 5, Lincoln, 1971); E. Mason, 'The role of the English parishioner, 1100-1500', *Journal of Ecclesiastical History* 27 (1976); E. Duffy, *The stripping of the altars. Traditional religion in England, c.1400-c.1580* (New Haven and London: Yale University Press, 1992); E. Duffy, *The voices of Morebath: reformation and rebellion in an English village* (New Haven and London: Yale University Press, 2001); K.L. French, *The people of the parish: community life in a late medieval English diocese* (Philadelphia: University of Pennsylvania Press, 2001); V. Bainbridge, *Gilds in the medieval countryside: social and religious change in Cambridgeshire c.1350-1558* (Woodbridge: Boydell, 1997). On manifestation of moral teaching, see for example M.K. McIntosh, *Controlling misbehavior in England, 1370-1600* (Cambridge: Cambridge University Press, 1998).

Conclusion

For discussion of different disciplinary approaches to study of the medieval peasantry, see, for example, in terms of archaeology as one instance, C. Dyer, 'The material world of English peasants, 1200-1540: archaeological perspectives on rural economy and welfare', *Agricultural History Review* 62 (2014), 1-22; R. Hodges, 'Parachutists and truffle-hunters: at the frontiers of archaeology and history', in M. Aston, D. Austin and C. Dyer, eds, *The rural settlements of medieval England. Studies dedicated to Maurice Beresford and John Hurst* (Oxford, 1989), pp. 287-305; D.A. Hinton, *Archaeology, economy and society. England from the fifth to the fifteenth century* (London: Routledge, 1998).

INDEX

Abel, W. 13
Abingdon (Oxfordshire) 243
adolescence 174, 177, 183
Alrewas (Staffordshire) 188
American Historical Review 20, 37
ancient demesne 96, 203, 235
anthropology 14, 29 (n. 56), 172, 197, 205, 226
anticlericalism 240
apprenticeship 176
archaeology 9, 135, 139, 199, 227, 229, 257-8
Ashley, W.J. 3, 60, 117, 259
Aston, M. 101
Aston, T.H. 199
Ault, W.O. 200

Bailey, M. 104, 108, 115 (n. 105), 136, 139, 166-7, 171 (n. 60), 244
Bainbridge, V. 241
Bardsley, S. 188-9
Barron, C. 188
Barry, L. 158
Bartley, K. 107
Barton Blount (Derbyshire) 257
Battle Abbey, estates of 46
Bec, abbey of, estates of 234
Bedfordshire (county) 76
Bennett, H.S. 4-5, 11, 49, 114 (n. 93)
Bennett, J.M. 15, 29 (nn. 52, 55), 136, 183, 185, 187-8, 190-1, 193 (n. 38), 195 (n. 72), 211, 262 (n. 24)
Berg, M. 20
Berkeley (Gloucestershire), estates of 23 (n. 1)
Biddick, K. 15
biographies (peasant) 162, 211-12
Birmingham, University of 6, 18, 20, 96, 112 (n. 52), 209, 247 (n. 24)
Birrell, J. 228
birth 166, 167, 182
    extra-marital 166, 177
    rate 165

Bishop, T.A.M. 5
Black Death 2, 38, 42, 43, 62, 67, 68, 69, 73, 102, 104, 138, 140, 155, 161, 162, 163, 164, 165, 177, 188, 196, 201, 215
    see also plague
Blanchard, I. 27 (n. 37), 136, 146 (n. 79), 215
Bloch, M. 28 (n. 46)
Breckland (Norfolk/Suffolk) 136
Brenner, R. 92-3, 96, 97-8, 107, 115 (n. 103), 120-3
Brenner debate, the 6, 97-8
brewers and brewing 125, 136, 184, 187-8, 190, 191
Briggs, C. 132, 185, 186-7, 231
Brigstock (Northamptonshire) 183, 211
Britnell, R. 69, 103-4, 114 (n. 87), 125, 126-7, 140, 227
Britton, E. 105, 123
Broadberry, S. 134
Brooks, N. 101
Buckinghamshire (county) 186
Bury St Edmunds, abbey of, estates of 133, 212, 213, 224
by-laws 200, 207

Cam, H. 198, 202-3, 204, 210
Cambridge (Cambridgeshire) 137
Cambridge Group for the History of Population and Social Structure 19, 155, 165
Cambridge, University of 7, 19, 20, 155
    Girton College 20
Cambridgeshire (county) 186, 241
Campbell, B.M.S. 72-4, 107-8, 115 (n. 103), 132, 133-4, 140, 157-8
Canterbury, archbishopric, estates of 153
capital 41, 74, 77, 97, 106, 121, 124, 130, 131-2, 137, 140, 186, 187, 188, 212
Carpenter, C. 197

Carpenter, D.A. 238, 250 (n. 69)
Chaucer, Geoffrey 225
Chayanov, A.V. 129-30
chevage 94
Chevington (Suffolk) 212, 224
Cheyney, E.P. 38
Childers, B.D. 162
children and child-care 183, 189, 207
church 10, 84, 205, 237, 239, 240, 242
Clark, E. 231
Clark, G. 74, 140
class (peasant) 18, 84, 88, 89, 94-6, 106, 112 (n. 51), 206, 209-11, 224, 225, 233-4, 236
class struggle 11, 84, 95, 96-8, 99, 101, 104-5, 118, 185, 210
cloth 69
  industry and trade 66, 72, 81 (n. 57), 242
commerce 40, 41, 42, 57, 64, 66, 72, 74, 98, 118, 120, 121, 124, 125, 126, 128, 136, 139-40, 175
commercialisation 8, 115 (n. 103), 126, 127, 140, 143 (n. 32), 227, 262 (n. 21)
community 33, 44-7, 94, 105, 142, 149-50, 191, 196-216, 231, 254
  'community of the realm' 105, 236-7, 238
  village 33, 44-7, 94, 149-50, 196-216
commutation 3, 6, 8, 21, 38-9, 52 (n. 30), 85-90, 94, 97, 102
  see also rent
consuetudines non taxatas 94
consumption 13, 75, 97, 120, 122, 126, 133, 135, 136, 138-9, 142-3 (n. 32), 147 (n. 90), 159, 223, 224, 225, 227-31, 247 (n. 24), 255, 260
  see also diet and nutrition; crops; housing
Cornwall (county) 136
Cornwall, Duchy of 153
Corpus Christi, feast of 101-2
Coss, P. 238
Cotswolds 211, 255
Coulton, G.C. 4-5, 11, 49
coverture 186
crafts and craftsmen 75, 101, 134
credit and debt 41, 74-5, 77, 119, 125, 128, 132, 137, 139, 184, 186, 216, 231, 248 (n. 34), 260
crisis 64, 69, 132, 239, 262-3 (n. 25)
  see also mortality, crisis

crops (peasant) 71, 73, 136
  cash 68, 119, 147 (n. 90)
  grain and pulses 41, 42, 155, 158, 159, 228
  storage 200
  yield 62, 64, 71, 72, 73, 157, 158
Crowland abbey, estates of 71
culture (peasant) 15, 23 (n. 2), 48-9, 149, 223-45
Cunningham, W.A. 53 (n. 49), 60, 102, 117
Cuxham (Oxfordshire) 202

Dahlman, C.J. 257
Davenport, F. 34, 37, 44, 49
dearth *see* famine
debt *see* credit and debt
demesnes 16, 34, 37, 70, 72, 73, 86, 89, 90, 91, 102, 106, 107, 109 (n. 6), 119, 137, 140, 185, 189
  direct management of 34, 71, 86, 89, 90, 226
  leasing of 43, 76, 91, 202, 224, 226
demography 7, 8, 14, 33, 42-4, 66-8, 141, 149, 151-67, 181, 183, 184, 239
  see also fertility; mobility; morbidity; mortality; population
Derbyshire (county) 215
deserted medieval settlements 257, 261-2 (n. 15)
DeWindt, A.R. 105, 123
DeWindt, E. 27 (n. 37), 105, 106, 123, 124-5, 226, 231, 260 (n. 2)
DeWitte, S. 80 (n. 33)
diet and nutrition 69, 80 (n. 33), 139, 158, 228, 257, 258, 262 (n. 16)
disease 43, 66, 67, 68, 73, 80, 164, 182
  see also Black Death; morbidity; plague
Dobb, M. 6, 92
Dodds, B. 71
Domesday Book 34, 35, 39, 47-8, 95, 235
Doughty, H.M. 49
DuBoulay, F.R.H. 153
Duby, G. 13
Duffy, E. 240, 242
Durham, bishop of, estates of 8, 104
Durham, cathedral priory of, estates of 8, 12, 71, 90, 137
Durham, palatinate 76, 104, 234
Dyer, C.C. 6, 71-2, 96, 101, 125-6, 127, 139, 154, 201-2, 208, 210, 211-12, 215-16, 224-5, 227-9, 235, 247 (n. 24), 257-8

INDEX

Dyffryn Clwyd, Welsh marcher lordship of 187

East Anglia 43, 76, 130, 201
Ecclestone, M. 160
economics, discipline of 2, 226, 256-7
Economic History, Second International Conference of (1962) 20
Economic History Review 4, 110 (n. 29), 235
education 10, 16-18, 20, 30-1 (n. 62), 249 (n. 48)
Edward I, king of England 87, 232
Edward II, king of England 237
Eiden, H. 101
elites (peasant) 76, 95, 101, 105, 107, 182, 207, 208, 243
  see also 'kulaks'
elves 241
Ely, abbey and bishopric of, estates of 50 (n. 3), 90
enclosure 47, 201-2, 218 (n. 15)
Engels, F. 53 (n. 54)
English Historical Review 19, 31 (n. 66)
English Rising (1381) *see* Peasants' Revolt (1381)
entrepreneurialism/entrepreneurship (peasant) 41, 108, 117, 124, 131, 133, 140, 198, 215, 216
entry fines (*gersuma*) 94
Essex (county) 101, 103, 104, 154, 161, 166, 171 (n. 54), 173, 174, 187, 203, 241, 243
Evans, R. 96
Exeter (Devon) 137

Fagan, H. 99, 100
Faith, R. 76, 91, 96, 210, 235
family and household 37, 47, 132, 133, 172-82, 183
  formation 138, 156, 163, 172, 173-6, 177-8, 181, 182, 183
    models of 173-5, 178
  income and expenditure 40-1, 64, 94, 120, 126, 183, 185, 190-1
  reconstitution 8, 151, 160
  size 7, 48, 65, 75, 129, 130, 149, 159, 169 (n. 27), 172, 175, 178-81
  structure 5, 75, 130, 141, 167, 168 (n. 16), 172, 175, 178-81, 183, 189, 205, 226

nuclear 179, 181-2, 200, 216
  see also neolocality
family-land bond 132-3, 205-6, 214, 215-16
famine 67, 79 (n. 32), 160, 161, 165, 262
famuli 86, 109 (n. 6)
feminism 20, 260, 262 (n. 24)
Fenland 177, 180
fertility 59, 67, 68, 73, 141, 149, 152, 154, 164, 165-7, 171 (nn. 60, 61), 172, 174, 176, 177, 178, 182, 239
  rate 165, 166, 172, 176
feudal reaction 102-4
field systems
  open 44, 46-7, 180, 199-201, 205, 218 (n. 15), 256-7
food 49, 62, 67, 68, 73, 76, 120, 135, 136, 138, 139, 140, 155, 157, 164, 223, 227, 228
  availability 67, 68, 138, 140, 159
  see also crops; diet and nutrition; livestock (peasant)
Ford lectures, University of Oxford 19, 42, 119, 125-6, 184, 236
Forncett (Norfolk) 37-8, 44, 49
Forrest, I. 243
Fortnightly Review 42
France 162
Franklin, P. 96, 184, 234
frankpledge, view of 153, 160, 203
  see also sources, tithing lists; tithing penny
fraternities *see* guilds
Freedman, P. 224
freedom 65, 233, 255, 259
  see also tenantry, free
French historians 13, 28 (n. 46)
Fryde, E.B. 255

garciones 160
Gasquet, Cardinal F. 4, 12, 25 (n. 16), 42-3, 241
Gattrell, P. 13
gender 2, 10, 48, 172, 182-91, 193 (n. 38)
geography 14, 19, 228
German historians 13
Germany 179
Glastonbury abbey, estates of 89, 110 (n. 22), 160
Gloucester, abbey of, estates of 227
Goldberg, P.J.P. 165, 166, 176, 188, 189
Goltho (Lincolnshire) 257
Gomme, G.L. 2, 45, 46, 47, 87, 201

274

INDEX

Gottfried, R. 67
government, central/royal 60, 66, 101, 189, 202, 203–4, 210, 232, 236, 237–8, 243, 250 (n. 69)
Graham, H. 188
Gras, N.S.B. 41, 117, 127
Gray, H.L. 3, 26, 38, 87, 201
Gressenhall (Norfolk) 159, 169 (n. 31)
Gross, C. 241
gross domestic product (GDP) 128, 133–5, 136, 145 (n. 70)
guilds 204, 213, 218 (n. 26), 241, 242, 244

Hajnal, J. 173, 176, 177, 191 (n. 2)
Halesowen (Worcestershire) 159, 161, 163, 164, 175, 176, 177, 180, 192 (n. 20)
Hall, D. 201
Hallam, H.E. 158–9, 161, 169 (n. 27), 177–8, 179, 180, 192 (n. 20), 221 (n. 72), 215
Hanawalt, B.A. 183, 185
Harlcrow, E.M. 90
Harvard, university 5
harvest
  failure 64, 132, 163, 239
  work 139, 188, 189, 228, 247
Harvey, B.F. 69, 90 (n. 22), 131, 171 (n. 61), 244–5
Harvey, P.D.A. 129, 130, 202
Hasleton (Gloucestershire) 242
Hatcher, J. 107, 136, 138, 139, 146 (n. 79), 153, 156, 158, 166, 171 (n. 61), 188–9
Havering-atte-Bower (Essex) 187, 203
Henry III, king of England 212, 238
heresy *see* lollards and lollardy; Wycliffe, John, Wycliffites
heriot 163
Heritage, John, merchant, grazier and farmer 211–12
Hilton, R.H. 6, 11, 19, 20, 21, 22, 28 (n. 46), 75, 76, 86, 88, 92–103, 112 (n. 48), 118–20, 138, 147 (n. 90), 184–6, 198, 209–10, 214, 224–6, 227, 233–6, 238, 247 (n. 24)
history
  administrative 2, 34, 37, 161, 198, 199, 202
  constitutional 2, 4, 16, 37, 199, 238
  cultural 2, 49, 212, 216, 223–4, 226, 256

economic 2, 3, 4, 11, 13, 14, 17, 19, 20, 25 (n. 12), 30 (n. 61), 85, 93, 129, 150, 154, 228, 257
'from below' 99, 113 (n. 65)
gender 2, 8, 193 (n. 38)
institutional 2, 3, 7, 15, 16, 18, 60, 85, 128, 198–204, 210
legal 2, 7, 14, 16, 18, 29 (n. 53), 34–5, 37, 232
'new social (scientific)' 6, 14, 27 (n. 35), 106, 152, 206, 254
social 8, 11, 13, 14, 17, 19, 58, 129, 150, 154, 212, 243
women's 193 (n. 38)
Holt, J.C. 225, 226, 246 (n. 10)
Holywell-cum-Needingworth (Huntingdonshire) 106, 124, 226
Homans, G.C. 5, 6, 11, 13, 16, 25 (n. 22), 27 (n. 35), 29 (n. 56), 75, 168 (n. 16), 174–5, 178–9, 180, 205–6, 214, 241
Hood, Robin 225–6, 246 (n. 10)
household *see* family and household
housing (peasant) 23 (n. 2), 138, 139, 229, 247 (nn. 24, 27)
Howell, C. 178–9, 181
Hudson, W. 117, 213
hunting 49, 229, 230, 244
Hyams, P.R. 77, 131, 132, 231

individualism 22–3, 45, 47, 74, 132, 186, 197, 198, 204–5, 211–16
inheritance 5, 7, 8, 132–3, 153, 164, 168 (n. 16), 173, 174, 177, 178, 180, 182, 205, 206, 207, 214
  impartible 174, 177, 180, 205
  partible 180, 214
inventories, peasant 71, 229

Jack Cade's rebellion (1450) 105
Japanese historians 12, 27–8 (n. 44)
Jessop, Reverend A. 4, 11–12, 43, 48, 53 (n. 49)
Jones, A. 76
journals and periodicals 19
  see also American Historical Review; Economic History Review; English Historical Review; Fortnightly Review; Law and History Review; Past and Present
Justice, S. 256

275

INDEX

Kanzaka, J. 107
Keen, M. 225
Kent (county) 153, 201, 229
Kett's rebellion (1549) 105
Keynes, J.M. and Keynesian economics 61, 62
Kibworth Harcourt (Leicestershire) 179, 181
kin and kinship 7, 8, 14, 45, 129, 173, 175, 176, 205, 206, 214, 215–16
King, E. 124, 131, 144 (n. 57)
Kosminsky, E.A. 4, 13, 16, 42, 85–9, 92, 94, 97, 107, 110 (n. 29)
Kowaleski, M. 137
Kuhn, T.S. 8–9, 15, 18
'kulaks' 131, 213
  see also elites (peasant)
Kümin, B. 241

Labour Studies, Institute of 21
Lancaster, Thomas of 237
land
  accumulation of 65, 76, 189, 214
  common 201
  fragmentation/morcellisation of 40, 65, 76, 119, 122, 214
  market in 13, 21, 23, 40, 64, 66, 74–7, 117–18, 124, 128–33, 140, 143 (n. 43), 144 (n. 53), 144 (n. 57), 206, 212, 213–14, 216, 230, 240, 260
  use 3, 44, 69, 90, 200–1, 258
  see also family-land bond; inheritance; tenantry; tenure
Langdon, J. 72, 73, 140, 189
Langland, William 225, 235
Larson, P. 104, 234
law 34–5, 37, 39, 45, 47, 48, 49, 139, 187, 203, 210, 216, 225, 230–1, 236, 255
  canon 166
  common 2, 40, 184, 203–4, 235, 236
  customary 26 (n. 33), 34, 184, 186, 203
  and litigation 34, 166, 184, 216, 231, 234, 235
  Welsh 54 (n. 70)
Law and History Review 161
lawyers and legal advice 5, 139, 202, 210, 230–1, 235
le Play, F. 205, 219 (n. 39)
le Roy Ladurie, E. 97
Lee, J. 137
Leicester, abbey of 224
Leicestershire (county) 76, 93, 118

leisure 49, 138, 226, 244
Lennard, R. 89–90, 95, 245–6 (n. 8)
Levett, A.E. 2, 4, 43, 44, 233–4, 249 (n. 48)
Liberal Party 20
liberi homines see tenantry, free
life expectancy 67, 152, 154, 160, 162, 164, 171 (n. 61)
Lincolnshire (county) 158, 177
Lipson, E.A. 3, 60, 102, 127
literacy 231, 239, 242, 255, 256
literary studies 5, 113, 224, 256, 261 (n. 5)
livestock (peasant) 63–4, 71, 72, 79 (n. 26), 139
Lock, R. 160
Lollards and Lollardy 242–3, 252 (n. 96)
  see also Wycliffites
Lomas, T. 76
London 114 (n. 87), 137
London School of Economics 20
Longden, J. 155, 162
lordship 2–3, 16, 33–9, 40, 41–2, 44, 58, 64, 66, 84–108, 118, 120, 121, 126, 127, 128, 131, 132, 133, 138, 153, 173, 182, 185–7, 203, 205, 206, 209, 210, 211, 216, 224, 225, 226, 227, 228, 233–5, 237, 259
Loschky, D. 162

McCloskey, D. 200, 218 (n. 16)
MacFarlane, A. 22–3, 133, 198, 214–15, 216
McIntosh, M.K. 185, 187, 203, 244
Maddicott, J.R. 203, 204, 237–8
Maine, H.S. 46, 47, 203, 215
Maitland, F.W. 2, 16, 29 (n. 53), 34, 35, 37, 39, 40, 42, 47, 48, 49, 95, 111, 199, 202, 206, 215, 218 (n. 26)
Malthus, T. and Malthusianism 61, 122, 123, 160
manor 2–3, 9, 10, 11, 16, 34, 35, 37, 40, 46, 75, 85, 94, 98, 124, 149, 160, 164, 175, 184, 185–6, 187, 198–9, 202, 203–4, 206, 207, 209, 224, 230, 254, 255, 259
  manorial officers 35, 90, 202, 207, 208, 210–11, 221 (n. 64), 234, 235, 239
market 40–1, 57, 66, 70, 73, 74–7, 117–41, 149
  credit 132, 140, 200
  labour 70 75, 131, 137–8, 140, 177, 181, 182
  see also land, market in
marriage 8, 10, 48, 94, 156, 163, 166, 168 (n. 16), 172–8, 182, 183, 186, 239, 240, 242, 243

age at 166, 172, 173, 174, 176–8, 183, 192 (n. 20)
    patterns 138, 176–7
Marshall, A. 61
Marx, K. 50 (n. 1), 53 (n. 54), 97, 256
Marxism/Marxist approaches to history 6, 7, 18, 62, 80 (n. 38), 88, 92–3, 95–9, 104, 110 (n. 29), 111 (n. 32), 112 (n. 48), 112 (n. 53), 118–23, 139–40, 141 (n. 5), 198, 206, 209–11, 213, 233–4, 260
Masschaele, J. 73, 134–5, 140, 204
Mayhew, N.J. 133, 134, 135, 145 (n. 70)
merchet 48, 94, 239
Middleton, C. 185–6
Miller, E. 50 (n. 3), 81 (n. 57), 90, 117–18, 254
mills 72
mining 136, 146 (n. 79), 215
mobility 59, 97, 103, 138, 153, 154, 164, 166, 181–2, 197, 226, 247 (n. 29)
money and money economy 38, 50 (n. 3), 60, 61, 85, 86, 87, 102, 103, 117, 119, 120, 121, 128, 133, 137, 214, 225
monks and monastic houses 2, 12, 67, 106, 107, 135, 137, 156, 171 (n. 61), 244
Montfort, Simon de 237
morbidity 67, 171 (n. 61), 244
    see also disease
Morebath (Devon) 240
Morgan, M. 234
mortality 7, 42–4, 53 (n. 49), 64, 66–8, 79 (n. 32), 80 (n. 33), 149, 152–6, 157, 160–1, 162–5, 167 (n. 4), 171 (nn. 54, 61), 182
    background 68, 163, 164
    crisis 42, 43, 68, 79 (n. 32), 80 (n. 33), 157, 160–1, 163–4, 165
    infant 68, 153, 167 (n. 4)
    rate 7, 152, 153, 155, 160, 163
mortgages 77, 144 (n. 59)
Musson, A. 231

neifs and neifty 36
    see also tenants, unfree
neighbours and neighbourliness *see* reciprocity
Neilson, N. 20–1, 25–6 (n. 22), 36–7, 51 (nn. 18, 19)
neolocality 173, 174–5, 177, 178
    see also family and household, formation

'Neo-Smithian Marxism' 121–2
New Mexico, university of 152
Nichols, J.F. 235
Norfolk (county) 11, 12, 37, 44, 48, 49, 76, 101, 105, 159, 169 (n. 31)
'normal science' and scientific revolutions 8–9, 15
    see also Kuhn, T.S.; paradigms
North, D. 257–8
Norwich 242
Norwich priory, estates of 72
numeracy 231
nuptiality *see* marriage; family and household, formation

Oakington (Cambs.) 71
Ohlin, G. 162
Olson, S. 15, 29 (n. 52), 203, 231–2
Oman, Sir C. 100, 101
Orwin, C.S. and C.S. 199
Oxford Studies in Social and Legal History 36
Oxfordshire (county) 20, 189, 202

Page, T.W. 3, 38, 52 (n. 26), 87, 95, 102
paradigms 8–10, 15, 259
Parman, Robert 212
parish 10, 151, 153, 167, 171, 239–41, 243
Past and Present 97, 209, 216
Paston, William (I), wife of 212
patriarchy 183, 185–6, 191
peasantry
    definition of 1, 21–3, 133, 214
    representations of 224–5
Peasants' Revolt (1381) 13, 28 (n. 46), 88, 96, 99–102, 104, 105, 233, 234, 238–9, 256
Penifader, Cecilia 211
Perkins, William (Jack Sharp of Wigmoreland) 243
Peterborough abbey, estates of 64, 124, 131
piety 237–9, 240, 242
plague 38, 42–4, 60–1, 62, 67, 80 (n. 33), 99, 100, 102, 104, 107, 108, 153, 157, 160–1, 162, 163, 166, 177, 179, 180, 183, 188, 208, 234
    see also Black Death
Pontifical Institute, University of Toronto *see* Toronto, University of

INDEX

Poos, L.R. 101, 103, 104, 154, 160–1, 164–6, 169 (n. 29), 173–4, 176, 178, 189, 243
population 7, 11, 13, 33, 42–4, 57, 58, 59–77, 98, 108, 115 (n. 103), 118, 122, 123, 127, 133, 134, 138, 140, 144 (n. 53), 149, 150, 151–67, 168 (n. 19), 171 (n. 61), 174, 176, 179, 181, 198
   age structure 155, 160
   estimates 29 (n. 55), 73, 74, 157–61, 168 (nn. 19, 21), 170 (n. 36)
   see also fertility; mobility; mortality
population-resources model 61, 62–3, 66–7, 68, 73–4, 77, 155
Postan, C. 13
Postan, M.M. 4, 7, 11, 13, 20, 57, 58, 60–77, 81 (nn. 46, 56), 85–6, 87, 88, 89–90, 91, 97, 122, 123, 129, 130, 131, 136, 144 (n. 57), 154–5, 158, 160, 162, 163, 175, 178, 180, 197–8, 214
postmodernism 2
pottery 136
poverty 12, 20, 49, 174
   see also wealth and relative wealth
Powell, E. 100
Power, E. 42, 211
Prescott, A. 113 (n. 66)
prices 4, 62, 64, 65, 68, 71, 74, 121, 123, 138, 140, 155
production 70, 73, 93, 96, 101, 103, 120, 122, 126, 133–5, 136, 147 (n. 90), 185, 223, 227
proto-industry 69, 70, 120, 143 (n. 37), 181, 191
   see also brewers and brewing; cloth, industry and trade

Raftis, J.A. 6, 7, 8, 11, 13–14, 16, 105–6, 123–4, 150, 198, 206–7, 213, 214, 231
Ramsey, abbey of, estates of 6, 16, 18, 21, 36, 105–6, 123, 124, 206, 207, 208, 226
Ramsey (Huntingdonshire) 106
Razi, Z. 96, 159–61, 163–5, 175–6, 177–8, 179, 180, 181, 192 (n. 20), 209, 215, 216, 220 (n. 59)
reciprocity 47, 96, 106, 120, 124, 197, 198, 200, 207, 208, 209, 231, 244
Redfield, R. 206
Redgrave (Suffolk) 213–14
Rees, W. 43

rent 3–4, 6, 7, 14, 18, 23 (n. 1), 34, 36, 38, 39–40, 41–2, 43, 58, 60, 65, 69, 85–91, 92, 93, 94, 97, 101, 103, 107–8, 110 (n. 22), 120, 133, 135, 147 (n. 90), 153, 154, 184, 210, 225, 244, 254, 259
   boon works 21, 36, 37, 51 (n. 18), 228, 234
   labour services 3, 6, 34, 38, 42, 44, 52 (n. 30), 58, 60, 85–91, 94, 97, 102, 103, 210, 233, 234
   money 3, 38, 40, 42, 58, 60, 68, 85, 86–91, 94, 103, 107–8
   rent in kind 38, 60, 85, 89, 102
   see also chevage; commutation; *consuetudines non taxatas*; heriot; merchet; tallage
replacement rates 7, 14, 162–3, 164, 176
Réville, A. 28, 99–100, 101, 113 (n. 66), 249 (n. 51)
revolts and uprisings *see* Jack Cade's rebellion (1450); Kett's rebellion (1549); Peasants' Revolt (1381)
Reynolds, S. 205
Ricardo, D. 61, 256
Richard II, king of England 234
Richardson, G. 200
Rickinghall (Suffolk) 27–8 (n. 44)
Rigby, S.H. 98, 110 (n. 30), 113 (n. 74), 169 (n. 24), 185–6
Rogers, J.E.T 4, 12, 20, 22, 38–9, 40, 41, 42, 43, 44, 46, 48, 49, 54 (n. 78), 84, 100, 102, 117, 138, 157, 259, 260 (n. 1)
Round, J.H. 35
Rubin, M. 29 (n. 52)
Russell, J.C. 152–3, 158, 161, 167 (n. 4), 168 (n. 19), 179
Ruthin (Denbighshire) 187–8
Russia 58, 129, 256
Russian historians 12–13, 85, 92–3, 110 (n. 29), 129

St Albans, abbey of, estates of 234
St Paul's cathedral, estates of 46, 91
Salzmann, L.F. 127
Sapoznik, A. 71
Scase, W. 232–3
Schofield, P.R. 132, 231, 232, 239, 250 (n. 65)
Schofield, R.S. 165, 171 (n. 61)
seals and sigillography 226–7, 246 (n. 15), 247 (n. 16)

INDEX

Seebohm, F. 2, 16, 22, 42, 43, 44, 45, 46, 47, 87, 157, 199, 201
Selden Society 34
serfdom *see* villeinage and villeins
servants and service 70, 134, 137, 138, 166, 174, 176, 178, 182, 189, 195 (n. 72), 214
sex ratios 152
Shanin, T. 22
Slavin, P. 80 (n. 33)
Slicher-Van Bath, B.H. 13
Smith, Adam 60, 117, 122, 256
    see also 'Neo-Smithian Marxism'
Smith, R.M. 14, 46, 129-33, 144 (nn. 53, 57), 158, 161, 164-5, 166, 170 (n. 45), 179, 184, 197, 204, 213-15, 239
sochemanni/sokemen *see* tenantry, free
social structure 6, 14, 59, 120, 149, 150, 151, 156, 172, 175, 176, 182, 183, 206, 208, 214
social structuralists/structural approaches 7, 8, 75-6, 106-7, 118, 152, 176, 180, 191, 198, 204-9
sociology/sociological approaches to the past 5, 8, 11, 29 (n. 56), 104, 105, 106, 123-5, 150, 168 (n. 16), 172, 178, 204-9
Solzhenitsyn, A. 213
sources 3, 9, 10, 13, 16, 42-3, 89, 90, 91, 106, 114 (n. 93), 134, 151, 153, 156, 159, 161, 163, 165, 166-7, 171 (n. 61), 176, 179, 183, 198, 209, 212, 214, 221 (n. 72), 232, 233, 236, 245-6 (n. 8), 254-6, 258-9, 261 (n. 5)
account books 10, 27 (n. 33), 211-12
accounts, church wardens 240-1
accounts, manorial 5, 10, 16, 34, 40, 43, 106, 127, 157-8, 255, 232, 238
accounts, obedientiary 16
ballads, poems, political songs 224, 225-6, 246 (n. 10), 249 (n. 42)
Bishops' registers 242
cartularies 5, 16, 46
    Carte Nativorum 64, 77
chancery rolls 210, 255
coroners' rolls 183
court books, consistory 165
court rolls 5, 6, 10, 12, 13, 15, 16, 40, 43, 46, 71, 77, 106, 143 (n. 43), 124, 159, 160, 161, 162, 163, 165, 167, 180, 183, 207, 208, 209, 232, 255, 256

curia regis rolls 210
custumals 46, 255
extents 16, 73, 90
Hundred rolls 16, 46, 87, 107, 238
inquisitions *post mortem* 38, 87, 107
lay subsidies 63, 71, 157, 160, 174
Modus tenendi parliamentum 236
muster rolls 160
parish registers 151, 167, 171 (n. 61)
poll-tax listings 160, 168 (n. 19), 174
Psalter, Luttrell 225
rentals 10, 161, 228, 255
surveys 46, 89-90, 255
tithing lists 160, 165, 180, 255
wills 153
Spalding, priory of 158, 169 (n. 27), 179
standard of living 66, 67, 68-70, 80 (n. 38), 126, 133-4, 139, 140, 188, 189, 227, 228, 230, 258, 23 (n. 2)
Stenton, F.M. 199
Stevens, M. 187-8
Stone, D. 73, 158
Stone, E. 90
Suffolk (county) 14, 27-8 (n. 44), 108, 160, 187, 212, 224, 232
superstition 241-2
Sweezy, P. 121

tallage 232
Tawney, R.H. 3, 19, 22, 23, 41, 84, 95, 117, 129, 213
taxation 63, 69, 71, 100, 134, 157, 160, 174, 203, 204, 232
Taylor, C.C. 199-200
technology 66, 70-4, 127, 134, 140, 190
tenantry 2, 6, 9, 10, 11, 12, 14, 16, 21, 22, 34-40, 42, 43-4, 46, 47, 48, 49, 51 (n. 21), 58, 64, 71, 84-108, 118, 120, 121, 124, 126, 131, 132, 137, 149, 150, 153, 154, 155, 160, 162, 163, 176, 182, 184, 202, 206, 209, 210, 211, 212, 226, 228, 233, 234, 235, 238, 239, 254, 258, 265-6, 267
free 3, 21, 36, 39, 48, 84-108
unfree 3, 21, 35-6, 38, 42, 48, 58, 84-108, 158, 203, 225, 232, 233, 235
tenure 2, 3, 8, 22, 23 (n. 1), 35-6, 38-9, 40, 49, 52 (n. 28), 65, 84, 85, 87, 89, 90, 101, 104, 106, 107, 115 (n. 105), 119, 184, 216, 235, 259

279

tenure (*cont.*)
  copyhold 34
  customary 76, 128, 131, 184
  free 35, 107, 235
  jointure 184
  leasehold 91, 227
  villein 36, 40, 85, 104, 106, 108, 128, 131, 143 (n. 43)
  see also tenure, customary; villeinage and villeins
Thirsk, J. 199
Thomas, R.P. 256-7
Thomson, J.A.F. 242
Thornbury (Gloucestershire) 120, 184, 234
Thorner, D. 22-3
Threlfall-Thompson, M. 137
Thrupp, S. 162, 163, 164
tithes 71
tithing penny 153, 160, 165
  see also frankpledge, view of; sources, tithing lists
Titow, J.Z. 64, 155, 162, 163
Tittleshall (Norfolk) 12
Tönnies, G. 204, 205, 206, 218 (n. 26)
Toronto, university of 7, 8, 11, 18, 123, 207, 208, 209
towns 10, 67, 69, 70, 73, 75, 76, 82 (n. 62), 120, 126, 134, 135-7, 138, 140, 176, 181, 182, 187, 189-90, 218 (n. 26), 242, 244
Townsend, R.M. 257
trade 41, 42, 45, 61, 67, 69, 175, 120, 126, 127, 128, 135-9, 140, 227
transition debate 6, 91-3, 123, 125
  see also Brenner debate, the

Victoria County History 2, 34, 50 (n. 3)
vill 198, 202, 203, 220 (n. 64), 255
villeinage and villeins 3, 13, 19, 31 (n. 66), 34-9, 40, 46, 51 (n. 21), 58, 60, 65, 91-108, 110 (n. 29), 115 (n. 105), 139, 232, 234, 254, 255, 259
  see also tenantry, unfree

Vinogradoff, Sir Paul 2, 13, 35, 36, 37, 39, 40, 48, 49, 87, 95, 199

waged-labour 50 (n. 1), 86, 108 109 (n. 6), 130, 131, 138, 244
  legislation and 189, 244
  see also famuli; market, labour; servants and service
wages 4, 54 (n. 78), 65, 66, 68, 69, 74, 102, 123, 134, 138, 140, 173, 174, 175, 178, 184-5, 188, 189, 190
Walcote, John, shepherd 242
Wales and the Welsh Marches 43, 165, 229
Walsham-le-Willows (Suffolk) 160
wealth and relative wealth 13, 21, 42, 64, 74-5, 76, 81 (n. 46), 85, 95, 99, 106-7, 126, 131, 156, 174, 175-6, 180, 181, 182, 186, 188, 189, 201, 207, 209, 213, 226, 228-9, 239
  see also elites (peasant); poverty
weather 12, 64, 66, 69
Wharram Percy (Yorkshire) 257
Whittle, J. 105
widows and wives 48, 182, 183, 184, 186
Wilburton (Cambridgeshire) 34, 40, 42
Williamson, J. 76, 143 (n. 53)
Willis, James, weaver 252 (n. 96)
Wiltshire (county) 187
Winchester, bishopric of, estates of 2, 43, 64, 155, 162
women 15, 20, 48, 54 (n. 78), 136, 141, 166, 172, 177, 180, 182-91, 193 (n. 38), 211, 262 (n. 24)
Woodstock (Oxfordshire) 189
wool 42, 135, 211, 255
Worcester, bishopric of, estates of 154
Wrigley, E.A. 165, 171 (n. 61)
Wycliffe, John 102, 235
Wycliffites 242
  see also Lollards and Lollardy

York (Yorkshire) 166